Racism and Anti-Racism in World Perspective

SAGE SERIES ON RACE AND ETHNIC RELATIONS

Series Editor:

JOHN H. STANFIELD II

College of William and Mary

This series is designed for scholars working in creative theoretical areas related to race and ethnic relations. The series will publish books and collections of original articles that critically assess and expand upon race and ethnic relations issues from American and comparative points of view.

Racism and Anti-Racism in World Perspective

Editor

Benjamin P. Bowser

**Sage Series on Race
and Ethnic Relations**

v o l u m e   13

SAGE Publications
International Educational and Professional Publisher
Thousand Oaks   London   New Delhi

For information address:

SAGE Publications, Inc.
2455 Teller Road
Thousand Oaks, California 91320
E-mail: order@sagepub.com

SAGE Publications Ltd.
6 Bonhill Street
London EC2A 4PU
United Kingdom

SAGE Publications India Pvt. Ltd.
M-32 Market
Greater Kailash I
New Delhi 110 048 India

Printed in the United States of America

Library of Congress Cataloging-in-Publication Data

Main entry under title:
Racism and anti-racism in world perspective / edited by Benjamin P.
   Bowser.
         p. cm.—(Sage series on race and ethnic relations; v. 13)
      Includes bibliographical references and index.
      ISBN 0-8039-4953-7 (alk. paper).—ISBN 0-8039-4954-5 (pbk. :
   alk. paper)
      1. Racism. I. Bowser, Benjamin P. II. Series.
   HT1521.R325   1995
   305.8—dc20   95-16620

This book is printed on acid-free paper.

95 96 97 98 99 10 9 8 7 6 5 4 3 2 1

Sage Production Editor: Astrid Virding

Contents

Series Editor's Introduction

We are finally beginning to realize that race, racism, and anti-racism are global phenomena. In keeping with that realization, there is a growing demand for scholarship that offers comparative analyses of these social and political economic phenomena. This fascinating anthology project, under the guidance of distinguished sociologist Benjamin P. Bowser, offers the first post-1960s comparative analysis of race, racism, and anti-racism. Whereas Bowser offers valuable analytical overviews of global trends of racism and anti-racism in the introductory and concluding chapters and part introductions, the individual chapters are theoretically grounded, nationally and regionally based essays. This volume will be an important research resource in the race and ethnicity field for many years to come.

John H. Stanfield II
Series Editor

Introduction:
The Global Community,
Racism, and Anti-Racism

Benjamin P. Bowser

As this century has unfolded, direct colonialism and formal racial control have given way to indirect neo-colonialism at home and abroad (Blauner, 1972; Nkrumah, 1965). "Jim Crow" has been defeated, and formal racial segregation has been outlawed in the United States. Women may vote and own property, and their subordinate role in patriarchy is being challenged. Virtually all of Europe's overseas colonies are now politically independent. Most of the former Western European colonial nations no longer have the ability to project at will their military power outside of Europe, and the war in Vietnam ended the post-World War II belief in U.S. overseas military invincibility. The former European colonial powers (and the United States) are becoming economically interdependent, as well as trade partners with the Asian, Middle Eastern, and Latin American regional economies (Berry, 1987). Virtually all the 19th-century symbols of European national and racial supremacy are gone.

Whereas the 20th century was the era of national states, the 21st century appears to be the century of the global economy. In the coming century, the nation-state will no longer be the primary unit of economic growth and self-interest (Frieden & Lake, 1987; Hollifield, 1992). Formerly self-sufficient nation-states are joining together already. The trend is toward forming regional economies and more formidable competitive units in the Pacific Rim, Western Europe, and North and South America. Nations that fought wars and historically devised ideologies against one another now find themselves united through economic self-interest. Absolutely critical to the organization, growth, and maintenance of these new world economies are communications technologies, access to information, a common language for discourse, thousands of working agreements and protocols, and cross-cultural management (Belous & Hartley, 1990). If Americans and Europeans can define the emerging culture of international trade and control communications in the world economy, they will continue to have a powerful yet subtle advantage. Our concern in this book is that modern Western racism is a part of this continued Western influence and contribution to the emerging world community and is having profound and far-reaching effects. What, then, is racism in the emerging postmodern global community?

RACISM AND ANTI-RACISM DEFINED

The term *racism* has many meanings. For some people, the term is synonymous with "White people." For others, the term *racism* stands for personal prejudice and discrimination. For still others, it stands for any race consciousness or the absence of color blindness. For yet another group, racism stands for institutional practices that maintain racial inequalities (Blauner, 1989). More often, individuals use one or the other of these meanings. The fact is that none of these meanings are mutually exclusive. The formal theoretical definition of racism links individual acts of racially motivated prejudice and discrimination with institutional "laws, customs, and practices that systematically reflect and produce racial inequalities" (Jones, 1972, p. 172). In turn, institutional racism is reinforced and called for by cultural beliefs in the generalized and assumed inferiority of ascribed racial groups that are in fact arbitrarily defined. The individual, institutional, and cultural levels are interrelated in one hypothesis defining racism: "Racism results from the transformation of race prejudice and/or ethnocentrism through the exercise of power against a racial group defined as inferior, by individuals and institutions with the intentional or unintentional support of the entire (race or) culture" (Jones, 1972, p. 172).

There are other definitions of racism, but all the definitions have in common an emphasis on a level of action (cultural, institutional, or personal) and articulation of interrelations (Jones, 1981). But for most people in the world community, racism describes race relations unique and isolated to the United States and Western Europe (see Guimarães, this volume).

In contrast, *anti-racism* is not well-defined. From its historical presence in the United States, anti-racism can be defined as a conscious rejection of the belief in any one race's inferiority or superiority, which in turn leads to a rejection of the necessity for institutional reinforcement of racism and for personal acts of prejudice and discrimination to affirm racial superiority (Aptheker, 1993). One might argue that anti-racism need not be a conscious action; one could unconsciously reject racism or never have acquired the belief in the first place. But at this point, the historic evidence of White anti-racism shows conscious acts of rejecting racial hierarchy that range from simple defiance—not behaving within one's racially prescribed role—to armed rebellion against institutional racism. An unconscious rejection of racism remains to be demonstrated either historically or in the present.

Whatever racism means in popular thought, it is a social construct that describes a very real human phenomenon and cannot be dismissed as delusion, nor can it always be demonstrated directly and concretely (Jones, 1981). One illustration of how the underlying reality of racism plays on perception and experience is evident in the United States. Laws were passed in the 1960s and briefly enforced against formal racial discrimination in the South and racially discriminatory outcomes in education, housing, and employment in the rest of the nation. A decade of social reform eliminated one racial barrier after the other and gave the impression that the bases of racial inequalities were being addressed. Yet after all these reforms, African Americans and other people of color continue to experience racial prejudice and discrimination, simply in more subtle and indirect ways. Institutional racism now appears to be an indirect expression of social class barriers, and is just as effective in maintaining historic racial inequalities as the old practices (Dunbar, 1984). This failure of legal and other state efforts to eliminate racism, rather than just some of its institutional expressions, has set the stage for the current impasse in efforts to improve race relations in the United States (Bell, 1992). It has also divided the nation by differing perceptions. Many people believe enough has been done to address racial inequality, whereas others believe not enough has been done.

The disappointments over past attempts to eliminate racism in the United States and elsewhere are partly due to confusion about the concept of racism. First, there is the continued presumption that, if racism exists, it is a one-dimensional social phenomenon. If racism exists, anyone can see it (see interviews in Blauner, 1989). If racism is not evident, it either has been successfully eliminated or did not exist in the first place. What is missing in this underlying assumption is that racism can change and take on different expressions. Second, many believe that racism is simply a flaw in social organization and practice (Myrdal, 1944). People who come out of legal backgrounds are particularly prone to this belief (Bell, 1992). They believe that if institutional practices are changed by law or otherwise, racism can be eliminated. This assumption confuses cause with effect, and presumes that institutional racism is not itself an outcome of history and culture. It is argued in this book that institutional practices with racist outcomes are themselves outcomes and are not the root cause of racism. Finally, there is the belief that racism is the behavior of a few individuals who are certainly antisocial and possibly mentally ill. This point is thoroughly explored and found wanting by Pettigrew (1981).

These false underlying assumptions about racism have led the general public, scholars, and activists all over the world to misread and misunderstand contemporary racism. The most notable of these well-intended misreadings in the United States is Wilson's mistitled book, *The Declining Significance of Race* (1978). Wilson's key point is that the apparent division of African Americans into a then-growing middle class and a large and stagnant underclass meant that social class opportunities and barriers were becoming more prominent than racial ones. In contrast, Bell's recent bestseller, *Faces at the Bottom of the Well* (1992), presents the opposite view. According to Bell, racial discrimination continues to be evident in personal lives and institutional practices. Racism continues unabated but in new ways. Both Wilson and Bell are accurate in recognizing that changes have occurred in race relations in the United States, but neither view accurately assesses the complexity of the underlying perceptions and realities of racism as both a social construct and a dynamic phenomenon. Instances of the same debate can be found in attempts to understand racial hierarchy in Brazil, South Africa, the United Kingdom, and Western Europe.

Wherever racism is articulated in the world community, what is missing in most views is, first, a recognition that racism's underlying reality can be changed in response to economic and organizational transitions in society (Van den Berghe, 1969). Like all other social phenomena, racism's underlying realities are not independent, self-actuated social processes with a life of their own. However one defines racism, it exists, transforms, continues, increases, and declines. Racism is a dynamic, not a static, phenomenon. Racism's realities are more like moving and hiding targets than still objects out in the open. Past victories against racism any place in the world in this century have not been absolute gains any more than defeats have been absolute losses. In the struggle against racism, conditional advancements and strategic retreats have been made. With each victory and retreat, new ground has been sought for future battles.

Second, what is missing in most views of racism is recognition that all social change is due to human action and inaction (Berger, 1962). Progress and regression in race relations do not just happen because of some impersonal cosmic force or fate. People create outcomes. This does not mean that all people can be simply divided into being part of the problem or part of the solution—racists versus anti-racists. We know about people who are clearly racist by all definitions—members of the Ku Klux Klan, neo-Nazis, and Adolf Hitler. We also know about people who were clearly anti-racist—Martin Luther King, Jr., John Brown, and Raoul Wallenberg. We know about the decisive actions of colonial elites in the Western world in creating modern racism as ideology and state practice to justify their continued enslavement of Africans and the genocide of native people (Allen, 1994; Mintz, 1974; Richardson, 1968; Williams, 1944). We suspect the hand of contemporary economic power brokers in creating the conditions that have intensified present racial conflicts (Goldsmith & Blakely, 1992). What we do not know specifically is how the rest of us, who are neither elite nor clearly racist or anti-racist, contribute to and affect the dynamic realities referred to as racism. An up-to-date description of racism's dynamic and human-created realities in the contemporary world is needed.

RACISM AND ANTI-RACISM
IN WORLD PERSPECTIVE

The failure to address racial inequalities effectively through institutional reform is partly due to not addressing simultaneously the very close relationship between institutional racism and culture. The underlying social phenomenon described by the many references to racism are by-products of efforts to create, maintain, or advance historic and national worldviews (Fredrickson, 1971). These worldviews are based on unexamined and often unsubstantiated assumptions about one's own historic group's nationality, "race," customs, and contributions to the modern world. *Cultural racism* is the belief that one's own people and ways are categorically superior, and that other people, things, and ways are categorically inferior to those of others (Jones, 1981). This definition is not the same as being able to see or accept strengths and weaknesses or advantages and disadvantages in one's own and other's cultures. Nor is this the same as simply preferring one's own familiar and well-known world. It is quite possible to be ethnocentric and not racist (as we will see in Chapter 1).

Cultural racism, then, is an expression of nationalist ideologies that define the world categorically (King, 1995). In the racism of dominant groups, one's own people are THE people. One's own customs are THE customs. In a society that is founded by THE people with THE customs, all institutions that constitute the organization of society (government, economy, religion, family, and education) are intended to defend and advance the superiority of THE people and their ways. Regardless of the diversity of all the people in a nation, or that others might have predated one's own group's presence and made crucial contributions, the nation belongs only to THE people. So THE people categorically deserve and reserve the right to lead the nation and are privileged over all lesser peoples and ways. This is what Gramsci (1985) calls "cultural domination hegemony." This is why Christopher Columbus and the early Spanish and English settlers could not even imagine becoming a part of Native Indian societies. Nor could European settlers imagine forming a new society blending their own and Indian ways. Instead, Native Americans were immediately seen as not having nations and cultures worth respecting, as an inferior people, and as having only one purpose—to serve the new European societies as servants, laborers, and slaves.

In dominant group anti-racism, one does not believe that one's own people are THE people or that one's own customs are THE customs. An undetermined number of individuals within the dominant group do not believe in their own group's racism, and some proportion of these individuals are in fact anti-racist—they have taken consistent action against racist institutional and individual practices. Efforts to identify and understand anti-racism among dominant group Europeans in the world community have yet to begin. There is clearly a need for historic and contemporary studies of dominant group anti-racism in other racialized societies besides the United States (Aptheker, 1993). In one of the only attempts to estimate the number of White anti-racists based on decades of survey research, Pettigrew (1981) suggests that up to one-fifth of White Americans are in fact anti-racist.

But there is yet another side to racism: subordinate group racism. In this form of racism, one's own people are the TRUE people. One's own customs are the TRUE customs. But in a society dominated by OTHER people, all of the OTHER people's institutions hide the superiority and pervert and steal the genius and cultural virtues of the TRUE people (Essien-Udom, 1962; Patterson, 1977). Subordinate group racists concede the state to the OTHER people and believe that there will be no justice or true community until a fully separate nation is established for the TRUE people. If this new nationalist nation ever comes into being, the TRUE people will deserve and reserve the right to lead it and be privileged regardless of whoever else also makes up that state. Once a subordinate group has acquired a national state, subordinate group racism transforms into a dominant group racism.

I hypothesize that subordinate group anti-racism also exists. There are those within subordinate groups who reject both dominant and subordinate group racial hierarchy. They, like their dominant group anti-racist peers, see through the claims of racial nationalists and embrace some higher social principle as the basis of the state and of access to resources and privilege. Yet all of the writing on subordinate group opposition and struggle against racism is about efforts against dominant group racism. We know virtually nothing about subordinate group struggles and conflict against their own racism. There is a need for a parallel study to Aptheker's *Anti-Racism in U.S. History* (1993) that looks at subordinate group anti-racism in the contemporary United States and world community.

In its social necessity to dominate in fact or in potential, racism as a part of nationalist cultural ideology places highest value on the humanity, creations, sensitivities, and potential of THE (TRUE) people. Furthermore, the categorical superiority of THE (TRUE) people calls for and cannot exist without human hierarchy. There must be privilege and lack of privilege or else racism as part of the worldview of dominant or subordinate groups could easily be negated, along with its justification for monopolizing advantages and benefits. In all racist ideation, THE people are the privileged or the TRUE people should be privileged. Lesser people should lack privilege because they are inferior.

But equally as important as the worldview from which racism comes is that racists seek translation of their view into concrete realities (Takaki, 1990). To make certain that reality confirms the dominant racist's belief in his or her own supremacy, the nation's institutional life must be organized and managed to produce the desired hierarchy and "racial" privilege for THE people—institutional racism. With cultural and institutional racism in place, THE people can demonstrate that they are superior to inferior people, regardless of whether specific members of THE people have appropriate personal and individual attributes such as intelligence, honor, morals, and virtue (Carmichael & Hamilton, 1967). In fact, the only way lesser people can be seen as having any value is to conform to THE customs of THE superior people. The more complete their conformity, the higher their worth—up to a point. The customs of lesser people are valuable only in terms of what can be appropriated as entertainment, innovations, and fads for THE people (Habermas, 1990). Regardless of the extent of lesser people's conformity or their contribution to THE superior people's ways, a lesser person will never be equal to THE people short of complete physical and cultural assimilation.

It is often assumed that the victims of dominant group racism are automatically anti-racist. This is another common misconception. Not all people of European or any other descent are racist any more than all people of African, Native American, or Asian descent are anti-racist. The construction of acceptable social identities for members of subordinate groups in a racially hierarchical society is intended to maintain their subordination and keep them from becoming anti-racist. In the same way, the construction of the dominant group's social identity has a complementary intent—to maintain dominant group superiority and to prevent anti-racism (Aptheker, 1993).

In a racist social system, to be faithfully and uncritically a member of any racial group is to perpetuate and reinforce racism. Furthermore, dominant and subordinate group racisms are complementary and mutually reinforcing. Racists are people with essentially the same worldviews, even if they are at different ends of the power spectrum. Just as dominant group racists are threatened by anti-racists regardless of racial background, subordinate group racists cannot accept or work with anti-racists from the dominant group. Neither dominant nor subordinate group racists have a vision of, interest in, or trust that an inclusive society is attainable by recreating the existing social system. Subordinate group racists, just like dominant group racists, oppose the creation of the necessary cross-racial coalitions necessary to struggle for a principled inclusive society where hierarchy based on race might be dismantled.

This understanding of racism suggests that all people and cultures have the capacity and potential to be racist. This does not say that all people are racist and actualize this potential. Racism in the postmodern world is more than ethnocentrism or the appearance and disappearance of racial discrimination. Modern racism does not require that THE people dominate "inferior" people directly through overt physical force, political control, or economic dominance. Control is exercised by defining and redefining through all the media the perceptions and cultural images of inferior groups.

In the modern world, it is more efficient and effective to exercise power and maintain domination by controlling the worldviews of others and by selectively incorporating aspects of their cultures into one's own (Gramsci, 1985). For example, people outside Western European cultures who come into contact with the West soon find that they no longer are in control of their own worldviews (see McLean, this volume). They are quickly transformed into consumers and, when needed, aspiring workers. Modern racism requires the elimination of other, presumed inferior worldviews. Lesser people may only have the identity THE people's worldview confers on them—and that is as less developed and inferior.

THE CULTURAL ROOTS OF MODERN RACISM

Racism is first and foremost a cultural assumption—it is rooted deeply in culture. In North America, the early North Carolina slave holders had to justify slavery and indefinitely maintain control over the then-majority population of African slaves and White indentured laborers (Cecil-Fronsman, 1992, pp. 69-82). It was their intent that their ideation about superior and inferior peoples become cultural (Allen, 1994; Cecil-Fronsman, 1992; Mintz, 1974; Richardson, 1968; Takaki, 1990). In this way, the economic benefits of racial hierarchy would become part of the common White identity (Cecil-Fronsman, 1992). In time, the very character of the nation and ideation of what was taken for granted as normal in successive generations would reproduce racial categories and hierarchy. The very same cultural process has produced and reinforced patriarchy. Long after the old slave masters are gone, their definition of reality and social advantages, derived from being "White," are still taken for granted despite centuries of social change. Prior to the 17th century, slavery in the Western world was practiced without racism as we now know it (see Wood, this volume).

One implication of cultural racism is the following. Although institutions change constantly, unless underlying cultural assumptions also change, new institutional arrangements will continue to reproduce what is historically expected (Carmichael & Hamilton, 1967). Furthermore, nothing really changes if the base cultural assumptions remain the same— "the more things change, the more they remain the same." This point might lead one to say that, indeed, racism is permanent because culture cannot be changed by passing a law and then enforcing it, nor can racism be changed simply by reorganizing a corporation and branch of government. So the question arises, "If racism is at core cultural, can a cultural attribute be changed?" The answer is, "Yes." But the way in which cultural beliefs are changed requires very different strategies and approaches from those used to change institutional or individual behaviors.

First, to change culture it must be understood that cultural assumptions are not innate givens. They are social constructs and are compelling only as long as they are unexamined and believed (Essed, 1991). The seeming permanence of cultural traits lies in the fact that these traits are taken for granted and used to define expected reality. Individuals and groups that question and examine base cultural assumptions are no longer automatically compelled by them. Witness the successive "cultural" liberation of some stigmatized groups in the United States such as Blacks, women, Indians, and gays.

Second, well into this century there was little change in base European cultures, despite the radical transformation of the commercial and industrial revolutions (Stein, 1960). Things were done as they had been for centuries and expectations for most people did not change. The changes that occurred in family life, work, and community happened slowly and due to what was thought of as social evolutionary rules, as suggested by Ward's *Dynamic Sociology* (1868) and Giddings' *Principles of Sociology* (1896). At the turn of the century, it was radical to think that culture changed, whether spontaneously, by evolution, in a unilinear way, or irreversibly, as described by Sumner in his essay, "The Absurd Effort to Make the World Over" (1924). Now social change is taken for granted and expected, and an entire generation exists who knows nothing else.

Contemporary disappointment at racism's seeming permanence is contrary to the extraordinary potential in the modern world for change. Not even conservatives, who wish to reverse history and are fearful of the future, believe that rapid change can be stopped. The communications revolution, which is still gaining momentum, has already obliterated cultural complacency and isolation virtually everywhere on earth. As time and distance between people are reduced, economic and other interdependencies increase (Hodgkinson, 1995). This does not mean that racism will simply disappear with increasing interdependence. Communications tools and potential are now available as never before to call the assumed necessity of racial hierarchy into question and reduce, if not eliminate, it as a basis for long-term social oppression.

APPROACHES AND BIASES

This book's authors come from the fields of anthropology, classics, sociology, political science, communications, and history. The chapters are highly interdisciplinary and have underlying theoretical bases. It has become a ritual to acknowledge that the study of race relations in the social sciences in general and in sociology in particular suffers from poor theory (Van den Berghe, 1969). The formal study of race is not driven by established scientific theories and quantitative methodologies. Instead, the subject and the desire for social change (to reduce racial hatred and inequalities) come first, and we use the perspectives, evidence, and best guesses of all disciplines to understand and address racism. This book is part of this topical approach, but not because we wish to follow tradition.

Racism and anti-racism provide organizational and structural analyses about how race relations are actualized and responded to. In the past, self-conscious scientific approaches to race relations have had to focus on specific aspects of intra- and interracial interactions (Blalock, 1967; Jaynes & Williams, 1989). Where race relations can be decomposed into fragmented microrealities, testable scientific techniques are applicable because sufficient controls can be excersized at the microlevel to test hypotheses and generate theory, as found in articles on race published in *American Sociological Review.* Extraordinary work has been done in this way. But even where microracial realities can be translated into data and studied statistically, a pressing need for macroanalysis and explanation continues. What are the possible connections between individual and group prejudice, discriminatory organizational practices, government and private sector decision making, and changes in social and economic organization? We cannot even conceive of empirical tests of these kinds of complex interrelationships without sufficient macrohypothetical descriptions and explanations about these relationships. Our examination of racism is an attempt to answer these important macroquestions.

Students of race relations need to be reminded that the empirical scientific method that utilizes probability theory and statistical techniques to determine whether or not generalizations will be accepted or rejected is not the only scientific method or the only disciplined way to explore human realities systematically (Bulmer, 1984). The work reflected in this book is based on systematic inquiry through current and past literature, government and historic records, and the observations of hundreds of people from all over the world at different points in time. Chapter references provide evidence. The work presented in this book is neither fiction nor THE truth. But we believe that what we have here is much better than good guesses. Furthermore, to write passionately in a dispassionate way about racism and to be well-informed requires experience, a scholarly frame of reference, and broad cultural exposure. Each author's biases are clear. Each author shows interest in the best evidence grounded in human experience; that knowledge can eliminate racism. As editor of this collection, I bring to the table two open biases. First, I believe that, even in the most chaotic of social circumstances, an underlying logic and order exists (Suttles, 1970). Second, social change does not just happen, it is a complex mix of surprise, circumstance, and decision making. We create our own realities and futures, or they are created for us.

Prior Literature

Soper's *Racism, A World Issue* (1947) may be the first attempt to look specifically at race relations as a worldwide and comparable phenomenon using racism as an organizing concept. Other attempts soon after that saw the growing importance of race relations as a comparable world phenomenon include Frazier's *Race and Culture Contacts in the Modern World* (1957) and Shibutani and Kwan's *Ethnic Stratification: A Comparative Approach* (1965). Shibutani and Kwan look more specifically at inequalities around the world than does Frazier, but Frazier looks more specifically at cultural differences. Neither work uses racism to interpret the relation among culture, social systems, and inequality. The book that makes this connection most clearly is Van den Berghe's *Race and Racism: A Comparative Perspective* (1969). Of specific importance is Van den Berghe's thesis that race relations is changing worldwide due to transitions of societies from paternalistic to competitive structures. These transitions are closely linked to changes in cultural and economic events that have resulted in covert, indirect forms of racial stratification based on economic practices and cultural identity.

Van den Berghe's suppositions about the role and manner in which racism would transform racial inequality was not surpassed by the explosion of books and journals on international comparative race and ethnic relations that came into being during the 1970s. Much of this work focused on case studies of relations between culturally and/or racially distinct national groups. Examples are Baker (1983); Francis (1976); the journal *Research in Race and Ethnic Relations,* started in 1979; Kuper and Smith (1969); LeVine and Campbell (1972); and Smith (1992). A summary of much of this world comparative literature can be found in Weinberg's *World Racism and Related Inhumanities: A Country-by-Country Bibliography* (1992).

Another fascinating development that came out of this international and comparative literature is stated by Van den Berghe in *The Ethnic Phenomenon* (1981). Questions arose about the utility of race as an explanatory concept. If race is a social concept that describes alleged differences between groups that cannot be supported in science, what is the utility of race other than being a part of the ongoing cultural code to maintain social inequalities? There is no such thing, in fact, as Black, White, or Asian races. Since 1980, the concept of race has been used in conjunction with ethnicity or not at all in the international and comparative literature.

Since 1981, three new developments have pushed beyond Van den Berghe's important insights. First, there is the world-systems literature that has emerged from Wallerstein's two volumes, *The Modern World-System* (Part I, 1974; and Part II, 1980). Wallerstein outlines and notes the specific class and group decisions and historic events that have lead to the emergence of the modern world economy. The movement and accumulation of capital from nation to nation and region to region that make and break national states and enrich or impoverish national labor forces in quick succession are also explained in Wallerstein's *Labor in the World Social Structure* (1983) and in Hopkins and Wallerstein's *Processes of the World-System* (1980).

A second and parallel development to the world-system approach is the work describing the global economy. This work is not informed by the Marxist tradition of macroanalysis. It comes out of policy analysis of government decision making, foreign trade and aid practices, and studies of corporate international investment, trade, and labor practices. Examples of work in this area are Beeman and Frank, *New Dynamics in the Global Economy* (1988), Berry, *Economic Geography* (1987), and Bosworth, *Saving and Investment in a Global Economy* (1993). Despite the very different perspectives and points of departure, they portray the global economy in a manner that is amazingly consistent with the descriptions of historically projected processes in the work on world-systems. This work provides a confirmation of the world-systems themes, and world-systems analysis provides the historic background for the emerging global economy.

A third development is the increasing potential to use the concept of culture as it has never been used before. Both the world-systems and the global economy literature introduces the central role of culture in maintaining global social systems and potentially challenging them. The communications revolution is occurring after the commercial and industrial revolutions, and may have as profound a social effect as the others did. A by-product of the communications revolution is that a commonly held global culture is emerging, despite cross-cultural differences and national and ethnic boundaries. Multiculturalism may very well become the norm, and most people will have at least one subculture in common. Works such as Jencks' *The Post-Modern Reader* (1992), Habermas' *Moral Consciousness and Communicative Action* (1990), and Gramsci's *Selections From Cultural Writings* (1985) are vital to understanding the role of communications and culture in maintaining modern social systems.

Finally, one might ask, "What does any of this literature have to do with racism and anti-racism?" The answer is, "Everything." Racism describes the dynamic relations between racial prejudice, institutional discrimination, the economy, and culture. These relations have been transformed from paternalistic to competitive social structures, as Van den Berghe (1969) predicted. But what the world-systems and global economy literature suggests is that another structural transformation is underway. Or, one might argue, the old structure is continuing to be transformed (Frieden & Lake, 1987). Either way, racism is continuing to be transformed beyond what now may be recognized as racism and the social context Van den Berghe described in 1969. Racism and the most effective actions that can be taken against it are becoming transnational or global on at least the cultural and institutional levels.

ABOUT THIS BOOK

Part I

In the first of three parts, the focus is on the history of racism and an introduction to anti-racism. Did racism exist in the ancient world? If so, why? If not, when did it come into being and how? Frank Snowden, Jr., begins Part I with "Europe's Oldest Chapter in the History of Black-White Relations." This is a most important response to the belief that racism has been with us for all time and in all places. Snowden argues persuasively that racism has not always existed, and that the early Greeks and Romans were relatively sophisticated in their knowledge of physical and cultural differences among people. They understood that physical differences were a function of climate and exposure to the sun—effectively predating our best modern scientific evidence.

In Chapter 2, Peter H. Wood explains "How the Myth of Race Took Hold and Flourished in the Minds of Europe's Renaissance Colonizers." Both positive and negative images of Africans existed in precolonizing Europe. Once colonization began, the notion of European innate superiority evolved slowly. Racism grew out of the need to control slaves, to justify slavery, to create a racial identity that would unify diverse Europeans, and to obscure the real motive for slavery and White superiority—the maintenance of wealth and privilege for a small elite.

Wood's chapter is based primarily on English history. In Chapter 3, Laura A. Lewis takes a parallel look at the development of racism in the Hispanic colonies, in particular Mexico. In "Spanish Ideology and the Practice of Inequality in the New World," Lewis traces the origin of modern racism in the Hispanic world from two sources: the Spanish efforts to purge their nation of the Moorish and Jewish presence in the 15th century, and the New World colonial elite's interest in maintaining economic gain and privilege through the exploitation of native people and Africans.

In the final chapter of Part I, Herbert Aptheker looks at some of the evidence of White anti-racism in U.S. history after the Civil War ("Anti-Racism in the United States: 1865-1900"). During this critical period, when successful efforts were made to disenfranchise African Americans through sharecropping and a comprehensive and formal system of racial segregation (Jim Crow), there were Whites who opposed these efforts and spoke out against the presumption of racism. It was not popular or convenient to be anti-racist in the South after the Civil War. Like the African Americans who opposed disenfranchisement, many of these Whites gave their lives for their beliefs. Although this evidence is limited to the United States, it presents a challenge to look more carefully at characteristics of anti-racism in other places in the world. Is the transracial characteristic of anti-racism in the United States unique to the United States? What implications does dominant group anti-racism have for more effective anti-racism mobilization in the future?

Part II

Part I focuses on the historical background of racism and introduces the important missing perspective in studies of racial inequality—opposition to racism, or anti-racism. In Part II, three topical chapters provide analyses of issues related to anti-racism. As with Chapter 4, these chapters primarily draw on experiences and developments in the United States. But each author points out that parallel developments have occurred in other world communities and a need exists to do comparative analysis.

Polly E. McLean writes about "Mass Communication, Popular Culture, and Racism" in Chapter 5. Control of mass communications and popular images is crucial to social control in the postmodern world community. Modern communications have been vital to advancing modern racism. It is through the mass media that the rest of the world has been socialized to primarily North American racial imagery. McLean points out that the media have the potential to be a formidable tool for anti-racism, and on occasions have showed this potential.

In Chapter 6, Bob Blauner provides an initial analysis of why there has not been an effective anti-racist movement in the United States. In "White Radicals, White Liberals, and White People: Rebuilding the Anti-Racist Coalition," Blauner goes to the heart of the matter and asserts that liberal Whites, who in principle are opposed to racism, have been alienated from anti-racist coalitions by radical Blacks and Whites, who have categorically dismissed all liberals and liberal concerns as racist. The cause of anti-racism in the United States has suffered greatly from this strategic error. Blauner points out that it is not too late to begin coalition building.

People are oppressed and hierarchy is maintained by a number of other bases, besides race—sex, class, ethnicity, sexual orientation. By no means does this book's focus on race suggest that race is mutually exclusive or even more important than these other bases for organizing and justifying systematic inequality. A full treatment of all the bases of inequality is beyond the scope of this book.

But one connection must be addressed: the relation between anti-racism and feminism. Frederick Douglass spoke of the close relation between racial and sexual oppression, and said that liberation in one area could not occur without liberation in the other (Foner, 1976). Aptheker (1993) points out that, throughout U.S. history, women tended to be more anti-racist than men.

In Chapter 7, "Changing the Subject: Race and Gender in Feminist Discourse," Karen Dugger looks at the struggle to define a basis of collective discourse and common ground between White women and women of color. She suggests that postmodern feminism presents some promise to bridge the gap, and she address deficiencies in women's progressive efforts.

These topical chapters in Part II are only samples of the analysis that needs to be done, based on the historic implications that racism is not innate but conditional and that racism is opposed, not simply by members of oppressed groups, but by dominant group members as well.

Part III

Part III presents area analyses of contemporary developments of racism and anti-racism in the world community. One can see the extent to which historic cultural conditioning and unique circumstances have contributed to variations in contemporary racism and anti-racism, and the extent to which the national expressions of racism are converging, as suggested by Van den Berghe (1969). Part III provides evidence of the extent to which racism is evolving into a form of social control and stratification in the postmodern global community. This time, the scope of analysis is expanded to Great Britain, Western Europe, the Caribbean, South Africa, and Brazil. A subsequent volume is needed to present analyses of racism and anti-racism in Australia, Japan, China, India, Canada, Eastern Europe, the Middle East, and the rest of Latin America.

John Solomos leads off Part III in Chapter 8 with "Racism and Anti-Racism in Great Britain: Historical Trends and Contemporary Issues." Unlike nations in the Western hemisphere, Great Britain did not have clearly recognizable communities of color until the post-World War II labor shortages were filled by Afro-Caribbean and East Indian immigrants. Solomos very aptly shows that state racism has played on nativistic fears and English racial nationalism. The result is a modern racism in Great Britain.

Louis Kushnick continues this line of analysis in Chapter 9, "Racism and Anti-Racism in Western Europe." He examines the post-World War II need for service labor in Western Europe that was filled primarily by Turks and North Africans. He also points out that European economic exploitation of Third World nations is driving Third World immigrants to jobs in Europe despite increasingly hostile treatment. Kushnick provides a number of very useful comments about the effectiveness and potential of anti-racist efforts in Western Europe.

Chapter 10 is an introduction to racism and anti-racism in Brazil by Rosana Heringer. An introduction is needed because of the complexity and scope of issues related to race relations in Brazil. In Chapter 11, Antonio Sérgio Alfredo Guimarães writes on "Racism and Anti-Racism in Brazil: A Postmodern Perspective." According to Guimarães, it is a myth that racism does not exist in Brazil. In fact, attempts earlier in this century to forge a unique and modern Brazilian identity led students of race not to see the racism embedded in the "Brazilian way." In Chapter 12, "Black Resistance in Brazil: A Matter of Necessity," Rosângela Maria Vieira shows that race consciousness and community among African Brazilians has existed and does exist. In fact, this is the largest and strategically most important community of African descent in the West, with extraordinary potential to influence change both at home and abroad.

In Europe and in North and South America, people of color are dominated by people of European descent. In Chapter 13, "Racism and Anti-Racism in the Caribbean," Ralph R. Premdas shows how historically subordinate groups struggle with racism. As the politically dominant group in a number of Caribbean nations, the Afro-Caribbean elite's efforts to reward political allies and to use the government to maintain group privileges have resulted in charges and counter-charges of racism between Afro-, Asian-, and Hispanic-Indian Caribbeans. This issue is especially critical in nations where the Native Indian population is growing due to immigration, while the African-origin population continues to emigrate. Premdas suggests that Europeans versus people of color is not the only way that racism can occur. Afro-Caribbeans can express dominant group racism, and East Indian Caribbeans can in turn articulate subordinate group racism.

Mokubung Nkomo and associates write in Chapter 14 about "The Long Shadow of Apartheid Ideology: The Case of Open Schools in South Africa." Anti-racism both in and outside of South Africa has resulted in the dismantling of overt apartheid. But the authors point out that what is replacing it is not a racially impartial democratic process. A new system of racial control to maintain historic inequalities is emerging. The authors use the desegregation of "open" (private) schools as an illustrative case.

Finally, Chapter 15 is my synthesis of all three parts. Racism is unique in each location. Clearly, no two historical backgrounds are exactly alike, and cultural differences exist between nations. But what is extraordinary is the extent to which each national expression of racism appears to be converging into a common model. Painfully evident is the extent to which racism is now international and has been influenced by U.S. racial imagery and history. In contrast, the local scope and range of anti-racism has yet to be realized, is still limited largely to subordinate group opposition in each nation, and lacks the organization and comprehensiveness necessary to address the international scope of racism effectively. In effect, the new racism calls for nothing short of rethinking anti-racism, broadening its scope, and building coalitions between principled dominant and subordinate group anti-racists.

REFERENCES

Allen, T. (1994). *The invention of the White race: Racial oppression and social control.* New York: Verso.

Aptheker, H. (1993). *Anti-racism in U.S. history.* Westport, CT: Praeger.

Baker, D. (1983). *Race, ethnicity, and power: A comparative study.* Boston: Routledge & Kegan Paul.

Beeman, W., & Frank, I. (1988). *New dynamics in the global economy.* New York: Committee for Economic Development.

Bell, D. (1992). *Faces at the bottom of the well: The permanence of racism.* New York: Basic Books.

Belous, R., & Hartley, R. (Eds.). (1990). *The growth of regional trading blocs in the global economy.* Washington, DC: National Planning Associates.

Berger, P. (1962). *Invitation to sociology.* Garden City, NY: Anchor.

Berry, B. J. L. (1987). *Economic geography: Resource use, locational choices, and regional specialization in the global economy.* Englewood Cliffs, NJ: Prentice Hall.

Blalock, H. (1967). *Toward a theory of minority group relations.* New York: John Wiley.

Blauner, B. (1972). *Racial oppression in America.* New York: Harper & Row.

Blauner, B. (1989). *Black lives, White lives: Three decades of race relations in America.* Berkeley: University of California Press.

Bosworth, B. (1993). *Savings and investment in a global economy.* Washington, DC: Brookings Institution.

Bulmer, M. (1984). *Sociological research methods.* New Brunswick, NJ: Transaction Books.

Carmichael, S., & Hamilton, C. (1967). *Black power: The politics of liberation in America.* New York: Random House.

Cecil-Fronsman, B. (1992). *Common Whites: Class and culture in antebellum North Carolina.* Lexington: University Press of Kentucky.

Dunbar, L. (Ed.). (1984). *Minority report: What happened to Blacks, Hispanics, and American Indians, and other minorities in the eighties.* New York: Pantheon.

Essed, P. (1991). *Understanding everyday racism: An interdisciplinary theory.* Newbury Park, CA: Sage.

Essien-Udom, E. U. (1962). *Black nationalism: A search for identity in America.* New York: Dell.

Foner, P. (1976). *Frederick Douglass on women's rights.* Westport, CT: Greenwood.

Francis, E. (1976). *Interethnic relations.* New York: Elsevier North-Holland.

Frazier, E. (1957). *Race and culture contacts in the modern world.* Boston: Beacon.

Fredrickson, G. (1971). *The Black image in the White mind.* New York: Harper & Row.

Frieden, J., & Lake, D. (1987). *International political economy: Perspective on global power and wealth.* New York: St. Martin's.

Giddings, F. (1896). *The principles of sociology.* New York: Macmillan.

Goldsmith, W., & Blakely, E. (1992). *Separate societies: Poverty and inequality in U.S. cities.* Philadelphia: Temple University Press.

Gramsci, A. (1985). *Selections from cultural writings.* (D. Forgacs & G. Nowell-Smith, Eds.). Cambridge, MA: Harvard University Press.

Habermas, J. (1990). *Moral consciousness and communicative action.* Cambridge: MIT Press.

Hodgkinson, H. (1995). Demographic imperatives for the future. In B. Bowser, T. Jones, & G. Auletta (Eds.), *Toward the multicultural university* (pp. 3-19). Westport, CT: Praeger.

Hollifield, J. (1992). *Immigrants, markets, and states: The political economy of postwar Europe.* Cambridge, MA: Harvard University Press.

Hopkins, T., & Wallerstein, I. (Eds.). (1980). *Processes of the world-system.* Beverly Hills, CA: Sage.

Jaynes, G., & Williams, R., Jr. (Eds.). (1989). *A common destiny: Blacks and American society.* Washington, DC: National Academy Press.

Jencks, C. (Ed.). (1992). *The post-modern reader.* New York: St. Martin's.

Jones, J. (1972). *Prejudice and racism.* Reading, MA: Addison-Wesley.

Jones, J. (1981). The concept of racism and its changing reality. In B. Bowser & R. Hunt (Eds.), *Impacts of racism on White Americans* (pp. 27-49). Beverly Hills, CA: Sage.

King, W. (1995). The triumph of tribalism: The modern American university as a reflection of Eurocentric culture. In B. Bowser, T. Jones, & G. Auletta (Eds.), *Toward the multicultural university* (pp. 21-39). Westport, CT: Praeger.

Kuper, L., & Smith, M. (Eds.). (1969). *Pluralism in Africa.* Berkeley: University of California Press.

LeVine, R., & Campbell, D. (1972). *Ethnocentrism.* New York: John Wiley.

Mintz, S. (Ed.). (1974). *Slavery, colonialism, and racism.* New York: Norton.

Myrdal, G. (1944). *An American dilemma.* New York: Harper & Row.

Nkrumah, K. (1965). *Neo-colonialism: The last stage of imperialism.* New York: International Publishers.

Patterson, O. (1977). *Ethnic chauvinism: The reactionary impulse.* New York: Stein & Day.

Pettigrew, T. (1981). The mental health impact. In B. Bowser & R. Hunt (Eds.), *Impacts of racism on White Americans* (pp. 97-118). Beverly Hills, CA: Sage.

Richardson, P. (1968). *Empire and slavery.* New York: Harper & Row.

Shibutani, T., & Kwan, K. (1965). *Ethnic stratification: A comparative approach.* New York: Macmillan.

Smith, J. (1992). *The politics of ethnic and racial inequality: A systematic comparative macro-analysis from the colonial period to the present.* Dubuque, IA: Kendall/Hunt.

Soper, E. (1947). *Racism, a world issue.* New York: Abingdon-Cokesbury.

Stein, M. (1960). *The eclipse of community: An interpretation of American studies.* New York: Harper & Row.

Sumner, W. (1924). The absurd effort to make the world over. In A. Keller & M. Davie (eds.), *Selected essays of William Graham Sumner.* New Haven, CT: Yale University Press.

Suttles, G. (1970). *The social order of the slum: Ethnicity and territory in the inner city.* Chicago: University of Chicago Press.

Takaki, R. (1990). *Iron cages: Race and culture in 19th century America.* New York: Oxford University Press.

Van den Berghe, P. (1969). *Race and racism: A comparative perspective.* New York: John Wiley.

Van den Berghe, P. (1981). *The ethnic phenomenon.* New York: Elsevier North-Holland.

Wallerstein, I. (1974). *The modern world-system.* New York: Academic Press.

Wallerstein, I. (1980). *The modern world-system II.* New York: Academic Press.

Wallerstein, I. (Ed.). (1983). *Labor in the world social structure.* Beverly Hills, CA: Sage.

Ward, L. (1868). *Dynamic sociology.* New York: Johnson Reprint.

Weinberg, M. (1992). *World racism and related inhumanities: A country-by-country bibliography.* New York: Greenwood.

Williams, E. (1944). *Capitalism and slavery.* New York: Capricorn Books.

Wilson, W. (1978). *The declining significance of race.* Chicago: University of Chicago Press.

PART I

WHAT IS INNATE ABOUT IT?

If racism is an innate part of our human character, it has always existed and it should be clearly evident in history. Furthermore, if it is innate, there is very little that we can do about racism that would be long term and effective. Our struggles against racism are like our struggles against sin—racism will be with us for as long as we are human and alive. This is precisely what many well-intended scholars and ordinary people believe. There are people whose life circumstances and daily experiences have been minimized by their racial membership who have also come to believe in racism's permanence. But they see it as an inevitable and innate characteristic of people of European descent.

In Chapter 1, Frank M. Snowden, Jr., explores the origins of racism. He revisits the Greeks and Romans and examines the very foundations of Western culture and civilization. Using original sources and meanings, he finds that racism was not a given in the ancient world, where Europeans and Africans traveled, exchanged, and lived with one another, as well as fought wars against and with one another. Color prejudice did exist in the ancient world, but racism as we know it today did not—the distinction between racism and color prejudice is an important one. In Chapter 2, Peter H. Wood traces the development of modern racism, primarily in the English colonial world. In comparison with all the other problems of civilization and exchange between people, European racism is relatively recent, and came into being as a justification for Indian and African slavery and as a way to maintain social control and elite privilege in colonial American societies. In Chapter 3, Laura A. Lewis takes a parallel look at the development of racism in the Hispanic world.

1

Modern European racism was inherited from the recent colonial past. It is not innate in anyone's genes, any more than a specific language or food preference is. Racism is cultural and conditional, and what is cultural and conditional can be changed and does not have to be lived with. In Chapter 4, Herbert Aptheker provides the best evidence of racism's conditionality. He provides a history from 1865 to 1900 of the actions of Whites who not only rejected racism but worked against it and, in some cases, gave their lives for it. Aptheker uncovers the erroneous effort to characterize anti-racism as White versus Black, effectively using race to prevent what those who benefit from racism fear most—that racism is essentially repulsive and that transracial coalitions have the greatest chance of ending racism both during colonial times and now. Chapter 4 provides a challenge as to how racism and efforts to oppose it are analyzed in the United States as well as in the rest of the world.

1

Europe's Oldest Chapter in the History of Black-White Relations

Frank M. Snowden, Jr.

INTRODUCTION AND TERMINOLOGY

In the late twentieth-century atmosphere of "racial and political correctness" the use of the color-term black as an ethnic designation without an explanatory note might be misinterpreted as "racist" in tone. The Greeks and Romans, the subject of this chapter, however, in the first European accounts of the physical characteristics of certain African peoples, frequently used a color-term— *Aithiops, Aethiops, Ethiopian*— literally a burnt-faced person— as a designation for the blackest and most woolly-haired people known to them. But it is not generally known that *Ethiopian* carried no stigma of inferiority similar to that associated with color-terms in post-classical societies which have subjected dark and

AUTHOR'S NOTE: In addition to the publications cited herein, the following provide additional information on many points treated in this chapter: "Aethiopes" (1981), *Lexicon Iconographicum Mythologiae Classicae* I, 1. Zurich and Munich: AARA-APHLAD, pp. 413-419; I, 2 (plates) pp. 321-326; *"Melas-leukos and Niger-candidus* Contrasts in Classical Literature" (1988), *The Ancient History Bulletin,* 2(3), 60-64; "Romans and Blacks: A Review Essay" (1990), *American Journal of Philology, 111*(4), 543-557; "Review of *Blacks in Ancient Cypriot Art* by Vassos Karageorghis" (1990), *American Journal of Archaeology, 94,* 72-74; "Whither Afrocentrism?" (1992, Winter), *Georgetown,* pp. 7-8; "Response" (1993), *Arethusa, 26*(3), 319-327.

black-skinned peoples to social, economic and political discrimination on the basis of the color of their skin. The written accounts and artistic portrayals of African blacks by Greeks and Romans have received primarily the attention of specialists in classical studies and ancient art. The history of black-white relations in Greco-Roman antiquity, however, has a special relevance for the modern world. It sheds light on the reasons not only for the vast differences in attitudes toward blacks in ancient and modern societies, but also for the absence in antiquity of the "color line" which W.E.B. Du Bois referred to as "the problem of the twentieth century."

"Negro," and "black" (which in general replaced "Negro" in the United States in the 1960s) have long been used in the modern world to describe people closely resembling the Ethiopians of Greco-Roman texts and similar ethnic types depicted by classical artists. In these same sources, the color of people with lighter pigmentation, like Europeans, has been commonly described as white. The Arabic historian Ibn Khaldûn made a comment pertinent to the Greco-Roman use of a color-term as an ethnic designation when he observed that whites did not designate inhabitants of the north, like those of the south, by their color because "whiteness was something usual and common (to them), and they did not see anything sufficiently remarkable in it to cause them to use it as a specific term" (The Muqaddimah, trans F. Rosenthal, 1958, I, p. 172).

In this chapter I have followed a common historical and anthropological practice of using "black" and sometimes "Negro" in referring to the Ethiopians of classical texts and to the ethnic types in Greco-Roman art resembling "textual" Ethiopians. "Black" and "Negro" are more meaningful in certain modern contexts than Kushites, used by Egyptians, or Ethiopians and Nubians, used by Greeks and Romans for people inhabiting the Nile Valley south of Egypt.

THE PHYSICAL CHARACTERISTICS OF AFRICAN BLACKS

Aithiops-Aethiops (Ethiopian) was the most common generic word used by Greeks and Romans when writing about the dark- and black-skinned peoples who lived south of Egypt and on the southern fringes of northwest Africa. The word Ethiopian was in origin a reflection of an environment theory that attributed the Ethiopian's color as well as his woolly or tightly curled hair to the intense heat of the southern sun. The

Ethiopians most often mentioned in Greek and Roman records lived in the Nile Valley south of Egypt. This region was known as Kush in Egyptian and Old Testament texts and was designated by Greeks, Romans, and early Christians as Ethiopia (not to be confused with present-day Ethiopia). The area has also been referred to as Nubia, often divided into Lower Nubia, extending from the First to the Second Cataract, and Upper Nubia, stretching southward from the Second Cataract to the area in the vicinity of Meroë, situated north of Khartoum, the capital of present-day Sudan. Other people, also known as Ethiopians, are reported to have lived in northwest Africa, roughly from the present-day Fezzan in southwest Libya and the oases of southern Tunisia to the Atlantic coast of south Morocco.

The color of Ethiopians was regarded as their most characteristic and identifiable feature, a trait highlighted in the words Ethiopian and Ethiopia (Land of the Burnt Face). Some Ethiopians were described as the blackest people on earth ([Aristotle] *Prob.* 66.898b; Arrian, *Anab.* 5.4.4); others were exceedingly dark and pure Ethiopians (Ptolemy, *Geog.* 1.9.7) and those near the Egyptian-Ethiopian boundary were not so black as Ethiopians, but darker than Egyptians (Philostratus, *VA* 6.2). As early as about 700 B.C. the poet Hesiod (*Op.* 527) wrote of nameless dark men living in the south; somewhat later, Xenophanes, the philosopher-poet, described Ethiopians as black and flat-nosed (*Frg.* 16); in the fifth century B.C. Herodotus observed that the Ethiopian's hair was the woolliest of all mankind (7.70); and in the late first century B.C. the historian Diodorus (3.8.2) described Ethiopians who lived near the Nile as black, flat-nosed, and woolly-haired. But by far the most detailed description of a black comes from a poem, the *Moretum* (31-35), attributed in antiquity to Vergil, which described a woman with these characteristics: hair tightly curled, lips thick, color dark, chest broad, breasts pendulous, belly somewhat pinched, legs thin, and feet broad and ample. Long before the advent of modern anthropology, this description adumbrated the traits appearing in some later anthropological classifications of so-called Negroid types (Snowden, 1970, pp. 9-11, 14). And as Clyde Kluckhohn has emphasized (1961, pp. 27-28) "Greek descriptive anthropology was carried further and carried out more systematically than that of any other ancient people whose records have survived."

Realistic portrayals of several black ethnic types depicted by Greek and Roman artists from the early second millennium B.C. until late in the Roman Empire (Vercoutter *et al.*, 1976, pp. 133-285) parallel the textual descriptions of Ethiopian Negroid traits. The combined written descriptions and the realistic and highly individualized portraits of numerous blacks point to direct observation and an intimate acquaintance with several black types. The accuracy of Greco-Roman portrayals of blacks, and the remarkable range of types have been noted by many specialists acquainted with present-day Africa, E. Mveng (1972, pp. 67-70) of the Federal University of Cameroon, for example, describing the Greco-Roman portrayal as a vast and authentic tableau of the principal types of African Negroes. Neither the blacks of artists nor those of classical authors were all portrayed monolithically as if cast from a single mold. All blacks did not look alike to Greeks and Romans, and variations in physical types were attributed, some to the influence of environment, and others to racial mixture (Snowden, 1993, pp. 322-326).

In addition to their accurate descriptions of the physical traits of African blacks, Greeks and Romans called attention to a number of Ethiopian cultural practices. Petronius, the author of the *Satyricon* (102), noted the custom of facial scarification, when he wrote that one cannot "pass for" an Ethiopian merely by blackening one's face: a complete Ethiopian disguise requires thick lips, tightly curled hair, and cicatrices (scarification) on the forehead (Snowden, 1983, p. 15 and figs. 22a-b). A knowledge of circumcision among Ethiopians, mentioned by Herodotus (2.104), is also attested by a fifth-century B.C. vase-painter, who contrasted the uncircumcised Heracles and the circumcised Ethiopian attendants of the Egyptian king Busiris (Snowden, 1983, p. 15 and fig. 19).

Greeks and Romans differentiated clearly between the physical characteristics of people they described as darker than themselves, and used Ethiopians as the yardstick by which these people were measured. In the first century A.D., for example, Manilius, author of the *Astronomica*, described Ethiopians (4.722-730) as the blackest; Indians, less sun-burnt; Egyptians, mildly dark; and Moors, the lightest. In other words, all Ethiopians were dark or black, but all people described as black or dark were not Ethiopians. Further, the Greco-Roman practice of using Ethiopians as a yardstick for measuring not only coloration but also the hair-type of peoples darker than themselves is illustrated by an emphasis on the contrast between the woolly hair of Ethiopians and the "non-woolly" hair of dark-skinned Egyptians (Strabo, 15.1.13; Arrian, *Ind.* 6.9). The claim that the Egyptians were predominantly black and that Hannibal, Cleopatra, and Septimius Severus were black is supported by neither the iconographical and written evidence relative to the physical characteristics of Ethiopians (the only word used as the regular equivalent of blacks or Negroes in the modern world) nor by copious other archaeological and historical evidence (Snowden, 1989, pp. 83-93; 1992, pp. 7-8).

GREEK AND ROMAN ENCOUNTERS WITH BLACKS

Under what circumstances did Greeks and Romans become acquainted with Ethiopia and Ethiopians? Although blacks are known from iconographical evidence as early as the second millennium B.C., and although Ethiopians are mentioned in Homer, it was not until the seventh century B.C. and later that most Greeks had occasion to encounter Ethiopians face-to-face. Military encounters provided a major avenue for Greek and Roman contacts with blacks, and accounted for the presence of blacks in many parts of the ancient world. Greek mercenaries in the army of Psammetichus II (595-581 B.C.) were the first Europeans reported to have actually confronted Ethiopian warriors on African soil. They had been recruited by the pharaoh for his expedition into Nubia (Herodotus, 2.161; Kitchen, 1973, p. 406), undertaken to eliminate a threat to Egypt from the Ethiopians who had ruled Egypt during the Twenty-fifth Dynasty (ca. 747 B.C.-656 B.C.). A certain Pabis from Colophon in Asia Minor was one of the Greek mercenaries whose names are known from graffiti scratched on a colossal statue of an Egyptian pharaoh at Abu Simbel, seven hundred miles up the Nile (Tod, 1946, no. 4,6-7). Worthy of note is the fact that another Colophonian, the philosopher Xenophanes, was the first European to identify Ethiopians by a feature other than color, their flat noses (*Frg.* 16 Diels). Pabis and his fellow Greeks upon their return to Asia Minor had apparently related to their countrymen accounts of what they had learned about the flat-nosed Ethiopians, once rulers of Egypt and of an empire that extended from deep in the interior of Africa to the Mediterranean. Greek military experience in Egypt is also strikingly reflected by the prominence given to Negro warriors in Greek art of the sixth century B.C. and by continuing Greek interest in the Twenty-fifth Dynasty.

The popularity of Negroes as subjects in Greek art and of Ethiopian themes in the theater in the fifth century B.C. was stimulated no doubt by the presence of Ethiopian soldiers among the troops of Xerxes (480-479 B.C.) during his invasion of Greece (Herodotus, 7.69-70, 9.32). For the majority of mainland Greeks these Ethiopians were the first blacks whom they had actually seen in the flesh. Encounters with black warriors continued in the Ptolemaic period. In fact, Ethiopians created substantial obstacles to implementation of plans which the Ptolemies had for the military occupation of Nubia and/or commercial activity there. At times Ethiopians besieged Ptolemaic positions (Preisigke, no. 5111). In some of the Egyptian rebellions that plagued the later Ptolemies, Ethiopians also played a role (Préaux, 1936, pp. 535-536; Pestman, 1965, pp. 168-169). Although Ptolemy Philadelphus according to Theocritus (*Id*. 17.87), had conquered a part of the country of the black Ethiopians, Ethiopia was nevertheless a threat to Egyptian autonomy. An unnamed Ptolemy, perhaps Epiphanes, according to the geographer Agatharchides, recruited a corps of five hundred horsemen from Greece for his war against the Ethiopians. It was also perhaps a threat of the Ethiopian military that Agatharchides was referring to in his account of the advice of an experienced regent to a young Ptolemy recommending caution against undertaking an expedition into Nubia (*De Mari Erythraeo*, 11-20).

In his account of Roman encounters with Ethiopians in the last quarter of the first century B.C., the historian Strabo reinforced the image of Ethiopians as a substantial military force. Ethiopians, according to Strabo, crossed the Roman boundary in Egypt, captured several towns, defeated three cohorts, enslaved the inhabitants, and seized statues of Augustus. Although Roman countermeasures reportedly resulted in the capture of Napata and the sale of Ethiopian prisoners, the extremely favorable terms of Augustus' peace settlement suggest that some details of Strabo's account may have been exaggerated because, according to the historian's report, Augustus granted the envoys of the Ethiopian queen everything they requested, including the remission of the tribute he had imposed (Strabo, 17.1.53-54). The many terra-cotta figurines of Negro warriors from the Roman period provide vivid illustrations of Ethiopian adversaries mentioned by authors of the early Roman Empire (Vercoutter *et al.*, pp. 213-214). And Josephus' references to Ethiopians in *Jewish Antiquities* (2.252-254; 8.165, pp. 254, 292-294; 10.15-17) reinforced the recurrent images of black warriors and may have reminded the historian's contemporaries of events closer to their own era (Snowden, 1983, pp. 53-54). Encounters with blacks in northwest Africa in the late first century B.C. and later enlarged the Roman knowledge of Ethiopian soldiers (Snowden, 1970, pp. 141-143; 1983, pp. 31-33). Blacks like the Ethiopian auxiliaries recruited by the Moorish chieftain Firmus in 372 A.D. participated in revolts that broke out sporadically during the Roman occupation of northwest Africa (Ammianus Marcellinus, 29.5.37).

Not all blacks in the Greco-Roman world were slaves. The advantages of cosmopolitan centers like Alexandria and Rome were as attractive to enterprising blacks as to others—Greek, Syrian, or Jew—who had voluntarily left their native lands in search of a better life. Some Ethiopians left Nubia and settled elsewhere to further their commercial interests which had always been an important factor in the Nubian economy. Others knew the value of knowledge of the language and culture of the Mediterranean world and sent their children to Alexandria, Athens, and Rome to study. Some black warriors who had escaped capture, attracted by what they had seen, returned later in a spirit of adventure or in the pursuit of economic gain. Another source of black settlers abroad may have been diplomats like those in attendance at the palace of the emperor Constantine, some of whom may have decided to return to their foreign posts after the completion of their assignments and may have encouraged others to join them (Eusebius, *De Vita Constantini*, 4.7).

THE IMAGE OF BLACKS IN GREEK AND ROMAN LITERATURE

Greeks and Romans had highly positive images of the blacks whom they encountered in their daily lives. This point is illustrated in classical literature from Homer to the sixth century A.D. Although a large part of this favorable image pertained to the Ethiopians of the Napatan-Meroïtic kingdom of Kush, Greeks and Romans in their day-to-day contact with Ethiopians must have at some time associated the blacks of their daily experiences with the people of Nubia and their African homeland. The first impressions of blacks among many Greeks and Romans were frequently not of slaves or "savages" but of soldiers who like themselves were warriors protecting their own territory against foreign invasion or pursuing their national or personal interests in other lands. A continuing image of blacks in classical literature was that of Ethiopian warriors— facing the Greeks in Egypt and during the Persian Wars, and opposing Romans in the Carthaginian Wars and Augustus' troops in Egypt. Ethiopian resistance caused both the Ptolemies and the Romans to rethink their commercial and military policy in Nubia. Even though these latter day Ethiopians were not as successful as those that had conquered and had ruled Egypt, they must have reminded many Greek and Roman veterans of the more formidable Twenty-fifth Dynasty (Snowden, 1983, pp. 25-26, 41-42). And even in the early Empire echoes of the Twenty-fifth Dynasty were still heard and reported with apparent admiration. The historian and geographer Strabo (1.3.21; 15.1.6) included Tearco (Taharqa), the fifth ruler of the Ethiopian Twenty-fifth Dynasty, among the world's great monarchs. Freedom-loving Ethiopians, according to Seneca (*De Ira* 3.20.2) who had talked with centurions after their return from an Ethiopian mission under Nero's auspices, rejected the Persian king Cambyses' threat of slavery in words befitting the free and insulting to kings.

Ethiopians were fleshed out for the first time in Herodotus according to whom Greeks had accurate knowledge of Egyptian history from the time of Psammetichus I onward (Herodotus, 2.154). And this knowledge included what the historian had learned about Ethiopians during his visit to Egypt which, he said, took him as far south as the First Cataract (Herodotus, 2.29). Meroë, the capital of Ethiopia, was described as a great city whose inhabitants paid high honor to Zeus and Dionysus (Herodotus, 2.29). Ethiopia was an independent country which had been ruled by only one Egyptian king, while eighteen Ethiopian kings had ruled Egypt (Herodotus, 2.100, 110). One of these, Sabacos, after invading Egypt with a great army, ruled for fifty years in a humane manner, never putting evildoers to death but instead required them to perform worthwhile civic undertakings (Herodotus, 2.137, 139). And the perspicacious king of the Macrobian Ethiopians, the tallest and most handsome men on earth, rebuked the Persian king Cambyses for coveting territory that did not belong to him and for attempting to enslave a people who had not wronged him (Herodotus, 3.17-26).

The figures of Herodotus are obviously incorrect as to the number of Ethiopian kings in Egypt and Egyptian kings in Ethiopia. The historian's account of Sabacos, however, stresses an element of piety attested by other documents relative to the pharaohs of the Twenty-fifth Ethiopian Dynasty. Sabacos' piety and respect for human life as reported by Herodotus are reminiscent of the temperament and generosity of the second pharaoh of the Ethiopian Dynasty, Piye (ca. 751-716 B.C.) as recorded on a stele which describes him as attentive to religious ritual, respectful of the temples and gods of Egypt, and moderate in his relations with the vanquished (Breasted, 1912, pp. 541-545). Hence, Herodotus was apparently reporting on African realities more often than has been realized. In his account of Cambyses' plan for an Ethiopian campaign, Herodotus describes a "table of the sun," said to have been a meadow outside the city (Herodotus, 3. 17-18). His account of Macrobian expertise in archery and his description of the bows of Xerxes' Ethiopian auxiliaries (3.21, 7.69) antedated Heliodorus' description of the Ethiopians' unerring skill in hitting their adversaries' eyes (Heliodorus, *Aethiop*.9.18). His history points to a fifth-century B.C. knowledge of an ancient Ethiopian military tradition: the bow had been the typical weapon of southerners since the days of the formidable black archers recruited from Ta Sety, the "Land of the Bow" (Lower Nubia) by Egyptians as early as about 2000 B.C. (Vercoutter *et al.,* 1976, p. 43 and ills. 10-12).

The presence of Ethiopian soldiers on Greek soil in the army of Xerxes (480-479 B.C.) provided an opportunity for the tragic poets of the fifth century B.C. to play to a curiosity about "a far-away country of a black race that lived by the fountains of the sun" (Asechylus *PV* 807-812). Plays by the tragic poets familiarized spectators with Ethiopian ethnic types and legends, the popularity of which is attested by scenes depicted on vases, some probably from the workshops of vase-painters who had actually witnessed performances (Vercoutter *et al.*, 1976, ills. 167-177, and Snowden, 1983, figs. 17, 19, 20-21). *Andromeda*, a play of both Sophocles and Euripides, dealt with a legend in which Perseus, a son of Zeus, rescued and married a daughter of a king of the Ethiopians. Although the Danaids, the fifty black maidens in the *Suppliants* of Aeschylus, fleeing from their Egyptian cousins, were described as differing from Greeks in both color and form, and as "black and smitten by the sun" (*Supp.*, pp. 154-155, 496), they experienced no antipathy because of their color. In fact, they received a sympathetic hearing of their request for asylum although the Greek king realized that he and his countrymen ran the risk of war by his decision. Following performances of the plays on Ethiopian themes, theatergoers may well have concerned themselves with related questions such as the identity of the Negro on coins of Athens and Delphi. Was he Delphos, the eponymous founder of Delphi, the son of Apollo or Poseidon and a woman, the variants of whose name in all instances but one meant the Black Woman, and did his features resemble those of Ethiopians in Xerxes' army?

Ethiopians were not only pioneers in religion but also originators of many Egyptian beliefs and customs, according to Diodorus (3.2-7). Lucian's statement that Ethiopians invented astrology (*Astr.* 3-5) may have stemmed in part from reports of travelers who visited Meroë, where astronomical equipment and graffiti representing sketches of astronomi-cal calculations have been found (Garstang, 1944, pp. 4-6). It is tempting to suggest that visitors to Meroë, impressed by "discoveries" of this kind at the southern periphery of Egypt, circulated a report that astrology was an Ethiopian invention and gave rise to further speculation that a number of Egyptian institutions had an Ethiopian origin. References to Ethiopian justice and the Ethiopian origin of Egyptian customs should perhaps be interpreted as evidence of the writers' objectivity in reporting what they had learned from their sources rather than as an idealization of an unknown, distant people, as some have argued. The Greek image of Ethiopians, even when not always based on historical fact, must have had an enormous impact on the day-to-day attitudes toward Ethiopians: perceptions are often influential in shaping social attitudes.

Even after Ethiopians had been encountered as enemies, Greek authors continued to record, without rancor, familiar "Ethiopian themes"—military power, love of freedom and justice, piety, and wisdom. Ethiopians, according to Diodorus, were not only the first of all men but also the first to worship the gods who looked upon them with such favor that they doomed to failure attempts of foreign rulers like Cambyses to invade and rule their country (3.2.2-3.3.1). In his novel entitled *Aethiopica*, Heliodorus painted a full vignette of a just Ethiopian king, reminiscent of Herodotus' Sabacos. Heliodorus' Ethiopian ruler, Hydaspes, was a model of wisdom and righteousness, shunned putting men to death, and instructed his warriors to refrain from slaughter and to take the enemy alive. In a charitable spirit he heeded the plea of his bleeding Persian foe to spare his life, and having no desire to expand his kingdom, was content because of his reverence for justice to withdraw within the natural boundaries of the Cataracts (Heliodorus, *Aethiop*. 9.20-21, 10.39). As late as the fifth century A.D. the anthology of Stobaeus (4.2.25) preserved the tradition of Ethiopian piety and justice: Ethiopian houses were without doors and no one stole things left in the streets.

In the course of time, along with continuing highly favorable reports about Ethiopians, stories were circulated about Ethiopians living beyond Napata and Meroë whose customs differed widely from those of northern Ethiopians. Some of these were reported to be completely or partially nude, some to have wives in common, and some to be without belief in any gods (Diodorus, 3.8.5; 3.9.2; 3.15.2). Differences between Ethiopians inhabiting Meroë and the land adjoining Egypt and those who lived beyond Meroë were explained in terms of an environment theory which was first spelled out in detail in the Hippocratic Corpus (Hippocrates, *Aër*. xii, xvii-xxiv; *Vict*. 2.37). After describing the effects of the extreme cold of the north on Scythia and its inhabitants and of the torrid southern heat on Ethiopia and Ethiopians, Diodorus stated "it is not at all surprising that both the fare and manner of life as well as the bodies of the inhabitants of both regions should be very different from those that prevail among us" (Diodorus, 3.34). The wild habits of certain Scythians and Ethiopians were attributed by Ptolemy to the excessive cold in one instance and the torrid heat in the other (Ptolemy, *Tetr.* 2.2.56). In other words, according to the environment theory, people, regardless of their color, who lived in the outer regions of the earth, followed customs that differed from those of populations in temperate climes. Ethiopians, however, were not stereotyped as primitive or cannibalistic. In fact, it was fair northerners, not black southerners who, according to Strabo, were said to be among the most savage people in the world—more savage than the Britons were the inhabitants of ancient Ireland who considered it honorable to devour their fathers when they died and to have intercourse with their mothers and sisters (Strabo, 4.5.4).

GRECO-ROMAN ATTITUDES TOWARD THE BLACK MAN'S COLOR

How did the Greeks and Romans account for the black man's color and his woolly hair? What significance did they attach to the obviously different physical features and mores of people in various regions of the world? The widespread environment theory, cited by Diodorus and others, was one of the reasons that Greeks developed no special theory of the inferiority of blacks qua blacks. Setting forth the effects of the environment on the physical characteristics of peoples and their mores, this explanation of racial differences was applied in a uniform manner to all peoples. Ethiopians, Pliny the Elder wrote (2.80.189), are clearly burnt by the sun and at birth have a scorched appearance, curly beards and hair, whereas inhabitants of the opposite region of the world have white, frosty skin and straight yellow hair. And Ethiopians are wise because of the mobility of their climate, whereas northerners are fierce because of the rigidity of theirs. The basic human substance—the same in all—was tempered differently in different climes.

The black, woolly haired Ethiopians of the deep south and the fair, straight-haired Scythians of the far north who were frequently cited as favorite anthropological and geographical illustrations of the environment theory figured prominently in contexts emphasizing inclusiveness and equality. It makes no difference whether one is Scythian or Ethiopian, wrote Menander, it is natural bent, not race that determines nobility (*Frg.* 612 Koerte). Origen, in his statement that all whom God created He created equal and alike, extended the traditional Scythian-Ethiopian formula by adding Hebrews, Greeks, and Taurians (Origen, *Princ.* 2.9 5-6).

And Menander, like the early Christians in their pronouncements on the equality of all in God's eyes, employed the familiar Ethiopian-Scythian contrasts of the environment theory because it made unmistakably clear an unprejudiced view of ethnic physical differences. The popularity of the environment theory did not prevent Greeks from classifying foreign peoples and their country as barbarians. The Greek-barbarian antithesis, however, was based on cultural differences, not on color or physical appearances and was a manifestation of ethnocentrism, a characteristic of many people—the view that "one's own group is the center of everything, and all others are scaled and ruled with reference to it" (W. G. Sumner, 1960, pp. 27-28).

It has been difficult for some scholars to recognize that in the ancient world blackness did not evoke the hostilities which have developed in more color-conscious societies. An idée fixe—black as the immutable equivalent of slave or inferior—has not been without its influence. As H.C. Baldry has pointed out, "In treating a subject which is so alive today, nothing is easier than to read back twentieth-century ideas into documents which in reality have quite another meaning" (Baldry, 1965, p. 6). And this is exactly what some scholars have done in their interpretations of blacks in the ancient world—consciously or unconsciously they have seen color prejudice where none existed. In the entire corpus of classical literature, with its many references to Ethiopians, often confirmed by repeated events of history, there are, however, only a few concepts or notions which some scholars have claimed as antiblack in sentiment.

In spite of Herodotus' description of some Ethiopians as the most handsome men on earth and of tributes to dark and black beauties in Greek poetry, some critics have attributed to Greek artists an unproved aesthetic antipathy to blacks in comments such as these: as a rule the Negro is most absurdly drawn in Greek vases (Bates, 1904, p. 50); the ugliness of the Negro seems to have appealed alike to sculptor, engraver, and painter (Seltman, 1920, p. 14); Memnon was represented as white because of a Greek aversion to Negroid features (Robertson, 1959, p. 67; "plastic" vases are always best when the subject, like the Negro's head, is itself grotesque (Lane, 1963, p. 55); and most of the Negroes depicted by Greek and Roman artists are "hideous and implicitly racist" (Patterson, 1982, p. 421, note 16). Some scholars have curiously regarded simple realistic portrayals of blacks as revealing a "degree of antipathy . . . [and] a sensory aversion to the physiognomy of blacks" (Thompson, 1989, p. 160).

Interpretations such as those just cited show a complete misunderstanding of the classical artists' interest in Negroid types, and have overlooked the varied and often sympathetic treatment which blacks received over many centuries in several media and art-forms. By far a majority of scholars have seen in classical art an astonishing variety and vitality. There are penetrating depictions of a racial type which artists perceived as a challenge to their skill to represent by texture and by paint the distinctive features of Negroes, and to contrast blacks with other Mediterranean types in order to express the infinite variety of a common human nature. The popularity of blacks as subjects and the high quality of many pieces—some of the finest from ancient workshops—have given rise to a common view that ancient artists were as free from color prejudice as their literary counterparts (Snowden, 1983, pp. 79-82).

Some scholars have mistakenly seen color prejudice in certain references to the Ethiopian's color as evidence of a "child-psychology" theory which regarded black skin as unpleasant. Though obviously aware of the Ethiopian's color, Greek authors attached no significance to the color of the skin. Ethiopians do not astonish Greeks because of their color and physical appearance: such a reaction, Agatharchides wrote, ceases at childhood (*De Mari Erythraeo* 16). This statement was not only an accurate assessment of Greek reaction to the Ethiopian's color, but a sound observation on an aspect of child behavior noted by modern psychologists, according to whom "four-year olds are normally interested, curious, and appreciative of differences in racial groups" (Allport, 1964, p. 304). In other words, Agatharchides was no misguided purveyor of racist dogma but was merely recording the normal reaction of young children to observed differences in skin color, and he was not setting forth, as A. Dihle has suggested (Dihle, 1962, pp. 214-215), a theory of aversion to the black man's color rooted in childhood.

In light of the fact that both Greeks and Romans regarded black and white skin as mere geographic accidents, with no stigma attached to the color of the skin, it is strange that some references to ethnocentric aesthetic preferences have been interpreted as evidence of color prejudice. Like many people, Greeks and Romans had narcissistic canons of physical beauty—what H. Hoetink has called a "somatic norm image" (Hoetink, 1967, p. 120). Classical authors, while recognizing the subjectivity of their ethnocentric criteria, frequently stated a preference for a "Mediterranean" complexion and features—a middle point between the extremes of fair, blue-eyed northerners, and black woolly-haired southerners. There is nothing odd or pejorative about preferences for a white type in a predominantly white society, or for dark- or black-skinned beauties in a predominantly black society.

What was notable in the Greco-Roman world was the spirit of those who observed that classical standards of beauty were relative. Dio Chrysostom's discourse on beauty raised the question as to whether there was not a foreign type of beauty, just as there was a Hellenic type (Dio Chrysostom, *Or.* 21, 16-17). Sextus Empiricus (*Math.*xi.43) noted that men differ in definitions of beauty—Ethiopians preferring the blackest and most flat-nosed; Persians, the whitest and most hooked-nosed; and others considering those intermediate in color and features as the most beautiful. And perhaps most surprising from the point of view of some twentieth-century commentators were those who openly expressed a preference for dark- or black-skinned women. A poem of Philodemus to a certain Philaenion describing her as short, black, with hair more curled than parsley and skin more tender than down, concluded: "May I love such a Philaenion, golden Cypris, until I find another more perfect" (*Anth.Pal.* 5.121). Asclepiades praised the beauty of one Didyme: "Gazing at her beauty, I melt like wax before the fire. And if she is black, what difference to me? So are coals, but when we light them, they shine like rose buds" (Asclepiades, *Anth. Pal.* 5.210). Martial (1.115) wrote that, though he was sought by a girl whiter than a washed swan, than silver, snow, lily, or privet, he pursued a girl blacker than night, than an ant, pitch, a jackdaw, or a cicada. Those who stated their preference for dark-skinned women were not apologetic, as L.A. Thompson (1989, p. 134) has argued, in describing them as "black but beautiful," but were describing the beauty of blackness in language that epitomized the spirit of those who rejected the Mediterranean norm image.

In a tribute to a famous animal fighter, Luxorius, a poet of the sixth century A.D., wrote that Olympius had suffered no harm because of his blackness but, on the contrary, his glory would live ever after him in Carthage because of the popular admiration for his skill in the amphitheatre. The poem was not an exaltation of the white man's whiteness illustrating Roman worship of the Mediterranean somatic norm image (Thompson, 1989, p. 31), but was conceived in the spirit of poets like Vergil, Ovid, and Martial who had earlier rejected prevailing standards of beauty. In addition, Luxorius was also expressing another important classical concept: excellence is found in all men, whatever their race. Menander (*Frg.* 612), a writer of New Comedy, had said that natural bent, not whether one was Scythian or Ethiopian, determined nobility; Agatharchides (*De Mari Erythraeo* 16), that success in battle depends not upon color, but upon courage and knowledge of warfare. Similarly, for Luxorius, it was Olympius' strength and skill in the amphitheater, not his color that mattered.

The satirist Juvenal (13.163-173) wrote that the Ethiopian's blackness, the pygmy's small stature, and the German's blue eyes and yellow hair do not provoke laughter in their own countries because their physical characteristics are common to all. But not all Romans saw, as Juvenal did, a reason for astonishment or laughter in somatic differences. Like Diodorus (3.34.8) who saw nothing surprising in such differences, Seneca (*De Ira* 3.26.3) observed that neither the German's red hair nor the Ethiopian's color is to be considered odd because these traits are characteristic of their countrymen. In short, it is doubtful that either Germans or Ethiopians and other northerners and southerners suffered seriously as a result of classical narcissistic standards of beauty.

Convincing testimony as to the rejection of the prevailing somatic norm image is also provided by the number of mixed black-white types depicted in Greek and Roman art which confirm in a most striking manner the textual evidence of interracial mixture. Realistic portrayals of mulattoes and various mixed race black-white types in Greek and Roman art illustrate various steps in the disappearance of Negroid physical traits, and references to racial mixture in classical texts offer dramatic confirmation of the fact that there were those who rejected the prevailing norm image. Aristotle (*HA* 7.6.585b; *Gen. An.* 1.18.722a) and Plutarch (*Sera* 21.563) in references to the transmission of inherited physical characteristics or to supposed evidence of adultery, included no strictures on black-white racial mixture. In the *Aethiopica* of Heliodorus (4.8) a descendant of Achilles was enamored of a girl whose Ethiopian mother had exposed her at birth to avoid being accused of adultery for having given birth to a white child. The eventual discovery that her parents were the black king and queen of Ethiopia did not matter to her Greek beloved. In short, black-white sexual relations were not the cause of great emotional crises.

Some scholars have seen an anti-black bias in the Roman association of the Ethiopian's color with ill omens and the early Christian black-white imagery. Social scientists, however, have pointed out that there seems to be a "widespread communality in feelings about black and white," that among both Negroes and whites the color white tends to evoke a positive and black a negative reaction, and that both colors figure prominently in the areas of human experience concerned with superstition and religion (e.g., K. J. Gergen, 1968, pp. 112-115). Although similar associations with the color black and white among Greeks and Romans had in origin nothing to do with the color of the skin, some writers of the early Roman Empire placed dark-skinned peoples—Ethiopians, Egyptians, Garamantians—in ill-omened contexts. Among the several omens, for example, which Brutus and Cassius encountered as they were proceeding to the battle of Philippi was an Ethiopian (Appian, *B.Civ.* 4.17.134; Florus, 2.17.7.7-8; Plutarch, *Brut.* 48). At the time of the emperor Caligula's death a nocturnal performance was being rehearsed in which Egyptians and Ethiopians were reenacting scenes from the Lower World (Suetonius, *Calig*, 57.4).

Interpretations that have seen a significant anti-black sentiment in classical associations of Ethiopians with death and the Underworld are questionable. In the first place, research in the social sciences has raised the question of whether individuals who react negatively to the color black also develop antipathy toward dark-skinned people, and suggests that though such a reaction is theoretically plausible, the evidence is far from convincing (K. J. Gergen, 1968, p. 121). Furthermore, it was not until the literature of the early Empire that the association of dark-skinned peoples with omens of disaster was reported. By that time, however, the favorable image of Ethiopians had long been established, and the unbiased environment explanations of racial differences had been deeply rooted. At the same time that these notions about the color black were being circulated, the popular environment theory was being revived; the ancient image of just Ethiopians was being reinforced; and, perhaps most importantly, Christian writings and sermons were using a rich black-white imagery emphasizing the black man's membership in the Christian brotherhood and, in one sense, granting a privileged position to Ethiopians.

BLACKS AND EARLY CHRISTIANITY

Black-white symbolism figured prominently in early Christian authors in two major contexts, demonological and exegetical. In apocryphal and patristic literature black was the color of the devil and of some demons who tempted saints and monks or troubled them in visions or dreams. Whether these incarnations of evil and temptation appeared in the shape of Ethiopians or Egyptians, or crows, or as merely black, the emphasis was on the color black and the evil spirits did not resemble real Ethiopians (Courtès, 1979, pp. 9-10, 19). Also perhaps related to the emphasis on color and the absence of any similarity to real Ethiopians is the fact that skin coloration seems to be the only physical trait mentioned in early Christian accounts. It is significant that later medieval iconography, in spite of the black and Ethiopian apparitions of apocryphal and patristic literature, portrayed so few demons with Negroid features (Vercoutter *et al.*, 1976, p. 14). This demonological use of black was obviously related to the earlier classical association of the color black with evil. A similar origin perhaps explains the contrast of the blackness of evil with the light of God. The devil is black, according to Didymus the Blind (*Sur Zacharie* 4.312) because he fell from the splendor and virtue of spiritual whiteness that only those who have been "whitened" by God can possess. In the demonological contexts, however, there was no stereotypical image of Ethiopians as personifications of demons or the devil (Snowden, 1983, pp. 100-107).

The fundamental Christian attitude toward blacks, however, is clearly reflected in the black-white symbolism of exegetical writers. The influential theologian Origen of Alexandria became the model for the later patristic treatment of "Ethiopian" themes. By adapting a classical black-white imagery and by relying on familiar patterns of thought, Origen and others realized that they could interpret scriptural references more meaningfully and could explicate their message more convincingly. The essential spirit of Origen's "Ethiopian" interpretations appears in his commentary on the Song of Songs, in which he also includes observations on other important scriptural references to Ethiopians. In his commentary on the "black and beautiful" maiden, Origen illustrates the applicability of black-white imagery to *all* peoples: "We ask in what way is she black and in what way fair without whiteness. She has repented of her sins; conversion has bestowed beauty upon her and she is sung as 'beautiful' . . . If you repent, your soul will be 'black' because of your former sins, but because of your penitence your soul will have something of what I may call an Ethiopian beauty" (*Homiliae in Canticum Canticorum* 1.6). The mystery of the church arising from the Gentiles and calling itself black and beautiful, Origen points out, is adumbrated in the marriage of Moses to a black Ethiopian woman which he interprets as a symbolic union of the spiritual law (Moses) and the church (the Ethiopian woman)—a foreshadowing of the universal church (*Commentarium in Canticum Canticorum* 2.362, pp. 366-367). Origen expressed a basic Christian tenet when he declared that it makes no difference whether a man is born among Hebrews, Greeks, Ethiopians, Scythians, or Taurians, all whom God created He created equal and alike (*De principiis* 2.9.5-6).

A few other examples of Ethiopian symbolism in early Christian writers will suffice to give an idea of the range and spirit of this Ethiopian theme. Christ came into the world, wrote Gregory of Nyssa, to make blacks whites (*Commentarium in Canticum Canticorum* 1,5-6). Ethiopians, in the interpretation of Cyril of Alexandria, are those whose dark minds have not yet been illumined by divine light (*Expositio in Psalmos* 73.14). In explicating a verse from the Psalms, St. Augustine states that under the name "Ethiopia" all nations are signified, a part representing the whole and "properly by black men, for Ethiopians are black. Those are called to the faith who were black, just they, so that it may be said to them 'Ye were sometimes darkness but now are ye light in the Lord'" (*Enarrationes in Psalmos* 73.16). When Augustine declared that the church was not to be limited to a particular region of the earth but would reach even the Ethiopians, the remotest and blackest of men (*Enarrationes in Psalmos* 71.12), he was not only recalling Homer's distant Ethiopians, but he also had in mind perhaps those Ethiopians on the southernmost fringes of his own bishopric in northwest Africa. The Ethiopian imagery dramatically emphasized the ecumenical character of Christianity and was a dramatic means of presenting cardinal tenets of Christianity. Nor is there any evidence that the Ethiopians of the first centuries after Christ suffered in their day-to-day contacts with whites as result of metaphorical associations of this symbolism. Nor did the early Christians alter the classical symbolism or the teachings of the church to fit a notion of blacks as inferior, or to sanction segregated worship.

THE DAILY LIFE OF BLACKS
IN THE GRECO-ROMAN WORLD

How did blacks, obviously conspicuous because of their blackness and other facial features, actually fare in their day-to-day contacts with Greeks, Romans, and others? There is no evidence that blacks were excluded solely on the basis of color from opportunities—occupational, economic, cultural, social, or religious—available to other newcomers of comparable origin. Like many other slaves or freedmen, blacks engaged in occupations at the lower end of the economic scale—servants, house-boys, cooks, bath attendants, day laborers of various sorts, musicians, singers, dancers. But blacks with special qualifications found a place for their talent and industry. In Egypt blacks had for centuries found a career in the army a means of achieving positions of security and prestige. Blacks who served in the army of Septimius Severus in Britain and elsewhere enjoyed the same advantages upon discharge as other soldiers in the Roman *numeri*. One of these black soldiers was depicted on a sarcophagus dating from the time of Septimius Severus and was one of the Emperor's elite guard (L. Salerno, 1965, p. 259; Vercoutter *et al.*, 1976, p. 214 and fig. 281). In northwest Africa at Thaenae (in modern Tunisia) C. Julius Serenus, a black, had attained sufficient financial means to enable him to adorn his villa with a mosaic which depicted him and his white wife drinking from golden goblets (Snowden, 1983, p. 92). Northwest Africa has also provided evidence of the success of black athletes— charioteers, gladiators, wrestlers, and *venatores*. One of these athletes, Olympius, attained great popularity and became the idol of Carthage. His fame received tribute from the poet Luxorius (Snowden, 1983, pp. 77-79).

There were blacks who were culturally and physically assimilated in their new homes. Some blacks learned Greek before they left Nubia, where archaeological remains found at Meroë suggest that Greek was taught. The Ethiopian King Ergamenes, according to Diodorus (3.6.3) had a Greek education and studied Greek philosophy. Where Ergamenes studied is not known but Alexandria was a likely center for the education of children of well-to-do Nubians. Reported among the disciples of Aristippus, a Cyrenaic philosopher, was a certain Aethiops, and included among the distinguished followers of Epicurus were two from Alexandria, one black and one white (Diogenes Laertius, 2.86; 10.25). The dark- or black-skinned playwright Terence, who might have been of Negroid extraction (Snowden, 1970, p. 270, note 3), arrived in Rome as a slave from Carthage, received his freedom from his owner, a Roman senator, and achieved fame as a comic poet. Juba II, king of Mauretania, whose features in some likenesses suggest Negroid admixture (J. Vercoutter *et al.*, 1976, p. 265, figs. 363-364), wrote many works in Greek, including a history of Rome, books on Libya, and strove to introduce Greek and Roman culture into his African kingdom. A Negro, known only as Memnon, a protégé of Herodes Atticus, was one of the most talented disciples of the celebrated sophist and patron of art in the second century A.D. (Philostratus, *VA*, 3.11 and *VS*, 2.588).

Many blacks were physically assimilated into the population of the Greco-Roman world in which there were no institutional barriers or social pressures against black-white unions, although it is difficult to estimate the extent of this assimilation. References to black-white racial mixture included no theorizing of "white purity" and nothing resembling later strictures on miscegenation. Little is known about the dark- and black-skinned ladies praised in Greek and Roman poetry, such as Didyme whose blackness reminded the epigrammatic poet Asclepiades of burning coals that shine like rose-buds (*Anthologia Palatina* 5.210 and Snowden, 1991, pp. 239-253) or the unnamed "super-black" lady of Martial's epigram (1.115, pp. 4-5) preferred to a white beauty. One point is certain, however: all Greeks and Romans did not accept the prevailing ethnocentric norm of Mediterranean whiteness.

When blacks sought spiritual comfort in their new homes, they were welcomed on the same terms as whites in both the Isiac and Christian worship, not only as converts but as priests and monks. Blacks frequently played an influential role in the spread of the Isiac ritual, in Egypt at Philae because it was within the reach of large numbers of Ethiopians, situated near the First Cataract. The temple at Philae, the Mecca or Jerusalem of Isiac worship, attracted worshippers of many classes and nationalities who welcomed the expert ritualistic knowledge of Ethiopians. These worshippers expressed their devotion to the "Queen of the Southern Peoples" at one of the most sacred shrines of the popular goddess (R.E. Witt, 1971, pp. 61-63). Murals depicting Isiac worship at Herculaneum depicted blacks and whites among the worshippers and priests. One black is a choirmaster directing a chorus of the faithful of both sexes, and in another scene the eyes of most worshippers are focused upon a central figure, a black, executing a dance (J. Vercoutter *et al.*, 1976, figs. 288-289). Ethiopians may have been strangers when they arrived in Italy or Greece, but the reception of fellow cultists gave them a spiritual security in their new homes like the blacks depicted on a sarcophagus found on the Appian Way (J. Vercoutter *et al.*, 1976, figs. 383-384).

The strong bond that had united blacks and whites in the common worship of Isis was reinforced by Christianity. Like the Isiac cult, Christianity swept ethnic distinctions aside. During the first six centuries of Christianity blacks were summoned to salvation and were welcomed in the Christian brotherhood on the same terms as others. In fact, Ethiopians and Scythians, as stated earlier, figured prominently in a deeply spiritual imagery and in basic pronouncements of the early Christian credo (Snowden, 1970, pp. 196-215; 1983, pp. 99-108). Philip's baptism of the Ethiopian, a high official of the Ethiopian queen, was a landmark in the book of Acts (8.26-40) proclaiming that color was to be of no significance in determining membership in the church. Blacks were among humble converts like the Ethiopian slave "not yet whitened by the shining grace of Christ," whose spiritual welfare was the subject of concern in a correspondence between Fulgentius (*Epistulae* 11-12), Bishop of Ruspe (in modern Tunisia) and a deacon. St. Menas, sometimes portrayed as a Negro on flasks bearing his name and effigy, was a national saint of Egypt, where pilgrims from Asia and Europe as well as from Africa came to worship at his shrine west of Alexandria (Snowden, 1970, fig. 62, pp. 211-212). One of the most outstanding Fathers of the Egyptian desert was a tall, black man, Abba Moses, who was known as a model of humility and the monastic life, an excellent teacher, and a Father's Father (Snowden, 1983, p. 106). In short, in the early church blacks found equality in both theory and practice.

SUMMATION

In summary, both Greeks and Romans, not withstanding a few concepts and ideas sometimes misinterpreted as anti-black in sentiment, had the ability to see and to comment on the obviously different physical characteristics of Ethiopians without developing an elaborate and rigid system of discrimination based on color of the skin. Color did not acquire in the Greco-Roman world the great importance it has assumed in some post-classical societies either in the self-image of many people, or in the denial of equality to blacks in theory or practice. Unlike commentators who have read back modern racist concepts into classical documents and have seen color prejudice where none existed, scholars who have allowed the Greeks and Romans to speak for themselves have emphasized the unbiased Greco-Roman attitude toward blacks. And D. L. Noel (1984, p. 227) has recently stated that the arguments for an overall absence of color prejudice in antiquity are sound and complement Stephen Jay Gould's assessment of "latter day scientists who perceive and interpret racial differences through lenses severely distorted by prevailing racism."

In brief, the written and iconographical evidence relating to blacks in antiquity when considered in its entirety, demonstrates the soundness of W. R. Connor's description of the Greco-Roman world as "a society which for all its faults and failures never made color the basis for judging a man," and the aptness of his observation that "the signs of bigotry which we find in studying the history of classical antiquity are almost always among the modern scholars, not among their ancient subjects" (Connor, 1970, p. 4).

REFERENCES

Allport, G. W. (1964). *The nature of prejudice*. Reading, MA: Addison-Wesley.

Baldry, H. C. (1965). *The unity of mankind in Greek thought*. Cambridge, UK: Cambridge University Press.

Bates, W. N. (1904). Scenes from the Aethiopis on a Black-figured Amphora from Orvieto. Transactions of the Department of Archaeology, University of Pennsylvania, Free Museum of Science and Art, Philadelphia, parts. I and II, 50.

Breasted, J. H. (1912). *Ancient records of Egypt: From the earliest times to the Persian conquest*. New York: Scribner.

Connor, W. R. (1970). Review of "Blacks in antiquity: Ethiopians in the Greco-Roman experience." *Good Reading: Review of Books Recommended by the Princeton Faculty, 21*(3), 4.

Courtès, J. M. (1979). The theme of "Ethiopia" and "Ethiopians" in patristic literature. In J. Devisse (Ed.), *The image of the black in Western art II: From the early Christian era to the "age of discovery"* (Vol. 1, pp. 9-32). New York: William Morrow.

Dihle, A. (1962). Zur hellenistischen Ethnographie. In *Grecs et barbares: Six exposés et discussions Entretiens sur l'antiquité classique VIII*. Vandoeuvres-Genève: Fondation Hardt.

Garstang, J. (1944). Fifth interim report on the excavations at Meroë in Ethiopia. *Annals of Archaeology and Anthropology, 7,* 4-6.

Gergen, K. J. (1968). The significance of skin color in human relations. In J. H. Franklin (Ed.), *Color and race* (pp. 112-125). Boston: Houghton Mifflin.

Hoetink, H. (1967). *The two variants in Caribbean race relations: A contribution to the sociology of segmented societies* (E. M. Hookykaas, Trans.). New York: Institute of Race Relations.

Kitchen, K. A. (1973). *The third intermediate period of Egypt, 1100-650 B.C.* Warminster, UK: Aris & Phillips Ltd.

Kluckhohn, C. (1961). *Anthropology and the classics*. Providence, RI: Brown University Press.

Lane, A. (1963). *Greek pottery* (2nd ed.). London: Faber & Faber.

Mveng, E. (1972). *Les sources grecques de l'histoire négro-africaine depuis Homère jusqu'à Strabon*. Paris: Présence Africaine.

Noel, D. L. (1984). Review of "Before color prejudice: The ancient view of blacks." *American Journal of Sociology, 90,* 227.

Patterson, O. (1982). *Slavery and social death: A comparative study*. Cambridge, MA: Harvard University Press.

Pestman, P. W. (1965). Harmachis et Anchmachis, deux rois indigènes du temps des Ptolémées. *Chron. d'Egypte, 40,* 168-169.

Préaux, C. (1936). Esquisse d'une histoire des révolutions égyptiennes sous les Lagides. *Chron. d'Egypte, 11,* 535-536.

Preisigke, F. (1915). *Sammelbuch griechischer Urkunden aus Ägypten I*. Strasbourg, no. 5711.

Robertson, M. (1959). *Greek painting*. Geneva: Skira.

Rosenthal, F. (Trans.). (1958). *The Muqaddimah: An introduction to history* (Bollinger Series). New York: Pantheon.

Salerno, L. (1965). *Palazzo rondinini.* Rome: De Luca.

Seltman, C. T. (1920). Two heads of Negresses. *American Journal of Archaeology, 24,* 14.

Snowden, F. M., Jr. (1970). *Blacks in antiquity: Ethiopians in the Greco-Roman experience.* Cambridge, MA: Belknap Press of Harvard University Press.

Snowden, F. M., Jr. (1983). *Before color prejudice: The ancient view of blacks.* Cambridge, MA: Harvard University Press.

Snowden, F. M., Jr. (1989). Bernal's "Blacks," Herodotus, and Other Classical Evidence [Special Issue]. *Arethusa,* 83-95.

Snowden, F. M., Jr. (1991). Asclepiades and Didyme. *Greek, Roman and Byzantine Studies, 32*(3), 239-253.

Snowden, F. M., Jr. (1992). Whither Afrocentrism? *Georgetown 24*(1), 7-8.

Snowden, F. M., Jr. (1993). Response. *Arethusa, 26*(3), 322-326.

Sumner, W. G. (1960). *Folkways: A study of the sociological importance of usages, manners, customs, mores, and morals.* New York: New American Library.

Thompson, L. A. (1989). *Romans and blacks.* Norman, OK: University of Oklahoma Press.

Tod, M. N. (1946). *A selection of Greek historical inscriptions* (2nd ed.). Oxford, UK: Clarendon.

Vercoutter, J., Leclant, J., Snowden, F. M., Jr., & Desanges, J. (1976). *Image of the black in Western art I: From the pharaohs to the fall of the Roman Empire.* New York: William Morrow.

Witt, R. E. (1971). *Isis in the Greco-Roman world.* London: Thames & Hudson.

INDEX OF SOURCES

Acts of the Apostles, 8.26-40.

Aeschylus, Prometheus Vinctus 807-812; Supplices 154-155, 496.

Agatharchides, De Mari Erythraeo, 11-20 = GGM, 117-119.

Ammianus Marcellinus 29.5.37.

Anthologia Latina, nos. 183,353.

Appian, Bella civilia 4.17.134.

Aristotle, De generatione animalium 1.18.722a, Historia animalium 7.6.585b.

[Aristotle] Physiognomonica 6.812a; Problemata 20.66.898b.

Arrian, Anabasis 5.4.4; Indica 6.9.

Asclepiades, Anthologia Palatina 5.210.

Augustine, Enarrationes in Psalmos 71.12 = CCL 39.980; 73.6 = CCL 39.1014.

Asclepiades, Anthologia Palatina 5.210.

Cyril of Alexandria, Expositio in Psalmos 73.14 = PG.69.1188.

Didymus The Blind, Sur Zacharie 4.312, ed. L. Doutreleau, Sources chrétiennes, Vol. 3, no. 85 (Paris 1962) 964-965.

Dio Chrysostom, Orationes 21.16-17.

Diodorus, 3.2-3.9.2; 3.15.2; 3.34.1-8.

Diogenes Laertius, 2.86; 10.25.

Eusebius, De Vita Constantini 4.7 = PG 20.1156.

Florus, 2.17.7.7-8.

Fulgentius, Epistulae 11-12 = PL 65.378-392.

Gregory of Nyssa, Commentarium in Canticum Canticorum. 1, 5-6 Oratio 2 (PG 44.792).

Heliodorus, Aethiopica 4.8; 9.18; 9.20-25; 10.39.

Herodotus, 2.29; 2.100; 2.104; 2.110; 2.137,139; 2.154; 2.161; 3.17-26; 7.69-70; 9.32.

Hesiod, Opera et Dies 527.

Hippocrates, Aër xii, xvii-xxiv; Vict. 2.37.

Josephus, Antiquitates Judaicae 2.252-254; 8.165, 254, 292-294; 10.15-17.

Juvenal, 13.163-173.

Lucian, De astrologia 3-5.

Manilius, Astronomica 4.722-730.

Martial 1.115.

Menander, Frg. 612 Koerte = CAF III 157.

Moretum 31-35.

Musaeus (Philodemus) Frg. 13 = H. Diels and W. Kranz, Fragmente der Vorsokratiker, Berlin, 1961, 25.

Origen, Commentarium in Canticum Canticorum 2.362 = GCS Origen 8.115; 2.366-367 = GCS 8.117-118; De principiis 2.9.5-6 = GCS Origen 5.169-170; Homiliae in Canticum Canticorum 1.6 = GCS +Origen 8.36.

Ovid, Heroides 15.35-38; Metamorphoses 4.438.

Petronius, Satyricon 102.

Philodemus, Anthologia Palatina 5.121.

Philostratus, Vita Apollonii 3.11; Vitae Sophistarum 2.588.

Pliny, Naturalis historia 2.80.189.

Plutarch, Brutus 48; De sera numinis vindicta 21.563.

Ptolemy, Geographia 1.9.7; Tetrabiblos 2.2.56.

Rufinus, Historia monachorum, de Apollonio 7.151 = PL 21.415.

Scriptores Historiae Augustae, Septimius Severus 22.4-5.

Seneca, De Ira 3.20.2; 3.26.3, Hercules Oetaeus 1705.

Sextus Empiricus, Adversus Mathematicos xi. 43

Sidonius, Carmina 5.460.

Statius, Thebais 2.49; 4.291.

Stobaeus, 4.2.25.

Strabo 1.3.21; 4.5.4; 15.1.6; 17.1.53-54.

Suetonius, Caligula 57.4; Vita Terenti 5.

Theocritus, Idyls 17.87.

Vergil, Aeneid 6.298-299., Eclogues 2.16-18; 10.37-39.

Vitruvius, De architectura 6.1.3-4.

Xenophanes, Frg. 16 Diels-Kranz.

2

"If Toads Could Speak": How the Myth of Race Took Hold and Flourished in the Minds of Europe's Renaissance Colonizers

Peter H. Wood

In 1942, at the height of Adolph Hitler's ascendancy in Europe, anthropologist Ashley Montagu described "the fallacy of race" as "man's most dangerous myth." In the half-century since then, several generations of scholars have struggled to explain the tortuous history and devastating consequences of this pseudoscientific concept in the hope that increased understanding may assist in eradicating the disease. In the process, it has become clear that racist ideas, both primitive and complex, as a response to the manifest genetic and cultural diversity of humankind have a deep history and multiple roots throughout the world.

Since ancient times, wherever divergent societies came in contact, they usually characterized one another as "foreign," "barbarian," and "inhuman." Moreover, they lacked any clear understanding of the difference between cultural traits—such as language, religion, or social habits—learned by each generation, and biological traits—such as hair texture, facial appearance, or skin color—passed on genetically and hence much

AUTHOR'S NOTE: Portions of this chapter appeared in a longer article, "Race," in *Encyclopedia of American Social History,* Vol. 1 (New York, 1993), pp. 437-451.

less susceptible to rapid change. They were often quick to equate cultural differences with physical traits, and over centuries these hostile observations, though based upon mistaken assumptions, often evolved into deep-seated prejudices that still prove difficult to eradicate.

The ancient roots and global dimensions of the race concept have become increasingly obvious; it is also evident that European cultures have played a special role in the evolution, dissemination, and exploitation of this idea over the last six centuries. Indeed, the strain of racism that reached its most virulent form under Hitler has its complex origins, like so much else in the modern world, in the explosive mixture of new ideas, people, and institutions that historians characterize as the European Renaissance. In the period beginning around 1400, and accelerating dramatically after 1500, separate forces flowed together and intermingled, reinforcing one another in a tidal wave that transformed Europe and, within several centuries, engulfed much of the world.

The swirling ingredients that dictated this "rise of the West" included overseas exploration and military conquest, international banking and commercial capitalism, religious ferment and scientific investigation, systematic colonization and massive enslavement. Precisely how these vast forces interacted over centuries—in what order, with which proportions, and to what effect—remains a subject of vigorous, and seemingly endless, research and discussion. Over the past century, the story of Renaissance expansion has been ably told, both by those who celebrate and by those who deplore the direction and outcome of the Europeanization of the globe. The recent quincentennial of Columbus's misadventure prompted fresh reexaminations by admirers and detractors alike.

RACISM

Even those who judge the complicated fission that prompted European change and expansion as having been humane, or at least inevitable, now concede that this historical process yielded a new and different brand of racism as one of its most central components and long-term by-products. Like other toxic by-products, this one has proven hard to identify, trace, comprehend, and contain. It has spread and seeped, poisoned and changed, often defying the best removal efforts of those most ruined or most appalled by its corrosive powers. Although the complex chemistry of its origin and the elaborate leeching processes by which it spread may never be entirely understood, it now seems clear that European colonialism and the imposition of a vast, intercontinental network of forced labor played central roles in fostering and consolidating racism as we have come to know it in the West.

This chapter briefly sketches the emergence of a virulent and pervasive strain of racism in the Western world between 1500 and 1800. It pays special attention to the religious debates and scientific speculations among Europeans that resulted from their abrupt and jarring confrontation with "new worlds" that had no place in their inherited worldview. It looks first at the outlook and experience of Europeans before 1500. Then it examines the complicated adjustments—both intellectual and economic—that flowed in general from the so-called Columbian exchange and specifically from the extended encounter over several centuries with the indigenous people of the Americas. Thirdly, it surveys the implications of the regime of race-based enslavement that had come into being throughout much of the Americas by 1700. Finally, it examines the Enlightenment debates that saw the consolidation of racist practices and anti-racist activism in Western society toward the end of the 18th century.

IDEAS AND IMAGES OF RACE
IN LATE MEDIEVAL EUROPE

In Christian Europe in the 15th century, new sailing technologies enabled increased travel, and Christian rulers were beginning to compete for the secular wealth, religious glory, and strategic knowledge that could accompany exploration. Marco Polo's journey to Cathay in the late 13th century, a succession of crusades to the Near East, and the ongoing caravan trade with sub-Saharan Africa had slowly sensitized European courtiers to the problems and possibilities posed by varied people beyond the shores of the Mediterranean Sea. It is interesting to note that, as a result of these contacts, Italians started to employ the word *razza* before 1400, and during the 15th century the terms *raca* (Portuguese), *raza* (Spanish), and *race* (French) came into use. The English, removed from the Mediterranean and late to enter the theater of overseas exploration, would not utilize the word *race* until shortly after 1500.

In 1453—several years after the birth of Columbus in Genoa—the Ottoman Turks conquered Constantinople. They marked their victory by converting the famous Byzantine Christian church of Santa Sophia (built by the Emperor Justinian in the 6th century) into a mosque for the Muslim faithful. Cut off from the Orient by Muslim power, Europe's initial outward thrust in the 15th century was southward toward the "New World" of the southern hemisphere, rather than eastward or westward. As a result, European maps and paintings of the period reflect an increasing familiarity with the different-looking people of equatorial Africa. It was, of course, a renewed familiarity, for Egyptians, Greeks, and Romans in the ancient Mediterranean; each in succession had awareness of the people beyond the Sahara. But like much else from the classical world, this awareness was greatly diminished in Europe following the fall of the Roman Empire; it was kept alive largely in Muslim texts that would later pass back into the hands of Europeans.

The famed Catalan Atlas, for example, was drawn by the Jewish cartographer Abraham Cresques and presented to Charles VI of France in 1381 by Pedro IV of Aragon. It depicts a handsome Black king in West Africa. The figure wears a royal crown, carries a scepter, and holds an enormous nugget of gold in his right hand. The image derives from Mansa Musa, the king of Mali, who had traveled from Timbuktu to Mecca half a century earlier with such a fabulous retinue that his fame had spread across both the Islamic and the Christian world. "This Negro lord," states the inscription, "is called Musa Mali, lord of the Negroes of Guinea. This king is the richest, most noble lord in all this region on account of the abundance of gold that is gathered in his land" (Sanders, 1978, p. 6).

Militant Christians began to speculate about conquering or converting such distant rulers and locating others who had already acquired the Christian faith. Foremost among these potentates was the mythical Prester John, a wise and wealthy Christian ruler living somewhere to the east or south in the vague Indies, where St. Thomas had preached the Gospel. By the 14th century, Prester John was considered Black and associated with the broad region of Ethiopia. An inscription on the Catalan map describes a place south of Egypt where a Saracen king was "always at war with the Christians of Nubia who are under the rule of the Emperor of Ethiopia, of the land of Prester John" (Sanders, 1978, p. 39). In the second quarter of the 15th century, when Prince Henry the Navigator of Portugal sent ships southward along the African coast in the hope of outflanking Muslim power in the Middle East and reaching the Orient by sea, he desired to open up oceanic trade with Black Africa, to convert Muslim rulers, and to establish ties with Black Christians in the land of Prester John.

Meanwhile, Pope Eugenius IV, anxious to link the Church of Rome to eastern churches in the face of an increasing Ottoman threat, sent out invitations in 1439 to diverse patriarchs and Christian leaders—including "Prester John, illustrious emperor of the Ethiopians"—to convene in Italy

(Bugner, 1979, II, 2, p. 117). Delegates from an Ethiopian monastery in Jerusalem attended the Council of Florence in 1441, and the presence of these African dignitaries had an effect on the art of the early Renaissance. It soon became common throughout much of Europe to portray one of the three wise men from the New Testament as a pious and wealthy African. Indeed, the adoration of the magi became a favorite artistic theme of the late 15th century, and the Black king, resplendent and devout, was often depicted with an emblem of Africa near him, such as a camel or a chimpanzee. By the start of the 16th century, when reports of the explorations of da Gama and Columbus were exciting the Renaissance imagination, such masters as Hieronymous Bosch and Albrecht Dürer elevated this Black wise man, bearing an orb in his hand, into an emblem of the world of discovery that beckoned Europeans.

Not all 15th-century European depictions of Africans were so regal and positive, however. St. Maurice, the early Christian martyr from North Africa, who became a favored emblem of the Holy Roman Empire, continued to appear as a noble and militant Black defender of the faith in the churches of central Europe. But devils, executioners, and the biblical scourgers of Christ were commonly depicted as strong and dangerous African infidels. The Portuguese conquest of Ceuta in North Africa in 1415 is considered the beginning of successful European overseas expansion. The chronicler Gomez Eannes de Zurara describes a Moor, "very tall and of a most threatening complexion," who led the defense until pierced by a Portuguese lance:

> The aspect of this Moor was such as to inspire terror, since all his body was black as a crow, and he had very long and white teeth, and his lips, which were fleshy, were turned back. (Zurara, 1936, p. 99)

IMPERIALISM AND ANTHROPOLOGY BEFORE 1700

Columbus himself, having previously visited West Africa and perhaps Iceland, shared with most Europeans a sense that skin color correlated readily, if not exactly, with latitude. On 13 October 1492, after sailing west from the Canaries until he encountered the Bahamas, the admiral noted that the local inhabitants, "are not at all black, but the color of the Canarians, and nothing else could be expected, since this is in one line from east to west with the island of Hierro in the Canaries" (Colón, 1960, pp. 24-25). Believing that he had reached the Indies of Southeast Asia, Columbus designated as Indians all those living in the uncharted domain to which he laid claim. Before the enormity of his error became clear, this colossal misnomer had taken on an irrevocable life of its own.

Confident to the end of his life that he had reached the outskirts of Asia on his four voyages, Columbus felt little surprise regarding the people he encountered. But the contacts initiated in 1492 presented profound conceptual challenges for both Americans and Europeans. As Columbus's successors conceded the existence of a land mass they had not known (calling it America after the early explorer Amerigo Vespucci), the nature of its residents became more problematic for the newcomers. They had to wonder, as others were wondering of them, whether these unknown beings were mortal or immortal, human or nonhuman. (A century later, Shakespeare's *Hamlet* would illustrate Renaissance fascination with the unsettled boundaries of human life. When confronting the ghost of his father as a "worthy pioneer" and "welcome . . . stranger," Hamlet reminds his companion, "There are more things in heaven and earth, Horatio, than are dreamt of in your philosophy.")

Even as remote strangers on both sides of the Atlantic struggled to resolve the basic issue of the boundaries of humanity, the beginnings of continuous intercontinental contact led to a series of more specific questions among Europeans in America. The invaders asked themselves whether local inhabitants were heathens worthy of "salvation" who could be quickly and easily converted to the Catholic faith. Or should these strangers, on the other hand, be exterminated as dangerous animals with no souls? Alternatively, should the Indians be enslaved, if possible, following Aristotle's ancient dictum that some persons are by nature free, and others slaves, and that for these latter slavery is both expedient and right? After all, not only did slavery have sanction from respected ancient philosophers, the enslavement of non-Christians had royal and papal approval.

Resolution of these momentous questions did not come quickly. A tome published in Paris in 1510 by a Scotsman named John Major argues that Aristotle's doctrine of natural slavery applied to the Indians (Major, 1510). But the following year, a Dominican friar in Hispaniola denounced cruel Spanish practices of enslavement in a sermon. "Are these Indians not men?" asked Antonio de Montesinos. "Do they not have rational souls? Are you not obliged to love them as you love yourselves?" (Las Casas, 1951, II, pp. 441-444). In 1537, Pope Paul III decreed that Indians should not "be treated as dumb brutes created for our service . . . incapable of receiving the catholic faith . . . nor should they be in any way enslaved." His papal bull, *Sublimis Deus,* affirms that "the Indians are truly men and that they are not only capable of understanding the catholic faith but, according to our information, they desire exceedingly to receive it" (Hera, 1956). Five years later, the Spanish king prohibited Indian slavery in his colonies, due largely to the effective protests of priests led by Bartolomé de Las Casas.

Nevertheless, the use of forced Indian labor and the practice of importing enslaved Africans expanded and continued in New Spain. Moreover, since the beginnings of transatlantic contact, sexual coercion accompanied economic coercion, as illustrated by the following passage in a letter of 28 October 1495, written by Michele de Cuneo, who accompanied Columbus on his second voyage to the Caribbean. The young Italian told a European friend about his and others' pursuit of a native canoe:

> [They had] captured a very beautiful Carib woman, whom the said Lord Admiral [Columbus] gave to me, and with whom, having taken her into my cabin, she being naked according to their custom, I conceived desire to take pleasure . . ., but she did not want it and treated me with her fingernails in such a manner that I wished I had never begun. But seeing that (to tell you the end of it all), I took a rope and thrashed her well, for which she raised such unheard-of screams that you would not have believed your ears. Finally we came to an agreement in such manner that I can tell you that she seemed to have been brought up in a school of harlots. (Morison, 1963, p. 212)

The "proper place" of the Indian as viewed by Europeans was contested most sharply at Valladolid in Spain in 1550-51, during the extended debate that took place between Las Casas and Juan Genés de Sepúlveda. Throughout the century, Renaissance humanists, preoccupied with Aristotle's dictum that man is the measure of all things, disputed the origin and place of non-Europeans. For example, Paracelsus, the Swiss-born physician, surmised in 1520 that Negroes and other non-Europeans had not descended from Adam (Paracelsus, 1603). The French essayist Montaigne, on the other hand, argued forcefully that human beings were similar and equal, set apart only by minor differences of appearance, widely divergent customs, and deep-seated prejudices. Civilization is largely in the eye of the beholder, Montaigne contends: "each of us labels whatever is not among the customs of his own people as barbarism" (Montaigne, 1958, p. 152).

For Montaigne's contemporaries, intent upon understanding the true identity and nature of America's inhabitants, the question of Indian origins emerged as an intriguing and significant issue that would continue to vex future generations. A century after Columbus, a Jesuit missionary named Joseph de Acosta, who had spent 17 years in Peru and Mexico, cautiously surmised that Indians had come to the New World several thousand years ago, pushed by hunger or overpopulation. Building on the ideas of others, he speculated that Americans had originally arrived from Asia by crossing a narrow strait or using a land connection still unknown to 16th-century Europeans. The hypothesis expressed in Acosta's *Historia natural y moral de las Indias* (1590) was successfully countered within Spain by the more vague and contradictory speculations of Gregorio García, who published *Origen de los indios de el nuevo mundo* in 1607. But Acosta's views received considerable attention elsewhere in Europe.

After all, most Europeans now understood Americans to be human, and all humans were still thought to have descended from Adam and Eve no more than several thousand years ago. If, as Christians believed, the Garden of Eden lay far to the east of the European land mass, then America might be closer to that ancestral garden than Europe itself. Acosta's proposition of an Asiatic derivation for the Indians, therefore, kept open the possibility for affirming Holy Scripture, though Acosta himself dismissed the common speculation that Americans represented one of the biblical Lost Tribes of Israel. Acosta's *Historia natural y moral de las Indias* appeared in an English translation in 1604, when English interest in colonization and its attendant intellectual and cultural issues were reaching new heights. Within the following decade, England established its first permanent foothold in the New World at Jamestown in Virginia, and Shakespeare completed *The Tempest,* his brilliant play that deals fancifully, but profoundly, with issues of physical and cultural differences.

Having renounced papal authority when the Protestant Reformation reached England in the mid-16th century, and having staved off the Spanish Armada in 1588, the English set out to colonize North America in ways that would distinguish them from the conquistadors of Catholic Spain. They translated the descriptions of Spanish atrocities in America penned by Las Casas, and they used these shocking accounts to promote the vision of less violent efforts toward the Christianization of Indians in New England and elsewhere (Las Casas, 1583). The seal of the Massachusetts Bay Colony depicted a Native American calling out, "Come over and help me," and some early Puritans speculated that the local inhabitants were descendants of the Lost Tribes of Israel. Other English immigrants—hardened by hostile encounters with the Irish in earlier colonization efforts closer to home—suspected that the Indians might instead be imps of Satan, placed in their path to test and torment them.

From the start, the English were bent upon founding settler colonies, to which they sent not only young male soldiers but whole families. Relations with Indian women, therefore, were often viewed more as a sinful temptation than as a logical accommodation to circumstance, as in the early Spanish and French colonies. In Virginia, John Rolfe agonized at length before wedding the youthful Powhatan woman, Pocahontas (Hamor, 1615, pp. 61-68). For Rolfe and others, the issue turned much more on the heathen religious status of his potential bride than on her non-European features. Sanctioned and unsanctioned liaisons with Indians would remain a part of life in Anglo-America, but the doctrine of intermarriage would never gain such wide acceptance among the settler colonies of the Protestant English of northern Europe as it did among the Catholic French and Spanish, who by the 17th century had had greater contact with non-European peoples.

ENGLISH ACCEPTANCE OF RACE-BASED ENSLAVEMENT

At first, the English were hesitant to abuse or alienate the various eastern woodland Indian groups upon whom they found themselves notably dependent in the new and unfamiliar environment. They maintained pious fantasies of avoiding the hegemonic excesses of the Spanish and perhaps even converting local tribes into loyal Protestant allies against their papist rivals in Florida and the West Indies. When such European diseases as smallpox and measles devastated their Indian neighbors, sparing most colonists, the English had no knowledge of comparative immunities that could help them understand the phenomenon. Their ministers interpreted the devastation as a further sign of their Protestant God's favor to his chosen people. Catholic treatment of Africans also became an issue in Europe's religious debates, and even as Elizabethan Englishmen experimented with the risks and profits of shipping Africans to Hispanic America, Francis Drake and other English raiders liberated Black workers as part of their effort to destabilize New Spain.

Richard Hakluyt, the London propagandist and imperial strategist, hinted at this anti-racist approach when he published *The Principal Navigations of the English Nation* in 1589 (Hakluyt, 1935), following the defeat of the Spanish Armada. The Cimarrons of Central America, runaway African slaves with whom Drake had formed a connection, were, "a people detesting the prowde [sic] governance of the Spanyards." According to Hakluyt, they could "easily be induced to live subject to the gentle government of the English" (Hakluyt, 1935, pp. 142-143). But these pretensions for anti-racist solidarity with exploited non-Europeans did not last long. Faced with a rapid decline in Indian population and a decreasing availability of excess labor from England, the settlers gradually turned, during the 17th century, to the importation of African laborers. English colonists had partial access to the elaborate Atlantic slaving networks of other European colonial powers, such as the Spanish and Dutch, and by the 1660s, they had established their own Royal African Company.

At first, the rationale for exploiting Africans had little to do with appearance—non-Christians and captives taken in war could be enslaved according to accepted European principles. Moreover, it was easier to exploit persons when there was little "feedback" to the source of labor. Within each North American colony, the future supply of workers from Europe was linked in part to the current terms of labor. Word of harsh working conditions, high mortality, or increased years of indenture could cross the Atlantic promptly and turn the flow of immigrant labor elsewhere. Such feedback to West Africa was virtually nonexistent, however, and as a result there was no linkage between conditions and supply. Africans could be made to serve for life without reducing the likelihood of another boatload arriving the next year.

The emergence of lifelong servitude in turn rearranged punishments and incentives. Once Africans could be owned for life, no misdeed could lengthen their term of service. If English servants were implicated in the crime, they could be forced to serve additional time, as illustrated by an early Virginia law concerning "English running away with Negroes." "Be it enacted," stated the law of 1660-1661,

> that in case any English servant shall run away in the company with any negroes who are incapable of makeing satisfaction by addition of time . . . that the English so running away in company with them shall serve for the time of the said negroes absence as they are to do for their owne by a former act. (Hening, 1809-1823, II, p. 26)

In the frequent instances where there was no English coconspirator, penalties against lifetime African servants were increasingly meted out in the form of corporal punishment.

A loophole remained from these worsening conditions. Unable to prevent the extension of service to a lifetime or to stem the flow of additional workers, an African slave, according to custom, could convert to Christianity and thereby demand a release from bondage. It soon became clear to planters in Virginia and the Carolinas, aided by Spanish precedent, that if legal status could be tied to skin color, a genetic trait that changed far more slowly than the cultural attribute of faith, then African Americans and their offspring could be confined to perpetual bondage. The planters who dominated the Virginia assembly enacted a law in 1667 "declaring that baptisme of slaves doth not exempt them from bondage." The assemblymen argued, disingenuously, "that the conferring of baptisme doth not alter the condition of the person as to his bondage or freedome; that diverse masters, freed from this doubt, may more carefully endeavour the propagation of christianity" (Hening, 1809-1823, II, p. 260).

Five years earlier, another Virginia statute had been put in place that helped consolidate racial enslavement through a dramatic reversal of English legal precedent. Whereas in England children traditionally inherited the status of their father, it was reported that in Virginia "some doubts have arrisen whether children gotten by any Englishman upon a negro woman should be slave or free." To resolve the issue in favor of their own class, the assemblymen asserted in 1662 "that all children borne in this country shall be held bond or free only according to the condition of the mother" (Hening, 1809-1823, II, p. 170). The path was now set for the imposition of hereditary slavery; it is not surprising that in the social commentaries and legal documents of the next generation, English colonists who had traditionally identified themselves as Christians began for the first time to distinguish themselves as Whites.

The imposition of new racial categories, superseding traditional class hierarchies, met with considerable resistance. Before and during Bacon's Rebellion of 1676 in Virginia, African and European workers found common cause in resisting the onerous work conditions in the Virginia tobacco fields, and the threat to capital posed by their collaboration was duly noted. British troops had to come to the defense of the planter class, and in subsequent decades the line between White servitude and Black slavery was drawn ever more sharply. The bulk of plantation labor would fall increasingly to African Americans (an option that brought enormous profits to powerful Englishmen deeply invested in the Africa trade), and poor Whites were instilled with a sense of racial superiority that would become a key ingredient of American culture for hundreds of years. Harsh slave codes, following those already in place in the Caribbean, used brutal punishments and tortures to impose and sustain the new order.

The full transition to race slavery took scarcely more than a generation; it was accompanied by, and consolidated through, an intensified usage of derogatory racial stereotypes and epithets. By the early 18th century, the pattern of exploitation had been so thoroughly imposed as to be deemed "natural" by enforcers and beneficiaries. Writing in the 1720s, Virginia planter William Byrd boasted that the enormously lucrative system of racial enslavement was in place, and all he had to do was maintain this profitable engine and reap the proceeds. "Besides the advantage of pure Air," he wrote to a friend in England,

> we abound in all kinds of Provisions without expence (I mean we who have Plantations). I have a large Family of my own, and my doors are open to Every Body yet I have no Bills to pay, and half-a-Crown will rest undisturbed in my pocket for many Moons together. Like one of the Patriarchs, I have my Flocks and my Herds, my Bond-men and Bond-women, and every Soart [sort] of Trade amongst my own Servants, so that I live in a kind of Independence on every one but Providence. However . . . I must take care to keep all my people to their Duty, to set all the Springs in motion and to make every one draw his equal Share to carry the Machine forward. (Byrd, 1726/1924, p. 27)

Needless to say, the century that saw racism become ensconced in the English-speaking world also saw an immediate rise in anti-racism. Resistance to codified racial prejudice and exploitation came directly from those who were victimized, through covert opposition and occasional acts of overt rebellion despite overwhelming odds. In addition, some among the newly designated "White race" began to question the framework of racialist thought and behavior that was growing up around them. First through individual acts of conscience, then through the collective resistance of organized groups—both religious and secular—they asserted their opposition, planting seeds of doubt that would mature during future generations. Meanwhile, the intellectual and theological battles over human origins and diversity that had emerged during the Renaissance continued within a dramatically new context.

ENLIGHTENMENT EFFORTS
AT CLASSIFICATION

By the late 17th century, with the wholesale enslavement of Africans and coercion of Native Americans underway in the New World colonies, Europeans at home continued to grope for an understanding of the wider world they were moving so decisively and competitively to exploit. In 1684, French physician François Bernier suggested that it was possible to classify people not merely by country and region, but also according to differing conformations of the face and body (Bernier, 1684). He divided humans into four general classifications: Europeans, Far Easterners, Black Africans, and Lapps. Bernier's generation, although still acknowledging diversity among Europeans, was struck more by European physical similarities when contrasted with people from other continents.

Over the next half-century, descriptive natural history emerged as an increasingly serious pursuit and found its greatest champion in the botanist Carl Linnaeus. In *Systema Naturae,* first published in 1735, the young scholar put forward his own four-part list regarding humankind. At age 28, the Swedish naturalist had embarked upon his lifelong career of describing all living organisms and classifying them into fixed species. In each separate and immutable species, numerous varieties exist that have adapted to diverse geographic or climatic conditions. Within the human species, Linnaeus identified four general varieties: *Homo Europaeus, Homo Asiaticus, Homo Afer,* and *Homo Americanus.* These were all variations on a single theme. As the German philosopher Leibnitz put it, there

> is no reason why all men who inhabit the earth should not be of the same race, which has been altered by different climates, as we see that beasts and plants change their nature, and improve or degenerate. (Leibnitz, 1942, p. 19)

Georges Louis Leclerc Buffon, the leading French authority on natural history during the second half of the 18th century, proved to be of the same mind. Buffon argued that Africans had been gradually darkened by generations of living in the tropics. If they resided long enough in Europe, he surmised, their color would perhaps lighten eventually to become as white as that of native Europeans (Buffon, 1781-1785, III, 163-65, 201, VII, 394-95). For Buffon and others, such changes were not based upon temperature alone. Altitude, diet, and proximity to the ocean seemed to be significant forces shaping appearance, but so did social customs in general and "cross-breeding" in particular.

The problem for these 18th-century observers lay in differentiating between human changes caused by environmental, social, medical, and genetic factors. A boy's skin color, for example, might differ from that of his mother because he had been reared in a different climate, or because he had been obliged to work in the fields exposed to more sun and wind, or because he had suffered some malady, or because his biological father was of a different color. When similar results could derive from such different causes, it was not easy to unravel the underlying rules. Keen to address such problems and to encourage the progress of anthropology at a time of ongoing overseas exploration, a group of prominent French scientists founded the Society of the Observers of Man in 1800. Could acquired characteristics be inherited? Could inherited characteristics be changed? It is not surprising that one of the society's charter members, the naturalist Lamarck, came to the mistaken conclusion that traits obtained in life could be transmitted by heredity (Lamarck, 1914).

Another European puzzling over "whether a leopard could change its spots" was J. F. Blumenbach, a medical professor at the University of Göttingen often considered, with Buffon, the father of anthropology. "Innumerable varieties of mankind run into one another by insensible degrees," Blumenbach observed. Yet he was willing to divide humans into five basic varieties: Linnaeus's four, plus the Malays. The division, he believed, went far beyond color, for he collected and studied skeletons from around the world. He was especially interested in crania, and originated the comparative study of human skulls. Observing that one skull in his collection from the Caucasus Mountains of Russia resembled the crania of his fellow Germans, he coined the term *Caucasian* to describe light-skinned Europeans. But Blumenbach ridiculed those who tried to rank human differences in any hierarchy, usually one with themselves at the top. "If toads could speak," he wrote, they would no doubt modestly rank themselves as "the loveliest creature upon God's earth" (Blumenbach, 1865, pp. 30, 264-265).

In English North America, patterns of racial prejudice and discrimination against non-Whites had been well established since the late 17th century, gaining the weight of legal and intellectual precedent with each succeeding generation. Nevertheless, speculation persisted regarding the adaptability—and even the eventual amalgamation—of Europeans, Africans, and Native Americans in the so-called New World. Plantations and cities near the coast, frontier villages, and Indian towns in the interior all provided ample evidence that humans of different "varieties" could procreate at will. Moreover, Enlightenment belief in human perfectibility and brotherhood reinforced this egalitarian tendency as the century progressed. In this context, it was hardly surprising for the Declaration of Independence to underscore the ideal that all men are created equal, even if present circumstances revealed stark inequalities.

After all, most American leaders in the Revolutionary generation shared the environmentalist optimism of Buffon and Blumenbach. In 1787, the Reverend Samuel Stanhope Smith, a Presbyterian minister who later became president of the College of New Jersey, published *Essay on the Causes of the Variety of Complexion and Figure of the Human Species,* in which he speculates that human physiology is determined by latitude, along with elevation, soil, wind, and other factors. He explains apparent differences between African American field hands and house servants not in terms of miscegenation in the big house, but in terms of the harsh conditions in the fields. Not surprisingly, Smith and others became fascinated with the case of Henry Moss, a former slave from Virginia who, while living in the North after the Revolution, developed white spots on his body (Smith, 1810, pp. 92-95). Within the course of several years, Moss had nearly turned white, and he was exhibited in Philadelphia in 1796 as a living example of the fact that freedom and a cooler climate could draw out underlying similarities between Africans and Europeans.

Like Blumenbach's toads, these White observers had no hesitancy in seeing their own physical characteristics as the ideal norm. They accepted Buffon's ethnocentric notion that the pale skin of Europeans represented the real and natural color of the human race—giving an additional meaning to the term "enlightenment." Dr. Benjamin Rush of Philadelphia, familiar with Henry Moss, speculated that blackness might be viewed as a mild disease, an affliction, perhaps derived from leprosy, that could be cured by improved conditions (Rush, 1799). All humankind, such observers reasoned, had descended from the single creation of Adam and Eve (*monogenism*). Some human groups, long subjected to harsher environments, had diverged and degenerated more than others. Still, "The history of the creation of man and of the relation of our species to each other by birth, which is recorded in the Old Testament," Rush observed, "is the . . . strongest argument that can be used in favor of the original and natural equality of all mankind."

Some of Rush's contemporaries, such as the slave holder and deist Thomas Jefferson, were less confident about the unity of humankind as implied in the Bible. In *Notes on Virginia,* the master of Monticello imposed a crude hierarchy on perceived differences, finding Africans (whom he had only known in bondage) to be less beautiful, sensitive, artistic, and gifted than Europeans. Placing his own ancestors well above the forebears of his slaves on almost every count, Jefferson hedged on the crucial issue of separate origins and admitted his lingering uncertainty. "I advance it, therefore, as a suspicion only, that the blacks, whether originally a distinct race, or made distinct by time and circumstance, are inferior to the whites in the endowment both of body and of mind" (Jefferson, 1903-1905, II, pp. 199-201).

This growing propensity to rank, rather than merely differentiate, characterized the 19th century. The biological thinking of the late 18th century gave rise, in subsequent decades, to an increasingly concrete and damaging racist ideology, as scientists and scholars lent added credence to popular beliefs among Caucasians in the inherent inferiority of non-Whites. The 19th-century West saw the gradual emergence of a pseudo-scientific theory reinforcing Caucasian notions that Whites were innately and permanently superior. It no longer seemed certain, as written in Acts 17:26, that God "hath made of one blood all nations on the earth to dwell."

So-called scientific racism reached its peak in the second quarter of the 20th century, and has been on the decline ever since. Recent advances in archaeology, anthropology, and evolutionary genetics, however, have rekindled in new forms the Enlightenment debate over descent from a single Eve versus multiple origins for divergent human groups. Another generation of scientists, no less laden with cultural baggage than their ancestors, is attempting to assess our biological origins; the prospects for agreement seem more elusive than ever.

HISTORICAL REFERENCES

Acosta, Joseph de. (1590). *Historia natural y moral de las Indias.* Sevilla: En Casa de Juan de León,

Bernier, François. (1684, April 24) Nouvelle Division de la Terre, par les differentes Especes ou Races d'hommes qui l'habitent . . . . *Journal des Sçavans,* pp. 133-140.

Blumenbach, Johann Friedrich. (1865). (Trans. and Ed., Thomas Bendysshe). *The anthropological treatises of Johann Friedrich Blumenbach* . . . . London.

Buffon, Georges Louis Leclerc [Comte de]. (1781-1785). (Trans., William Smellie). *Natural history, general and particular.* London, 9 vol.

Bugner, Ladislas (Ed.). (1979). *The image of the Black in Western art: Vol. 2 (2 Parts), From the early Christian era to the "Age of Discovery."* New York: Morrow.

Byrd, William, II. (1924). Letter of William Byrd II to Charles, Earl of Orrery, July 5, 1726. *Virginia Magazine of History and Biography, XXXII,* 26-28.

Cayton, Mary Kupiek, Elliott J. Gorn, & Peter W. Williams (Eds.). (1993). *Encyclopedia of American social history, 3 vols.* New York: Scribners.

Colón, Cristobal. (1960). (Trans., Cecil Jane; Ed., L. A. Vigneras). *The journal of Christopher Columbus.* New York: Albert and Charles Boni.

García, Gregorio. (1607). *Origen de los indios de el nuevo mundo, e Indias occidentales . . . .* Madrid.

Hakluyt, Richard. (1935). (Ed., E. G. R. Taylor). *The original writings and correspondence of the two Richard Hakluyts.* London: Hakluyt Society. 2nd series, LXXVI, LXXVII.

Hamor, Ra[l]ph. (1615). *A true discourse of the present estate of Virginia . . . .* London.

Hening, William Waller, (Ed.) (1809-1823). *The statutes at large: Being a collection of all the laws of Virginia, from the first session of the Legislature in the year 1619,* 13 vols. Richmond: Franklin Press,

Hera, Alberto de la. (1956). El derecho do los Indios a la libertad y la fe. La bula *Sublimis Deus* y los problemas indianos que la motivaron. *Anuario de historia del derecho español, 26,* 119-139.

Jefferson, Thomas. (1903-1905). Notes on Virginia. In Andrew A. Lipscomb and Albert E. Bergh (eds.), *The writings of Thomas Jefferson.* Washington, DC.

Lamarck, J. B. (1914). (Trans., Hugh Elliot). *Zoological philosophy: An exposiiton with regard to the natural history of animals . . . .* London.

Las Casas, Bartolomé de. (1583). (Trans., M. M. S.) *The Spanish colonie, or briefe chronicle of the acts and gestes of the Spaniards in the West Indies, called the newe World.* London: Thomas Dawson for William Broome.

Las Casas, Bartolomé de. (1951). (Ed., Augustín Millares Carlo). *Historia de las Indias.* 3 vols. Mexico City.

Leibnitz, Gottfried W. von. (1942). Otium Hanoveranum sive Miscellanes ex ore . . . (Leipzig, 1718, p. 37). As quoted in M. F. Ashley Montagu. *Man's most dangerous myth: The fallacy of race.* New York: Columbia University Press.

Linnaeus, Carl (Carolus). (1735). *Systema naturae.* Lyon.

Major, John (Johannes). (1510). *In Secundum Librum Sententiarum.* Paris.

Montagu, M. F. A. (1942). *Man's most dangerous myth: The fallacy of race.* New York: Columbia University Press.

Montaigne, Michel de. (1958). (Trans., Donald M. Frame). Of cannibals. In *The complete works of Montaigne.* Palo Alto: Stanford University Press.

Morison, Samuel Eliot (Trans. & Ed.) (1963). *Journals and other documents on the life and voyages of Christopher Columbus.* New York: Heritage.

Paracelsus, Aureolus Theophrastus Bombast von Hohenheim. (1603). Liber de nymphis, sylphis, pygmaeis et salamamdris. *In Pera medico-chemicorum sive paradoxorum.* Frankfurt.

Rush, Benjamin. (1799). Observations intended to favour a supposition that the black Color (as it is called) of the Negroes is derived from the LEPROSY. (Read at a special meeting July 14, 1797). *Transactions,* American Philosophical Society, *IV,* pp. 289-297.

Sanders, Ronald. (1978). *Lost tribes and promised lands: The origins of American racism.* Boston: Little, Brown.

Smith, Samuel Stanhope. (1810). *Essay on the causes of the variety of complexion and figure of the human species* (rev. ed.). New Brunswick, NH.
Zurara, Gomes Eannes de. (1936). The conquest of Ceuta. In Azurara, *Conquests and discoveries of Henry the Navigator* (edited by Virginia de Castro e Almeida; translated by Bernard Miall). London.

SUGGESTED READING

Allen, T. W. (1994). *The invention of the White race: Racial oppression and social control.* London: Verso.
Bartlett, R. (1993). *The making of Europe: Conquest, colonization, and cultural change, 950-1350.* Princeton, NJ: Princeton University Press.
Bentley, J. H. (1993). *Old world encounters: Cross-cultural contacts and exchanges in pre-modern times.* New York: Oxford University Press.
Boville, E. W. (1970). *The golden trade of the Moors* (2nd ed.). London: Oxford University Press.
Brandon, W. (1986). *New worlds for old: Reports from the New World and their effect on the development of social thought in Europe, 1500-1800.* Athens: Ohio University Press.
Bugner, L. (Ed.). (1976). *The image of the Black in Western art.* Cambridge, MA: Harvard University Press.
Davis, D. B. (1966). *The problem of slavery in Western culture.* Ithaca, NY: Cornell University Press.
Dudley, E., & Novak, M. E. (Eds.). (1972). *The wild man within: An image of Western thought from the Renaissance to romanticism.* Pittsburgh, PA: University of Pittsburgh Press.
Forbes, J. D. (1993). *Africans and Native Americans: The language of race and the evolution of red-Black peoples* (2nd ed.). Urbana: University of Illinois Press.
Fredrickson, G. (1971). *The Black image in the White mind.* New York: Harper & Row.
Gossett, T. (1963). *Race: The history of an idea in America.* Dallas, TX: Southern Methodist University Press.
Gould, S. J. (1981). *The mismeasurement of man.* New York: Norton.
Haller, J. (1971). *Outcasts from evolution.* Urbana: University of Illinois Press.
Harris, M. (1964). *Pattern of race in the Americas.* New York: Walker Summit Library.
Honour, H. (1976). *The new golden land.* New York: Pantheon.
Huddleston, L. E. (1967). *Origins of the American Indians: European concepts, 1492-1729.* Austin: University of Texas Press.
Hulme, P. (1986). *Colonial encounters: Europe and the native Caribbean, 1492-1797.* New York: Methuen.
Hulme, P., & Whitehead, N. L. (Eds.). (1992). *Wild majesty: Encounters with Caribs from Columbus to the present day.* New York: Oxford University Press.
Jordan, W. D. (1968). *White over Black: American attitudes toward the Negro, 1550-1812.* Chapel Hill: University of North Carolina Press.
Mintz, S. W. (Ed.). (1974). *Slavery, colonialism, and racism.* New York: Norton.
Nash, G., & Weiss, R. (Eds.). (1979). *The great fear: Race in the mind of America.* New York: Holt, Rinehart & Winston.

Pagden, A. (1986). *The fall of natural man: The American Indian and the origins of comparative anthropology.* Cambridge, UK: Cambridge University Press.

Parry, J. H. (1963). *The age of Reconnaisance: Discovery, exploration, and settlement, 1450-1650.* Cleveland, OH: World Publishing Company.

Retamar, R. F. (1989). *Caliban and other essays.* Minneapolis: University of Minnesota Press.

Rose, P. I. (1968). *The subject is race: Traditional ideologies and the teaching of race relations.* New York: Oxford University Press.

Ruchames, L. (1969). *Racial thought in America: From the Puritans to Abraham Lincoln.* Amherst: University of Massachusetts Press.

Sanders, R. (1978). *Lost tribes and promised lands: The origins of American racism.* Boston: Little, Brown.

Segal, D. (Ed.). (1992). *Crossing cultures: Essays in the displacement of Western civilization.* Tucson: University of Arizona Press.

Stanton, W. (1960). *The leopard's spots: Scientific attitudes toward race in America, 1815-59.* Chicago: University of Chicago Press.

Stocking, G. W., Jr. (1968). *Race, culture, and evolution.* New York: Free Press.

Tyler, S. L. (1988). *Two worlds: The Indian encounter with the European, 1492-1509.* Salt Lake City: University of Utah Press.

Van Deburg, W. L. (1984). *Slavery and race in American popular culture.* Madison: University of Wisconsin Press.

Wolf, E. (1982). *Europe and the people without history.* Berkeley: University of California Press.

Wood, F. G. (1990). *The arrogance of faith: Christianity and race in America from the colonial era to the twentieth century.* New York: Knopf.

3

Spanish Ideology and the Practice of Inequality in the New World

Laura A. Lewis

The culture and history of New Spain, a region that today includes Mexico, illustrate the ways in which early modern Iberian imperialism came to rest on the domination and degradation of vanquished Indians and on the enslavement and debasement of blacks.[1] This essay examines Spanish ideology and the practice of inequality in that colony, one of Spain's most important possessions in the 16th and 17th centuries.

Although Spanish ideology was not "racist" in the modern sense, it was grounded in the superiority of "things Spanish," including whiteness, Christian "reason," purity of blood, and Hispanization. Deviation from these standards connoted social difference and made non-Spaniards threatening and inferior to Spaniards. Social difference, in turn, was the foundation for the formation of a colonial hierarchy in which Spaniards, blacks, Indians, and mixed-race mulattos and mestizos were assigned distinct, yet fundamentally interdependent, statuses.

AUTHOR'S NOTE: This chapter is part of a larger project titled "Race, Witchcraft, and Power in Colonial Mexico." I am grateful to the Organization of American States, the Wenner Gren Foundation for Anthropological Research, and the American Bar Foundation for their support during all phases of research and writing. Archival sources are available upon request.

LINEAGE, NATIONALISM,
AND IBERIAN RECONQUEST

To understand Spanish attitudes in the New World, it is helpful to look first to medieval Spain, where an "organic" social model evolved from the well-defined rights and obligations of groups or "estates" of clergy, nobility, and commoners. At the pinnacle of this model was the Crown, which realized divine will through judicial procedures. Crown subjects— the majority landless peasants—were expected to fulfill preordained roles in an orderly way, with the Crown as their benevolent guide and the Church and judiciary as interdependent and usually supporting forces (MacLachlan, 1988, pp. 1-19).

Although Spain was predominantly Christian, it accommodated populations—such as Muslim Moors and Jews—that could not properly belong to the social community (the *república*) because they were not Christians themselves. The Moors first crossed into the Iberian Peninsula early in the 8th century. For much of the next 800 years, they waged war with Christians over its possession. Yet during that time, Christians and Muslims also had periods of peaceful coexistence, and even after the Muslims' final defeat in 1492, Islam was for a while tolerated in Christian Spain.

Jews had also lived among Spanish Christians for hundreds of years when, beginning in the late 14th century, resentment of their notable material success—as financiers, merchants, artisans, and professionals— triggered an unprecedented wave of violence and anti-Jewish sentiment. Many converted to Christianity in response to persecution. In 1492, when the last Islamic stronghold at Granada fell to Christian forces united under the monarchs Ferdinand and Isabella, Jews were forced to convert or face expulsion from Spain. New Christians, or *conversos,* as converted Jews came to be known, were subsequently excluded from positions of prestige and power, and suspected of secret judaizing. The forced conversion of Moors followed that of Jews, and the expulsion of *moriscos* (little Moors), or converted Moors, ensued at the beginning of the 17th century. Thus, the defeat of Islam in the late 15th century, together with the Counter-Reformation that followed close on its heels, ushered in proto-nationalism and a desire for religious homogeneity. Accordingly, intolerance came to replace *convivencia* (coexistence) as ethnic minorities were exiled from Spain.

In 1478, Ferdinand and Isabella had established the Spanish Inquisition for the purpose of routing heretics who threatened national unity through their subversion of Christianity. As a political tool of the state and a papal tool for religious purification, the Inquisition played a fundamental role in defining what practices were deviant and therefore subject to persecution (Root, 1988). From early on, proof of Christian lineage was key to excluding those of Jewish or Muslim ancestry from important positions. Individuals aspiring to a church or state career were obliged to prove their genealogies, and therefore their legitimacy, by coming before the Inquisition to present a certificate attesting to their status as "Old Christians" of pure blood and noble birth (*hidalguía*). In this way, what had begun as Spanish "religious" anti-Semitism became "ethnic" anti-Semitism (Peters, 1988, p. 84), as religious heterodoxy was by turns related to cultural and then to genealogical "deviance" (Root, 1988, p. 118) or to the blood purity (*limpieza de sangre*) of Old Christians.

The shift that seems to have taken place in Spain during this period marked a transformation from a society that had at times accepted Muslims and Jews in a spirit of coexistence and converted Muslims and Jews as Christians to one that harbored suspicions of their inborn defectiveness, characterized by the persistent "Muslimness" or "Jewishness" of moriscos and conversos. Indeed the word *morisco* itself signifies the "residual Muslimness" of an ostensibly converted population (Root, 1988, p. 123). What therefore began as a general religious prejudice soon became primarily one about lineage, and blood became a pronounced idiom of socioracial difference. This change offers clues to the genesis of racial thinking in the 15th and 16th centuries not only in the Old World, but also in the New World, where Spaniards also confronted populations of non-Christians.

THE NEW WORLD

In the same year that Ferdinand and Isabella conquered the last remaining Islamic stronghold at Granada, Christopher Columbus sailed for what he thought was a new passage to Asia. In the process, he "discovered" America and opened the way for the domination of Spanish law and cultural concepts in the West. Already populated by indigenous peoples, America soon became home to thousands of enslaved Africans as well. Although denigrated, the conquered and enslaved populations of the New World were not amputated from the social body, as minorities were in Spain. Instead, colonial society—ostensibly free of Moors and Jews, whose passage to Spanish America was restricted by the Spanish monarchs—came to depend for its very survival on controlling non-Spaniards, who always presented a threat to Spanish domination, by including them in a social system that ensued from the application of Iberian hierarchical concepts to the multiethnic colonies (McAlister, 1963; Mörner, 1967, p. 48, 54). In the New World, defects of race, religion, and nationality were linked to skin color (not fully white) and ultimately to lineage (not fully Spanish/Christian) as Christian Spaniards came to govern dark-skinned, non-Christian people. The colonial regime that arose in this context codified inequality in law and cultivated it through social practice.

The land that is today known as Mexico was first invaded by Europeans in 1519, when Hernan Cortés led an expedition from Cuba to Mexico's eastern coast. At the time, the central part of Mexico was dominated by the Aztecs, who had themselves conquered other ethnic groups beginning in the mid-14th century. Directly ruling a small geographical area, they extended their influence through complex alliances with other polities. Within two years, Cortés and a small band of conquistadores had destroyed the Aztec empire and captured its leader, Moctezuma. By the middle of the 16th century, the indigenous population was, in effect, completely subordinated to the conquerors, who christened their new possession "New Spain."

In the Spanish colonies, wealth was systematically extracted from indigenous people to benefit a privileged Spanish class and the Spanish state. By the late 15th century, Spanish residents of the first colony, the Caribbean island then known as Hispaniola, had instituted the practice of dividing Indian groups among themselves and profiting from their labor. They also enslaved many who resisted Spanish encroachment. Under medieval canonical law, non-Christians were legitimately enslaved, yet the conversion of Indians to Christianity was also central to the conquest. In 1502, Isabella issued an order asserting the Indians' freedom once they accepted Christianity. But she also authorized the governor of Hispaniola to continue to utilize Indian labor to mine gold in the royal mines, to produce food for Spaniards, and to work on the construction of public buildings. In addition, many settlers continued to extract labor or tribute from Indians. This practice marked the beginning of the New World *encomienda,* an institution rooted in Spain, where grants of dues and services from commoners were traditionally made by the Crown to the nobility for specific periods of time (McAlister, 1984, p. 157).

The Church's desire to conquer indigenous Mexico spiritually often conflicted with settlers' desire to harness needed humanpower. During the early years of Spain's occupation of the Caribbean, ideological battles between the Crown, the colonists, and the clergy were triggered by the rapid extermination of the indigenous population through disease, over-work, and outright slaughter. Within a generation, that population was replaced with slaves imported from sub-Saharan Africa, already a source of slaves for Europeans. In New Spain, labor requirements grew as the Indian population—also decimated by epidemic disease and demoraliza-tion—became a less and less viable workforce. Prodded by the Dominican Bishop of Chiapas, Bartolomé de Las Casas, the Crown intervened in 1542 with the New Laws, which declared Indian enslavement illegal and limited the powers of those who held encomiendas.

Throughout the early colonial period, Mexico received on average two-thirds of all Africans brought to Spanish America. Initially these slaves, who at times outnumbered Spaniards, came principally from West Africa (Guinea-Bissau, Senegal, Gambia, and the coast of Sierra Leone). The source later shifted to Angola and the Congo in Central Africa (Aguirre Beltrán, 1972, pp. 240-241; Palmer, 1976, p. 20). By the early 17th century, there were more than 50,000 Africans in New Spain, with 20,000 of those in Mexico City and the surrounding Valley of Mexico. The rest were concentrated in the eastern Veracruz-Pánuco region, the Bajío silver mining regions and ranches to the north and west of Mexico City, and the sugar plantations, ranches, and mines that followed a southwestern belt running from the city of Puebla to the Pacific Coast (Aguirre Beltrán, 1972, Part IV; Palmer, 1976, p. 46).

In New Spain, slaves were utilized on the sugar plantations and *haciendas* (landed estates), and in mines, sweatshops, artisans' shops, and pearl fisheries. They could also be found in virtually every Spanish house. The practice of hiring slaves out for a daily wage (*jornal*), most of which went to the slave owner, was also common (see Palmer, 1976, chaps. 2 & 3). Spaniards enhanced their own status by possessing numerous slaves, and slave ownership extended to Indians of high rank and aspiring free blacks, who could rarely afford to purchase them. Manumission was attainable, but those who gained it were forbidden to bear arms, gather in groups, join certain craft guilds, or live outside the supervision of Spaniards. Thus, free blacks were also subject to discriminatory laws and regulations (Palmer, 1976, pp. 179 ff.).

Black slaves were considered by colonists to be robust and therefore superior to Indian laborers weakened by fragile constitutions, protected in theory by colonial law, and reluctant to work for Spaniards. But in New Spain, the cost of black slaves led to their use only as skilled workers because the highly profitable plantation economy that used blacks as the bulk of its labor force never took hold there as it did in the Caribbean and

Brazil. As a consequence, most labor in the colonial Mexican economy was provided by Indians, whose numbers began to rebound in the late 16th century.

THEOLOGICAL DOGMA AND CONTRADICTIONS IN CHRISTIAN THOUGHT

Charles V's New Laws generated resistance from the colonists and aroused unprecedented and far from undivided discussion about the legitimacy and aims of the Spanish colonial project. In 1550, the royal chaplain and philosopher Juan Gínes de Sepúlveda, one of the most virulent defenders of colonization, produced a treatise "proving" the innate inferiority of Indians, their inability to become Christians, and the right of Spaniards to enslave them. Often condemned as an extremist by modern historians (see Pagden, 1982, pp. 109 ff; Sepúlveda, 1941, p. 1, note 1), Sepúlveda in fact articulated what was at the time a pervasive view of the nature and status of the Indian in Christian and European intellectual thought (Pagden, 1982, p. 110).

As already mentioned, it was largely Bartolomé de Las Casas, the great "defender of the Indians," who precipitated Crown abolition of Indian slavery and the limiting of Spanish access to Indian labor through the implementation of the New Laws in 1542, after decades of campaigning for Indian rights. Soon Sepúlveda was summoned by Charles V to Valladolid, Spain, to debate Las Casas over Spanish aggression in the Americas.

Sepúlveda's position was that Indians lacked the capacity to reason, and therefore were similar to Aristotle's "barbarians" or natural slaves. This was also an appeal to the conventional Spanish definition of a barbarian, described later by the 17th-century Spanish lexicographer Covarrubias Orozco as someone who speaks Spanish badly or not at all, is unable to write, does not obey the law or behave according to Spanish custom, lacks "reason," and is "merciless and cruel" (Covarrubias Orozco, 1984, p. 194). Moreover, in a move reconciling Christian thought with what was believed to be Aristotelian, Sepúlveda framed his analysis in terms of the doctrine of natural law, which ground reason in the will of God and posited the divine origin of social norms. Thus, all human behavior was judged according to how closely it conformed to the norms of those judging such behavior. Differences in beliefs and practices meant not only that some were un-Spanish and un-Christian but also, as a consequence, that their ways of life were unacceptable.

Sepúlveda considered the behavior of Indians unacceptable for all of the conventional reasons: Indians were supposedly cruel, they were thought to practice cannibalism and human sacrifice, and they were considered sexually indiscriminate, allegedly committing sodomy and bestiality. Furthermore, according to Sepúlveda, their defectiveness was a characteristic not of individual sinners but of an entire people that did not recognize the natural law of God in their "customs and public institutions" (Sepúlveda, 1941, p. 123). Because Indians did not seem to be aware of what was "natural" and what was not, Sepúlveda considered them savage or inhuman people (*gente inhumana*; p. 85). This term indicated his ambivalence. It was clear to Sepúlveda that, although they might be barbarians, Aztecs had developed organized religion and warfare, a merchant class, a nobility, and a market economy—in short, the signs of civilization as the Spanish understood it.

Sepúlveda further advanced his argument of Indian inferiority by disparaging Indians for such "female" qualities as their second-rate minds and their cowardice (1941, p. 85, p. 107). Moreover, he associated Indians not only with women and children, who also allegedly lacked reason, but with animals as well:

> In prudence, talent, virtue and humanity [Indians] are as inferior to Spaniards as children are to adults and women to men. There is as much difference between them as there is between wild and cruel and very merciful people, between those who are intemperate and those who practice self-restraint and are moderate, and I am saying between monkeys and men. (p. 101)

Although he wavered in his belief in Indian defectiveness by noting that Indians did not completely lack reason and were not "bears" or "monkeys," Sepúlveda (1941, p. 109) ultimately interpreted Aristotle's argument to mean that inferior life forms, including Indians, women, children, and animals, should be subordinate to superior ones, defined as Spaniards, men, adults, and humans. Through the reciprocal associations of these constructs, he imagined not only women and children but Indians as "incomplete men," and men, in turn, as "civilized" and Spanish.

Other Spanish theologians of the time wrote invectives to capture what they considered the deviance of nonconformist groups such as the Moors, whom they typically likened to animals. For instance, a 17th-century Aragonese priest, Pedro Aznar Cardona, linked reason to full humanity when he stated that moriscos "raise their sons dirty as beasts . . . are clumsy in their reasoning, bestial in their discourse, barbaric in their language, ridiculous in their custom" (cited in Root, 1988, p. 130). Elsewhere, he characterized moriscos as wolves, ravens, and dogs, as well as heretics, and contrasted them to civilized Christian Spaniards (Boase, 1990, p. 18). Moriscos were also associated with disease (Root, 1988, p. 131) and undesirable, invasive plant life. Indeed, the same priest described them as "evil weeds" (cited in Root, 1988, p. 131).

In the New World, racial difference and social nonconformity were invoked through similar metaphors that, in effect, also dehumanized populations not considered Spanish, Christian, or civilized. Here colonial discourses linked "wild" Chichimec Indians, runaway black slaves (*cimarrones*), and vagabonds to animals, diseases, and undesirable plant life. These three groups had in common not only their dark skin, but also their lack of a fixed place in the colonial order.

Chichimec was the generic name given by the sedentary people of central Mexico to the nomadic Indian groups of the north. It was taken up by the Spaniards, who waged a long, drawn-out war of colonization against them. Reports from the northern frontier emphasized the Chichimecas' untamed and bestial nature. One Spanish miner, for instance, reported that the northern Guachichiles " . . . run around . . . like wild beasts" (cited in Behar, 1987, p. 116). The word *cimarrón* also ties blacks and Indians to animals. It was first used in the New World to refer to domestic cattle that had wandered away. It then came to designate Indian slaves who fled their Spanish captors, and finally it denoted runaway black slaves (Price, 1979, p. 1, note 1). Although its origins are unknown, cimarrón also means untamed, wild, savage, and uncultivated.

Vagabonds were usually mixed-race men of unknown parentage who lacked "income, houses, their own land, goods, jobs, parents, relatives to feed them or masters to serve," as one viceroy complained, and thus, in the Spanish view, a position that was understood to locate and fix man in a natural social order. Appearing to wander without purpose and without support, vagabonds "infested roads" that the authorities commanded be kept "clean" of them (Archivo General de la Nación [AGN] ramo General de Parte, tomo 11, expediente 367, 1663; also AGN ramo Reales Cédulas Duplicadas, tomo 3, expediente 7, 1587). As "exact opposites" of the Spanish idea of what was respectable (Baretta & Markoff, 1978, p. 595), vagabonds posed a constant threat to a civilization in which, as envisioned by Spaniards, everyone had a clear status.

Although unsettled individuals were excluded from the core of what Spaniards considered civilization, in the end even those encompassed within the colonial order were seen to threaten its stability. As one of the Crown's viceroys stated—without distinguishing slaves from freedmen from vagabonds—all blacks, mestizos and mulattos were "bad weeds [that] keep on increasing" (Archivo General de Indias [AGI] Mexico 27, N.52, 1608).

Yet visionaries such as Las Casas could almost see who the true "barbarians" were. In fact, Las Casas responded to Sepúlveda's arguments about Indian inferiority with an extraordinary essay describing the horrors the Spanish visited upon the Indians, the *Brevíssima relación de la destruición de las Indias* (The Devastation of the Indies) (1992). In this work, remarkable for its inversion of the relationship between Spaniards and Indians through Christian imagery and conventional metaphors of beastliness, Indians were portrayed as guileless and Spaniards as corrupt. Indians, as Las Casas wrote, "have no desire to possess worldly goods," and "their repasts are such that the food of the holy friars in the desert can scarcely be more parsimonious, scanty and poor" (p. 28). For Las Casas, Spaniards were the animals who came among these meek outcasts like "ravening beasts, wolves, tigers, or lions that had been starved for many days" (p. 29). For him, the uncivilized were the Spanish.

Moreover, Las Casas did not believe, as Sepúlveda did, that the concept of natural slavery could be universalized to encompass a whole people. "All the races of the world are men," wrote Las Casas, "and the definition of all men and of each of them, is only one and that is reason" (cited in Pagden, 1982, p. 140). For the Dominican friar, Indians not only could acquire Christian faith and therefore achieve reason, but in many ways they were the true Christians.

The debate between Sepúlveda and Las Casas suggests a pervasive conflict between two competing views signifying not only the historical contradictions of Spanish colonialism but also the Spanish treatment of minorities at home. According to Sepúlveda, a Christian could only be born, and Christian blood conveyed reason. But the messianic hope of Spaniards such as Las Casas was that everyone would ultimately become Christian. That hope resonated with the conviction that, theoretically at least, all people were capable of embracing Christianity of their own free will and, therefore, the enslavement and slaughter of Indians could not be justified.

Yet, slavery itself was not unconscionable for Las Casas, nor was it for other religious men of the day. In fact, when the enslavement of Indians became contested, Las Casas took for granted that blacks could take their place, even though blacks were routinely baptized upon enslavement and thus were ostensibly Christians. Not only did he obtain a license to import blacks two years after the New Laws freeing Indian slaves took effect, Las Casas also criticized the taking of Indian slaves, "as if [the Indies] were African lands" (cited in Friede, 1971, p. 165). Although some years later he began to doubt the legitimacy of blacks' enslavement, Las Casas did not consider the institution of slavery itself illegitimate. Rather, he seems to have believed that, like Indians, blacks had been enslaved "tyrannically" without regard for their right to freedom and their Christian potential (Bataillon, 1971, pp. 415-416; Friede, 1971, pp. 165-166). Among the smattering of other voices raised against that enslavement was that of the archbishop of Mexico, Alonso de Montúfar, whose request that the issue be officially addressed was unsuccessful (Friede, 1971, p. 166).

It has been suggested that the lack of concern by the Spanish monarchs for the welfare of blacks was due to the fact that Africans, unlike Indians, were not vassals of Spain and not, therefore, a Spanish responsibility (Pagden, 1982, p. 33). Such a position begs several questions. Why, for instance, were blacks perceived as hardier than Indians when in fact thousands died prematurely en route to and in the New World? Why were Indians and not blacks given their freedom, when both were subject to Christianization? The fact that there were many efforts to protect Indians, Las Casas' being only the most notable and most successful, whereas few spoke up against the enslavement of blacks suggests that distinctions between the two groups had already developed.

CIVILIZATION AND BARBARISM: INDIANS AND BLACKS COMPARED

Official terminologies for colonial categories of persons expose a consciousness of race linked in subtle ways to notions of civilization and barbarism. For instance, a Spaniard was known as an *español,* which referenced a native of Spain, a polity that in the early modern period implied an organized juridico-political body in the form of a province or kingdom. The term also indexed all the characteristics, in the Spanish mind, of a civilized being, including whiteness, Christian reason, and Hispanization.

The designation *indio* (Indian) signaled a complex early colonial view of the Indian as, at least in some respects, a creature who had rights separating him from "natural slaves," for, like Spaniards, Indians were marked by a label that referenced a polity and a place, and therefore a potential civilization. Well-known, of course, is Columbus' belief that he had come upon Asia by a new route, but more significant than the actual misidentification is the consideration of Indians as members of a juridico-political body that, however backward, was still identifiable as a polity.

Like Indians, blacks were considered a homogeneous group. There was little regard for internal social and ethnic distinctions except insofar as geographical origin was linked to character. Slaves were attributed with innate traits accorded with their place of birth, and some were less desirable than others (Aguirre Beltrán, 1972, pp. 186 ff; Zapata Olivella, 1989, p. 73). Unlike Indians, however, blacks were not considered members of a political entity. Europeans removed the conditions for blacks to be civilized and humane in the Spanish way as the sub-Saharan slave trade uprooted Africans from their lineages and families, the foundation upon which, in the Spanish view, cities and therefore civil life developed (Pagden, 1982, p. 71). To Spaniards, then, blacks had no identifiable social structure, religion, laws, government, or political economy. Although New World blacks seized every opportunity to construct family ties, the lack of recognition by colonial officials of those ties underscored blacks' social isolation and thus, in the Spanish mind, their lack of "civility."

However uncivilized they were thought to be, prevailing tradition nevertheless required the inclusion of blacks in the Christian universe, even as slaves. In fact, before the pressure for labor became too great, the Spanish monarchs insisted that all black slaves bound for the New World first reside for a time in Spain, where they could be baptized and civilized in Christian and Hispanic ways. By the mid-16th century, when slave importation directly from Africa to the colonies had become the norm, slaves were being baptized on the ships that carried them to the Americas.

Like the conversion of Indians to Christianity, the nominal Christianization of blacks ostensibly served to enlighten them and to integrate them into a world intelligible to other Christians. Yet although baptism was a way to draw all New World denizens into the same conceptual Christian universe, it did not make them all equal. As already noted, slavery itself was not incompatible with Christian doctrine, and the church justified making slaves of blacks through its belief that "equality in Christ would compensate for any inequalities in this world" (Sweet, 1978, p. 99). Furthermore, as the largest landowner in Spanish America, the church had an interest in legitimizing rather than contesting the social order (Sweet, 1978, p. 100). The fact that masters were seen to have a "Christian responsibility toward their slaves" (Sweet, 1978, p. 97) embodies the contradiction, and although slaves were denied their temporal rights, baptism provided them with inalienable spiritual rights to salvation.

COLOR AND THE
AESTHETICS OF PHYSICALITY

It was widely thought that the skin of blacks was a "sign of the sins of their fathers," as a Dominican friar told the Lima Inquisition in 1575 (cited in Bataillon, 1971, p. 417). Medieval Arab writers also believed in blacks descent from the biblical Canaanites and therefore in their fate as slaves. But according to the Dominican friar, it was not only blacks' fate that condemned them to slavery, it was also their temperament. "The condition of the blacks is not convenient for liberty," he continued, "because they are untamable and bellicose and would disturb themselves and others if they were free" (cited in Bataillon, 1971, p. 417). It is most significant that blacks were labeled according to the color of their skin "black" (*negro*), an "unlucky and sad color," wrote Covarrubias Orozco, who also cited a proverb, "although we are black, we are people" (1984, p. 826), that suggests a certain ambivalence in this respect as in others.

Blacks, Spaniards, and Indians engendered among themselves mixed-race offspring, the primary categories of which were *mestizos* and *mulatos*. Mestizos were of Spanish and Indian ancestry. The term derives from the Spanish word *mezcla* (mixture) or from the Latin *mixticius* (mixed) and signifies the belief that Indians and Spaniards were able to breed successfully because both belonged to the category "human." But the word *mulato*, which derives from *mula,* or mule, a cross between a donkey and a horse, referred to those with one black parent. It, in turn, suggests that blacks were considered a species apart, unable to breed successfully with Indians or Spaniards. Because the offspring of enslaved females could themselves be enslaved under Spanish law, many mulattos were also slaves.

In medieval Christianity, negative and positive images of blacks existed alongside one another. Dark skin color was the mark of the infidel, but consciousness of it was not highly diffused. The devil was sometimes, but by no means always, black, and at the same time black madonnas and saints were venerated by white Europeans. According to St. Clair Drake, it was only after the mid-15th century that blackness became a negative "master symbol" (1990, pp. 2, 192). In the New World, the linked physical and cultural traits of blackness came to be constructed in relation to ideas about Indians, who were more aesthetically appealing and less "savage" to Europeans (Fairchild, 1934, pp. 9-10; McAlister, 1984, p. 461).

Blacks seemed the very opposite of the Spanish ideal of beauty, as they did to other Europeans of the day (Jordan, 1977, pp. 4 ff.). The colonial Mexican elite expressed its distaste for blackness in physical descriptions notable for their exclusive focus on blacks and mulattos. For instance, a mulatto burned at the stake in 1605 for impersonating a priest was described by inquisitors with some fascination as, "a tall dark man with wide shoulders, a very ugly face, a wide, blunt nose, and thick lips like a black" (AGN, ramo Inquisición, tomo 275, expediente 14, 1605).

In another text, a priest described two blacks who allegedly wandered the northern zone of Nueva Vizcaya, preaching "the devil's words" to the Indians, as "ugly" with small, sunken eyes (AGN, ramo Historia, tomo 19, "Noticia de la annua del año 1598, primera misión de Jesuita en la Nueva Vizcaya"). One notary described a mulatto woman suspected of witchcraft as "fat with an ugly face" (AGN ramo Inquisición, tomo 296, expediente 3, 1612).

Spanish preoccupation with blackness is most notable, however, in the blatantly color-conscious terms for blacks and mulattos, including *mulato claro* (light mulatto), *mulato blanco* (white mulatto), *mulato prieto* (dark mulatto), *mulato pardo* (brown mulatto), *mulato lobo* and *mulato alobado* (half-breed mulatto), *moreno* (dark-complexioned, brown, colored), *negro retinto* (very dark black, literally "redyed"), and *negro amulatado* (mulatto-like black) (Aguirre Beltrán, 1972, pp. 65ff; Palmer, 1976, pp. 41-42; Van den Berghe, 1978, p. 52). Moreover, several euphemisms for mulatto, such as coyote and *lobo* (wolf), are names of animals, and are reminiscent of the conventional metaphors of beastliness that denoted socioracial difference and inferiority.

LEGAL STATUS AND SOCIAL STATUS IN THE NEW WORLD

The Spanish word *raza,* which is derived from the Latin word *ratio,* or reason, first appeared in 1438 in the phrase "good race" (Corominas & Pascual, 1980, vol. 4, p. 800). Although it did not have the pseudoscientific connotations it gained in the 19th century in Europe and North America, from the 16th century on race was always linked by Spanish writers to lineage and therefore to purity of blood (Corominas & Pascual,

1980, vol. 4, p. 800). Race quickly became as important as, and closely related to, nobility and orthodoxy, as the Spanish Crown battled to rid Spain of its religious and ethnic deviants following the *reconquista*. Jews and Moors had, in fact, sometimes been referred to as of *mala raza,* of bad or defective race, in 15th-century Spain. Covarrubias Orozco strengthened the link when he associated *raza* with a non-Christian lineage, "like having some raza of a Moor or a Jew" (Covarrubias Orozco, 1984, pp. 896-897). By the beginning of the 16th century, the term had taken on a purely negative sense in Spanish that may have been related to a similar Spanish word, *raça,* which signified "defect or blemish in a piece of cloth" (Corominas & Pascual, 1980, vol. 4, p. 800). Covarrubias Orozco himself made this association and characterized that deviance as "the thread unlike the rest of the threads in the weft" (1984, p. 896).

In Spain and in the New World, *casta* (caste) was the more conventional designation for persons grouped by lineage. An Iberian word that in the Middle Ages denoted any group of humans or animals (Mörner, 1967, p. 53), *casta* had come to be defined by the early 17th century as "noble and pure-blooded lineage, he who is of good line and descent; notwithstanding that we say he is of good caste and bad caste" (Covarrubias Orozco, 1984, p. 316). Covarrubias Orozco also located "nature" in this quality: "Nature comes from caste and from native land or nation" (1984, p. 316). By extension, then, lineage and therefore blood conveyed essential qualities of the person.

The New World *sistema de castas* (system of castes) categorized persons by blood and ancestry, which came to be linked to skin color and juridical status as the traditional Old World distinction between Spanish nobility and Spanish commoners gave way to distinctions among Spaniards, Indians, mixed-races, and blacks. The social hierarchy in New Spain was dominated by the white (Spanish) elite, the index of legitimacy. Indians and mestizos, in turn, had more rights than blacks and mulattos, yet fewer rights than Spaniards; and black slaves had the fewest rights of all.

The Crown initially implemented legislation with the aim of creating two social entities in the colony, a *República de los indios* (Indian nation) and a *República de los españoles* (Spanish nation), subject to different laws and regulations. The legal status of blacks and mixed-races, despite the fact that they were collectively known as castas, depended for the most part on their ancestry and their status as free persons, and they never formed a third entity recognized by the law. Although some mestizos and mulattos were brought up among Indians, their residence in Indian villages was discouraged. Thus, mixed-races and blacks were primarily associated with the Spanish Republic.

As what one historian of colonial Mexico has called a "rudimentary apartheid policy" (Liss, 1975, p. 43), the notion of two republics masked an integral dependency that hierarchized two political entities so that, in practice, Indian political and economic structures were subordinated to Spanish ones. Although the indigenous population possessed a juridical status that granted it certain rights and a semi-protected rank, ultimately the colonists' economic survival depended on their ability to extract goods and labor from that population. This dependency in effect subordinated the conquered native population to the conquerors.

The sistema de castas was less obviously a system of social practice wherein Spaniards formed the elite and Indians the lowly masses. The castas came to mediate the relation between Spanish consumers and Indian producers of wealth as servants and slaves, overseers and estate managers, deputies and assistants, and in general as agents of Spaniards. The result was that although Indians ostensibly enjoyed more rights than persons with African ancestry, most of whom were slaves, all castas were dominant over Indians as the practice of socioracial hierarchy came to diverge from its sanction in law (Mörner, 1967, pp. 30-31, 60 ff.).

PUTTING DIFFERENCE TO WORK

Spanish ideas about blackness as they developed in the New World encompassed both physical and behavioral attributes. Not only was blackness aesthetically unpleasant to Spaniards, perceptions of blacks as particularly prone to aggression also informed early reports sent by colonial officials to Spanish monarchs. In 1579, for instance, Viceroy Enríquez wrote:

> blacks are one of the things of which one has to take special account in this land. Although arms are prohibited to them, they carry hidden knives, and whatever the offense they cause many deaths among themselves and among Indians and even among Spaniards. (AGI Mexico, 1579, p. 20 note 29)

Especially and "most cruelly," he continued, most deaths and injuries occurred among the Indians, whom he characterized as a "wretched" people without "resistance." A quarter of a century later, another viceroy wrote "blacks, as they are more powerful, will do anything they want to the Indian villagers, and they will oppress them" (AGI Mexico 25, n. 26, 1603). These dispatches illustrate the Spanish conviction that Indians were miserable, ignorant, and altogether lacking strength, and, in contrast, blacks were "naturally evil" (Palmer, 1976, p. 42).

Although blacks were thought to be the most aggressive of the dark-skinned peoples, mulattos were also "pugnacious" according to Viceroy Martín Enríquez (AGI Mexico 19, n. 125, 1574). According to Viceroy Mancera, who governed almost a century later, mestizos were "no less presumptuous" than blacks and mulattos. But because they had Spanish blood, "their presumption [was] better controlled and more subject to reason" (cited in Israel, 1975, pp. 64-65). In fact, as one Spanish colonist said of a mixed-raced man named Francisco, "he is mestizo . . . and does not get involved with blacks" (AGN ramo Inquisición, tomo 491, exp. 16, 1616, Mexico). Notwithstanding these distinctions, as a group castas were said to be "universally inclined to evil," and they were frequently accused of "treating [Indians] badly and making them serve them" (AGN ramo Reales Cédulas Originales 6, exp. 292, 1578).

As a result of the perception of Indians' weaknesses, as well as the widespread belief that Spaniards also mistreated them, Indians were supposed to be isolated in their villages, where they would govern themselves at the local level. Yet they routinely had contact with Spaniards, blacks, and mixed-races, and often brought court cases against them for harassment. These cases demonstrate that antagonism and violence were central to certain colonial social practices as Spaniards came to control Indians through castas.

In one case, a black slave named Domingo, described as "naturally unsettled and depraved" by one Indian official and "arrogant," "haughty," and "extremely bold" by another, was accused of terrorizing an Indian village as he forced residents to work on his Spanish master's hacienda (AGN ramo Criminal, tomo 265, exp. 26, 1647). The Indians of another village complained that the Spaniards who lived in the vicinity, frequently accompanied by their foremen and "other mulattos and mestizos," habitually took them from their houses by force, sometimes tying the Indians to the tails of their horses. They ordered the Indians to work for them "night and day" on their haciendas, treating them more cruelly than they treated their own slaves (AGN, ramo Indios, tomo 11, exp. 456, 1640). In another incident, the residents of an Indian village brought criminal charges against a mulatto village treasurer who "aggravated and oppressed" them by coming to their homes, threatening them, and tricking them into carrying messages up to Spanish haciendas. If they refused to go, the mulatto would catch and beat them. Once they reached the haciendas, they were made to work for weeks on end, treated badly, insulted, and not paid. The Indians claimed the mulatto was paid by the Spaniards for the work the Indians themselves did as if the Indians were his slaves (AGN ramo Criminal, tomo 105, exp. 18, 1644).

In other cases, an Indian woman was assaulted and jailed by a black slave on orders of the Spanish district official (*alcalde mayor*) to whom she had appealed when her husband was allegedly murdered by one of the official's assistants (AGN ramo Criminal, tomo 57, exp. 5, 1650). An abusive priest, angered by what he perceived as the disobedience of residents of an Indian village, ordered his slaves to have them confined to the church. One of the slaves wielded a machete, with which he pursued the Indians (AGN ramo Bienes Nacionales, tomo 596, exp. 13, 1682). In yet another incident, the mother of a district official was accused of sending her female black slaves to catch "rebellious" Indians and take them to jail (AGN ramo Criminal, tomo 34, exp. 13, 1639). Not only did Spaniards stand behind the aggressors in the majority of cases, but as we see in the final example, even black women were considered capable of dominating Indians, who lacked the force to resist them.

Colonial law called for the separation of Indians from others. But, as demonstrated above, Indians routinely came into contact with Spaniards and castas. Moreover, in order to control Indians and extract labor from them, Spaniards used free and enslaved blacks, as well as mulattos and mestizos, to force compliance. Thus, while those of African descent had fewer rights than Indians, they were also considered stronger and more evil than Indians, and therefore the perfect intermediaries between Spaniards and the conquered native population.

One can conclude that, although inequality in New Spain was conferred through cultural notions of blood and race, as it also was in Spain, the results were somewhat dissimilar. In Spain, religious and ethnic minorities were amputated from the social body and expelled from the peninsula. In contrast, New Spain needed its "impure" populations and incorporated them into the colonial order as various forms of labor. One sees in the colony the creation of a society where "race" played a major role in the determination of a subject's position and where inequality and inferiority based on racial ascriptions were sanctioned both in law and in everyday practice.

CONCLUSION:
INDEPENDENCE AND BEYOND

Although the enslavement of blacks was legal in Mexico until 1829, the importation of black slaves peaked in the mid-17th century. By the end of that century, the indigenous population had rebounded from its early devastation and mixed-race populations grew as the slave trade all but trickled to a halt. Therefore, for all intents and purposes, by the time slavery was legally abolished, the trade in Africans had already ended.

Nevertheless, the abolition of slavery was part of the rhetoric of the independence movement of the early 19th century as non-whites attempted to rid Mexico of its colonial legacies of racism and ethnocentrism (Carroll, 1991, p. 133). Leaders such as Miguel Hidalgo and the mixed-race José María Morelos, both insurgent priests, challenged the Spanish elite by calling for slave emancipation and the dismantling of the caste system as it was written into law. Not surprisingly, non-whites were drawn to the insurgent movement led by Hidalgo and Morelos, and later by Vicente Guerrero, who was himself of partial African ancestry and became one of the new nation's first presidents.

Independence brought change at the level of national and local politics, as slavery and the caste system were legally abolished and all those besides Spaniards were permitted to vote and hold public office (Carroll, 1991, pp. 134 ff.). Yet whites still held much of the power and they feared that Indians, in particular, would rise up and take over. Non-whites continued to have a lower social status as whites "held the color line" and even gained control of the independence movement. In many ways, the elite modeled the new government on the colonial one and resisted popular forces for a change that did not come until the revolution, nearly a century later (Carroll, 1991, pp. 142-143).

Following independence, racial classifications were no longer a part of Mexican census data. The black population—which had shrunk dramatically from its mid-16th-century levels—rapidly disappeared from the historical record, not to reemerge until the mid-20th century, when some anthropological interest arose in the Afro-Mexican population of Mexico's Pacific Coast (see Aguirre Beltrán, 1958). As a consequence, the debates about race and nation that accompanied the Revolution of 1910 focused on Spaniards, Indians, and mestizos.

By the late 19th century, the official definition of an Indian had come to include ethnic characteristics such as language, dress, and social organization, and many Mexicans had come to consider themselves mestizos. The "heyday of European racist thought" (Knight, 1990, p. 78) also coincided with Mexico's late 19th- and early 20th-century economic development and the creation of a reliable labor force that once again depended on the Indian masses. A sort of internal colonialism came to characterize the state-building process of this period, as the Europeanized elite sought once again to forcibly draw what it viewed as "lazy" natives into the political economy (Knight, 1990, pp. 78-79).

Knight (1990) argues that even the ostensibly anti-racist rhetoric of the 1910 Revolution and the nation building that followed was infused with ideas that not only essentialized "Indian" characteristics, but continued to identify Indians as a problem. Indians were to be either integrated in an "enlightened [and] noncoercive fashion" (p. 80) into the revolutionary state (revolutionary *indigenismo*) and eventually to be assimilated into a "cosmic race" of mestizos (*mestizaje*), or alternatively, encouraged to assert their national autonomy, as was the position of the "Indiannists."

In contrast to 19th-century ones, these ideological alternatives valued rather than denigrated Indians and mestizos. But racist paradigms continued to imprison the intellectuals of the new state, most of whom conceived of Indians as a "race," and some of whom actually sought to whiten Mexico's population though assimilation. Racism, for instance, pervades the rhetoric of the philosopher and politician José Vasconcelos, the most vocal proponent of *mestizaje*, for whom mestizos were "the bridge to the future" (cited in Knight, 1990, p. 86). Vasconcelos argued that North Americans and Latin Americans were the offspring of different "parental races" possessed of "racial, temperamental and spiritual differences" (Knight, 1990, p. 95). He also denigrated blacks' appearance. No one, he argued, would voluntarily mate with this "inferior race" or "with types whom the instinct for beauty will signal as fundamentally recessive and unworthy of perpetuation" (cited in Stepan, 1991, p. 151). But other groups were greater victims of the nationalistic fervor that gripped Mexico in the early 20th century. In 1931, for instance, there were mass expulsions of Chinese, stereotyped as "filthy, disease-ridden money-grubbing, parasitic and sexually threatening" (Knight, 1990, p. 96).

By the middle of the 20th century, "Indianism" typified the elite view of the Indian "problem." At the other extreme, some whites and mestizos who felt victimized by Indian "uppishness" sought to reassert their

" 'racial' superiority" (Knight, 1990, p. 99). Today, although most Mexican intellectuals would deny that racism is a problem in Mexico, "whitening" continues to be the ideal.

Although Afro-Mexicans have not been a prominent part of the national consciousness, and many Mexicans do not even realize they have historically been part of the population, there are still communities of Afro-Mexicans on the Pacific coast of Mexico, as well as in other parts of the country. They have generally remained isolated, and have not presented a major "social problem" (Rout, 1977, p. 282). Whether this will change in the future remains to be seen, but for now the Indian is "the officially recognized sufferer from oppression" (p. 282), and local Afro-Mexicans generally do not view themselves as part of a national dialogue. Instead, for many, the rhetoric of the revolution and beyond has made it clear that, whatever the contribution of blacks to a national culture, "the Mexican is an Indian."

NOTE

1. Throughout this chapter, I follow colonial terminology and refer to people of African descent as blacks (*negros*), indigenous Americans as Indians (*indios*), and Spaniards as Spaniards (*españoles*). The cultural and historical significance of these terms, as well as those designating mixed races, are discussed fully later in the chapter.

REFERENCES

Aguirre Beltrán, G. (1958). *Cuijla: Esbozo etnográfico de un pueblo negro*. Mexico City: Fondo de Cultura Económica.

Aguirre Beltrán, G. (1972). *La población negra de México*. Mexico City: Fondo de Cultura Económica.

Baretta, S. R., & Markoff, J. (1978). Civilization and barbarism: Cattle frontiers in Latin America. *Comparative Studies in Society and History, 20*(4), 587-620.

Bataillon, M. (1971). The clérigo Casas, colonist and colonial reformer. In J. Friede & B. Keen (Eds.), *Bartolomé de Las Casas in history* (pp. 353-440). DeKalb: Northern Illinois University Press.

Behar, R. (1987). The visions of a Guachichil witch in 1599: A window on the subjugation of Mexico's hunter-gatherers. *Ethnohistory, 34*(2), 115-138.

Boase, R. (1990). The morisco expulsion and diaspora: An example of racial and religious intolerance. In D. Hook & B. Taylor (Eds.), *Cultures in contact in medieval Spain* (pp. 9-28). London: King's College London Medieval Studies.

Carroll, P. (1991). *Blacks in colonial Veracruz: Race, ethnicity and regional development*. Austin: University of Texas Press.

Corominas, J. & Pascual, J. A. (1980). *Diccionario crítico etimológico Castellano e Hispánico*. Madrid: Editorial Gredor.

Covarrubias Orozco, S. (1984/1611). *Tesoro de la lengua castellana o española*. Madrid: Ediciones Turner.

Drake, S. (1990). *Black folk here and there* (2 vols.). Los Angeles: University of California Center for Afro-American Studies.

Fairchild, H. (1934). *The noble savage*. New York: Russell & Russell.

Friede, J. (1971). Las Casas and indigenism in the sixteenth century. In J. Friede & B. Keen (Eds.), *Bartolomé de Las Casas in history* (pp. 127-234). DeKalb: Northern Illinois University Press.

Israel, J. (1975). *Race, class and politics in colonial Mexico, 1610-1670*. Oxford, UK: Oxford University Press.

Jordan, W. (1977). *White over black: American attitudes toward the Negro, 1550-1812*. Chapel Hill: University of North Carolina Press.

Knight, A. (1990). Racism, revolution and indigenismo: Mexico, 1910-1940. In R. Graham (Ed.), *The idea of race in Latin America, 1870-1940* (pp. 71-113). Austin: University of Texas Press.

Las Casas, B. (1992). *The devastation of the Indies* (Herma Briffault, Trans.). Baltimore: Johns Hopkins University Press.

Liss, P. (1975). *Mexico under Spain, 1521-1556: Society and the origins of nationality*. Chicago: University of Chicago Press.

MacLachlan, C. (1988). *Spain's empire in the New World: The role of ideas in institutional and social change*. Berkeley: University of California Press.

McAlister, L. N. (1963). Social structure and social change in New Spain. *Hispanic American Historical Review, 43*(3), 349-370.

McAlister, L. N. (1984). *Spain and Portugal in the New World: 1492-1700*. Minneapolis: University of Minnesota Press.

Mörner, M. (1967). *Race mixture in the history of Latin America*. Boston: Little, Brown.

Pagden, A. (1982). *The fall of natural man: The American Indian and the origins of comparative ethnology*. Cambridge, UK: Cambridge University Press.

Palmer, C. (1976). *Slaves of the white God: Blacks in Mexico, 1570-1650*. Cambridge, MA: Harvard University Press.

Peters, E. (1988). *Inquisition*. New York: Free Press.

Price, R. (1979). Introduction: Maroons and their communities. In R. Price (Ed.), *Maroon societies* (2nd ed., pp. 1-30). Baltimore: Johns Hopkins University Press.

Root, D. (1988). Speaking Christian: Orthodoxy and difference in sixteenth-century Spain. *Representations, 23*, 118-134.

Rout, L., Jr. (1977). *The African experience in Spanish America*. Cambridge, UK: Cambridge University Press.

Sepúlveda, J. G. de (1941). *Tratado sobre las justas causas de la guerra contra los indios*. Mexico City: Fondo de Cultura Económica.

Stepan, N. L. (1991). *The hour of eugenics: Race, gender and nation in Latin America*. Ithaca, NY: Cornell University Press.

Sweet, D. G. (1978). Black robes and "Black destiny": Jesuit views of African slavery in 17th-century Latin America. *Revista de historia de América, 86*, 84-133.

Van den Berghe, P. L. (1978). *Race and racism: A comparative perspective* (2nd ed.). New York: John Wiley.

Zapata Olivella, M. (1989). *Las claves mágicas de América*. Bogotá: Plaza y Janés.

4

Anti-Racism in the United States: 1865-1900

Herbert Aptheker

The predominant view in U.S. historiography presents racism as being unchallenged among White people. This idea is false; it also is pernicious, for it tends to disarm present-day advocates of egalitarianism among White people. This idea also disheartens Black people, fostering among them tendencies toward hopelessness or other forms of extremism—which really is another expression of hopelessness.

In earlier works, I challenge this view, most recently in a 1992 volume tracing anti-racism in the United States from the colonial period to the conclusion of the Civil War. For some years I have been examining evidence of anti-racism among White people in the United States since the reconstruction era. This chapter is a brief summary of some of the evidence so far accumulated.

Burnham (1972) writes that, faced with the egalitarianism common among "most of today's intellectuals," they might wish that this consensus had existed in the late 19th century, but the opposite was true. In fact, he asserts, in that period "none" challenged racism's validity.

Dyer (1992), writing about the time of Theodore Roosevelt, affirms that "anti-Black thought existed in virtually every area of scholarly inquiry . . . nearly all the American thinkers wrote in a White supremacist vein," differing only "in their antipathy toward Blacks." He mentions that this attitude prevailed among White Americans—and the modifier "virtually every" disappears (p. 91).

Haller (1971), dealing with views among scientists, writes,

> The subject of race inferiority was beyond critical reach in the late nineteenth century. Having accepted science and its exalted doctrinaire, American society betrayed no statement, popular or otherwise, that looked to a remodeling of its social or political habits of race. (p. 210)

These sources ignore the existence of African Americans, but it is important to note that from Benjamin Banneker to Frederick Douglass to W.E.B. Du Bois, the denial of inferiority runs through Black history. In addition to the above examples, one might add the speech made in 1858 by John S. Rock, who, satirizing the posture of White racial superiority, contrasted the splendid features of his Black comrades with "the delicate physical organization, wan color, sharp features and lank hair of the Caucasian," and concluded that "when the White man was created, nature was pretty well exhausted—but, determined to keep up appearances, she pinched up his features and did the best she could under the circumstances" (cited in Aptheker, 1951, p. 405).

In a more serious vein, the National Medical Society, in a memorial to Congress in 1870, protested the Jim Crowism then characteristic of the medical profession and added, "Science knows no race, color, or condition; and we protest against the Medical Society of the District of Columbia maintaining such a relic of barbarism" (cited in Aptheker, 1951, p. 618).

In an earlier work dealing with the Abolitionist movement (1989), I emphasize that, although the elimination of slavery was, of course, the movement's central aim, it also sought to elevate the condition of the free Black population and denied the inferiority of the African American people—though some of its White adherents doubted this.

Both Frederick Douglass and Wendell Phillips devoted much of the final years of their lives to opposing racism. This chapter discusses opposition to racism from 1866 to the creation of the National Association for the Advancement of Colored People (NAACP) and the convening of the First Universal Races Congress in London in 1911. A book is needed to do this period and topic justice, but for now let me suggest something of what its contents would be.

EVIDENCE OF ANTI-RACISM
AFTER THE CIVIL WAR

A purpose in the launching of the weekly newspaper *Nation* was to attack racism. In its early pages this is evident, but by about 1868 its anti-racist intent became muted, and the magazine rationalized the abortion of the vision of the pre-Civil War Abolitionists.

Several White men—Thaddeus Stevens and Charles Sumner, Oliver Morton of Indiana, George W. Julian of Ohio, Henry Wilson of Massachusetts—actively sought anti-racist legislation. To convey their argumentation and passion, Henry Wilson, speaking in the U.S. Congress in 1869, said of the Black man: "I recognize him not only as a countryman, a fellow citizen, but as a brother, given by his creator the same rights that belong to me." Ending slavery was necessary, said this future vice-president, but equality must be assured. He wanted the "black man in this country made equal with the White man. . . . I believe in equality among citizens— equality in the broad and most comprehensive democratic sense. No man should have rights depending on the accidents of life" (Fortieth Congress, 1869; Pole, 1973).

Thaddeus Stevens wrote this epitaph for his tombstone in a cemetery for Black people:

> I repose in this quiet and secluded spot, not from any natural preference for solitude, but finding other cemeteries limited as to race by charter rules, I have chosen this that I might illustrate in my death the principles which I advocated through a long life, equality of man before his creator. (Trefousse, 1968, p. 344)

Lydia Maria Child, one of the most effective and courageous fighters against slavery, detested racism. She wrote to Wendell Phillips in 1860 to see to it that she not be buried in a cemetery that practiced Jim Crow.

Child lived to see slavery's end; in its aftermath, she was the editor of *The Freedman's Book,* widely used in the South immediately after the Civil War. Not only does the book reject racism, as Bond (1939) writes, but,

> The teachers in these (postwar) schools taught the (Black) children the social graces by precept, but also by example; part of their technique consisted in living with the Negroes, eating with them, and treating them in accordance with the egalitarian principles that were characteristic of their code. (p. 117)

Bond (1939) deals with Alabama; what he describes about anti-racism in that state in the 1860s and 1870s was characteristic in those years throughout the South. Even more than Bond, Tunnell (1984) shows the reality of Black-White unity and the repudiation of racism not merely in words but in action—even, in more than one case, unto death.

Swint (1941/1967) notes that in 1869 there were about 10,000 teachers in the South (all of them White and the majority women) dedicated to eliminating the literary blindness with which slavery had afflicted Black people. Swint describes abysmal racism. But the vivid examples of anti-racism persist, perhaps all the more dramatically given the author's stark prejudice against Blacks. Thus, quoting the first issue of the *American Freedman* (April 1866), which was the organ of the Union Commission of the American Freedman, one finds the assertion that the superiority of the White person is unproven. It added that the Commission "was pledged to the maintenance of the doctrine of equal rights." The motto of the movement was: "No distinction of race, caste or color in the republic." The teacher "must educate not white nor blacks specifically but all men equally as members of the same great commonwealth." Overwhelmingly, the teachers were White women; despite ominous hostility from plantation owners, they persevered; inspired, as one of them wrote in 1864, that in her seven years as a teacher she had "not seen a parallel to their appetite for learning, and their active progress" (cited in Swint, 1941/1967).

It is refreshing and inspiring to observe that the platform of the Republican Party in Texas adopted on July 4, 1867 affirms,

> That as a measure of State policy, we will endeavor to establish, at the earliest practicable time, a system of free common schools for the equal benefit of all children and youths of the scholastic age, without distinction of race or color, to be supported by equal and uniform taxation, until a school fund can be made available for this purpose. (Eby, 1918)

E. M. Wheelock, Texas superintendent of public instruction, in an 1868 report to Governor E. M. Pease, affirms that, as a result of the "late War we have an altered destiny." Now, he says, "in line with the 19th century" we must "re-adjust the course of" Texas. The chief need "is the education of our youth." For this, "no sacrifice, whether of money or of prejudice" is excessive. He called for universal suffrage, which necessitated universal education (cited in Eby, 1918).

J. C. Dunlap came down from the North to teach Black people in Tennessee. He believed in and practiced equality of all people. The Ku

Klux Klan (KKK) celebrated July 4, 1868, by kidnapping Dunlap and bestowing 200 lashes upon him—fittingly celebrating the Declaration of Independence. He was cared for—says the source—by a prominent Democrat before leaving the South.

Despite his physical handicaps, George W. Ashburn, a White man prominent in the Republican Party in Georgia, had come South to teach Black people in 1868. He was flogged into unconsciousness. A White Southerner also named Ashburn joined the Union Army and later participated in Black-White political efforts. He lived with Black people and was severely beaten.

George W. Smith fought for equality after serving in the Union forces. He was dragged from his Texas home by a mob and killed after fiercely resisting in October 1868. Two unnamed Black men were also killed with him (Trelease, 1971). Smith, reported a local paper, "lived almost entirely with Negroes on terms of perfect equality." He headed the local Union League.

Governor Ridgely C. Powers of Mississippi told the state senate in 1870 that he could "see some reason for refusing to ride in the same car or steamboat, or for declining to sit in the same assembly with drunkards, gamblers, robbers and murderers" but, he continued, "to refuse to come into such proximity with men because they happen to have a different complexion from my own, would be to acknowledge a mean prejudice, unworthy of an age of intelligence." Surely, "the time has passed for estimating a man by the color of his skin, rather than by the qualities of his heart, or the strength of his intellect" (Harrison, 1974).

The 1870s—especially the later half—are correctly depicted as marked by the revival and intensification of racism, but the mistaken impression exists that this racism was accomplished without resistance. I remind the reader that I am referring to resistance against racism from White people; of course, the African American population continued its resistance.

Following are some evidences of the rejection of racism by White people in the 1870s. In South Carolina, as Bourbon terror mounted, the Charleston *Daily Republican* editorialized against the idea that White men and only White men must control the state.

> Such talk [of White supremacy] is as wickedly idle as for colored men to say that their race shall have complete control. It is not a matter of race at all. It is a matter of citizenship, in which colored and white are to have their rights and their due share of power; not because they are white, not because they are colored, but because they are American citizens. By-and-by

we shall stop talking of the color of a man in relation to citizenship and power, and shall look at his wealth of mind and soul. (cited in Trelease, 1971, p. xxviii)

John W. Stephens was a wartime Unionist in Rockingham County, North Carolina. After the war he joined the Republican Party, taught school, and advocated equality of Blacks and Whites. He was expelled from his church (Methodist) for such beliefs, but neighbors did elect him to the state senate. He was constantly threatened and fortified his home, but in May 1870 he was killed by "a considerable number of reasonably prominent men" (Trelease, 1971, pp. 212-213).

Robert W. Flournoy served as a teacher in Pontotoc County, Mississippi. Born in Georgia, he moved to Mississippi in 1856; he had served in the Confederate army, but after the war he became a Republican and edited a newspaper with the subversive title *Equal Rights.* In his school, he had Black and White students. The KKK attacked him; Flournoy resisted and killed one of the marauders in 1871; after that he fades from available records. The likelihood is that he was killed.

Somewhat similar is the case of John Q. Johnson, who let it be known in Florida that racism was vile. Though constantly threatened, he refused to leave. Johnson was gunned down in April 1871. Other acts of terrorism—and heroic resistance—by White opponents of racism met martyrdom in 1870 and 1871 (Trelease, 1971, pp. 311, 336-337, 356).

There is little documentation of the lives of White (or Black) martyrs to anti-racism's cause. An exception is Howard's (1984) study of the murder by KKK terrorists of five men—four Black and one White—in Alabama. The White man was William Luke, who was killed on July 11, 1870. His crime was fraternization with Black people. There was a grand jury investigation but no one was indicted.

In 1870, the widely circulated *Lippincott's Magazine* published an absorbing account by a White Southerner, E. A. Pollard. The essay discloses a patriarchal tone, but it apologizes for racist conduct. It closes by advocating "the cause of the rights and progress of the colored people of the South"; this offers "a field of great weight and usefulness" (Pollard, 1870, 1871).

Jesse Henry Jones, associated with Wendell Phillips in the labor movement, created the Christian Labor Union with George Edwin McNeill in 1871. Its locale was Boston and, in addition to seeking greater rights for working people, it actively promoted the civil rights of Black people. It attracted few supporters, although one unnamed Black minister in Arkansas conveyed sympathy (Luker, 1991).

A historical work that is unusual in the extensive and sympathetic treatment of evidences of Black-White unity in the post-Civil War South is Williamson's (1965) discussion of the work conducted by members of the Northern Methodist Church. In the early 1870s, member Timothy Willard Lewis labored courageously and effectively in South Carolina seeking fellowship between Black and White. In 1871, the South Carolina Conference of the Methodist Church adopted a report that states:

> We re-affirm our solemn conviction that the true basis of organization in State and Church is without distinction of *race* or *color;* and to pander to the prejudice of the white or black race in this regard, will displease our common Father, and bring only evil and disaster in the end.

Williamson observes, "So thoroughly was the program executed that it is difficult to determine the color of members or ministers within the Conference, because the records are mute on the point."

Gilbert Haven, the bishop of this church, was a devoted opponent of racism; he continued his work in the South throughout the 1870s. Another prominent White person in South Carolina who vigorously opposed racism throughout the 1870s was Justus K. Jellson. From 1874 through 1876, Jellson was chairman of the education committee of the South Carolina Senate. In that key position, he labored for an anti-racist educational system, but in vain (Williamson, 1965).[1]

A significant attack on racism came from France; A. De Quatrefages, a leading scientist, professor, and member of the Institute of France, in an essay in the first volume of the influential *Popular Science Monthly* (1872) concludes that *"there exists but one species of men."* His conclusion, based on current scientific investigation, was "of great and serious importance, for it gives to the thought of universal brotherhood the only foundation that many people now recognize, that of science and reason."

From science to religion, attacks upon racism were not unusual in the latter part of the 19th century. Ochs (1980) discusses how the Catholic Church ordained African Americans as priests. The first was James Augustine Healy, who was ordained in 1854 and in 1875 was consecrated as bishop of Portland, Maine. Healy tended to emphasize his Irish heritage, but he never denied his African American reality. Two of his brothers served the church with distinction: Alexander Sherwood Healy was ordained in 1858 and served as rector of Holy Cross Cathedral in Boston from the end of the Civil War until his death in 1875; Patrick James Healy, Jesuit, served as rector of Georgetown University from 1874 to 1882.

Another African American whose African heritage was strikingly evident was Augustine Tolton. He was born a slave and received holy orders in Rome in 1886. He returned to the United States and served as a priest in Quincy, Illinois, and in Chicago. Carles Randolph Uncles was ordained in 1891 and was the first Black man to receive holy orders in the United States.

Och's (1980) study makes clear the dominant nature of racism in the church; it also illuminates the fact that these exceptions occurred, and that numerous White people found solace in the ministrations of those African American priests.

Peabody (1875) writes that racism certainly "is real, extensive and deep." Still, he insists, "This feeling cannot by any possibility be regarded as natural, innate, and inevitable" for, in other areas of the world, "there are not traces of it." Perhaps Black people belong "to an inferior race," but where the coeducation of Afro-Americans and White people has existed, it has not confirmed this conjecture. On the contrary, at Oberlin College in Ohio, at Lincoln University in Pennsylvania, and at Berea College in Kentucky, such practice prevailed and, on the whole, had been successful. The sense of this essay is that such anti-racist practices are wholesome and democratic and should be universal (pp. 593-601).

Bigglestone (1971) demonstrates Oberlin's sincere commitment to the coeducation of Blacks and Whites; in much of the period covered, the commitment was less than fulfilled, but it existed and in some cases turned out well. This was particularly true with Mary Church (later Mary Church Terrell), who attended Oberlin from 1879 to 1885. There she experienced prejudice, she felt, when an honor she deserved was withheld from her; but she had "very dear and intimate friends among the white girls." For a time she boarded at the college's main dormitory and felt no discrimination. At all college exercises and social functions, she was "cordially received." The Oberlin experience as a whole certainly was tainted with racism, but an effort was made to combat it and, to some extent, that effort was successful.

Louisiana has an exceptional history in terms of race relations—perhaps due to its mixed Spanish, French, and American history. This is especially true of New Orleans, where the absence—or, better, the denial—of racism in theory and practice was striking. This state and city history is told well by Harlan (1962), Somers (1974), and Rosenberg (1988). An illustration is the remark by Somers (1974) that "for at least two decades after the war many residents (of New Orleans) from the rank and file of both races, played and worked together on amicable, harmonious, even egalitarian terms."

During the worst excesses of the ruling-class-inspired terrorism of the KKK and other such monstrous racist organizations, one occasionally reads of bursts of shame from White people—particularly women—at the display of barbarism. Mixed in with these bursts are acknowledgments of the racism used to rationalize the terrorism. Marie Benchley, writing to Wendell Phillips on January 19, 1875 states,

> I have lived at the South for years and *know* that the *worst* reports of outrages against the colored people are true. The hatred of whites is so virulent, so limitless, and so utterly unscrupulous, it makes me ashamed of my race. I am burning to do something for the negroes. I have studied them faithfully while teaching them and *know* them to be superior in all that constitutes Christlessness. (cited in Bartlett, 1979)

Reflective of the betrayal of democratic and egalitarian goals of Radical Reconstruction, which crystallized politically by the end of the 1870s, was the proliferation of rationalizations for its betrayal. The influential *North American Review* devoted 60 pages of one issue (March 1879) to the views of eight luminaries of the period. With the exception of James A. Garfield and Wendell Phillips, the others regretted enfranchisement and argued, in effect, for institutionalized second-class citizenship for African Americans. The opening and closing essays were apologia for the betrayal, and came from James G. Blaine, then the most powerful Republican politician in the nation. The most vigorous and principled defense of democratic principles, and therefore of full equality in the life of the Black people, came from the aged but still redoubtable Phillips. He writes that emancipation is not enough—the land of the slave-holding class should have been given to the former slave. "Small enough compensation it would have been for the labor and suffering of generations. Now let us not compound our injustice through disfranchisement. Empower him and enhance the nation; re-enslave him and desecrate our country's flag." Phillips ends hopefully with, "Barbarism melts and crumbles before civilization."

"Right is stronger than wrong" insists Phillips (1879); perhaps, but vindication does not come speedily. Five years later, the valedictorian at a small-town Massachusetts high school devoted his graduation remarks to the memory of Wendell Phillips: W.E.B. Du Bois would sacrifice his life to the belief that right is stronger than wrong.

Pearne (1877), a leading figure in the Methodist church, presents a vigorous defense of equality for Black people. He vividly describes the hellish character of the system that oppressed Black people. He believed that not enough was being done to prevent this oppression and the nation was slipping backwards. The struggle must be intensified,

> until color-caste is stamped out, and the Freedman is as really *free* as the freest and the whitest. . . . These Freedmen have augmented the wealth of this nation by billions of dollars, yet we requite all their wasting toil through "centuries of oppression" with paltry sums.

The essay closes with demands for real commitment to the enhancement of Black people: "If it was right to emancipate the slave, it is right to enable them to maintain their freedom." This merits and demands a commitment to real education for the Black multitude. The author concludes, "The safety of our institutions demands that they [Black people] be educated" (pp. 462-482).

During the close of the 1870s and culminating in the Populist effort of the 1890s, militant resistance against Jim Crowism characterizes Black history. Much of this resistance, especially in Southern cities such as New Orleans, Richmond, and Savannah involved Black-White unity. An excellent account of this development is offered by Hair (1969). But this Black-White unity and militancy were shattered by wholesale violence, frequent lynchings, terrible tortures, and mass slaughters, as in the crushing of a Black-White strike in Thibodeaux, Louisiana, in 1887, where scores were killed. Some White people protested these outrages, among them Auel Arnand, a member of the state legislature, John A. Tetts, and Thomas J. Guice of the Louisiana Farmers Union. In Louisiana, as throughout the South, fraud, violence, and the vilest demagogic employment of racism broke mass resistance to the taking over of vast resources by the burgeoning monopolies that absorbed coal, iron, timber, and other wealth. It is in this context that Andrew Carnegie, Booker T. Washington, and W.E.B. Du Bois must be understood. But explicating this point is beyond the intent of this essay.

Returning to a chronological account of some highlights reflecting the reality of anti-racism, one finds a personality like Ora Langhorne of

Lynchburg, Virginia. This Southerner from a slave-holding family appeals for the rejection of racism and insists that this requires not segregation but unity—especially in the educational system. "The next great need of the South," she said in 1879, "is a system of education that shall include the mixed schools—which are needed not only for their [Blacks'] sake but for that of the country" (cited in Langhorne, 1880).

In the *New York Tribune* of February 17, 1879, William Lloyd Garrison expresses his vehement opposition to proposed legislation barring Chinese emigrants. The opposition, he writes, is "based on contempt of race" such as the arguments used to keep Black people in slavery. Such views "are not born of reason, or justice, or historical experience." This "hateful spirit of caste" is "an offense to God, and a curse to the world" (cited in Garrison, 1969, p. 297).

On April 24, 1879, the *Boston Traveler* published a letter by Garrison in which he excoriated the federal government for failing to protect its Black citizens. Are they, he asked "to be left without protection, as sheep in the midst of wolves?" He wrote, "the battle of liberty and equal rights is to be fought over again." His final word was to demand "a speedy end to all this bloody misrule" (cited in Garrison, 1969, pp. 301-304).

The labor movement before, during, and after the Civil War to the early years of the American Federation of Labor (A.F. of L.) was anti-racist in pronouncement and, generally, in practice. Foner and Lewis' (1989) study of that movement emphasizes this reality. Illustrative is the young Samuel Gompers, who took a principled anti-racist position. For example, during the Tenth Annual Convention of the A.F. of L., held in Detroit in December 1890, James Frank Moxley, a Black bricklayer representing the Sewer and Bricklayers' Local of Cleveland was called to the chair "to a burst of applause." While Moxley was in the chair, a debate arose from discussion as to whether a Southern local that desired affiliation should be admitted, because its constitution confined admission to White men. Such racism, a delegate insisted, "was not the policy of trade unionists." An argument ensued, and "Chairman Gompers said that while the convention could not force the point, it could express its conviction on the question looking to the influencing of the machinists by argument to strike the clause from southern constitutions" (Kaufman, 1987, pp. 409-411).

Marxist individuals and Marxist organization from the 1850s to the present have taken and continue to take anti-racist positions. Anti-racism has been and continues to be among the most significant characteristics of Marxists.

The decades of the 1880s and 1890s witnessed the nadir of racism and atrocious expressions of that poison, chronicled by Logan (1954). The same period also witnessed mounting resistance to racist barbarism. (Again, I am referring to White people. The mere mention of the names of Du Bois and the Niagara Movement [1905-1909] demonstrates the opposition to racism from Black people.) The mention of Du Bois brings to mind the fact that White people were influenced by him as they in turn influenced him. This is true, for example, of Franz Boas and George Washington Cable, not to mention Moorfield Storey, whose opposition to American imperialism first brought him to Du Bois' attention while he was a teacher in Atlanta. Soon both men were comrades in the creation of the NAACP—then considered, by those who ruled the country, to be a veritable den of subversion.

The first decade of the 20th century saw not only the Niagara Movement but also John Milholland's Constitution League and a growing awareness of the monstrosity of racism among people like Mary White Ovington, William English Walling, Eugene Victor Debs, Florence Kelley, Felix Adler, Jane Addams, Charles Edward Russell, and Oswald Garrison Villard. They benefited from and carried forward the heroic work of Albion Winegar Tourgee, thoroughly documented by Olsen (1971). McPherson (1975) and Sinkler (1971) add significantly to this history of anti-racism in the United States.

The rejection of racism, both as an idea and as a practice, has been a significant aspect of U.S. history. This rejection has come, in the first place, from African American people. But it also has come from a legion of White men and women.

The struggle against racism in the United States has been a significant aspect of the effort to advance democratic practice and economic justice. Its history is a precious heritage. It behooves present-day egalitarians to arm themselves with this knowledge and, thus strengthened, continue the effort to purify our land.

NOTE

1. In this work (Williamson, 1965), the author notes: "There were a surprisingly large number of cases in which white women gave birth to children from Negro fathers" (p. 207).

REFERENCES

Aptheker, H. (Ed.). (1951). *A documentary history of the Negro people in the U.S.* New York: Citadel.

Aptheker, H. (1989). *Abolitionism: A revolutionary movement.* Boston: Twayne.

Aptheker, H. (1992). *Anti-racism in U.S. history: The first two hundred years.* Westport, CT: Praeger.

Bartlett, I. H. (1979). *Wendell and Ann Phillips: The community of reform, 1840-1880.* New York: Norton.

Bigglestone, W. E. (1971). Oberlin college and the Negro student. *Journal of Negro History, 56*(1), 198-219.

Bond, H. M. (1939). *Negro education in Alabama.* Washington, DC: Associated Publishers.

Burnham, J. C. (1972). Book review: A discarded consensus. *Science, 175,* 506.

De Quatrefages, A. (1872). The unity of the human species. *Popular Science Monthly, 1,* 59-75.

Dyer, T. (1992). *Theodore Roosevelt and the idea of race.* Baton Rouge: University of Louisiana Press.

Eby, F. (1918). *Education in Texas: Source materials* (Bulletin No. 1824). Austin: University of Texas.

Foner, P. S., & Lewis, R. L. (1989). *Black workers: A documentary history from colonial times to the present.* Philadelphia: Temple University Press.

Fortieth Congress. (1869). *Congressional record, Third Session, 1326.*

Garrison, W. L. (1969). *William Lloyd Garrison, 1805-1879: The story of his life told by his children.* New York: Negro University Press.

Hair, W. L. (1969). *Bourbonism and agrarism protest: Louisiana politics, 1877-1900.* Baton Rouge: Louisiana State University Press.

Haller, J. S., Jr. (1971). *Outcasts from evolution: Scientific attitudes of racial inferiority, 1859-1900.* Urbana: University of Illinois Press.

Harlan, L. (1962). Desegregation in New Orleans public schools during reconstruction. *American Historical Review, 67,* 663-675.

Harrison, W. C. (1974). The creed of the carpetbagger: The case of Mississippi. *Mississippi Education Journal, 40,* 215.

Howard, G. L. (1984). *Death at Cross Plains: An Alabama reconstruction tragedy.* University: University of Alabama Press.

Kaufman, S. B. (Ed.). (1987). *The Samuel Gompers Papers, 1887-1890.* Urbana: University of Illinois Press.

Langhorne, O. (1880). Colored schools in Virginia. *Journal of Social Science, 11*(1), 36-45.

Logan, R. W. (1954). *The Negro in American life and thought: The nadir, 1877-1901.* New York: Dial Press.

Luker, R. E. (1991). *The social gospel in Black and White: American racial reform, 1885-1912.* Chapel Hill: University of North Carolina Press.

McPherson, J. M. (1975). *The abolitionist legacy: From reconstruction to the NAACP.* Princeton, NJ: Princeton University Press.

Ochs, S. J. (1980). *Desegregating the altar: The Josephites and the struggle for Black priests, 1871-1960.* Baton Rouge: University of Louisiana Press.

Olsen, O. H. (1971). *The Negro question: From slavery to caste, 1863-1910.* New York: Putnam.

Peabody, A. P. (1875).The co-education of the White and colored races. *Unitarian Review,* 593-601.

Pearne, T. H. (1877). The freedmen. *Methodist Quarterly Review, 59,* 462-482.

Pole, J. R. (1973). *The pursuit of equality in American history.* Berkeley: University of California Press.

Pollard, E. A. (1870). The Negro in the south. *Lippincott's Magazine, 383,* 91.

Pollard, E. A. (1871). The romance of the Negro. *Galaxy, 12,* 470-478.

Rosenberg, D. (1988). *New Orleans dockworkers: Race, labor, and unionism, 1892-1923.* Albany: State University of New York Press.

Sinkler, G. (1971). *The racial attitudes of American presidents from Lincoln to Theodore Roosevelt.* New York: Doubleday.

Somers, D. A. (1974). Black and White in New Orleans: A study in race relations, 1865-1900. *Journal of Southern History, 40*(1), 24-33.

Swint, H. L. (1967). *The Northern teacher in the South.* New York: Octagon Press. (Original work published 1941)

Trefousse, H. L. (1968). *The radical Republicans: Lincoln's vanguard for racial justice.* Baton Rouge: University of Louisiana Press.

Trelease, A. W. (1971). *White terror: The Ku Klux Klan conspiracy against Southern Whites.* New York: Harper & Row.

Tunnell, T. (1984). *Crucible of reconstruction: War, radicalism, and race in Louisiana, 1862-1877.* Baton Rouge: University of Louisiana Press.

Williamson, J. (1965). *The Negro in South Carolina during reconstruction.* Chapel Hill: University of North Carolina Press.

PART II

RACISM AND ANTI-RACISM: ESSENTIAL ISSUES

There are enormous implications to the fact that racism is recent and conditional and does not have absolute support among Whites. The first implication is that where racism exists, so does anti-racism. In Chapter 5, Polly McLean suggests that there is an Americanization of racism in the world community due to the scope and popularity of American film, television, and music. In fact, the largest market for these products is the international community. Where Western racism did not exist, it is being learned through American media, and where it already exists, American racial stereotypes are providing new distorted images. Although the export of racist media overseas has gone unchallenged, racist film media in the United States has been challenged by prominent Whites in the film industry, since World War II.

In Chapter 6, Bob Blauner explores the potential for more proactive and organized White anti-racism by reviewing the recent history of the demise of White radical and liberal coalitions in the United States, which can be traced partly to strategic errors made by Black and White radicals in the 1960s. This is an excellent case history of demobilization and disarray among Whites who share a common disgust and opposition to racism. In a similar vein, there is potential for coalitions against racism among White feminists and women of color. In Chapter 7, Karen Dugger explores this potential and suggests that postmodern analysis holds a key to bridging the conceptual differences between them.

These three chapters are introductions to and samples of the kind of analyses that are called for by the historic evidence in Part I. More work like that which follows is needed to take a new look at racism and to better understand anti-racism in the United States, as well as in other national communities.

5

Mass Communication, Popular Culture, and Racism

Polly E. McLean

For some time, the study of racism has dominated scholarly inquiry in the popular media (Bogle, 1973, 1988; Cripps, 1977, 1978; Dates & Barlow, 1990; Fife, 1974; Hill, 1986; Leab, 1976; MacDonald, 1983; Null, 1975; Poindexter & Stroman, 1981). Within this body of literature, researchers have also examined resistance from the victim (Archer, 1973), but as Aptheker (1987) suggests, "opposition to racism as an ideology and practice from Whites has been largely unexamined" (p. 4). This chapter will pay particular attention to the role of Whites and multiethnic groups in their efforts to combat racism in popular media.

This chapter is based on several assumptions. First, the character of racism has changed in U.S. popular culture as a result of the legal and political changes stemming from the passage of the 1943 antilynching laws and the 1964 Civil Rights Act. This is not to suggest that there has been a complete break with the old-fashioned racism prevalent during the first 50 years of this century. What it does suggest is that a more subtle, indirect form of racism has entered the public arena. As a result, "images and articulations that on the surface seem positive and empowering can tap into deeply embedded racist types and can function in racist ways in the dominant culture" (Cloud, 1992, p. 314). Second, the new visibility of African Americans in television and film has led to a false sense of denial and assertion that racism is all but gone in the United States, blurring the lines between the media and social reality. Third, since the beginning of this century, U.S. popular culture has been an international business. Despite various restrictions imposed by some countries, the United States continues to be the major player in the international cultural marketplace. Therefore, it is important to examine the stereotypes prevalent in media culture that have helped shape the construction of social reality on both the domestic and the international fronts.

THE RANGE OF
U.S. POPULAR MEDIA

Since the fall of European communism in the 1980s and with the privatization and deregulation boom, primarily in Western Europe, a new international audience has emerged with a tremendous appetite for U.S. cultural products. Although certain restrictions apply, the European Community (EC) market represents 100 million more customers than the United States alone. Burgeoning delivery systems into the home are growing, along with an entrenched video-cassette (VCR) market. "Estimates project that VCRs are in nearly 50% of EC households, cable TV in nearly 40% and satellite delivery in 25%" (Squire, 1992, p. 29).

The bestseller book *Megatrends 2000* (Naisbitt & Aburdene, 1990) reports that 75% of all imported television programs come from the United States. *Dallas* and *The Cosby Show* are distributed in nearly 100 countries. The nomadic Tuaregs in the Sahara delayed their annual migration for 10 days in 1983 to catch the last episode of *Dallas*; New Zealand's privately owned television service purchased 45% of its television programs from the United States in 1988, picking up such television shows as *Amen* and *227*. *Matlock* and *Spenser: For Hire* were tied as the number-one shows in South Africa in January 1989. *Boomerang* and *Lethal Weapon 3* were the top-grossing films in Australia, Tokyo, and Germany in 1992; *White Men Can't Jump* was the number-one hit in Madrid in 1992; *Coming to America* was viewed by 6.5 million Italians on Canale 5, making it the sixth most-viewed television program for the week ending January 23, 1993. Similarly, *Guess Who's Coming to Dinner* was the sixth most-viewed program on Denmark's TV-2 for the week ending March 14, 1993 (Doyle, 1992; Naisbitt & Aburdene, 1990; *Variety*, 1992a, 1992b, 1992c, 1992d, 1993a, 1993b).

In some cases, audiences appear to be playing catch-up with U.S. media laden with distorted images of people with whom they have had little or no contact. Russian audiences are a good example. "It appears that the Russians can't get enough of *Gone with the Wind*. The 50-year-old movie reportedly sold out a 2,500-seat Moscow theater during the first two months of its run" (Doyle, 1992, p. 80).

What should be apparent is the potential of a global culture, along with the prejudices, stereotypes, ideology, and values embedded in U.S. popular media. This potential raises many questions that scholars have never before had to consider. Will people with no prejudices or experiences with African Americans learn to relegate them to the buffoonery and cartoonish exaggeration that is often the standard fare of media offerings? Do representations of African Americans in popular media reinforce and spread the racist stereotypes held by Whites? How do viewers, both Black and White, decode covert racism in a U.S. film in South Africa? How do cultures with no indigenous meaning assigned to race and racism deconstruct ideas of race and racism from U.S. popular media? How does popular media reproduce the racism written into the culture? How do African Americans and their White allies question social injustice and challenge the moral, ethical, and ideological principles in such representations?

It would be presumptuous to suggest that a satisfactory answer to any of these questions can be offered here. The relationships between culture and values depicted in television programming and films are complex. Furthermore, little is known about how imported programs are decoded by audiences abroad. Available evidence permits only tentative comments about the relationship between racial stereotyping and an audience's construction of social reality. According to Real (1989), however, some indication is possible, because media texts do provide a vehicle for "constructing our interpretations of existence and social reality with regard to gender and ethnicity" (p. 254).

RACIAL STEREOTYPING

To understand the influence of racism in U.S. and foreign popular media, some understanding of stereotypes and their intricacies is useful. When dealing with people from a different sociocultural background— and there is limited information available—many gaps must be filled and, therefore, numerous inferences are necessary (Koltuv, 1962). The information generated originates in stereotypes that emerge from categorizations that are derived from the "pictures we carry about in our heads" to perceive the world around us (Lippmann, 1981). Stereotypic images result from an "economy of effort" that is useful and not always undesirable. Even so, stereotypes are not neutral, and it would be a mistake to underestimate their influence. Stereotypes serve as practical ideologies, transferred in "each generation from parent to child," making them "seem almost like a biological fact" (Lippmann, 1981, p. 36). Ashmore (1970) contends that expressed beliefs of negative stereotypes are one of two ways in which racism has most frequently appeared in U.S. history.

For most of the 20th century, stereotypes in U.S. popular culture have perpetuated a false sense of White superiority and a false sense of African American inferiority (Staples & Jones, 1985). Spigner (1991) argues that the prevalence of such racial imagery maintains White hegemony. These negative images also affect the victims of such depiction. Batts (1989) states that, "it is difficult not to buy into, at some level, the misinformation that society has perpetuated about victim status" (p. 14). In other words, when a group is given no other identity than what the dominant culture provides, it tends to internalize the negative expectations, which in turn reinforces the prejudice. For example, to earn a living, African American performers and filmmakers alike have had to conform to the stereotypes that audiences have become accustomed to seeing on the screen. Performers "learned to walk with a shuffle, to pop and roll their eyeballs, and to emit high-pitched giggles. These distinctive personalities, for White audiences, made Black characters so funny, lovable and controllable" (Evuleocha & Ugbah, 1989, p. 200). These roles have become so internalized that, even given artistic liberty, many performers are not able to recognize the buffoonish minstrelsy characterizations that seem to persist generation after generation.

THE EARLY 20th CENTURY

Through the Depression Years (1900-1939)

The beginning of the 20th century through the Depression years was marked by burgeoning new forms of mass communication and popular culture in film, radio broadcasting, postcard collecting, children's play objects, home items, recorded music, and other expressions of everyday culture. It was also a period that was one of the worst for African Americans, encompassing the retreat from post-Civil War Reconstruction, the rise of the second Klan, hundreds of lynchings, the Great Black Migration north, the race riots during and after World War I, and the wholesale denial of political and civil rights to African Americans. During this period, "new structures and new routines had to be developed and practiced to create and sustain a 'new' or different racial ideology based not on slavery, but on the concepts of racial inferiority" (Goings, 1990, p. 70).

Influenced by 19th-century U.S. popular literature and theater, in which blackfaced portrayals of slavery were prominent, new 20th-century stereotypes were developed that reinforced the idea that African Americans were inferior. These myths fixed an image in the minds of Whites that African Americans were primitive and comical subhumans. African Americans were either simple, childlike, docile, suffering victims or beastlike and thus a direct threat to Whites. The diffusion of these ideas through popular entertainment brought "mass audiences into the tents, town halls, and theaters of new population centers. Many of these messages would creep later into vaudeville, cinema and other forms of popular culture" (Saxton, 1990, p. 180).

Nowhere did these myths become more entrenched than in the newly emerging film industry. Beginning with Thomas Edison's Kinetoscope *The Pickaninnies Doing a Dance* (1894), African American images have been subjected to systematic distortion. In 1903, Louis Lumière of France brought his film with "the callous title, *Niggers Bathing,* to the United States. It was advertised as a 'humorous' subject" (Platt, 1949, p. 191). From this point on, films depicting Africans or African Americans continued the biased and perverse tradition of producing racist images and symbols.

The cultural window through which Whites were given a view of Africans and African Americans obscured, distorted, and misinformed more than it revealed. With skin color, these myths and images became inextricably connected to the popular cultural assumptions that people of African descent are bound to an irremediable savage past and consigned to an irrevocably demeaning destiny.

It was in this tradition of racism and cultural prejudice that D. W. Griffith's silent film *The Birth of a Nation* had its world premiere in Los Angeles on February 8, 1915. It was considered a milestone in filmmaking history from the point of view of technical skill, cinematic technique, and acting. It was also one of the most financially successful films ever made. With an initial investment of $110,000, *The Birth of a Nation* eventually returned at least $20 million. Donahue (1987) points out that, "since the film was distributed on a state's rights basis, the actual cash generated by the film might have been as much as $50 million to $100 million" (p. 12).

The film's success on the domestic market was partly attributed to Griffith's marketing strategy and distribution method, as well as to controversy. Nearly 10 years after its release, *The Birth of a Nation* was still breaking attendance records in larger movie houses (Donahue, 1987). On the international market, its success had to do with distribution, production values, and timing. In 1915 (the year the film was released) and in early 1916, U.S. film exports greatly increased and the United States was well on its way to dominating the world's film industry. The war had severely curtailed production in the single biggest film-producing country, France, and the resulting gap in supplies to film-consuming countries allowed American exporters to step in. Thus, feature films such as *The Birth of a Nation* produced during this period began the U.S. ascendancy in dominating the world's cinema and "the most remarkable hegemony in the history of intercultural communication" (Sklar, 1975, p. 215).

The Central and South American market is a good example. Before World War I, U.S.-made films had difficulty gaining entry into this market. The major obstacles stemmed from distribution monopolies and the high costs of U.S. films. U.S. producers were also accused of sending poor quality prints in comparison to their European competitors. The tide turned dramatically with *The Birth of a Nation*. Griffith, the producer and distributor, decided to bypass the middlemen and deal directly with the individual countries. In so doing, he sent his representative, Guy Croswell Smith, with *The Birth of a Nation* to Buenos Aires in the winter of 1915-1916. The film ran for over 200 performances. Its success was repeated in theaters in Chile, Peru, Bolivia, and Uruguay. The YMCA in the Panama Canal Zone also showed *The Birth of a Nation* (Thompson, 1985). By the end of World War I, Central and South American countries had either switched almost entirely to U.S. films or were well on their way to doing so. *The Birth of a Nation* was one of the very first films that helped pave the way for U.S. entertainment expansion overseas.

The Beginning of Anti-Racist Activity in Film

The Birth of a Nation proved to be one of the most detrimental, anti-Black films ever produced. The film depicts a South ravaged by the Civil War, corrupted by Black Reconstruction and the desire of African Americans to gain political rights, and eventually redeemed by the hooded Ku Klux Klan. Its plot rests on fervid racism and fear of miscegenation between Blacks and Whites. Reddick (1944) suggests that it provided influential propaganda that has been singled out as one factor enabling the Klan to enter its period of greatest expansion, reaching a total membership of 5 million.

Resistance to *The Birth of a Nation* began almost simultaneously with the film's opening. It was a resistance that involved both African Americans and progressive Whites. More important, the resistance came at a time when Black intellectuals in the United States, the Caribbean, Britain, and France had begun to develop a wealth of information on the histories and cultures of people of African descent. Their research and subsequent writings in the early part of the 20th century helped unmask the ideological framework of slavery and the dominant racist mythology prevalent in the stereotypes, symbols, and codes in U.S. popular literature and eventually in film. This new anti-racism literature also helped support the resistance movement. As a result, the organized and unorganized resistance was based on a coherent set of ideas and history that would empower people of African descent to reestablish their dignity in the world community.

The first level of resistance was to discredit the filmmaker and Rev. Thomas Dixon, the author of the novel upon which the film was based. Also analyzed were the principles that formed the image and content of the representation. According to Cobleigh (1971), Dixon's novel falsifies history, glorifies crime (especially lynching), invites prejudice against Blacks, and is a propagandistic tool designed to sell the doctrine of White supremacy and the repatriation of Blacks to Africa or South America. Rabbi Stephen S. Wise, of the Free Synagogue in New York City, blamed both Griffith and Dixon for coining prejudice and bitterness and described the film as "foul and loathsome libel on a race of human beings" ("Protests on Photo Play," 1915). Oswald Garrison Villard, grandson of Abolitionist William Lloyd Garrison and vice-president of the National Association for the Advancement of Colored People (NAACP), said *The Birth of a Nation* was "improper, immoral and unjust" ("Protests on Photo Play," 1915).

In addition to insisting that the film's representation did violence to Blacks, resistance also took the form of political pressure, organized and spearheaded by the six-year-old and predominantly White NAACP. For example, on March 30, 1915, less than one month after the film's New York premiere, a "delegation of five hundred of the most prominent White and Colored people in the city filled the Council Chamber at City Hall for an hour of terse, tense speeches and urged the mayor to act to suppress the film" ("The Clansman," 1915).

The Boston Branch of the NAACP, under the leadership of Morefield Storey, president of the American Bar Association and the NAACP, upheld the Black Abolitionist tradition by issuing a pamphlet condemning the film and circulating it widely around the country. This was followed by three booklets, *Fighting a Vicious Lie, Why the Negro Was Enfranchised,* and *The English Leaflet,* that were sent to 63 local branches and college chapters and high school principals (Reddick, 1944).

Resistance also took the form of direct action by citizens unconnected with the NAACP's efforts. The *New York Times* reported an egg-throwing demonstration by a crowd of Black and White men at the Liberty Theater. Howard Schaeffle, described as a Southerner and a libertarian, was arrested ("Egg Negro Scenes in Liberty Film Play," 1915). Later the same week, the police were called to disperse 500 Blacks who were denied tickets to view *The Birth of a Nation* by the management of the Tremont Theater in Boston. The demonstration led to the arrest of 11 people ("Negroes Mob Photo Play," 1915).

In the international market, resistance to *The Birth of a Nation* was stifled by a number of factors. To begin with, the intelligentsia of the Caribbean- and African-born populations residing in Europe were the most likely to spearhead resistance. But they were preoccupied with anticolonialism and Pan-African unity activities (Thompson, 1969). Outside Europe, few who were subject to European colonization (India being the exception) were exposed to U.S. films.

France was one country where the government banned *The Birth of a Nation.* The film was shown during World War I without any incidents. In 1923, however, when the film was rereleased, French Premier Raymond Poincaré "personally ordered *The Birth of a Nation* suppressed." Between the war and 1923, the numbers of Africans in France had greatly increased. Fearing racial demonstrations by French-speaking Africans and "foreign visitors," the government intervened and banned the film (Brown, 1984). It was this kind of fear that had led the South African government to ban in 1910 *The Johnson-Jeffries Fight,* which had incited race riots in the United States (Tomaselli, 1983). Fearing a similar outcome, the British-controlled Uganda Board of Censors in 1953 banned a Tarzan film (Brown, 1984).

The final resistance effort began in 1915, shortly after the release of *The Birth of a Nation.* Emmett J. Scott, Booker T. Washington's secretary, formed the Birth of a Race Photoplay Corporation with money raised by the Black middle class and some Whites. The group was formed to release *The Birth of a Race* (originally titled *Lincoln's Dream*) as an anti-racist answer to Griffith. The film was intended to depict the evils and cruelties of slavery, the bravery of Blacks during the Civil War, and the heroic efforts Blacks employed to educate themselves for this new freedom during Reconstruction. Three years later, however, the three-hour epic film that emerged had little to do with slavery, Black achievement, or Reconstruction (American Film Institute, 1988). Although it was a virtual flop, the film gave impetus to other African Americans to develop an independent cinema. These "race movies," which were not without stereotypes, vanished in the late 1940s.

The kind of opposition stemming from African Americans and White progressives to the showing of *The Birth of a Nation* was unprecedented. Specifically, it laid the foundation for subsequent anti-racist activities in popular media. These activities challenged the emerging film industry to produce, codify, and accurately represent the histories and lives of African Americans, and included picketing, letter-writing campaigns, developing an independent Black cinema, using legal means, employing both the Black and the White press to frame arguments, utilizing pressure, and making threats to the industry and to individuals promoting racist films. A largely unknown side of anti-racism was individual and collective action by members of the film industry.

Post-World War I

With the introduction of the "talkies" in 1927, Hollywood virtually took over the world film markets, and the number of acting parts requiring African American talent greatly increased. During this period, all-Black features appeared. The first two films of this genre were produced in 1929—*Hallelujah* (the first all-Black feature) and *Hearts of Dixie*. *Hallelujah* was praised in some circles for its cinematic quality (e.g., W. E. B. Du Bois referred to it as epoch-making) and for refraining from crude insults to African Americans. It was condemned in other circles for not advancing very far beyond the usual stereotypes of Blacks (Reddick, 1944). On the other hand, *The Hearts of Dixie*, featuring a lazy, good-for-nothing, good-natured slave on a Southern plantation, introduced a stereotype that would last much longer than anyone could have imagined at that time.

From 1927 through the 1930s, Hollywood continued to produce a number of all-Black or mixed-race stereotypical films for domestic and international consumption. *Trader Horn* (1930) introduced the "savage Black"; *King Kong* (1933) and *Baboona* (1933) emphasize the "naked and primitive" African savages who consider every White person a god; *Imitation of Life* (1934) stresses the self-effacing, faithful, kind-hearted servant and her mulatto daughter; *The Frisco Kid* (1935) and *Barbary Coast* (1935) glorify lynching. *The Prisoner of Shark Island* (1936) accentuates Blacks as inferiors and cowards. *Hypnotized* (1933) continues the blackface minstrel tradition; *Judge Priest* (1934) and *Caroline* (1934) parade the stereotypical shuffling, eye-rolling, crap-shooting, head-bobbing Uncle Tom.

Resistance With a Twist

Economic considerations, not moral value, helped shape the formation of the U.S. film industry. For example, the top-grossing film of the teens and twenties and the most heavily exported was also the most racist film—*The Birth of a Nation. Gone with the Wind,* the 1930s top-grossing film, was also imbued with racist images and became the next film targeted for anti-racist activity.

Even before production was completed, *Gone with the Wind* was opposed by the NAACP, the National Negro Congress, the National Urban League, the Black press, some trade unions, and the Communist Party. Many believed that the film was a sequel to *The Birth of a Nation.* Based on a popular novel, the film romanticizes the defeated Confederacy and depicts African Americans as liars, would-be rapists, mammies, and devoted field hands. Du Bois, editor of *The Crisis,* announced the opening dates of the film and asked readers to protest against the showing. He wrote, "These openings of the motion picture are of great interest to the colored people because the book from which the film is taken was judged by many critics to be full of anti-Negro propaganda" (cited in Archer, 1973, p. 206). As with *The Birth of a Nation,* the NAACP's vigorous objections led to the editing of some of the most offensive scenes, or at least to the softening of them.

The Communist Party took on the strongest role in late 1939. Designating its efforts as the "battle for cultural development" as a part of the fight for "political expression," the Communist Party launched a number of new initiatives to challenge the place of African Americans in mass cultural institutions. Benjamin Davis, councilman from Harlem and editor of the *Daily Worker,* pressed the party to launch a boycott and educational campaign against *Gone with the Wind.* In a show of personal conviction that impressed many African Americans in New York City, "Davis forced the resignation of a White *Daily Worker* critic who gave the film a positive review and commissioned David Platt to do a seven-part series analyzing the 'Negro in Hollywood Films' " (Naison, 1983, p. 299).

Until this time, showing Africans or African Americans to European audiences in a demeaning and stereotypical manner was never a concern for the industry. In the same way, it was not a concern for European filmmakers to portray Africans in an undignified light. Moreover, as Hollywood gained greater international prominence, Europeans became more concerned about the deleterious effect and sinister influence that American movies would have not on Europeans but on non-Europeans. Sklar (1975) suggests that Hollywood's constant "emphasis on crime and sex . . . stripped Caucasians of their aura of rectitude and moral power, and subverted the doctrine of White superiority" (p. 225).

For example, at a cinema in Poona, an Indian turned to an Englishman (who reported the incident to *The Spectator*) and said,

> I supposed you White people would call me a nigger. I am unacquainted with other sides of Western civilization, but what I have seen to-night, and on numerous other occasions in these places, convince me that the ordinary middle-classes in England and America are the most debased and immoral cretins any race or nation has ever produced. (cited in Sklar, 1975, p. 226)

The resounding cry was not that the word "nigger" was now international but the fear that Hollywood films might upset the hegemony of Europeans who now had territories spread all over the non-White world.

THE WAR AND POSTWAR YEARS
(1940-1950)

Until the 1940s, the film industry did not accept as its responsibility the function of helping destroy racial prejudice and stereotypes. "The Production Code of Ethics, established in 1934 and comprising the only stated rules and guidelines for Hollywood filmmaking, mentions the word race only once, forbidding the depiction in films of 'miscegenation' between Black and White races" (McManus & Kronenberger, 1946, p. 77).

Hollywood justified its stereotypic film images of African Americans by the "Dixie box office" returns, suggesting that to portray Blacks as ordinary human beings would have negative economic consequences. Jones (1947) takes exception to this, noting,

> The Southern box office represents roughly 8 per cent of the average national gross of a motion picture. Against this New York State, which has a law against discrimination, pulls 14.6 per cent of the national box office. Even more impressive is the total take of American movies abroad. In 1945, world box office returns were $2,235,000,000. Of that $885,000,000 or 37 per cent came from foreign markets. (p. 5)

Beginning in the early to mid-1940s, Hollywood envisioned a "new deal" for African Americans in film. This new deal was the first effort by progressive Whites in the film industry to address cinematic racial caricatures of African Americans. McManus and Kronenberger (1946) suggest that Hollywood's acceptance of responsibility for fostering racism through film was a spillover of the war effort:

> The exploitation of prejudice by the enemy evoked a response through films that was especially noteworthy in respect to anti-Semitic, anti-British, and anti-Soviet thinking and, to a considerably lesser degree, in helping to challenge anti-Negro and anti-labor prejudice. (p. 78)

Jones (1947), however, reiterates that Hollywood's change of heart was based more on financial factors than wanting to demonstrate racial tolerance. He notes that in 1946 some 45 cents of every dollar came from foreign audiences. By 1947 the figure had dropped to 30 cents. Studios were receiving feedback that foreign audiences laughed at the wrong places, and sometimes even walked out on U.S. films. It was assumed that audiences in China, Africa, India, the Philippines, Malaya, Japan, and even Europe, where color lines are hazy, were resentful of Hollywood's short-sighted policy on stereotyping people of color. It was, therefore, the thought of losing money from such vast audiences that made studio executives take notice of the negative depiction of African Americans. Likewise, Dore Schary, head of productions for RKO, acknowledges that the change was not purely altruistic: "We find we made more money if we didn't offend so many people" (1948, p. 52).

Walter White, executive secretary of the NAACP, and Wendell Wilkie, chair of the board of Twentieth Century-Fox and the 1940 Republican presidential candidate, launched a concerted campaign in 1942 to end negative and racist stereotypes in motion pictures. White and Wilkie wanted the major studios to establish an ad hoc committee of Black actors, private citizens, and White liberals to monitor the image and portrayal of Blacks in motion pictures (NAACP, 1991; White, 1948). This committee was never established due to Wilkie's sudden death, but the twosome was able to convince Hollywood's top brass about the harm pejorative stereotypes inflict upon Blacks and the American movie-going public in general (NAACP, 1991). Cripps notes that this watershed year was a major breakthrough in that the studios agreed "to abandon pejorative racial roles, to place Negroes in positions as extras they could reasonably be expected to occupy in society, and to begin the slow task of integrating Blacks into the ranks of studio technicians" (cited in Rodgers, 1993, p. 7).

Hollywood Responds

From 1942 through 1947, Hollywood began a concerted effort to bring about a better understanding among African Americans and Whites. Several of Hollywood's leading film directors, writers, and performers took very strong anti-racist positions through their writing and speeches. Many of these articles appeared in the *Negro Digest* as original articles or as reprints from other publications. In some cases, they appeared under the bylines of Dalton Trumbo, Orson Welles, Marsha Hunt, or John Garfield.

In writing about "Blackface, Hollywood Style," screenwriter Trumbo says that between the 1915 *The Birth of a Nation* and the 1939 *Gone with the Wind*, Hollywood produced,

> turgid floods of sickening and libelous treacle. We have made tarts of the Negro's daughters, crap-shooters of his sons, obsequious Uncle Toms of his fathers, superstitious and grotesque crones of his mothers, strutting peacocks of his successful men, psalm-singing mountebanks of his priests and Barnum and Bailey sideshows of his religion. (1943, p. 37)

Actor Welles wrote several emotionally charged anti-racist articles that appeared in the *Digest*. Many dealt not with Hollywood but with larger social issues besetting African Americans. In his article titled "Outlaw the Sin of Race Hate," he calls for avenging lynchings in Monroe, Georgia, and says, "race hate is the abandonment of human nature" and "where there is hate there is shame and where the racist lie there is corruption" (1946, p. 75).

In an article published in 1947, actor Garfield says,

There are many films in which minority groups are caricatured to the point where truth is all together lost. There are many more films, good in general, but untrue in their presentation of the Negro's life as totally divorced from the Caucasian's or the Caucasian's from the Negro. I often think that people in other countries must have an awfully distorted idea about what goes on over here! Certain films may be fine, but the sum total of our cinema as it comes across is generally untrue and very mediocre film. (p. 6)

Although some noted Hollywood talents were doing their individual part to encourage racial tolerance, the powerful Screen Actors Guild unanimously voted to oppose discrimination against African Americans in the motion picture industry. This was followed by a combined Actors, Writers, and Directors Guild policy that mapped out a three-pronged program that specified:

if a Negro part is indicated in a script, it will be played by a Negro, and the racial character will not be changed; subject, of course to normal judgment on story values. Second, that the Negro will be portrayed on the screen not as a caricature, but as a simple human being, a normal member of the community. Third, that some thought will be given to casting Negroes in the routine, unnamed bits in a script, as mechanics, secretaries, nurses, and so forth. (cited in Jones, 1947, p. 8)

Although a large part of Hollywood's anti-racist activities, especially during the war years, were orchestrated by the U.S. government, they did have a positive effect. For example, in an effort to boost morale, the War Department's Office of War Information mounted a propaganda campaign targeted at African Americans from which came the first model of race-consciousness films, *The Negro Soldier* (1944), produced by the U.S. Army. Other branches of the military followed with their own race-conscious films (e.g., the U.S. Navy produced *The Negro Sailor* in 1945). The war genre films of the 1940s helped usher in some of the first Hollywood films to dignify African Americans and to portray the problems of racial inequality. *Home of the Brave* (1949) explores the issue of racism in the military and is one of the first films to touch on anti-Black bias; misce-genation is the focus of *Lost Boundaries* (1949) and *Pinky* (1949); a Black man is saved from being lynched in *Intruder in the Dust* (1951).

But by no means did this "new awakening" suggest a break with the past. In 1945, "20th Century Fox shipped overseas an Agatha Christie mystery film called *Ten Little Niggers,* all in fun" (Platt, 1949, p. 191).

Evidently the enduring stereotypes still persisted. To these were added "new abnormalities: the zoot-suiters and the Afro-maniacs, as well as a variety of ingratiating new talents and faces, all helping to perpetuate the concept of the happy-go-lucky ward of democracy" (McManus, 1943, p. 18). Yet due to an overwhelming consciousness relating to the power of the media to shape attitudes, the studios were taken to task at every infringement.

In the summer of 1942, the editors of two African American newspapers, the *Los Angeles Sentinel* and the *Los Angeles Tribune,* organized and led a picket line at Loew's State Theater against the film *Tales of Manhattan,* in which they claimed the portrayals of Paul Robeson, Ethel Waters, Rochester, the Hall Johnson Choir, and others were of an undesirable "Uncle Tom" nature (Archer, 1973, p. 216). In the same fashion, *Tennessee Johnson* (1943), another anti-Black film, which glorifies President Andrew Johnson and his cooperation with the Southern Bourbon aristocracy, met with strong anti-racist protests. As with *Gone with the Wind,* the NAACP did not engage in the public fight, which was led by the National Negro Congress, the Communist Party, and trade unions. Instead, the NAACP was able to have certain scenes modified prior to the film's release. Reddick (1944) notes that "the film received more other-than-Black support than ever before attributing it to possible box-office failure" (p. 378). Disney's *Song of the South* (1946), a live-animated cartoon version of the Uncle Remus stories, was also on the NAACP and National Urban League hit list because of the impression it gave of an idyllic master-slave relationship and the stereotype of casting a Black male as an indolent servant.

THE CIVIL RIGHTS ERA
(1950-1964)

As a carryover from post-World War II liberalism, the beginning of the civil rights era saw remarkable anti-racist activity against racial stereotypes. Hollywood began to capitalize on the social and race relations that were hinted at in the late 1940s. *Native Son* (1951) shows the effect of White bigotry on Blacks and the impossibility of escaping the consequences. *No Way Out* (1950) deals with the insults and humiliation of being the only African American doctor at an all-White metropolitan hospital. *Cry, the Beloved Country* (1951), set in racially torn South

Africa, shows that through grief and suffering society may purge itself of the hate and fear that cause race prejudice. Positive change came to an abrupt halt, however, with the McCarthy hysteria, which blacklisted many progressive Whites in Hollywood and the broadcast industry who were interested in supporting anti-racism in the popular media.

With many White progressives preoccupied with blacklisting, the Black press continued its role as media watchdog. Black editors and reporters did not hesitate to use their influence to call attention to anti-Black caricatures and employment discrimination. An October 1955 editorial in the *Los Angeles Tribune* charges Walt Disney with "continued production of material that slyly, but unmistakably slurs the Negro race—as well as other non-Whites" and asks Disney to cease the libelous behavior. The editorial cleverly points out that, despite Disney's use of animals, "the wall-eyed Black crows, liver-lipped alligators, and other animals, all sounding like reincarnated Amos and Andies, Scatman Crotherses, etc., is lost to no one." The editorial also notes the lack of Blacks employed at the Disney studios in positions other than actor, who appeared to be hired for their "authentic dialect." A TV broadcast of Dumbo is singled-out for anti-Black caricatures that were "a gratuitous insult to the Negro race, more especially painful and harmful in light of the millions of Negro children, to their parents' embarrassment are Disney fans" ("The Anti-Negro Caricatures," 1955).

The advances in the 1950s were not without a price. To avoid accepting responsibility for their own actions, Hollywood blamed African American performers for perpetuating stereotypes and contributing to the Uncle Tom caricature (Schary, 1948). What Schary fails to understand is that African American performers who bought into many of the degrading stereotypes did so for reasons they had no control over. They were responding to policies and practices of the motion picture industry, an industry that systematically excluded African Americans from employment if they didn't deliver the very stereotypes that they were accused of perpetuating. Eventually, when caricatures in films were pointed out, producers simply scripted-out African American actors and then failed to reintroduce them in nonstereotypical roles. So prevalent was this pattern that, in 1957, Roy Wilkins, executive secretary of the NAACP, blasted the Association of Motion Picture Producers for using "NAACP discussions as an excuse for restricting employment of Negro actors" (cited in Archer, 1973, p. 223). This posture enabled the industry to consider racism as the "victims' problem" and not its own.

TELEVISION:
NEW MEDIUM, OLD STEREOTYPES

Television began as radio with pictures. A number of shows that originated on radio made their way into television. Several of these shows featured African American performers in the 1950s and depicted them with one of the most dominant stereotypes: that of the subservient servant—Rochester in *The Jack Benny Show,* Louise on *The Danny Thomas Show,* and Willi on *The Trouble with Father Show.* Staples and Jones (1985) comment that "Blacks were allowed to appear on television as long as their roles fostered the traditional stereotypes of Blacks as happy, carefree, musical and lazy" (p. 11).

The next prevalent stereotype was the "entertainer." Performers such as Nat King Cole, The Ink Spots, Count Basie, Sarah Vaughan, and Pearl Bailey were featured as early as 1949 in Ed Sullivan's *Toast of the Town.* An all-Black quartet featuring Billy Williams sang regularly on Sid Caesar's show. Arthur Godfrey employed The Mariners, an interracial quartet. In 1954, Fred Waring employed an African American tenor, Ron Sperman, to sing on his weekly General Electric program. "When Steve Allen took over the *Tonight Show,* he used African American performers as frequently and generously as Ed Sullivan" (Archer, 1973, p. 249).

With this new medium, optimism was very high, so much so that in projecting the future of television, *Ebony Magazine* asserted that the appearance of so many Blacks on television indicated a "sure sign that television is free of racial barriers" ("Television, the Miraculous," 1950). In the same way, the NAACP hoped television would accept Black talent and radio would offer Blacks more opportunities because of the competition offered by television (Archer, 1973).

By 1951, however, the hope had all but disappeared. The new medium simply adopted the racial stereotyping that flourished in radio and films, so much so that the NAACP passed a resolution at its annual convention in June against the *Beulah Show* on radio and the *Amos 'n' Andy Show,* scheduled for television broadcast on June 18, 1951, for perpetuating derogatory stereotypes and hampering racial justice. According to the resolution, "*Amos 'n' Andy* depicts Negroes in a stereotypical and derogatory manner . . . (and) the *Beulah Show,* or other shows of this type, are condemned" (NAACP, 1991, p. 3). After producing 81 half-hour episodes, the Blatz Brewing Company discontinued sponsorship, and *Amos 'n' Andy* was dropped from CBS-TV in June 1953. It went into syndication until

1966, when CBS decided to withdraw the show after five years of litigation (NAACP, 1991).

"Besides objecting to stereotypes, the NAACP also registered protests against television's alleged misrepresentations of Negro life, whether in fiction or fact" (Archer, 1973, p. 247). In 1953, the Philadelphia branch registered a complaint against WCAU-TV's *March of Time* program, which dramatized the racially segregated housing development Levittown as a model American community. The NAACP also lodged opposition to television programs or films that included all-Black casts.

The integration of television was not without condemnation. In 1952, Herman Talmadge, governor of Georgia, criticized television shows that featured African American performers on an equal basis with White performers and alluded to a sponsor boycott of such shows ("Talmadge Hits TV," 1952). Ed Sullivan responded:

> Statements of Georgia's Governor Talmadge that Negro performers should be barred from TV shows on which White performers appear is both stupid and vicious. Television has been a tremendous force in bringing about a finer American understanding throughout the country. From my personal experience, the South has been delighted by the great Negro performers who have brought their songs, dancing and dramatic talents into Southern living rooms. ("Ed Sullivan Leads TV Blast at Governor Talmadge," 1952, p. 13)

Arthur Godfrey defended his interracial quartet against Talmadge by stating,

> Would you kindly tell Governor Talmadge for me that if these young fellows could fight together through a war on behalf of our United States where bullets didn't bother with segregation, that I'm afraid I can't be bothered either. ("Talmadge Hits TV," 1952, p. 59)

The Coordinating Council of Negro Performers also protested, calling the governor's remarks "inflammatory diatribes."

During the early years of the civil rights period, anti-racist activities were focused primarily on the representational aspects of racism. As the 1960s approached, there was greater recognition of the problems of depiction and coverage of African Americans, which were closely associated with discriminatory hiring practices and were part of the institutional expression of racism. Thus, anti-racist activists broadened their agenda to include a greater condemnation of the abysmal hiring practices of the popular media industries. Some of the same issues from the previous decades, however, surfaced at the beginning of the 1960s.

On June 18, 1963, the NAACP, tired of the behind-the-scenes token appeasement to change, threatened to stage a nationwide boycott against the "lily White" policy of the many craft unions and the electronic arts' refusal to revise its portrayal of African Americans. The NAACP criticized Hollywood's continued policy on miscegenation and trifling excuse that films dealing with miscegenation or romance between Blacks and Whites would have "no market in the South and be badly hampered in the North." The NAACP also criticized the broadcast industry's arguments that "a Black on a small-sized television screen tends to draw attention from White actors" (Schumach, 1963, p. 23).

Almost a month after the NAACP's charge, at a meeting of the American Civil Liberties Union Art Division, actors Marlon Brando, Paul Newman, Burt Lancaster, James Whitmore, Charlton Heston, and Anthony Franciosa, along with other writers and producers, called for a boycott by performers of production companies that maintained policies of discrimination. Brando denounced the industry for using old excuses such as "people aren't ready for [integration] . . . we have a moral responsibility to the bankers . . . up to 40% of the market might be lost if more Negro actors are used," and their avowed policy on blocking any implication of miscegenation (*Variety,* 1963, p. 6). Brando and the other actors were well aware of the discrimination policies and tactics of the industry as well as its failure to make any efforts to contribute to the civil rights struggle. The actors' meeting was the first of its kind since the 1942 meeting in which many Hollywood elites were taken to task by one of their own for their inertia on anti-racism.

By the mid- to late 1960s, the film industry has been hit by a combination of White guilt, the empowerment of citizens' groups, the Black revolution, the death of King, and the recognition of the spending power of the Black consumer. It began presenting for the first time previously unexplored and taboo topics. The film industry touched on interracial marriages/romances (*One Potato, Two Potato,* 1964; *A Patch of Blue,* 1966; *Guess Who's Coming to Dinner,* 1967), a world of racist sickness (*The Learning Tree,* 1969), Black despair and rage (*Dutchman,* 1967; *Hurry Sundown,* 1967), ghettos (*The Cool World,* 1963), the state of being Black (*Nothing But a Man,* 1964), Black revolutionaries and the separatist movement (*Uptight,* 1969; *The Lost Man,* 1969), and racism and civil rights (*To Kill a Mockingbird,* 1962; *The Intruder,* 1963; *Black Like Me,* 1964; *In the Heat of the Night,* 1968) (see Bogle, 1973).

Again, this is not to suggest that the pejorative stereotypes of African Americans through images and symbols in the U.S. film industry had ceased. In the same way, not all of Hollywood's attempts to present their interpretation of African American life and history went unchallenged. The Black Anti-Defamation Association (BADA), an ad hoc group consisting of writers and performers in the Los Angeles area, led the campaign against a production on the life of slave insurrectionist Nat Turner. Like *The Birth of a Nation* and *Gone with the Wind,* the film is based on a controversial book—William Styron's, *The Confessions of Nat Turner.* The book portrays Black men as Sambos and Black women as sluts, and suggests that Turner's insurrection was based more on his repressed sexual desires than on his hatred for slavery. The pressure from BADA and the African American community forced some basic changes in the title and the use of more historical sources than the original interpretation for the film version (Roberts, 1969).

As for television, attempts to continue integration were frequently met with criticism from sponsors. Evuleocha and Ugbah (1989) assert that there were:

> instances of major advertisers withdrawing sponsorship from single broadcasters when a series focused on Blacks. Especially prone to this habit were corporations such as Gulf Oil and Metropolitan Life Insurance which were afraid of becoming associated with programs showing racial struggle. (p. 201)

Occasionally, television producers, writers, and performers attempted to handle racism and the racial strife of the 1960s either through individual action or by fusing into a single program theme a challenge to racism. In this spirit the cast of *Bonanza,* the highest-rated serial on the air for most of the 1960s, decided not to make a personal appearance in front of a segregated audience in Jackson, Mississippi. Likewise, the producers and writers entered the racial debate in a 1964 episode, "Enter Thomas Bowers." When the episode was announced, the sponsor, General Motors, was apprehensive about the controversial nature of the program, but NBC refused to budge. The plot concerns the appearance of a singer who is invited to Virginia City without advance knowledge of his color. The singer encounters different forms of prejudice and is jailed after the sheriff receives a wire that an escaped slave of similar appearance is sought for murder. Within the story structure, writers inserted valid commentary on the evils of prejudice, heard through the voice of the lead actors, and the importance of the "uncommitted middle" in achieving a solution to racial problems (Gould, 1964, p. L55).

Similarly, an episode of *Perry Mason* in 1963 cast a Black male as a judge before whom Perry Mason pleads his case. Despite protests, the program producer explained that her action was in line with the judiciary climate in California, where the series originated. Challenges also came in 1967, when "White reporters pointedly asked CBS-TV executives to account for the lily-White staff in their *In Black America* series" (Cripps, 1975, p. 690).

Undoubtedly, the most significant anti-racist action occurred in 1964 when the Office of Communication of the predominantly White United Church of Christ (UCC) began an action for the purpose of denying license renewal against station WLBT-TV for discriminating against the 45% Black population of Jackson, Mississippi. This case led to the landmark ruling by Circuit Court Judge Warren E. Burger that gave citizens' groups the right to challenge licenses before the Federal Communications Commission. This action by the UCC helped empower numerous citizens' groups, who were able to make inroads in television programming and fair employment over the next two decades (Office of Communication of the United Church of Christ v. FCC, 1966, p. 994).

BLACK POWER AND
POST-BLACK POWER PERIOD
(1965-1993)

Plus ça change, plus c'est la même chose—the more things change, the more they stay the same—best describes the media and popular culture of the Black power and post-Black power decades. This was a politically charged period that saw the passage of the 1965 Voting Rights Act, the assassination of Martin Luther King, and the ordeal of Rodney King. In the midst of marches, sit-ins, boycotts, demands for peace and justice, and outright struggle, television in the 1960s gave the American public the model of racial harmony with *Julia.* Two decades later in the midst of renewed struggle, racial tension, and demands for peace and justice, television gave the public *The Cosby Show.*

Beginning in the mid- to late 1960s, the popular media conveyed the impression that the Civil Rights Movement had all but solved past inequities. The increased visibility of African Americans in film and television programming, the rise of the second Black Renaissance, and the passage of the 1964 Civil Rights Act all gave the impression that African Americans had gained an equal place in society as well as in the media. Batts (1989) suggests that the dismantling of the old-fashioned racism was replaced by a new kind of modern racism. This new racism is defined by McConahay and Hough (1976) as "the expression in terms of abstract ideological symbols and symbolic behaviors of the feeling that Blacks are violating cherished values and making illegitimate demands for changes in the racial status quo" (p. 38).

As the 1970s began, anti-racist activity in the popular media, except on rare occasions, was more or less in the hands of African Americans. There was a growing silence on racial issues in popular culture. The visibility of African American performers and television personalities helped create the false impression that equality had finally arrived. Alliances with progressive Whites, more evident in the pre-civil rights and civil rights era, diminished, and a plethora of new African American-led media groups emerged as the watchdogs of an all-consuming popular media culture—Black Citizens for Fair Media, National Black Media Coalition, Black Artists Alliance, the Committee to Eliminate Media Offensive to African American People, National Black Network, and the Black Media Association. These groups continued to press for the same two demands that their predecessors sought: the abolition of demeaning stereotypes and fair employment opportunities for African Americans.

Not only were African Americans being abandoned by their former allies, but the qualitative improvements in film and television in the 1960s gave way in the 1970s to the "Blaxploitation Era" in cinema and the return to post-1960s stereotypes that were inserted in numerous situation comedies (*Good Times, That's My Mama, What's Happening*). Nonetheless, some gains were made.

As for the networks, they attempted to deal with anti-racism in a number of made-for-television specials—*Firehouse* (1973), *The Autobiography of Miss Jane Pittman* (1974), *Roots* (1977), *A Woman Called Moses* (1978). Even with good intentions, the media tended to negate and make trivial the experience of African Americans. Russell (1991) makes a good case for analyzing these television specials and subsequent media fare by suggesting the presence of a "dominant gaze" that "subtly invites the viewer to empathize and identify with its viewpoint as natural . . . it marginalizes other perspectives to bolster its own legitimacy in defining narratives and images" (p. 244).

One way in which the dominant gaze manifests itself is in altering the characterizations, content, and theme of story lines to make them more acceptable for the White television audience and repackaging them as essential truths. This was certainly evident in the made-for-television specials of the 1970s that purported to tell the story of racism and oppression. For example, the televised drama of Ernest J. Gaines' novel, *The Autobiography of Miss Jane Pittman*, mutilated the novel's images and symbols and inserted a White reporter/narrator into the story. Tucker and Shah (1992) suggest producers and network executives changed Alex Haley's epic slave narrative *Roots* into a classic immigrant story. In doing so, "the creators ignore the distinctiveness of Kunta Kinte's struggle—and the struggle of all Black Americans—against the institution of slavery and oppression in favor of an idea of universal assimilation implicit in the image of the immigrant myth" (p. 335).

The 1980s and Beyond

Since the beginning of U.S. popular media, African and African American experiences, histories, and lives have been interpreted and controlled by the dominant myths of a White-centered society. These myths have not disappeared, but have become more subtle in the midst of the new racism. It was not surprising then, that the 1980s brought to the United States and to the international public films centering on independent and heroic White women, with Africa serving as an exotic background. *Gorillas in the Mist* (1988) and *Out of Africa* (1986) fuse a supposedly liberal discourse on gender with a racist-imperialist depiction of Africa. In each case, the White goddess, delegate of a superior culture with all of its imperialist heritage, is pitted against greedy Africans, narrow-minded Blacks who are either engaged in petty economic struggles or immersed in little wars, as in *Gorillas*. Alternatively, Blacks are portrayed as mere caricatures of complacency given to occasional comic intransigence, as in *Out of Africa* (Bonavoglia, 1986). In reviewing *Out of Africa*, Bonavoglia contends that this is a story worth telling; however, the film presents a "whitewashed and one-dimensional view" (p. 45).

Films with U.S. themes were not much better, and in some instances outright harmful. *Soul Man* (1987) is a post-Bakke fantasy about the perilous possibilities of affirmative action and minority scholarships. It tells the story of an affluent young White male, who, when his father refuses to pay his tuition to Harvard Law School, takes tanning pills to turn his skin dark so he can masquerade as an African American and obtain a minority scholarship to Harvard Law School. Along the way he falls in love with the African American female law student who should have been awarded the scholarship that he received under false pretenses. In the end they fall in love, she forgives him, and they live happily ever after.

Benjamin Hooks, former executive director of the NAACP, calls the film,

> a crude exploitation that panders to the lowest racist feelings and has no redeeming values . . . and feeds the divisive false idea that special benefits are given to Blacks and denied to Whites because of their race, thus constituting reverse discrimination. (Williams & Adams, 1987, p. 42)

The strongest and most adverse criticism, however, came from the African American community and university students—University of California at Los Angeles (UCLA) Black Student Alliance, the Black American Law Students Association, UCLA, the Black Harvard Law Students—who attacked the film's distortion of being Black in the United States.

Representing the summit of the civil rights genre films, *Mississippi Burning* (1989) attempts to capture racial strife through a fictionalized account of the FBI involvement in the murder of three civil rights workers in the summer of 1964, and holds up as the protagonists two White males. Not only does the film distort the realities of that history, it demeans African Americans by casting them as background to the struggle, as noble victims, in a range from historical agents to props. In responding to the whitewashing of the film, Alan Parker, the director, believes that the heroes had to be White males, because White heroes are more acceptable to the largely White film-going public as well as to the profit-driven film industry than African American heroes. Similarly, *Cry Freedom* (1987), advertised as a story about South African antiapartheid leader Steve Biko, is more about a White newspaper editor and his family than the Black revolutionary leader. Richard Attenborough, the director, expressed a similar perspective for disregarding the real heroes of the story, "White audiences would not be interested in a film about Biko" (Spigner, 1991, p. 75).

Likewise, from 1980 to 1984, negative stereotypes continued on television. NBC's *Beulah Land* (1980) is a six-hour, three-part Civil War drama where slaves are depicted as happy and not having any problems with slavery. The Washington-based National Black Media Coalition protested the drama at local levels, putting picket lines at NBC stations, setting up a phone bank, and calling the advertisers ("The Recent Furor Surrounding the Way," 1992). An ad hoc group, The Coalition Against the Airing of *Beulah Land,* sponsored by the NAACP, labeled the series "demeaning to Blacks" (Bogle, 1988).

Regular network programming was not much better. A survey of ABC television programs in 1984 affirmed that 49% of African Americans were portrayed as criminals, servants, entertainers, or athletes (Douglas, 1984). Cummings (1988) suggests that, in addition to the latter, another particular theme was evident: "If Blacks were to be successful, well educated, properly brought up in a supportive, nourishing middle class environment, it was necessary for there to be White people at the head of each of the households—*Diff'rent Strokes, Webster*" (p. 79). Beginning in 1984, there were several notable exceptions to the traditional stereotyping that had plagued African Americans since the inception of television. These more accurate portrayals suggest that stereotyping is not inevitable, necessary for success, or the only alternative. These exceptions were *The Cosby Show, I'll Fly Away, A Different World, Roc, 227,* and the short-lived *Frank's Place.* In addition, *Frontline,* produced by a consortium of Public Broadcast System stations (KCTS, Seattle; WGBH, Boston; WNET, New York; WPBT, Miami; and WVTS, Detroit), has demonstrated an unusual sense of social responsibility in concentrating 10% of its television programs on racial strife and prejudice in U.S. society.

In some cases, the dismantling of negative stereotypes and replacement of them with positive ones can be counter-productive. *The Cosby Show* has received high praises for recoding ethnicity (Real, 1989) and introducing positive images for African American families (Dates & Barlow, 1990; Fuller, 1992). Indeed, *The Cosby Show* did dismantle the racist mythology and negative stereotypes prevalent in previous decades. Yet for all its praises, the show had its share of criticisms. Fuller (1992) has conducted the most extensive cross-cultural audience analyses of *The Cosby Show.* One of her most notable findings from the 13 countries participating in her survey is that the show is not about "a Black family" or "about being Black." Most respondents saw the family as "without color." Batts (1989) suggests that the color-blind thesis discounts the Black American experience by presenting a world where racism no longer exists and providing Whites, in the era of Reaganomics, reassurance that with hard work anyone can attain the American dream.

The success of *The Cosby Show* ushered in a plethora of African American situation comedies. Many of these new programs have been attacked for returning to the stock buffoonery of the 1970s. On *Hanging with Mr. Cooper,* substitute teacher Mark Cooper engages in juvenile antics—such as gluing a student to his chair—and expresses surprise with the bug-eyed shout "DAAAAMN!" NBC's short-lived *Rhythm and Blues* features a White deejay hired to lead the struggling WBLZ to the promised land. Besides unflattering portraits of bigoted Blacks and cartoonish exaggeration of jive, the show is a throwback to *Diff'rent Strokes* and *Webster,* in which "Black children were socialized, or 'saved' by more knowledgeable Whites" (Hammer, 1992, pp. 70-71).

The 1980s and the beginning of the 1990s also saw African American performers and filmmakers move forward in a number of significant ways. Eddie Murphy's movies have generated more than $1 billion worldwide—more than any other actor's in history. Filmmakers Kenyan Ivory Wayans, Euzhan Palcy, John Singleton, Robert Townsend, and Spike Lee have added a new, irreverent voice that speaks the language of Hollywood—profit. Between January 25 and October 25, 1993, films staring or costaring African Americans, such as *The Bodyguard, The Distinguished Gentleman, Sister Act, Made in America, Passenger 57, Cop and a Half, White Men Can't Jump, Malcolm X, Posse, The Long Walk Home, Mo' Money, Lethal Weapon 1, The Crying Game,* and *What's Love Got to Do With It,* were shown in the major international markets.

What does this international pattern suggest? According to Dekom (1992), the worldwide marketplace has become an A-title business. Whether selling pay television, home video, or syndicated products in the United States, or trying to secure presale financing in foreign territories, the revenues for low-level B or C pictures are rapidly disappearing. This means that movies with significant recognizable stars such as Eddie Murphy, Wesley Snipes, Whoopie Goldberg, and Whitney Houston and established directors such as Spike Lee and Richard Attenborough are more likely to do better in the overseas markets. Will films depicting Africans and African Americans in a stereotypical manner continue to be picked up by overseas sales agents and distributors? Will the racism inherent in other cultures determine what is purchased? Yes and no. *Out of Africa* did 65% of its business outside the United States (Pollack, 1992). Yet, in 1984, Egypt took offense at a miniseries portraying Anwar Sadat and banned it and any other films produced or distributed by Columbia Pictures. The *New York Times* reported that an objection in some circles was the selection of Lou Gossett, an African American, to play Sadat (Ganley & Ganley, 1987).

VIEW FROM THE OUTSIDE

Racism and negative stereotyping in the popular cultures of Africans and African Americans are not peculiar to the United States. According to Tomaselli (1983, p. 13), "since the inception of feature filmmaking in South Africa in 1916, Blacks have been portrayed in subservient roles." When not cast in these roles, Blacks are either absent or parodied. The popular *De Vorrtrekkers or Winning a Continent* (1916) adopted some of the same stereotypes that emerged in *The Birth of a Nation.* Directed by an American filmmaker for local and British consumption, Blacks in this film are depicted as "irredeemably savage [and] egged on by scheming, oily, idolatrous Portuguese East African traders" (Tomaselli, 1983, p. 13).

When Blacks are not depicted as the savage enemy or in traditional roles, they are invisible, particularly in films produced for White or Afrikaner audiences. Tomaselli does suggest, however, that when a Black South African is included, more than likely, it is a male and he is depicted as a "comic, solid, trustworthy and faithful to authority" (e.g., *The Wild Geese*; Tomaselli, 1983, p. 14).

Although considered a smashing worldwide success, the South African import *The Gods Must Be Crazy* was not viewed by all African Americans and White progressives as humorous (Davis, 1985). Despite some protests at movie houses, people flocked to see this slapstick comedy. Davis feels that films like *The Gods Must Be Crazy* belong to a "gray area"; it is difficult to understand the underlying racist assumptions without knowing something about "South Africa's past history, its [preindependence] domestic and foreign policies, and the single-mindedness with which South Africa used to shape the system of apartheid. It is within this context that *The Gods Must Be Crazy,* must be seen and only then, it will be recognized as 'not a harmless little comedy' " (Davis, 1985, p. 53).

Australia's peculiar history with indigenous people also helped shape a racism that was not unlike that in the United States or South Africa. Naturally, this racism became filtered through the lens of the filmmaker. More important, none of these countries' cultural industries developed in a vacuum. For example, "*Uncle Tom's Cabin* was as popular in the Australian theater in the last century as *Phantom of the Opera* is today" (McFarlane & Mayer, 1992, p. 5).

Early Australian filmmakers depicted "Aboriginals as rara avis along with other exotic birds and animal life" (Lewis, 1987, p. 20). In addition, Aborigines became stereotyped early as Stone Age killers or as noble savages. So much so that, with the release of the "Last Wave" in 1979, *New Yorker* critic Pauline Kael suggested that the treatment of the Aborigines was "still racist" (Kael, 1980, p. 102).

Two films, *The Chant of Jimmie Blacksmith* (1978) and *Wrong Side of the Road* (1981), attempt to present the Aborigines' racial experiences. *Wrong Side* is a musical documentary about the Aboriginal reggae rock band No Fixed Address. The film shows how the band's experiences of "racial illegitimacy and harassment from outside both test and sustain the 'inside' sense of Black community, undiminished by physical distance" (Dermody & Jacka, 1988, p. 116).

Jimmy Blacksmith was, according to Dermody and Jacka (1988), "bred purposely to be a champion of the film industry, of Australian culture, of raised consciousness about race and of Australia's first feature entered into competition at the Cannes festival" (p. 116). Based on the real-life experiences of Jimmie Governor, an Aborigine at the turn of the century, the film addresses the tension of race and gender in a society where the quest for dignity and "psychological, sexual and social autonomy is never completely granted Blacks" (p. 118).

The film's attempt to raise consciousness about race apparently did not work. Dermody and Jacka (1988) suggest that the violence directed toward Whites in the film far exceeded the expectation or capacity of the White Australian audiences. The "audience emerged angry, with the feeling that they had been misled, and were 'lambs to the slaughter' " (p. 11).

CONCLUSION

Since the beginning of the 20th century, the popular media has submitted to pejorative stereotyping and adoption of exploitative themes or modes of presentations concerning the histories and lives of African Americans. Simultaneously, the African American community and its White allies have not remained silent in the face of such depiction. Although in recent times, White progressives have abandoned the movement to keep the cultural industries in check, African Americans continue to wage battle in an industry that has responded only to political, financial, or social pressure for change. This chapter has shown that, despite variations and exceptions across this century, some stock racial characterizations of African Americans have persisted. Other characterizations have changed as the context of racism also changed. For example, the blatant representations of African Americans as simple, childlike, or beastly now operate on a more subtle, indirect level as modern racism has become anchored in the larger society. The tragic mulatto and her caring mammy stereotype has decreased in frequency. Television and film have not only reflected many social changes, they have also helped contribute to the production of modern racism by blurring the lines between the media world and social reality.

Today, U.S. export of popular media is second only to its export of aerospace technology. The dominance of the United States in the cultural marketplace suggests that international cultural standards are being communicated and reproduced. Such standards, far from being apolitical or value-free, form part of a larger network of ideas in which racism is positioned. The overwhelmingly biased images of African Americans that continue to dominate popular media culture are significant not only in what they say about African Americans but in what they imply about Western belief systems and the producers and consumers of such ideas. The power of images, coupled with their expansion into all corners of the globe, suggests more than ever a need for decolonizing the imagination.

REFERENCES

American Film Institute. (1988). *The American film institute catalogue of motion pictures produced in the United States: Feature films, 1911-1920.* Berkeley: University of California Press.

The anti-Negro caricatures that. (1955). *Los Angeles Tribune.*

Aptheker, H. (1987). Anti-racism in the US: An introduction. *Sage Race Relations Abstracts, 12*(4), 3-32.

Archer, L. C. (1973). *Black images in the American theater NAACP protest campaigns: Stage, screen, radio and television.* New York: Pageant-Poseidon.

Ashmore, R. D. (1970). Prejudice: Causes and cures. In B. E. Collins (Ed.), *Social psychology* (pp. 246-296). Reading, MA: Addison-Wesley.

Batts, V. (1989). *Modern racism: New melodies for the same old tunes.* Cambridge, MA: Visions.

Bogle, D. (1973). *Toms, coons, mulattos, mammies and bucks: An interpretive history of Blacks in American film.* New York: Viking.

Bogle, D. (1988). *Blacks in American films and television: An encyclopedia.* New York: Garland.

Bonavoglia, A. (1986, December). Out of Africa. *Cineaste, 14*(4), 44-45.

Brown, G. (1984). *The New York Times encyclopedia of film.* New York: Times Books.

Cloud, D. L. (1992). Ambivalence and stereotype in "Spenser: For hire." *Critical Studies in Mass Communication, 9,*(4), 311-324.

Cobleigh, R. (1971). Why I oppose *The Birth of a Nation*. In R. Gottesman & H. Geduld (Eds.), *Focus on* The Birth of a Nation (pp. 80-83). Englewood Cliffs, NJ: Prentice Hall.

Cripps, T. (1975). The noble Black savage: A problem in the politics of television art. *Journal of Popular Culture, 4,* 687-695.

Cripps, T. (1977). *Slow fade to Black: The Negro in American film, 1900-1942.* New York: Oxford University Press.

Cripps, T. (1978). *Black film as genre.* Bloomington: Indiana University Press.

Cummings, M. S. (1988). The changing image of the Black family on television. *Journal of Popular Culture, 22*(2), 75-85.

Dates, J. L., & Barlow, W. (1990). *Split image: African Americans in the mass media.* Washington, DC: Howard University Press.

Davis, P. (1985). The Gods Must Be Crazy. *Cineaste, 14*(1), 53-55.

Dekom, P. J. (1992). The global market. In J. E. Squire (Ed.), *The movie business book* (pp. 418-430). New York: Fireside.

Dermody, S., & Jacka, J. (1988). *The screening of Australia: Anatomy of a film industry* (Vol. 1). Sydney: Currency Press.

Donahue, S. (1987). *American film distribution: The changing marketplace.* Ann Arbor, MI: UMI Research Press.

Douglas, P. (1984, December). Minority groups push for Olympic ABC TV hirings. *The National Leader,* p. 5.

Doyle, M. (1992). *The future of television: A global overview of programming, advertising, technology, and growth.* Lincolnwood, IL: NTC Business Books.

Ed Sullivan leads TV blast at Governor Talmadge. (1952, January). *Pittsburg Courier,* p. 13.

Egg Negro scenes in liberty film play. (1915, April 15). *New York Times,* p. 1.

Evuleocha, S. U., & Ugbah, S. D. (1989). Stereotypes, counter-stereotypes, and Black television images in the 1990s. *The Western Journal of Black Studies, 13,* 197-205.

Fife, M. (1974). Black images in American TV: The first two decades. *The Black Scholar, 6*(3), 7-15.

Fuller, L. K. (1992). *The Cosby Show: Audiences, impact, and implications.* Westport, CT: Greenwood.

Ganley, G., & Ganley, O. (1987). *Global political fallout: The VCR's first decade.* Norwood, NJ: Ablex.

Garfield, J. (1947, November). How Hollywood can better race relations. *Negro Digest, 6,* 4-8.

Goings, K. W. (1990, February 14). Memorabilia that have perpetuated stereotypes about African Americans. *Chronicle of Higher Education, 36* B76.

Gould, S. (1964, April 26). Topical "bonanza." *New York Times,* p. L55.

Hammer, J. (1992, October 26). Must Blacks be buffoons? *Newsweek,* pp. 70-71.

Hill, G. H. (1986). *Ebony images: Black Americans and television.* Carson, CA: Daystar.

Jones, R. (1947, August). How Hollywood feels about Negroes. *Negro Digest, 5,* 4-8.

Kael, P. (1980). Doused. In *When the lights go down* (pp. 533-537). New York: Holt, Rinehart & Winston.

Koltuv, B. (1962). Some characteristics of intrajudge trait intercorrelations. *Psychological Monographs, 76*(33), 552.

Leab, D. (1976). *From Sambo to superspade: The Black experience in motion pictures.* Boston: Houghton Mifflin.

Lewis, G. (1987). *Australian movies and the American dream.* New York: Praeger.

Lippmann, W. (1981). Stereotypes. In M. Janowitz & P. Hirsch (Eds.), *Reader in public opinion and mass communication* (pp. 29-37). New York: Free Press.

MacDonald, J. F. (1983). *Blacks and White TV: Afro-Americans in television since 1948.* Chicago: Nelson-Hall.

McConahay, J. B., & Hough, J. C. (1976). Symbolic racism. *The Journal of Social Issues, 32*(2), 23-45.

McFarland, B., & Mayer, G. (1992). *New Australian cinema: Sources and parallels in American and British film.* Cambridge, UK: Cambridge University Press.

McManus, J. T. (1943, April). Is Hollywood fair to Negroes? *Negro Digest, 1,* 16-21.

McManus, J. T., & Kronenberger, L. (1946, June). Hollywood's new deal for Negroes. *Negro Digest, 4,* 77-80.

Naisbitt, J., & Aburdene, P. (1990). *Megatrends 2000: The new direction for the 1990s.* New York: Morrow.

Naison. M. (1983). *Communists in Harlem during the depression.* Urbana: University of Illinois Press.

NAACP. (1991). *Out of focus—out of sync: A report on the film and television industries.* Baltimore: NAACP.

Negroes mob photo play. (1915, April 18). *New York Times,* p. 15.

Null, G. (1975). *Blacks in Hollywood: The Negro in motion pictures.* Secaucus, NJ: Citadel.

Office of Communication of the United Church of Christ v. FCC (1966). 359 F.2d 994 (DC Cir.).

Platt, D. (1949). The Negro in films, March 11, 1946. In *Fighting words: Selections from twenty-five years of the* Daily Worker (pp. 191-192). New York: New Century Publishers.

Poindexter, P. M., & Stroman, C. A. (1981). Blacks and television: A review of the research literature. *Journal of Broadcasting, 25*(2), 103-122.

Pollack, S. (1992). The director. In J. E. Squire (Ed.), *The movie business book* (pp. 44-56). New York: Fireside.

Protests on photo play. (1915, April 15). *New York Times,* p. 1.

Real, M. (1989). *Super media: A cultural studies approach.* Newbury Park, CA: Sage.

Reddick, L. D. (1944). Educational programs for the improvement of race relations: Motion pictures, radio, the press, and libraries. *Journal of Negro Education, 13*(3), 367-389.

Roberts, S. V. (1969, March 31). Storm over "Nat Turner" screenplay subsides. *New York Times,* p. 28.

Rodgers, C. E. (1993). So you want to be in the movies? *The Crisis, 90*(1), 6-10.

Russell, M. M. (1991). Race and the dominant gaze: Narratives of law and inequality in popular film. *Legal Studies Forum, 15*(3), 243-254.

Saxton, A. (1990). *The rise and fall of the White republic: Class politics and mass culture in nineteenth century America.* New York: Verso.

Schary, D. (1948, February). Minorities and movies. *Negro Digest,* p. 52.

Schiller, H. (1989). The privatization of culture. In I. Angus & S. Jhally (Eds.), *Cultural politics in contemporary America* (pp. 317-332). New York: Routledge.

Schumach, M. (1963, June 26). NAACP seeks job equality in Hollywood film companies. *New York Times,* p. 23.

Sklar, R. (1975). *Movie-made America.* New York: Random House.

Spigner, C. (1991). Black impressions of people-of-color: A functionalist approach to film imagery. *The Western Journal of Black Studies, 15,* 69-78.

Squire, J. (1992). *The movie business book.* New York: Fireside.

Staples, R., & Jones, T. (1985). Culture, ideology and Black television images. *The Black Scholar, 3*(16), 10-20.

Talmadge hits TV for mixing races. (1952, January 6). *New York Times,* p. 59.

Television, the miraculous. (1950, June). *Ebony,* p. 22.

The Clansman. (1915, May). *The Crisis, 10*(1), 33.

The recent furor surrounding the way Blacks. (1992, April). *Jet,* pp. 56-58.

Thompson, K. (1985). *Exporting entertainment: America in the world film market, 1907-34.* London: British Film Institute.

Thompson, V. B. (1969). *Africa and unity: The evolution of pan-Africanism.* London: Longman.

Tomaselli, K. (1983). Racism in South African film. *Cineaste, 13*(1), 12-15.

Trumbo, D. (1943, February). Blackface, Hollywood style. *Negro Digest, 2,* 37-39.

Tucker, L. R., & Shah, H. (1992). Race and the transformation of culture: The making of the television miniseries *Roots. Critical Studies in Mass Communication, 9,* 325-336.

Variety. (1963, July 17). Talent feeds producers anti-Negro. *231*(80), 6.

Variety. (1992a, September 28). International box office. *348*(10), 33.

Variety. (1992b, Ocotber 19). International box office. *348*(13), 62.

Variety. (1992c, October 26). International box office. *348*(14), 62.

Variety. (1992d, September 28). International box office. *349*(1), 36.

Variety. (1993a, February 1). Italian toppers. *350*(1), 40.

Variety. (1993b, March 22). Danish toppers. *350*(8), 34.

Welles, O. (1946, November). Outlaw the sin of race hate. *Negro Digest, 5,* 74-76.

White, W. (1948). *A man called White: The autobiography of Walter White.* New York: Viking.

Williams, J. D., & Adams, S. H. (1987, January). NAACP focus. *The Crisis, 94,* 42.

6

White Radicals, White Liberals, and White People: Rebuilding the Anti-Racist Coalition

Bob Blauner

The modern Civil Rights Movement, spanning roughly the 20 years from 1955 to 1975, was the most important expression of mass anti-racist activity in the United States since 19th-century Abolitionism. These two decades and their racial politics had two phases. During the initial period, between 1955 and 1965, when the Montgomery, Alabama, bus boycott ushered in the Civil Rights Movement, anti-racist politics were centered in the American South. The expressed goal was the elimination of Jim Crow segregation laws and customs so that Black people could be integrated into mainstream America. The strategies and tactics were largely confined to nonviolence, even though "direct action" protest was becoming more militant. Although civil rights was for all intents and purposes a movement primarily of African American people, it included a significant, indeed sizable, participation of Whites, both as activists and as supporters.

During the second period, between 1965 and 1975, the locus of the anti-racist struggle shifted to the cities of the North and the West. This was much more difficult terrain. The core problems in the urban centers

---

tended to be tied to economic poverty rather than to the feudal-like patterns of legal discrimination in the South. Progress toward equality was not easy in either location or period. With high expectations frustrated in the second period, many of the movement's most dynamic and young Black leaders shifted away from integration to the pursuit of "Black Power." A spirit of racial nationalism blossomed, not only among many African Americans, but among other oppressed racial minorities in the United States as well—Mexican Americans, Puerto Ricans, Asian Americans, and Native Americans. Hand-in-hand with militant Black racial nationalism came a reevaluation of integrationist strategies and tactics. Many rejected Gandhian nonviolence. It was believed that, to achieve the new movement's goals, one must use any means necessary, including violence. The separatist spirit was directly expressed by rejecting the interracial character of such avant-garde militant organizations as the Student Nonviolent Coordinating Committee (SNCC) and the Congress of Racial Equality (CORE). White members were dismissed and told by SNCC leader Stokely Carmichael to organize in their own (White) communities (Carmichael & Hamilton, 1967).

The second phase of the Civil Rights Movement saw a steady decline in popular White support, referred to as the "White backlash." The exact timing, character, and causes of this so-called backlash have been much discussed and disputed by social commentators. But there is little doubt that a significant decline in the support of European Americans for the movement began in the late 1960s and continued into the 1970s. The White backlash contributed to the 1968 election of Richard Nixon as president of the United States. Many in the general public felt they had had enough of social unrest and yearned for law and order, and Nixon capitalized on this conservative trend. Racial backlash was also expressed in the support Alabama's segregationist Governor George Wallace garnered in his 1964 and 1968 presidential election campaigns.

How the alliance between African Americans and White American civil rights supporters declined and dissolved is complex, and needs to be carefully looked at. The aspect of this breakdown that has received the most attention is the demise of the coalition between African Americans and Jewish Americans, many of whom, throughout the first half of this century, were the most active supporters of efforts toward racial equity (Kaufman, 1988). Jewish-Black relations continue to receive attention, in large part due to the escalating rhetoric and tensions between these two groups in recent years and the Jewish perception that anti-Semitism has become especially prevalent in the African American community (Blauner, 1994).

THE SIGNIFICANCE OF LIBERALS AND RADICALS

As important as the crisis in Black-Jewish relations was for the larger anti-racist movement, I want to focus on another aspect of the demise of the civil rights coalition that took place in the late 1960s: the division that developed between White liberals and radicals, a split that I believe is even more significant in accounting for the seemingly permanent and complete demise of anti-racist coalition movements. To this day, the liberal-radical fissure continues to inhibit the mobilization of anti-racist coalitions and the participation of larger numbers of Whites in efforts toward racial justice.

The terms *liberals* and *radicals* are slippery and difficult to define, but they suggest two important political camps within the White population that have been committed historically to racial justice. Liberals and radicals share—and this distinguishes them from *conservatives*—a commitment to the expansion in practice of the ideals of democracy and equality. They do not characteristically look to the past for their visions of a better society, but to the future. Both liberals and radicals are responsive to the problems of disadvantaged groups and are open to some utilization of the state to intervene in providing a greater measure of economic and social justice. The meaning of liberal, radical, and conservative changes with political circumstances. Who identifies themselves and organizes around liberal, radical, and conservative issues also changes from place to place and through history.

The referents of these terms are contextual and relational rather than absolute. The radical will always be to the "left" of the liberal in that his or her critique of the status quo and political solutions will be more comprehensive, whereas those of the liberal will be more partial, piecemeal, and usually cautious. But the concrete details of specific positions—what distinguishes the two camps at any historical moment—will depend on the contingencies of time and place. Because this is a changing reality, new meanings of who and what is liberal and radical are regularly recreated by new historical circumstances.[1]

The present-day antagonism and lack of dialogue between most White liberals and White radicals is the American equivalent of the fault line between the Social Democratic and Communist movements that evolved in Europe in the years after the Russian Revolution. The inability of socialists and communists to work together is often seen as an important key to the ascendance of fascism in Europe in the 1930s. The liberal-radical split makes it impossible to develop a "united front" with a critical mass of White support against racism in the United States, and racism is America's fascism.

THE CONSEQUENCES OF THE LIBERAL-RADICAL DEMISE

From the Depression of the 1930s through the mid-1960s, liberals and radicals had an uneasy, but a working, relationship—despite their ideological and stylistic differences. True, the anti-Communist hysteria of the immediate post-World War II era, associated with Senator Joseph McCarthy, divided and weakened the American Left. But liberals and radicals tended to be on the same side regarding most of the great issues of social justice and economic change, and were allies especially in the struggle against racial bigotry, prejudice, and discrimination. All of this changed in the 1960s. Liberals and radicals began taking sharply different positions in the charged politics of the time. Race was the primary dividing point. The war in Vietnam, and conflicting attitudes toward the increasingly militant protest of White students and youth against the war were also important.

The legacy of this now 30-year-old split is present in the issues of racial politics that divide America in the 1990s. Most liberals and radicals tend to be on opposite sides of what are today called "the culture wars." The few liberals who still comment on race tend to oppose, either in principle or more often in operation, the present movement toward multiculturalism. They are often ambivalent about organized efforts to diversify the membership and the leadership of social institutions by race, gender, or any other form of social difference. Most of the intellectual arguments against affirmative action have come from White liberals (Glazer, 1975). (*Affirmative action* is a term describing a whole series of programs instituted since the late 1960s—particularly after the assassination of Martin Luther King, Jr.). Of particular concern have been programs implemented to increase the numbers of racial minorities and women in colleges and universities and in various occupations where minorities and women have been historically underrepresented.

In contrast, White radicals have been strong supporters of affirmative action and multiculturalism. Despite the small numbers of radicals in the general population and the greater numbers and influence of liberals, national affirmative action efforts have been sustained as the expressed goals of American businesses, colleges and universities, public associations, and government agencies. Of course, the White Left is not the only group that can take credit for this success. Radicals in alliance with more powerful Black and other minority movements, organized feminist groups, and a series of crucial court rulings have upheld the legitimacy of affirmative action.

LANGUAGE AND DISCOURSE

The influence of the White Left, Third World, and women's movements has been even greater in the area of language and discourse. During the past generation, a revolution has occurred in the way Americans talk about race and social difference in America. Perhaps the first sign was the success of Black militants in changing the term of reference for people of African descent from *Negro* to *Black*. Soon after, feminists educated the public—females as well as males—to refer to women as *women* and not as *girls*. Although in retrospect these highly publicized and conscious changes in speech may seem to be minor matters, they can be viewed as the origin of today's controversial "politically correct" language. But much less commented on, and much more important, is the way that the term *racism* emerged after the 1960s. Within less than a decade, racism became the most important idea in the language of race. The idea of racism, a word favored by White radicals as well as intellectuals and activists of color, replaced the concepts of prejudice and discrimination, terms that liberal Whites and moderate Blacks were more comfortable with.

Because discourse encompasses thought as well as language, the "victory" of the Left in this area is quite remarkable. But if there is a victory here, it is a Pyrrhic one. Changes in action and deep belief have not followed changes in the way Americans talk about race. This does not suggest that efforts toward affirmative action, diversity, or multiculturalism should be rolled back. As a radical, I personally believe in them. More important, these efforts have made a difference in upgrading the status of minorities and integrating and diversifying American society. I advocate a rethinking of and a retreat from using language and discourse as such major weapons in the fight for racial change. It is an anomalous and an unhealthy political development to have no mass anti-racist movement—today's is weak and almost nonexistent—and at the same time to have anti-racist thought virtually proscribed in everyday language. All indications are that the majority White population is opposed to and resentful of what it perceives as coercive language.

This situation of no anti-racist movement, no coalition between liberals and radicals, plus the use of language far in advance of action, has maintained a White backlash mentality long after the conditions that gave rise to it have passed into history. The discourse of racism predisposes White people to view themselves in terms of a "deficit model," one that focuses on human failings rather than on more positive potentials for growth and change. As with how Blacks react to White dialogue about Black family, community, and school achievement, the stance of Whites in the dialogue of race is also one of defensiveness. The contemporary discourse on White racism is counterproductive for coalition building.

Two things are needed: to describe the role of the Left in the liberal-radical split and to suggest ways to overcome this legacy of the 1960s to begin to heal the breach. I propose a series of arguments aimed at reversing the way Americans conceive of White people, so that it will be possible to look afresh at European Americans and see them in terms of their potentials for overcoming racism and for joining new democratizing movements, rather than continuing to look at them in terms of how racist and irredeemable they are.

HOW LIBERALS AND RADICALS SEPARATED: CONFLICT OVER RACE AND WAR

The history of the radical-liberal demise goes back to the 1950s. After eight years of the Eisenhower administration, Kennedy's election was viewed as a return to the liberal Democratic principles of the Roosevelt-Truman years. Kennedy's narrow victory over Nixon is often attributed to a sizable turnout at the polls of Blacks, who were impressed by Kennedy's pre-election gesture of solidarity with an imprisoned Martin Luther King, Jr. Expected to be responsive to their concerns, the new president was disappointing on civil rights issues, spoke out rarely, and, when he did, spoke with great moderation. Above all, he failed to protect the lives of civil rights activists against the racist terror they faced in the South (Golden, 1964).

The seeds of the radical-liberal tension were sown in the early 1960s, with growing disillusionment over President Kennedy's failure to act decisively in support of civil rights. The 1960s produced a new generation of liberals and radicals who had no experience with the 1930s' social programs, worldwide economic depression, world war, and the slow up-and-down pace of social reforms. The only issues for them were in the present—race, Vietnam, student and youth protest, and the best means of bringing about rapid social change. Women's liberation was also a critical divide for many. The conflicting positions of liberals and radicals became frozen and have remained hardened to this day.

Because Kennedy was viewed as a prototypical White liberal, criticism of this species of political being began to be heard more frequently in the early 1960s. A mistake that Third World activists and White radicals made was to generalize legitimate criticisms of Kennedy and other power holders to ordinary rank-and-file liberals. Rank-and-file liberals were still very much a part of the civil rights coalition during the first half of the 1960s.[2]

Rumblings of a liberal-radical break appeared after 1963, as "liberal bashing" was entering the political discourse. Murray Friedman wrote an article, published in 1964, with a prophetic title, "The White Liberal's Retreat." Friedman alleges that White liberals were great at supporting integration as long as the battleground remained in the South. But when the action moved North, and when their own schools, communities, and businesses were affected, their enthusiasm for racial justice weakened (also see Blauner, 1972; Fager, 1967; Levy, 1968).

There is certainly some truth to Friedman's charges. But the same criticisms applied to many radicals who put their personal interests before their commitments to racial justice. If liberals at this point were beginning to be turned off by the Black movement—earlier and in larger numbers than radicals would be later—it was largely because the rapidly developing trends in Black consciousness and movement strategies thoroughly challenged liberals' fundamental values. The hard edges of militant rhetoric, the undertones of violence, and the threat of violence were being justified by invoking Malcolm X's principle that Black people must achieve their freedom by any means necessary. At the same time, a new attitude was growing in the Black movement that targeted Whites generally and White liberals specifically as the enemy.

The assassination of President John F. Kennedy in November 1963 was a watershed event that would affect the entire decade that followed. Even with his limitations, Kennedy exemplified a youthful energy of hope and optimism. By mid-1963, he seemed to be becoming more committed to the Black cause. Kennedy's death served as the backdrop for the anger and alienation—especially among youth—that would mark political life in the late 1960s. The effect of the assassination cannot be overestimated.

But the radicalizing of Black civil rights activists that led to rejecting White radical and liberal support and to the demise of the radical-liberal coalition has another more specific source. We must remember that many White radical leaders gained their first social reform experiences during "Freedom Summer" in 1964, when they volunteered to help register Black voters in Mississippi. The predominantly Black Mississippi Freedom Democratic Party (MFDP) was formed that year as the only political party in the state that included Blacks and was based on "one man, one vote." The MFDP went to the Democratic National Convention in Atlantic City fully expecting to be seated as the official state body. But Kennedy's presidential successor, Lyndon B. Johnson, refused to select the MFDP over the all-White "official" state delegates because of his ties to conservative and "Dixiecrat" Southerners (all elected without Black representation). This betrayal was probably the single most important event that radicalized Black civil rights workers and their White allies during the eventful 1960s (McAdam, 1988).

Vice-President Hubert Humphrey, even more the prototypical White liberal than Kennedy, was the architect of a most unsatisfactory compromise offered to the MFDP. As a result, the image of the White liberal in the radical mind sank to a new low. Today, a number of movement veterans, notably Robert Moses, identify this event as precipitating the shift toward Black Power and Black Nationalism that would soon follow (Allen, 1969). Had the nation's top liberals not "sold out," had Johnson and Humphrey seated the MFDP, and had they directly challenged the Southern power structure, the Civil Rights Movement might have been incorporated into the nation's body politic today. Although other things contributed to militancy, much of the angry, "in your face" separatist rhetoric and style, which alienated the larger White population, might have been avoided.

Vietnam was the other great issue of the 1960s. For radicals, Vietnam was a quintessential liberal war, begun by Kennedy, escalated by Johnson, and run by a cabinet composed of the bulwarks of the Eastern liberal establishment: Robert McNamara, Dean Rusk, McGeorge Bundy, and William Bundy. So it is no surprise that it was primarily White radicals who first mobilized antiwar protest into a serious ongoing movement. An important oversight among radicals is that, within a few years, most rank-and-file liberals also opposed the war, including key members of the Johnson administration—even though this war was originally produced by liberal Democrats.

For many White youth in the 1960s, Vietnam was the key radicalizing experience. Despite the growth in the antiwar movement, many radicals were frustrated at their inability to stop the bloodshed. This led to increasingly aggressive tactics, such as breaking draft and public assembly laws, having violent confrontations with police, and harassing government officials (Wells, 1994). It was on this question of antiwar strategy that the liberals and radicals finally parted company. Liberals were repulsed by radical extremists, especially those who employed violent methods and were overtly supportive of North Vietnam. In their own opposition to the war, liberals did not want to sacrifice their commitments to due process, free speech and assembly, and civility. These were all values that were becoming more and more fragile during the turbulent 1960s and early 1970s.

Meanwhile, the most visible and vocal young civil rights protesters were continuing to move toward Black Nationalism, even separatism. Beginning in 1965, White members were dismissed from the SNCC and other militant organizations. In 1966, Stokely Carmichael's call for Black Power signaled the end of the civil rights focus of increasingly radical young Blacks, especially those whose focus was moving toward urban economic and political issues. Their new goal was to have Black people seek economic and political power on a group level and build autonomous communities of their own (Blair, 1977; Carmichael & Hamilton, 1967).

Most White supporters of civil rights were surprised and puzzled by these developments. Radical Whites did not like being told that they could no longer work with their Black comrades. They tried to understand the new situation; most, but not all, segments of the radical Left chose to support these new initiatives. White liberals could not. They were committed to interracial, rather than racially defined, organizations and the principle of integration. Central to the liberal tradition is a focus on the individual and the rights of individuals rather than on groups and group rights. Integration made sense to them because Blacks and other minorities were to assimilate as individuals rather than as members of an entire group. The call for Black Power turned off White liberals, as did the related tendency of African Americans (and later other Third World minorities) to form racially based caucuses within professional and other organizations.

Furthermore, Black Power and Black nationalism conflicted with the liberal vision of a colorblind society, where race should be irrelevant, ideally not even noticed, in daily life. Indeed, this liberal response may be faulted for seeing only the racial dimensions of the new Black consciousness movements and for minimizing the fact that Black nationalism was in large measure a claim for recognition of the ethnic realities of African Americans. In general, race appears more salient than ethnicity (Blauner, 1992). But at that time, few people of any political persuasion understood this.

Radicals, White and Black, also can be faulted for a hasty and arrogant dismissal of legitimate liberal concerns as "covert" or "objective racism." Just the opposite was the case. In many real-life contexts, a colorblind approach can be rightly criticized as unrealistic, even naive. But the ethic of colorblindness still stems from an outlook that is radically anti-racist in spirit. White liberals were not given sufficient credit for the integrity of their values. Instead, the very term *White liberal* was used with disdain by the mid-1970s.

White radicals need to do some soul searching to acknowledge how we have contributed to the isolation of White liberals from the anti-racist struggle by disparaging their values and underestimating their sincerity. White liberals have often been unfairly stereotyped as a unidimensional political type. Liberals have been viewed as White backlashers par excellence. The liberal backlash is seen by many, especially Black radicals, as nothing more than a polite cover for old-fashioned White racism. Liberals were prominent in the backlash against Black gains, but for the most part they left the Civil Rights Movement out of principled disagreement with its eventual racial, nationalist vision and physical and verbal violence. The response of the Left was to denigrate all opposition to Black militancy as derived from racism and Whites' unwillingness to give up racial privileges. It was only through listening carefully to some of the voices in my book, *Black Lives, White Lives* (1989), that I learned that Whites were also defending certain values that were meaningful to them and to the society as a whole.

Some Reflections

What lies behind the all or nothing approach? The answer is self-righteousness—the belief that we and only we have the correct political line. This position assumes that we know the truth that everyone else, sooner or later, must come to recognize. This righteousness is particularly disruptive in anti-racist politics, which requires a broad coalition of diverse constituencies and can only succeed if it is based on a pluralistic, polycentric tolerance of a wide variety of outlooks.

Most refreshing about the new Left of the 1960s was its new outlook and spontaneity, which manifested itself early on in a rejection of ideology. But its strong passion was also a weakness, making it easier for radicals to dismiss, even demonize, liberals for *their* relative lack of passion and "purity." The new Left was without the old Left's strengths, that penchant for long-term planning, as well as the latter's history of working with liberals that came from a commitment to and experience of building united fronts.

It is time to get rid of our righteousness, to see that the truth is multifaceted and complex, that all political positions, including our own, have blind spots, and that others can contribute important parts of the truth. Liberals and radicals might begin—if they have not already—the process of reevaluating the 1960s and 1970s to understand better what went wrong, how we are still locked in old positions, and what might be done about it.

I propose also to replace righteousness with a spirit of generosity, a willingness to credit and acknowledge the contributions of others, especially where they were right and we were wrong. We radicals, for example, deserve credit for our early, principled, and tenacious opposition to the Vietnam War. Liberals deserve more credit than we give them for their early recognition that there were dangers in Black Power and Black nationalism, and that angry anti-White rhetoric would have some negative long-term consequences.

This is not to suggest that mutual criticism should cease. I have already mentioned the difficulty that liberals have in recognizing the cultural distinctiveness of racial minorities. The motivation underlying this may often be benign: perhaps the desire to see non-Whites in terms of their universal human qualities or as American citizens. But such an attitude is too often accompanied by the belief that Blacks and other minorities lack rich histories, cultures, and values. This makes it easier for some liberals to dismiss ethnic studies classes as "feel-good" exercises devoid of serious academic content and to oppose multiculturalism in education automatically.

To bridge the gap, we need serious dialogue. Liberals and radicals rarely communicate today. Instead, we perceive each other through off-putting stereotypes. I applaud the efforts of Robert Pickus, a liberal critic of radicalism, who has organized dialogues and debates on multiculturalism through his project The Common Good. I would like to see radicals making similar overtures to liberals, setting up conferences and symposia for exchanges on contemporary problems and the history of the 1960s.

ON RACISM AND RACISTS:
THE NEED FOR NEW DIALOGUE

The term *racism* has its origins in the writings and speeches of Black intellectuals and the political Left, but it was hardly used in social science or American public life until the 1960s. The term does not appear, for example, in the classic work on race relations in the United States, Myrdal's *An American Dilemma* (1944). In the 1940s, the idea of racial inequity had much more limited connotations than today, referring to an ideology, an explicit system of beliefs postulating the superiority of Whites over non-Whites. During the 1950s and early 1960s, the ideological presumption of racial inferiority and superiority was discredited because it had been based largely on theories of biological inferiority. The focus shifted from systems of thought to a more individual approach to racially prejudiced attitudes and behavior. The model of prejudice and discrimination provided the language to name phenomena related to racial inequality and injustice. *Prejudice* referred to hostile feelings, beliefs, and stereotypes toward racial minorities. *Racial discrimination* referred to actions meant to harm members of another race.

By the mid-1960s, the terms *prejudice* and *discrimination* and the implicit causal relations between them were seen as too weak to explain the sweep of racial conflict and change, too limited in their analytical power, and, for some critics, too individualistic in their assumptions. These terms were heard less and less, as their original meanings tended to be absorbed by a new and more encompassing idea of racism. During the 1960s, the referents of racial oppression moved from individual actions and beliefs to group and institutional processes, from subjective ideas to objective structures or results. Instead of intent, there was now an emphasis on process: the more objective social processes of exclusion, exploitation, and discrimination that led to a racially stratified society.

As the idea of racism took hold, new and varied definitions of racism entered the political and racial lexicon, as if to guarantee that the entire landscape of social life and human affairs would be covered. First came *institutional racism,* introduced by Carmichael and Hamilton in *Black*

Power (1967), to highlight how racism is built into society, scarcely requiring prejudiced attitudes to be maintained. Of the new definitions, institutionalized racism has gained the most legitimacy, but other concepts less clearly named underscore even more how racism pervades institutions and social structures.

One of these other current racial concepts is *racism as atmosphere,* referring to the idea that an organization or an environment might be racist because its implicit, unconscious structures were devised for the exclusive use and comfort of White people. Such atmospheric racism explains why so many Blacks today say that the major feature of contemporary racism is its subtlety, in contrast to the explicit barriers that previously kept them outside organizations and institutions altogether. Perhaps the most radical definition of all is the concept, also unnamed, of *racism as result.* Here an institution or an occupation is racist simply because people of color are underrepresented in numbers or in positions of prestige and authority.

Thus, in the 1960s and especially in the 1970s, the words *racism* and *racist* entered into the nation's common parlance with a vengeance and transformed the way Americans talk about race relations—but not necessarily how we think about race.

The Left in the United States—and here I refer to radicals and progressives of all colors and to those intellectuals in and out of universities interested in anti-racism and multiculturalism—seized upon and developed the idea of racism into a master discourse. Racism became the chief weapon in the analysis of American race relations and in efforts to change a racially oppressive system. Now it is part of our general discourse as the politically correct way to talk about racial differences.

Much is positive about this. The discussion of racism has been part of massive public education about the history and present realities of racial oppression, an informal learning process that was initiated by the Civil Rights Movement. *Racism* as a term is much better than previous usages in cutting through obfuscation, especially the American tendency to deny, minimize, or trivialize the pervasive nature of racial oppression. The idea of racism works beautifully as a sensitizing concept, alerting us to the larger social and economic structures and institutional relationships that maintain a society still stratified by color, as well as alerting us to the more subtle interpersonal dynamics of relations across lines of race and color.

But powerful as the idea of racism is, the larger discourse has itself become obfuscating, as well as contentious and politically divisive. With the term being used so broadly to mean everything to everyone, people have absorbed only those meanings with which they feel comfortable.

Part of the culture wars is a contest between different groups as to which definition of racism will prevail in the larger society's meaning system. Because these differences are rarely spelled out, the battle over language takes place covertly, and in fact people talk about race past one another.

I first noticed how we talk past one another in classroom discussions, where Whites locate racism in color consciousness and its absence in colorblindness. In contrast, most Black, Latino, and Asian students see racism as a system of power. Thus it is fair to say that most (nonradical) Whites adhere to the old-fashioned and more limited meanings: racism as overt White supremacy, as prejudice, discrimination, or the imposition of the double standard in conduct and thought. People of color understand and accept those older meanings, but more and more—especially the younger college-educated generation—see racism as systematic, structural, and pervasive. The different ways that Blacks and Whites see racism underlies other gaps between the races. Blacks may see an act such as the Rodney King beating as "standard operating procedure," whereas for Whites it is an aberration. This difference partly explains why Blacks tend to be more negative about "racial progress" since the 1960s than Whites are.

The problem with inflation in the meanings of racism is that the concept loses practical utility as well as believability. If everything and every place is racist, we have no conceptual tools to distinguish what is important from what is not. We are lost in the confusion of multiple meanings. This leads to political pessimism, because if racism is everywhere, then effectively nothing can be done about it.

When college and university students talk about race these days, students of color tend to lead these discussions and Whites tend to be relatively quiet. In a sense, this is appropriate. Racial minorities have greater knowledge of the issues involved, both from their life experience and from studies. They are the experts, although many resent always having to "educate" White students. But a considerable part of the White silence comes from fear, the fear of saying the wrong thing and then being branded a racist. Thus, those Whites who do talk tend to express a safe Left-leaning line of thought.

This, of course, is politically correct (PC) language. Many on the Left typically dismiss the PC critique as a red herring, blown up by conservatives who for several years have been using PC as a screen to undermine their real targets: multiculturalism, affirmative action, and larger movements for diversity, inclusion, and social equality. I disassociate myself from such a view, but I have also found in my teaching that today's overheated racism discourse does inhibit openness and freedom of expression. Not only Whites but Asians, Latinos, and African Americans have privately expressed to me their frustrations in not being able to share serious reservations, deep feelings, and confusing personal experiences that they might have on the subject of race.

This is a serious matter. Freedom of expression is a basic, indispensable human value, one that supposedly defines American democracy. It is also absolutely essential for anti-racist education. If people cannot speak out, negative feelings and prejudices only harden. For people to gain the kind of personal growth and intellectual development out of which they come to understand and appreciate the experiences of racial others, we must have an atmosphere in which discussion of all views and experiences is possible.

I do not feel that the ambiguities and contradictions inherent in the idea of racism can be fully resolved. Racism by definition has to contain both the potential for divisiveness and the potential for reconciliation and healing. The discourse of racism challenges the basic character of the European American experience, forcing reevaluation of the historical meaning of being White in America. It implicates most European Americans in the history of colonialism and racial domination, even those whose families have not been in the country long. It therefore will inevitably bring forth resistance and anger. All this is part of the ambiguity and the dilemma we face, that the idea of racism and its larger discourse suggest that the nation has much unfinished business and that we all share a responsibility for the legacy of injustice and present-day inequalities.

In sum, the way we talk about racism more often reinforces the negative, divisive side rather than the positive possibilities for healing that an anti-racist movement must be centered around. People on the Left are often on a "racism alert," exhibiting a compulsive need to show how we have surmounted our own racism. The result is to highlight the racist tendencies of American people, lifestyles, and institutions, and to cut ourselves off from those ordinary Whites to whom racism does not seem pertinent to their everyday lives and who do not want to feel guilty about something over which they feel—rightly or wrongly—they have so little control. At the same time, radicals are neglecting the other pole, the possibilities for supporting and nurturing the inherent democratic anti-racist tendencies that most Americans, regardless of race, have within.

SOME SUGGESTIONS

Radicals have a responsibility in the area of discourse, because we played a major role in creating today's PC language. The discourse on race needs to be loosened and allowed to be more honest. I am not advocating license to use offensive group names and characterizations, but simply suggesting that we stop censoring the use of such common-place and commonsense terminology as racial prejudice, non-White, minority, and even Negro. Indeed, some White radicals today seem reluctant to use the word *Black,* feeling that only *African American* has the stamp of approval.[3] The Left's penchant to censor so many words, not just in race but throughout all dimensions of social difference, means that our speech and more of the nation's discourse have become unnatural and cumbersome.

The key term is *racism.* It is so entrenched in common speech that there is no way to eliminate its use or dethrone it from its central place, even if we wanted to. What I advocate instead is to push that word over to the side and make room for the occasional use of some older terms, especially when more precise and less inflammatory language will help begin and maintain dialogue.

Above all, we need to slow down, if not halt entirely, the tendency to call people racists when we do not like their views on racial issues. The escalating tendency of the past few decades to label people and positions racist has become counterproductive. When applied to individuals, the term should be limited to those who overtly advocate White supremacy or disseminate hate-filled characterizations of any racial or ethnic group. Otherwise, we need to give people the benefit of the doubt and assume that most of us are people of good will. Most Americans, whether they were born here or immigrated, inevitably absorb ideas, feelings, and assumptions about the superiority of White Westerners. We all harbor doubts at times about the equality of other races. In reality, we are all in a sense racist.

In addition to the racist in all of us, a resident belief in fairness and in our nation's historic commitment (at least in theory) to democracy exists. With such internal conflicts between racism and equality, the racial thinking of European Americans and people of color is inconsistent. I was continually struck in *Black Lives, White Lives* (Blauner, 1989) that the same person would in one breath utter a prejudiced, stereotyped platitude and in the next show a deep commitment to racial justice, a remarkable understanding of the racial politics of the day, or a profound belief in the fair and equal treatment of minority groups. Then would come another idea tinged with bias, distrust, or racial antagonism. Perhaps we need to find ways to encourage the democratic tendency rather than simply hammering away at hidden racist ones.

The issue of labeling particular policies and positions *racist* is more complex. It is important to be careful here, to think a situation through and analyze it before throwing around this double-edged term, which has such a potential to polarize. When charges of racism make sense because they strike a nerve, the ability to educate the public and force a constructive change in policy is also impressive. A recent example is Bertram Aristide's charge that U.S. policy toward Haiti was racist because immigrants who are Black were turned back whereas White Cuban immigrants were welcomed, despite fleeing Cuba for many of the same reasons Haitians were fleeing.

The trouble with the idea of racism is that it inevitably takes on a personal meaning, even when we try to use it impersonally to connote systems and structures of racial oppression, such as institutionalized racism. The popular mind does not understand the idea that racism refers to objective or structural realities, the meaning that social scientists and Third World activists tend to favor. For most ordinary people, especially European Americans, racism refers to feelings and attitudes and actions. I have tried to explain the larger idea of racism as an impersonal force to popular audiences without success. Many White college students have the same problem and immediately confuse objective with subjective racism. They feel they are being attacked personally as racists, even when that is not the intention.

Many African American intellectuals and militants have seized upon this objective-subjective distinction to argue that Black people cannot be racist because they lack the power to institute or uphold structures of domination. The assumption that Black people cannot be racist serves as a green light among some African Americans to legitimate the expression of crude stereotypes and hatreds of ethnic groups (most notably Jews), expressions that would be unacceptable if voiced by Whites. I do not think the Left should countenance such attitudes, or defend them. Black anti-Semitism is a form of racism and should be labeled as such.

THE ANTI-RACIST POTENTIAL OF WHITE PEOPLE

As I have suggested throughout this chapter, an anti-racist movement needs wide participation and support from the European American majority and cannot be successfully developed by people of color or radicals alone. The best strategy for gaining such wide support is to begin viewing

White people in terms of their strengths, that is, their possibilities for growth in consciousness and for the transcendence of racism. There have always been White Americans on the frontlines against racism. The anti-racist struggle has never been simply a Black against White event. Ignorance of this history and of the contemporary reality of principled White opposition to racism is essential to the belief that nothing can be done against racism (Aptheker, 1992).

I see two ways to approach this. The first is to emphasize the diversity of the European American population. Whites should not be viewed monolithically any more than Blacks or any other people are. When one looks at Whites in their particularity and diversity—rather than globally as "White people"—then one can see that White people in their distinct identities have many positive values. By building upon the strengths specific to a group's character and outlook, we can try to find ways to help its anti-racist possibilities blossom.

In the case of White liberals, I have tried to indicate the positive values in that group's outlook. These include an emphasis on individual rights, a commitment to integration and colorblindness, a strong moral sensitivity to the means of political action and the value of civility, and an abhorrence of violence. Like that of any group, the mentality of the liberal contains blind spots and limitations, some of which I have already alluded to. But for the purpose of nurturing anti-racist potential, the better strategy is to honor liberals' positive virtues, to take their contributions seriously, and to learn from them.

The radical Left as a politically conscious group has its virtues, having made immeasurable contributions to the struggle for racial justice. Because their political work is typically informed by social theory—Marxist or otherwise—radicals often see "the big picture" and are able to place racial phenomena in historical and international contexts. The radical penchant to see race as a structural rather than an individual matter has been illuminating, as well as the related insight that racial and ethnic conflicts need to be examined not only in their own right, but as part of larger systems of economic classes. In this context, the Left's critique of the culture of capitalism is important for anti-racist work, because the capitalist valuing of money, competition, and consumption helps keep racial and other hierarchies entrenched.

Jews are the White ethnic group with the most impressive history of commitment to racial equality. It has been estimated that 50% or more of the Whites who volunteered to work for civil rights in the South during the 1960s were Jewish Americans. This unique dedication stems from the group's identification as an oppressed minority and from a specific ethnic capacity to identify with "underdogs." Both of these traits have been encouraged and fortified by a religious tradition that strongly emphasizes social justice.

The much discussed Jewish-Black conflict stems from recent historical divisions and conflicts of interests, because many Jews occupy positions of authority and privilege that—in perception or reality—block the social and economic advance of African Americans. But part of the conflict is also psychological, in that the Jewish-Black alliance was too much of a big brother-little brother relationship, with all the paternalism, resentment, condescension, and envy inherent in such inequality. The key to welcoming greater numbers of Jews back into an anti-racist coalition is to acknowledge the special contributions that this ethnic and religious group has made to civil rights and social justice—in America and around the world—rather than to label it (or any other group) as particularly racist (Blauner, 1994).

Then there are "White ethnics"—a collective term that encompasses "hyphenated" Americans who immigrated to the United States from Europe in the past century. I will leave to others the task of discussing the anti-racist traditions of these groups, and instead say something about a related category that long has been seen as particularly bigoted, the White blue-collar worker. White blue-collar workers have derived such a reputation because of their visibility in attempting to keep Blacks out of "their" unions, jobs, and neighborhoods. Unlike middle-class Whites, they could not use class privilege to shield themselves from the tensions of racial change. They lived in the neighborhoods and attended the schools facing integration, and worked in the jobs where Blacks and other minorities could most easily enter the workforce. All this made the Archie Bunker stereotype plausible, but unjustifiable.

Blue-collar workers actually have been more "multicultural" than the rest of us for many decades. Working closely with people of color on the job, they get to know minorities on a more than superficial level. Because of their own class position, they are often able to identify with the experience of racial oppression. This ability to identify with Blacks is also historic (Cecil-Fronsman, 1992). Blue-collar Whites are also very job oriented and they judge people on how well they do their work. A strategy for nurturing the anti-racist potential of the White working class is to continue breaking down racial barriers in employment. White workers unlearn their racial stereotypes through equal-status contacts with people on the job. Like all working people, they need a thriving economy and full employment so that economic anxieties and class-based resentments are not channeled toward people of color.

Finally, a category with a particularly strong anti-racist potential is that of young people, including college students. Even though so much racial violence and bigotry has surfaced in the younger generation in recent decades, the anti-racist impulses among White youth and college students are very strong. White youth are like political liberals in their yearning for a colorblind society, and they have a strong desire to get to know people of all kinds. Youth are particularly open to new experiences and ways of seeing the world. They learn from these experiences as well as from books. Thus, it is important that White students at all levels be exposed to outstanding Black, Latino, Asian, and Native American instructors, as this in itself is a powerful education in anti-racism. It is essential that our classrooms provide a climate for free and open discussion about race and other sensitive topics.

The development of anti-racist consciousness in White people does not always require direct confrontation with racist beliefs, but is moved by any process that enhances self-knowledge and personal development. Thus, virtually all of today's personal growth, consciousness, self-help, and political movements can be viewed as allies in anti-racist work. Experiences sustained over time and supported by organizational involvement deepen awareness of the range of human feelings and expand consciousness. Whether the internal changes are political, emotional, spiritual, or some combination of the three, they enhance the potential for a greater understanding of racism. Personal racism is based on fear. Not simply fear of the unknown racial other, but fear also of our own unacceptable feelings and inner complexities.

An example of the type of movement I have in mind would be any of the ubiquitous 12-step or other recovery movements. The strength of such movements is that they are truly popular and cut across race and class. Directly multiracial experiences are especially valuable for enlarging the human capacity to identify across racial boundaries.

Countless examples could be cited of White people's capacity to "unlearn" racism from life experience simply as part of the process of becoming more fully human. Terkel (1992) presents many such cases in *Race*. One of the more dramatic stories is that of C. P. Ellis, a former Klan official, who developed a friendship with a Black female political opponent that in time undermined the entire structure of his beliefs. There have been several reports of young White Power activists "seeing the light" and converting to the cause of anti-racism. Lee Mun Wah's documentary film, *The Color of Fear,* depicts the case of David, a White fortyish Californian, whose prototypical liberal-conservative viewpoint on race seems invulnerable through most of a weekend of dialogue between men of different races. Despite all his defenses and rationalizations, the stories and feelings of the other men finally get to him. Central to his dramatic transformation is a new ability to listen to the experiences and the pain of men of color. In so doing, the racial other becomes like himself, a fellow human being. Something similar often happens with White college students when they see a documentary such as *Eyes on the Prize* and for the first time begin to understand the historical legacy of racism.

Finally, many White radicals and Third World theorists question the anti-racist potential of European Americans, stressing that "White skin privileges" give us an objective interest, a real stake in the continuance of the present system. Almost everyone has some interest in the status quo, if only because we have made some modicum of peace with it. And without doubt, White skin continues to provide many advantages. But Whites have an even greater interest in a just society. Given the average person's declining level of economic and social security and relative lack of real power, it is hard to argue that these White privileges can compare in importance with all the pain and loss everyone suffers from living in a society so divided, so lacking in real community, and so rent with underlying hatreds. These losses are political, moral, and spiritual and they are directly related to race. The potential for Whites to change exists and must be recognized and worked with. We have no other alternative to reverse the course of racial inequality in the United States and to form the coalitions that will be necessary to change the political and economic direction of this country.

POSTSCRIPT

In this chapter, I focused exclusively on the relationships between liberals and radicals in the United States. Those concerned with building transracial coalitions need to investigate the historic backgrounds of White liberal-radical coalitions in the world community as well as in the United States. Is the present liberal-radical split historically unprecedented, or was the 1960s' working coalition between White liberals and radicals against racism unprecedented and in need of explanation? Is the need for a liberal-radical relationship to progress in race relations unique to the United States, or does this same dynamic exist in other racially charged nations such as France, Germany, the United Kingdom, South Africa, or Brazil? It is the task of anti-racism scholars and activists alike to answer these questions.

NOTES

1. It also depends on whose perceptions we are talking about. Many Right-wing Republicans, as well as many in the general public, see liberals as far out and radical, lumping together the two segments of the Left. In the media today, liberal encompasses the entire range of Left politics. The word *radical* is rarely heard, as if this political species became extinct when the movements of the 1960s died out. Even radicals contribute to the blurring of the liberal-radical distinction in the public mind when they refer to political groupings as "liberals and progressives" in an attempt to court respectability. Perhaps the idea of liberal and radical became so blurred because conservative Republicans (above all, Ronald Reagan) were successful in portraying the liberal wing of the Democratic Party as far-out radicals who destroyed America's economy by giving us the welfare state and weakened our culture by encouraging the ethos of permissiveness and the victim mentality.

2. Rank-and-file liberals probably made up the bulk of the Whites who thronged to the 1963 March on Washington. Many liberal White college students volunteered for the Mississippi Freedom Summer in 1964, only to return North as newly radicalized (McAdam, 1988).

3. There is a certain compulsiveness in the tendency of White progressives to utilize the term *African American* all the time, even though Black Americans continue to use Black just as frequently. I would continue to honor, when appropriate historically, the word *Negro,* but draw the line at *colored* because it retains some offensive connotations. Having said that, I want to point out that "ordinary" White Americans have a lot of trouble understanding why, if *people of color* is so clearly the term of choice today, the term *colored people* is considered so objectionable.

REFERENCES

Allen, R. (1969). *Black awakening in capitalist America.* Garden City, NY: Doubleday.

Aptheker, H. (1992). *Anti-racism in U.S. history: The first two hundred years.* Westport, CT: Praeger.

Blair, T. (1977). *Retreat to the ghetto: The end of a dream?* London: Wildwood House.

Blauner, B. (1972). Race and the White professor. In B. Blauner (Ed.), *Racial oppression in America* (pp. 256-287). New York: Harper & Row.

Blauner, B. (1989). *Black lives, White lives: Three decades of race relations in America.* Berkeley: University of California Press.

Blauner, B. (1992). Talking past one another: Black and White languages of race. *The American Prospect, 10,* 55-64.

Blauner, B. (1994). That Black-Jewish thing: What's going on? *Tikkun, 9*(5), 27-32, 103.

Carmichael, S., & Hamilton, C. (1967). *Black power: The politics of liberation in America.* New York: Vintage.

Cecil-Fronsman, B. (1992). *Common Whites: Class and culture in antebellum North Carolina.* Lexington: University Press of Kentucky.

Fager, C. (1967). *White reflections on Black power.* Grand Rapids, MI: Eerdmans.

Friedman, M. (1964). The White liberal's retreat. In A. Westin (Ed.), *Freedom now* (pp. 320-328). New York: Basic Books.

Glazer, N. (1975). *Affirmative discrimination: Ethnic inequality and public policy.* New York: Basic Books.

Golden, H. (1964). *Mr. Kennedy and the Negroes.* Cleveland, OH: World Publications.

Kaufman, J. (1988). *Broken alliance: The turbulent times between Blacks and Jews in America.* New York: Scribner.

Levy, C. (1968). *Voluntary servitude.* New York: Appleton.

McAdam, D. (1988). *Freedom Summer.* New York: Oxford University Press.

Myrdal, G. (1944). *An American dilemma.* New York: Harper.

Terkel, S. (1992). *Race: How Blacks and Whites think and feel about the American obsession.* New York: New Press.

Wah, L. M. (Director and Producer). (1994). *The Color of Fear* [Film]. Oakland, CA: Stir Fried Productions.

Wells, T. (1994). *The war within: America's battle over Vietnam.* Berkeley: University of California Press.

7

Changing the Subject:
Race and Gender in Feminist Discourse

Karen Dugger

Several scholars have noted the integral relationship between theory, political practice, and organizing (Anzaldua, 1990b; Hewitt, 1992; Hill Collins, 1990; Knowles & Mercer, 1992; Mohanty, 1991). As a discursive practice, theory has the power to change the way individuals view their lives, their identity, and their interests, as well as the lives, interests, and identity of others. It has the power to create and mobilize political constituencies and to set the priorities around which these constituencies struggle. Thus, the theories we construct to illuminate the dynamics of social divisions organized around race and gender have political effects that can abet or disable anti-racist and feminist struggles. In this chapter, I review universalistic, intersections, and postmodern modes of feminist theorizing in terms of how each construes its theoretical subject. I examine the political implications of these analytical constructions of the subject of feminism in terms of the promise each holds for creating solidarity among members of the constituency it seeks to build, and the possibility of forging strategic coalitions across race, gender, and national boundaries that each sustains.

Many analyses of race and gender assume that individuals and groups possess coherent and stable identities and sets of interests grounded in some notion of concrete unmediated experience. Such analyses not only inhibit coalition politics but also generate internal divisions and conflicts within the very ranks of those whom such analyses mean to unify. The universalism that characterizes much of feminist theorizing has relied upon such a concept of collective and individual identity. The intersection and postmodern modes of feminist theory mark, in different ways, a break with this tradition and hence are more promising in terms of the politics they sustain.

UNIVERSALISTIC
FEMINIST THEORY

Although universalistic modes of feminist discourse are characterized by a multiplicity of perspectives, substantive focuses, and political concerns, underlying this variety is a common conceptualization of the subject of feminism. This subject is *gender* or, more specifically, woman as she is constituted in oppositional relationship to man. This definition of the subject of feminism, what Alarcon (1990) terms "an oppositional theory of the subject," understands womanhood and women's identity, subjectivity, social roles, and status as constructed solely in terms of relationships between men and women. Gender, defined in terms of the binary opposition man/woman, assumes women are subject to similar dynamics of gender subordination and consequently share similar interests and goals that transcend race, class, and national boundaries.

The exclusion of the lives, interests, and political priorities of women of color in both Western and non-Western societies ensues from this singular focus on gender differences (Alarcon, 1990; Amos & Parmar, 1984; Anzaldua, 1990b; Burnham, 1985; Carby, 1982; Chow, 1987; Garcia, 1990; Mohanty, 1991; Spelman, 1988). Feminist analyses of gender and gender hierarchy, which rely on the man/woman dualism, fail to recognize how race and nation differentially position European American women and women of color (as well as European American men and men of color) within a sex/gender system. Consequently, features of gender dynamics unique to socially dominant women who are White, Western, and middle/upper class are falsely generalized to others, further reinforcing their own privileged position while inhibiting theorizing about this privilege.

Concepts such as mothering, family, reproduction, patriarchy, and the assumption of universal female dependency and confinement to the domestic sphere have been employed by European American feminists in search of a singular gender dynamic that could explain women's subordination across time and cultures. Women of color have demonstrated how these concepts fail to recognize the specificities of their lives, resulting in the normative privileging of the political priorities of European American feminists and the patronizing dismissal of their own goals and objectives. In this chapter, I provide some illustrations of how these concepts have marginalized women of color and discuss the political effects of this marginalization.

The public/private sphere dualism informs much of the conceptual apparatus of universalistic analyses. Within this dualism, women's subordination and identity are construed as a product of their relegation to the private sphere of reproductive activities and their relative exclusion from the larger sphere of public/productive activities. The *ideology of separate spheres* defines women as too frail and dainty to undertake physical labor, as the chaste guardians of societal morality and the moral development of children, thereby valorizing women's roles as wives and mothers. The role that race and nation play in the social construction of womanhood and women's subordination in this dynamic is ignored completely.

Unlike White womanhood, Black womanhood was constructed not in terms of familial and domestic activities, but through Black women's role as laborer in slave, colonial, and market economies, and through their roles as domestics and surrogate mothers to White families (Carby, 1982; Dill, 1992; Higginbotham, 1992; Hurtado, 1989). As Higginbotham (1986) notes, Black women were never on a pedestal, as White women were. In dominant cultural discourse, they were viewed as "beasts of burden" and sexually licentious. They were excluded from the category of lady and not afforded the protection from sexual assault that the ideology of separate spheres granted White women (Higginbotham, 1992; Hurtado, 1989).

Nor was Black women's role as mother honored or protected. In contrast, the separate spheres ideology, though denying White women rights and privileges and limiting their potential for growth, does recognize, protect, and value their roles as mothers and wives. For Black women, however, existing laws and conditions of labor disrupted and undermined family life, reinforced their subordinate status, and constituted yet another assault on their humanness (Dill, 1992, p. 234). Thus, Black women carried out their roles as mothers under cultural and economic circumstances dramatically different from those of White women. These circumstances continue to undermine family stability and to reproduce images of Black women as mammies, matriarchs, and welfare queens—images not addressed or challenged in White feminist analyses of motherhood (Hill Collins, 1990). The failure to recognize the influence of racism on family life is also decried by women of color in Britain, who criticize White feminists for giving priority to practices such as arranged marriages and purdah within communities of color, while ignoring racist immigration practices that continue to separate families (Bourne, 1983).

For all women viewed through the framework of the public/private sphere dichotomy, the family becomes a major site of women's oppression, and their subsequent participation in wage labor becomes a liberating development. Although not denying that the family can serve as a source of oppression, women of color in both the United States and Britain contend that the family also serves as a place of refuge from and resistance to the racism of the larger society. The assumption of a traditional nuclear family in which women experience dependency also ignores the specificity of the position of women of color in regard to family structure. Many women of color, because they are single heads of households or because of their role as economic providers, are not in the same relationship of financial dependency on men as European American middle/upper class women (Carby, 1982; Dill, 1983; Hill Collins, 1990; hooks, 1990; Simons 1979). Hence, for women of color the demand for inclusion in the paid labor force did not have the same resonance as it did for White women. Denied protection and the cultural validation of their roles as wives and mothers and relegated to exploitative low-wage jobs, many women of color found domestic labor, in contrast to market work, more affirming of their humanity, and saw the role of housewife as a privilege and luxury (Dill, 1983; hooks, 1981; Lewis, 1977; Simons, 1979; White, 1984).

Similarly, Third World feminists have questioned the assumption that women's subordinate status is due to their lack of participation in the public sphere. Such an assumption fails to recognize the impoverished condition of the public sphere in dependent economies. For example, Mueller (1977) demonstrates that men's greater involvement in the public sphere of Lesotho was inconsequential in terms of power relations between men and women because the public sphere, controlled by White South Africans, was devoid of valued resources. Pala (1977) wonders whether African men or women suffer more from global processes of economic exploitation than from local traditions. The more relevant question, Pala contends, is how neo-colonial economic processes operate to subordinate both Third World women and men in the public and private spheres.

When race and nation are incorporated into the understanding of gender dynamics, the Western notion of an absolute patriarchy becomes problematic. By defining all men as oppressors and all women as victims, the concept of patriarchy obscures the position of men of color in gender hierarchies outside of European American middle-class social structures. By treating men as an undifferentiated category, the concept of patriarchy ignores the fact that men of color have been marginalized in the public sphere and consequently do not command the same kind of power or exercise the same control over resources that most European American men do. The concept of patriarchy also negates the racial and national oppression women and men of color have in common, thus rendering incomprehensible the bond between them and the interests they share (Carby, 1982; hooks, 1990; Lewis, 1977; Simons, 1979). By ignoring the intersection of race and nation with gender, the concept of an absolute patriarchy obliterates differences among social groups, thereby privileging gender over all other forms of social division.

UNIVERSALISM AND THE RELATIONSHIP BETWEEN RACE AND GENDER

The binary logic of the man/woman opposition limits the possibilities for understanding the relationships between race and gender. It does so by describing the effect of racism on the lives of women of color as constituting an additional burden. This is the additive model. Racism and sexism are conceived of as discrete phenomena and separable systems of power, whose effects are independent of one another (King, 1988; Simons, 1979; Smith & Stewart, 1983; Spelman, 1988). This understanding of the relationship between race and gender leaves intact the theoretical subject of feminism—gender—and in so doing demands no recasting of the central concepts of feminist theory or the political priorities derived from them.

By treating race and gender as discrete phenomena, the additive approach makes possible the assumption that a unique set of interests and concerns common to all women exists that warrants the label *women's issues*. These issues are then treated as separable or distinct from race issues, with the latter viewed as falling outside the province of the political objectives of feminism. Defining women's issues in this manner creates enormous divisions and conflicts within the women's movement that have severely damaged opportunities for building strategic coalitions across race and national boundaries. Concomitantly, it creates a theoretical opening within which national liberation, feminist, and anti-racist struggles can be pitted against each other.

POLITICAL CONSEQUENCES OF UNIVERSALISTIC FEMINIST THEORY

These political consequences of the man/woman binary opposition were in evidence everywhere during the first two United Nation Conferences on Women, held in 1975 in Mexico and in 1980 in Copenhagen. Western women who attended these conferences and the concurrent nongovernmental organization (NGO) meetings came with priorities derived from and limited by an exclusive focus on gender relations between men and women. Representations of Third World women by European American feminists were constructed by adding the man/woman dualism to the Western/non-Western dualism to produce what Mohanty (1991) terms the *Third World difference.* This difference presents a homogeneous portrait of Third World women as uneducated, tradition bound, less feminist, and more exploited and degraded than their Western counterparts, and hence in need of Western tutelage. Universalistic feminists were unable to see the class, regional, and cultural differences among Third World women, as well as the roles that racism, imperialism, and global economic processes play in their subordination (Mohanty, 1991; Ong, 1988). Consequently, European American women defined the struggle for gender equality in the Third World in terms of challenges to such gendered practices as clitoridectomies, seclusion, dowries, polygamy, and veiling.

When Third World women prioritized the influence of multinational corporations, racism, poverty, apartheid, dictatorship, and foreign domination on their lives, they were charged with being nonfeminists, of splitting the sisterhood, and of injecting politics into the conferences by subordinating their interests as women to the political concerns and priorities of their men (El Sadaawi, 1980). These two conferences were marred and coalition building was thwarted by damaging and demoralizing debates over what constituted a greater barrier to women's liberation—racism, sexism, economic exploitation, or Western imperialism. Because struggles for national independence and economic justice and struggles against sexism and racism were each conceived of as separate phenomena, a competitive struggle for legitimacy ensued.

The Anita Hill-Clarence Thomas controversy further dramatizes the disabling political consequences of the either/or framework that characterizes feminist and anti-racist discourse. The dualisms upon which these discourses rest allowed the Hill-Thomas hearings to be cast as a contest between racism and sexism. Much anti-racist discourse, like feminist discourse, is based on a binary opposition (Black/White) that does not recognize the social location of Black women. Most narratives of racist oppression and struggles for racial justice have been grounded in the experiences of Black men (Giddings, 1984; hooks, 1981, 1992; White, 1984, 1990). This equation of "blackness" with the particularistic experiences of Black men invested Thomas with racial authenticity, allowing him to become a representative of "the race" and, through his deployment of a lynching metaphor, to define the situation as an instance of racial harassment.

Existing at the unarticulated intersection of race and gender, Hill, on the other hand, "had no comparable tradition of a stereotype that had been recognized, analyzed, and subverted to draw upon" (Painter, 1992, p. 209). She eschewed the only roles available to her—mammy, matriarch, welfare queen, and Jezebel. Because "Hill chose not to make herself into a symbol America could recognize," writes Painter, "she seemed to disappear" (p. 210). She became visible only as a victim of sexual harassment, which, because of the way gender domination has been articulated, deraced Hill and constructed her as a generic (White) woman.

The discourses of race and gender have existed in relative isolation from one another. Consequently, claims emanating from each take on a mutually exclusive character. Such polarization of the categories Blacks and women inevitably facilitate polarized politics, in which demands for race and gender justice compete. As Crenshaw (1992) so poignantly argues, "When feminism does not explicitly oppose racism, and when anti-racism does not incorporate opposition to patriarchy, race and gender politics end up being antagonistic to each other and both interests lose" (p. 405).

THE INTERSECTION PARADIGM

Finding their history, identity, and interests devalued and marginalized in a variety of discourses, each of which vies for their allegiance and makes mutually exclusive claims on their identity, women of color have articulated a novel alternative paradigm. This paradigm decenters the oppositional subject of universalistic modes of theorizing. It contests the privileging of gender in feminist discourse and of race in anti-racist discourse by positing a plurality of overlapping and interconnected systems of domination. Here difference is conceptualized not in terms of polarities (Black/White, Western/non-Western, man/woman), but in terms of pluralities. Multiple meanings of race and gender are understood as being produced through a variety of both contradictory and mutually reinforcing discourses, practices, and social structures.

Although accepting that sexism oppresses all women and racism oppresses all people of color, the intersection model recognizes that the mechanisms through which this occurs are race and gender specific (Cole, 1986). For example, Hurtado (1989) discusses how the strategies of gender domination vary in accordance with women's relational position to White men. White women, who are destined to be the wives, lovers, mothers, or daughters of White men, are subordinated through seduction. On the other hand, women of color, who lack intimate or familial ties to White men, are subjugated through rejection. Similarly, whereas the separate spheres (public versus private) ideology legitimates the subordination of White women, the subordination of women of color is effected through a different though interrelated ideological apparatus. This was done through what Hill Collins (1990) terms the *controlling images* of mammy, matriarch, welfare mother, and Jezebel. Her analysis of these controlling images reveals the intersecting and mutually reinforcing nature of systems of race, class, and gender domination. Through the image of matriarch, Black women are portrayed as the source of Black economic subordination. This image then rationalizes racism. Its message is that if women only carried out their traditional roles, family stability and economic success would be guaranteed. This image and message support gender subordination. Similarly, the image of the welfare mother obscures the structural causes of poverty and justifies the control of Black female sexuality.

Understanding race, class, and gender as interlocking systems means that one is not simply a victim or an oppressor. Located at the intersection of a plurality of systems of domination, individuals and groups can be, and are, simultaneously both privileged and oppressed (Cole, 1986; Dill 1992; Hill Collins, 1990; hooks, 1989; Hurtado, 1989; Lorde, 1984; Moraga, 1983; White, 1990). Hence, identities, worldviews, and interests are multifaceted. By positing the coexistence of multiple and contradictory systems of oppression and privilege, the intersection model unsettles the notion that discrete and separable identities are based on the fixed divisions of race, class, and gender.

The multiple and contradictory locations any individual occupies, the situatedness and instability of any commonalties and differences we claim with others, are insightfully attested to by Jordon (1992). While on vacation in the Bahamas, she reflects on her own class privilege and the nexus of relationships that define her. She asks,

> who can doubt the ease, the sisterhood between that White girl and the Black women selling straw bags on the streets of paradise . . . is it not obvious that the wife of the Talmudic scholar and "Olive" (the Black woman), who cleans my room here at the hotel, have more in common than I can claim with either of them? (p. 30)

The political implications of the intersection paradigm are multiple. Recognizing that differences are inscribed in power relations, the intersection model renders these relations complex and contradictory, defying the idea that oppressions can be hierarchically ranked with any one notion (class, race, or gender) commanding greater political urgency or legitimacy than another. The political urgency or priority of any issue becomes contingent upon the particular sociopolitical context and phenomena under consideration, and is not decided *a priori* on the basis of abstract theoretical claims. Moreover, the understanding of the relationship between race and gender offered by the intersection paradigm refuses interpretations of events as singularly either a woman's issue or a race issue. This leads to a more inclusive politic that concurrently opposes multiple systems of domination. Finally, this approach opens an array of possibilities for coalitions by fragmenting the concept of identity, refusing totalizing claims that individuals and groups are either victims or oppressors. The intersection paradigm, however, does not preclude the tendency of "othering" fostered by conceptions of difference that rest on binary oppositions.

The weakness of the intersection paradigm is that it is not sufficiently critical of the concept of experience, but tends to rely upon a standpoint epistemology wherein knowledge, identity, and subjectivity are understood as given by material reality, that is, by one's concrete daily experiences (Hartsock, 1983). A reliance on standpoint epistemology threatens to reinscribe essentialist notions of identity and difference, to conceive of differences and identity as fixed and relatively impermeable or bounded. In other words, theories of gender grounded in a standpoint epistemology generate rigid and mutually exclusive subcategories of women, each demarcated by its particular location in the matrix of race, class, and gender relationships. The members of each subcategory are seen as sharing unique common experiences that give rise to claims and world-views inaccessible to the other subcategories. When scholars who work within the intersection paradigm assert some unique or singular stand-point grounded in a common experience (e.g., an Afrocentric, Latina, lesbian, or Asian feminist perspective), potential diversity is obscured.

Although giving voice to difference, the intersection paradigm still holds out the potential of suppressing it. When experience is conceived of as the source of knowledge, the perceptions and understandings of those deemed outside such experience are ipso facto excluded and de-moted to a lesser or subsidiary status. When experience authorizes or legitimates one's claims to the "truth" or to an "authentic" national, ethnic, racial, or gender identity, those who articulate differences become suspect and the authenticity of their identity is questioned.

Political unities constituted on some proclaimed commonality of expe-rience tend to become fragmented and disabled by conflict, because such "communality" can only rest on gaps and silences, repression of self, and exclusion of others. This is true regardless of the size or scale of the common group and regardless of whether the constructed political com-munity is women, women of color, Chicana women, or whatever. Harris and Ordona (1990) recount the factionalism that results from an inability to accept differences within communities of women of color. They write, "our definitions of unity mean sameness—same feelings, thoughts, ideas and behaviors" (p. 314). Similarly, Anzaldua (1990a) describes how othering, isolating and ostracizing those who fail to pass the ethnic legitimacy test, has divided the Chicana community. She contends that the possibility for unity demands that "we leave the boundaries of a fixed self" (p. 145).

POSTMODERN FEMINISM

Recently, some feminists have begun to explore the utility of postmod-ern thought for feminist theory and practice (Fraser, 1989; Fuss, 1989; Nicholson, 1990; Weedon, 1987). Particularly attractive is the postmod-ern emphasis on the constitutive role of discourse, because it disables "essentialist" notions of identity and difference. For postmodern femi-nism, discourse, not experience, constructs identities, worldviews, and political perspectives. Postmodern feminism accepts Althusser's (1971) understanding that experience, the concrete events of our daily lives and the contexts in which these occur, is never raw or transparent but always mediated by ideology. Ideology or discourse is the site where meaning is produced. Different discourses offer individuals a variety of modes of subjectivity, a variety of subject positions or ways of thinking, feeling, and being in the world. These discourses reflect and legitimate particular social relations, though they vary in their range and power depending on the political strengths of the interests they embody (Weedon, 1987). No discourse is, however, absolute. Nor are subjects passive in their discursive construction. Discourses contain gaps, silences, and ambiguities; spaces that provide for resistance and innovation, spaces in which dominant discourses can be challenged, innovations can be made, and a new discourse can be crafted (Weedon, 1987).

Given the existence of a plurality of discourses that compete for our identity and allegiance, knowledge or truth can never be guaranteed by experience, for experience is subject to competing and contradictory interpretations. Women experience their gender, as do people of color their race, in a variety of ways. Whether an experience, issue, or event is an instance of racism or sexism is a matter of political education, a matter of the subject position one assumes. As racism and sexism are political constructs, opposition to them comes not from experience, but from the adoption of a subject position within a particular discourse.

The understanding of identity and difference offered by postmodern feminism is one where neither identity nor difference is fixed, stable, or bounded. Both dimensions are constantly in process. In fact, there is an ongoing commerce between the current subject position assumed by individuals and positions being offered by alternative discourses to which individuals are constantly exposed. By recognizing the permeability and hybrid nature of identity, this understanding of subjectivity disallows any claim to authenticity. As Minh-ha (1989) writes,

> Whether I accept it or not, the natures of *I, i, you, s/he, We, we, they,* and *wo/man* constantly overlap. They all display a necessary ambivalence, for the line dividing *I* and *Not-I, us* and *them, him* and *her* is not, (cannot) always (be) as clear as we would like it to be. Despite our desperate, eternal attempt to separate, contain, and mend, categories always leak. Of all the layers that form the open (never finite) totality of "I," which is to be called pure, true, real, genuine, original, authentic? Which indeed, since all interchange, revolving in an endless process. (p. 94)

The conception of difference put forth by postmodern feminists is one where differences are always in process, where differences between and within entities are understood as a "multiple presence" (Minh-ha, 1989), and are constantly crossing and recrossing erected boundaries. This post-modern conception of difference contrasts with the idea of difference as the product of the unique experiences of subcategories of individuals, where individuals are assumed to possess a shared identity and conscious-ness by virtue of being situated in a particular position in the matrix of race, class, gender, and national hierarchies. Although constructing indi-vidual and collective identities as multifaceted assemblages, the intersec-tion model nonetheless reduces difference to a commonality that can be decisively demarcated from other assemblages of difference. This results in preserving, though in a new form, an oppositional theory of the subject.

IMPLICATIONS OF CONCEPTIONS OF DIFFERENCE FOR AN ANTI-RACIST FEMINIST POLITICS

How we conceptualize difference and identity has political conse-quences. Conceptualizing difference in terms of binary oppositions creates a space wherein various liberation struggles compete for pri-macy, where feminist, nationalist, and anti-racist politics are pitted against each other. On the other hand, understanding difference as the product of the unique experiences of identifiable subgroups, no matter how complex and contradictory such experiences may be, can lead to a suppres-sion of difference, thereby creating conflict and division within political communities.

A theory of gender domination that incorporates the insights of the intersection paradigm with a postmodern feminist understanding of iden-tity and difference appears to be more capable of sustaining unity within political constituencies, as well as fostering coalitions among them. A politics informed by an understanding of the subject as heterogeneous, incoherent, unstable, and porous has more difficulty constructing an official "other." It makes difficult the glorification or the demonization of particular identities, and instead allows us to choose among competing accounts of reality on the basis of their social implications. The ground of dialogue and debate shifts from discussions of whose experiences or claims to gender or racial authenticity are more real or legitimate to a discussion of what discourses are in play and the likely social and political implications of each. It is a politics that acknowledges that unity does not rest on mutual identification or demand that we recognize ourselves in others to admit them to the community (Young, 1990). Political constituencies are built on the basis of where one stands, what subject position one occupies, not on the basis of biogenetic categories or some putative commonality of experience. Potentially, all persons regardless of race, gender, or nationality could be allies in feminist, anti-racist, and national liberation struggles.

This is not to say, however, that the role of all participants in a coalition is the same. As groups, Blacks are the targets of racist practices and women the targets of sexist practices. Consequently, through political education, each has better access to understanding the effects and dynamics of racism and sexism, respectively, than those not subject to such practices. Hence, each is in a better position to lead initiatives against them. In other words, members of a coalition occupy varied subject positions that allow for differential apprehension of the gaps and silences, in particular discourses, and specific sociopolitical dynamics. Thus, in any coalition the role of all participants has its own particularity.

Some worry that a decentered subject is an unstable ground upon which to base politics (Benhabib, 1990; Bordo, 1990; Harding, 1990; Hartsock, 1990). Certainly, the history of the women's movement and Black resistance struggles demonstrates that grounding politics in a putatively common experience does not guarantee the internal stability of political constituencies or facilitate coalitions. This is not to deny the serious inroads anti-racist and feminist discourses have made into hegemonic racist and sexist ideology, or the efficacy of such discourses in mobilizing significant opposition to racist and sexist policies. Yet the gaps and silences in these discourses, and the differences they leave unarticulated, cultivate political fractiousness and provide the space wherein potential allies can be cast as enemies. Thus, the risk of a decentered subject is less hazardous than the "risk of essence" in building a more sustainable anti-racist feminist politics.

REFERENCES

Alarcon, N. (1990). The theoretical subject(s) of this bridge called my back and Anglo-American feminism. In G. Anzaldua (Ed.), *Making face, making soul/haciendo caras: Creative critical perspectives by women of color* (pp. 356-369). San Francisco: Aunt Lute Books.

Althusser, L. (1971). *Lenin and philosophy.* New York: Monthly Review Press.

Amos, V., & Parmar, P. (1984). Challenging imperial feminism. *Feminist Review, 17,* 3-19.

Anzaldua, G. (1990a). En rapport, in opposition: Combrado cuentas a las nuestras. In
   G. Anzaldua (Ed.), *Making face, making soul/haciendo caras: Creative and critical
   perspectives by women of color* (pp. 142-148). San Francisco: Aunt Lute Books.
Anzaldua, G. (1990b). Haciendo caras, una entranda: An introduction. In G. Anzaldua
   (Ed.), *Making face, making soul/haciendo caras: Creative and critical perspectives
   by women of color* (pp. xv-xxviii). San Francisco: Aunt Lute Books.
Benhabib, S. (1990). Epistemologies of postmodernism: A rejoinder to Jean-François
   Lyotard. In L. J. Nicholson (Ed.), *Feminism/postmodernism* (pp. 107-130). New
   York: Routledge.
Bordo, S. (1990). Feminism, postmodernism, and gender skepticism. In L. J. Nicholson
   (Ed.), *Feminism/postmodernism* (pp. 133-156). New York: Routledge.
Bourne, J. (1983). Toward an anti-racist feminism. *Race and Class, 25*(1), 1-21.
Burnham, L. (1985). Has poverty been feminized in Black America? *The Black Scholar,
   16*(2), 14-24.
Carby, H. V. (1982). White women listen! Black feminism and the boundaries of sister-
   hood. In Centre for Contemporary Cultural Studies (Ed.), *The empire strikes back:
   Race and racism in 70's Britain* (pp. 212-235). London: Hutchinson.
Chow, E. (1987). The development of feminist consciousness among Asian American
   women. *Gender & Society, 1,* 284-299.
Cole, J. B. (1986). Commonalities and differences. In J. B. Cole (Ed.), *All-American
   women: Lines that divide, ties that bind* (pp. 1-30). New York: Free Press.
Crenshaw, K. (1992). Whose story is it anyway? Feminist and antiracist appropriations
   of Anita Hill. In T. Morrison (Ed.), *Race-ing justice, en-gendering power: Essays
   on Anita Hill, Clarence Thomas, and the construction of social reality* (pp. 402-
   440). New York: Pantheon.
Dill, B. T. (1983). Race, class, and gender: Prospects for an all-inclusive sisterhood.
   Feminist Studies, 9(1), 131-150.
Dill, B. T. (1992). Our mothers' grief: Racial ethnic women and the maintenance of
   families. In M. L. Andersen & P. H. Collins (Eds.), *Race, class, and gender: An
   anthology* (pp. 215-238). Belmont, CA: Wadsworth.
El Sadaawi, N. (1980). Arab women and Western feminism: An interview with Nawal El
   Sadaawi. *Race and Class, 22*(2), 175-182.
Fraser, N. (1989). *Unruly practices: Power, discourse, and gender in contemporary social
   theory.* Minneapolis: University of Minnesota Press.
Fuss, D. (1989). *Essentially speaking.* New York: Routledge.
Garcia, A. M. (1990). The development of Chicana discourse, 1970-1980. In C. E. Dubois
   & V. L. Ruiz (Eds.), *Unequal sisters* (pp. 418-431). New York: Routledge.
Giddings, P. (1984). *Where and when I enter: The impact of Black women on race and
   class in America.* New York: William Morrow.
Harding, S. (1990). Feminism, science, and the anti-enlightenment critiques. In L. J.
   Nicholson (Ed.), *Feminism/postmodernism* (pp. 83-106). New York: Routledge.
Harris, V. R., & Ordona, T. A. (1990). Developing unity among women of color: Crossing
   the barriers of internalized racism and cross-racial hostility. In G. Anzaldua (Ed.),
   *Making face, making soul/haciendo caras: Creative and critical perspectives by
   women of color* (pp. 304-316). San Francisco: Aunt Lute Books.
Hartsock, N. (1983). The feminist standpoint: Developing the ground for a specifically
   feminist historical materialism. In S. Harding & M. B. Hintikka (Eds.), *Discovering
   reality* (pp. 283-310). Boston: D. Reidel.

Hartsock, N. (1990). Foucault on power: A theory for women? In L. J. Nicholson (Ed.), *Feminism/postmodernism* (pp. 157-175). New York: Routledge.

Hewitt, N. A. (1992). *Multiple truths: The personal, the political, and the postmodern in contemporary feminist scholarship* (Working Paper No. 5). Memphis: Memphis State University, Center for Research on Women.

Higginbotham, E. B. (1986). We were never on a pedestal: Women of color continue to struggle with poverty, racism and sexism. In R. Lefkowitz & A. Withorn (Eds.), *For crying out loud: Women and poverty in the United States* (pp. 99-110). New York: Pilgrim.

Higginbotham, E. B. (1992). African-American women's history and the metalanguage of race. *Signs: Journal of Women in Culture and Society, 17*(2), 251-274.

Hill Collins, P. (1990). *Black feminist thought: Knowledge, consciousness and the politics of empowerment.* Boston: Unwin Hyman.

hooks, b. (1981). *Ain't I a woman: Black women and feminism.* Boston: South End.

hooks, b. (1989). *Talking back: Thinking feminist, thinking Black.* Boston: South End.

hooks, b. (1990). *Yearning: Race, gender, and cultural politics.* Boston: South End.

hooks, b. (1992). *Black looks: Race and representation.* Boston: South End.

Hurtado, A. (1989). Relating to privilege: Seduction and rejection in the subordination of White women and women of color. *Signs: Journal of Women in Culture and Society, 14*(4), 833-855.

Jordon, J. (1992). Report from the Bahamas. In M. L. Andersen & H. Collins (Eds.), *Race, class, and gender: An anthology* (pp. 28-37). Belmont, CA: Wadsworth.

King, D. K. (1988). Multiple jeopardy, multiple consciousness: The context of a Black feminist ideology. *Signs: Journal of Women in Culture and Society, 14*(1), 42-72.

Knowles, C., & Mercer, S. (1992). Feminism and antiracism: An exploration of the political possibilities. In J. Donald & A. Rattansi (Eds.), *"Race," culture and difference* (pp. 104-125). London: Sage.

Lewis, D. K. (1977). A response to inequality: Black women, racism, and sexism. *Signs: Journal of Women in Culture and Society, 3*(2), 339-361.

Lorde, A. (1984). *Sister outsider.* Freedom, CA: Crossing Press.

Minh-ha, T. T. (1989). *Woman, native, other.* Bloomington: Indiana University Press.

Mohanty, C. T. (1991). Under Western eyes: Feminist scholarship and colonial discourses. In C. T. Mohanty, A. Russo, & L. Torres (Eds.), *Third World women and the politics of feminism* (pp. 51-80). Bloomington: Indiana University Press.

Moraga, C. (1983). La guera. In C. Moraga & G. Anzaldua (Eds.), *This bridge called my back: Writings by radical women of color* (pp. 27-34). New York: Kitchen Table.

Mueller, M. (1977). Women and men, power and powerlessness in Lesotho. *Signs: Journal of Women in Culture and Society, 3*(1), 154-166.

Nicholson, L. J. (Ed.). (1990). *Feminism/postmodernism.* New York: Routledge.

Ong, A. (1988). Colonialism and modernity: Feminist re-presentation of women in non-Western societies. *Inscriptions, 4*(3), 79-93.

Painter, N. I. (1992). Hill, Thomas, and the use of racial stereotype. In T. Morrison (Ed.), *Race-ing justice, en-gendering power: Essays on Anita Hill, Clarence Thomas, and the construction of social reality* (pp. 200-214). New York: Pantheon.

Pala, A. (1977). Definitions of women and development: An African perspective. *Signs: Journal of Women in Culture and Society, 3*(1), 9-13.

Simons, M. A. (1979). Racism and sexism: A schism in the sisterhood. *Feminist Studies, 5*(2), 384-401.

Smith, A., & Stewart, A. J. (1983). Approaches to studying racism and sexism in Black women's lives. *Journal of Social Issues, 39*(3), 1-15.

Spelman, E. V. (1988). *Inessential woman: Problems of exclusion in feminist thought.* Boston: Beacon.

Weedon, C. (1987). *Feminist practice and poststructuralist theory.* Oxford: Basil Black-well.

White, E. F. (1984). Listening to the voices of Black feminism. *Radical America, 18*(2), 7-25.

White, E. F. (1990). Africa on my mind: Gender, counter discourse, and African-American nationalism. *Journal of Men's History, 2*(3), 73-97.

Young, I. M. (1990). The ideal of community and the politics of difference. In L. J. Nicholson (Ed.), *Feminism/postmodernism* (pp. 300-323). New York: Routledge.

PART III

AREA STUDIES OF RACISM
AND ANTI-RACISM

There are five areas studied in Part III. Each author was asked to describe how racism is expressed in his or her national culture by focusing on the underlying dynamic of racism. What factors reinforce and motivate racism as a contemporary social issue? Each author was also asked to comment on the nature and extent of dominant group anti-racism. This latter request turned out to be a very difficult task, largely because of the lack of attention to anti-racism from scholars, newspapers, and activists alike.

In Chapters 8 and 9, John Solomos' look at Great Britain and Louis Kushnick's review of Western Europe, issues of racism are seen to revolve around the post-World War II immigration of people of color into largely single-racial national states. Immigrants have come for low-level domestic, service, and industrial jobs. With the current transition from national to international economies, immigrants are scapegoats for White working-class discontent and elite efforts to reduce the strategic importance of White labor. Racism is being used to shield from popular thinking the real underlying dynamics of European deindustrialization.

Racism in Brazil exists in fact but is denied in perception. Chapter 10 is an introduction by Rosana Heringer that provides the reader with a general economic picture of life for Brazilians and initial governmental efforts to address racism. In Chapter 11, Antonio Guimarães looks at the Brazilian denial of racism and provides a postmodern analysis of its role and place in maintaining the "Brazilian way." What is missing from most work on racism in Brazil is a description of the African Brazilian community. Rosângela Vieira provides this view in Chapter 12 by looking at the history of African Brazilian opposition to racism and the state of African Brazilian racial consciousness today.

In Chapter 13, Ralph Premdas looks at the Caribbean, where the issues of racism and anti-racism are waged between peoples of color in a microsetting within the larger world economy. The Caribbean provides evidence that racism is not limited to people of European descent. Racism is used as a way to maintain group control of the state and the material privileges that are derived from state control.

In Chapter 14, Mokubung Nkomo and associates write about the abolition of apartheid. Their main contribution is to point out that the end of apartheid does not mean the end of race-based inequality. In fact, apartheid is being replaced by another, potentially more effective, basis of inequality and control—differential historic participation in the South African economy virtually guarantees indefinite Black subordination.

In each case, the authors present evidence that racism is being updated in the world community.

8

Racism and Anti-Racism in Great Britain: Historical Trends and Contemporary Issues

John Solomos

The 1990s have witnessed important changes in the politics of race and racism in Britain and in many European societies. We have seen a resurgence of racist social and political movements in both Western and Eastern Europe, the development of new patterns of migration, and heated political debate about the best ways to respond to the challenge posed by these developments. Widespread reports in the media have highlighted the emergence of new forms of racism and their influence in a wide variety of specific national contexts. Indeed, in many societies questions about immigration and the position of minorities have become a key issue on the political agenda. At the same time, it has also become clear that debates about immigration are inextricably tied to wider changes in the social and political position of established ethnic and racial minorities. The future of minority communities that have established themselves in the period since World War II has been placed as much on the political agenda by recent developments as the question of how to respond to new waves of migrants and refugees. As second- and third-generation migrants establish themselves, their future social and political status is still the subject of intense, and in many cases hostile, public debate.

How have we arrived at this situation? What factors explain the present turmoil and conflict in societies such as Britain? To answer these and other questions, it is necessary to look back at the history of racism and anti-racism in British society, as well as to look forward to the future. This chapter seeks to do that by providing a detailed analysis of the changing terms of political discourse about race and racism in British society since 1945. In doing so, I shall also attempt to explore some of the developments likely to shape the future of race and racism in British society.

This chapter provides an overview of post-1945 immigration and political responses to it. It then moves on to explore the racialization of political life that took shape during the 1960s and 1970s, particularly through the development of immigration policy. From this account, it moves to an analysis of the changing politics of race and immigration in the past 15 years of Conservative rule, concentrating on the articulation of new forms of racialized politics. Finally, I touch on some aspects of contemporary debates about the possibilities for reform and the development of anti-racist politics.

MIGRANT LABOR AND THE STATE

Contemporary debates about race and racism in British society are inextricably linked to the question of immigration from the former British colonies. This feature of the British situation is somewhat different from other European societies, and it is the outcome of the specific legal and political circumstances that existed in Britain in the immediate post-1945 period. At the end of World War II, the British state had legislative powers to control the entry into Britain of non-British subjects and their access to the labor market. Such measures had been developed at the beginning of the 20th century in response to Jewish immigration. Very little control could be exercised, however, over the entry of the vast majority of British subjects living in the colonies and dominions. They retained a legal right to enter and settle in Britain, confirmed by the British Nationality Act of 1948. Although this act made a formal distinction between British subjects who were citizens of the United Kingdom and Colonies and those who were Commonwealth citizens, both categories of people had the right to enter, settle, and work in Britain. Additionally, citizens of the Republic of Ireland retained the right of unrestricted entry and settlement.

It is in this context that postwar migration from the colonies took place. Initially, most colonial migrants came from the West Indies, although by the 1950s workers from the Indian subcontinent began to arrive in relatively large numbers (James & Harris, 1993). In both cases, workers were attracted to Britain by a combination of push and pull factors relating to the economic situation in their countries of origin and in Britain. In general, they came to fill particular positions in the labor market created by the labor shortages that characterized the post-1945 British economy.

What became clear at an early stage, however, was that, despite the availability of colonial labor to meet demand in Britain, the state preferred to encourage the use of migrant labor from other European societies. Some British subjects from the colonies did arrive during this period, particularly from the West Indies, but almost as soon as they began to arrive, sections of political opinion perceived their arrival as a "problem." The relatively liberal attitude toward the arrival of European workers contrasted sharply with the fears expressed about the social and racial problems that were seen as arising from the arrival of colored colonial workers who were British subjects. Both the Labour governments of 1945-1951 and Conservative governments of the 1950s considered various ways to stop or reduce the number of Black migrants arriving and settling in Britain (Carter, Harris, & Joshi, 1987; Dean, 1987; Joshi & Carter, 1984).

The terms of political debate over immigration were established from 1945 to 1962. The close association between race and immigration in policy debates and in popular political and media discourses became an established feature of political debate at this time. Contrary to the arguments of some scholars, it seems inadequate to see this period as an "age of innocence" and lack of concern about Black immigration in the United Kingdom (Deakin, 1970; Patterson, 1969; Rose & Associates, 1969). Throughout this period, an increasingly racialized debate about immigration took place, focusing on the supposed "social problems" of having too many Black migrants and how they could be stopped from coming to Britain.

Much publicity was given to the arrival of 417 Jamaicans in May 1948, and subsequent arrivals by groups of West Indian workers. This focus on colored immigration helped obscure the fact that the majority of immigrants continued to come from the Irish Republic, White Commonwealth countries, and other European countries (Miles & Phizacklea, 1984, pp. 45-48; Patterson, 1969, chap. 1). The concentration on the number of West Indian immigrants, and later on the number of immigrants from India and Pakistan, was an issue of debate within the cabinet during the early to mid-1950s, when various measures to control Black immigration and dissuade Black workers from coming to the United Kingdom were considered. On the basis of a careful analysis of cabinet and ministerial debates about immigration from the colonies, a recent study concludes that, during the period from 1948 to 1962, the state was involved in complex political and ideological racialization of immigration policy that was to influence the politics of race in British society for decades to come (Carter, Harris, & Joshi, 1987).

The period between the 1948 Nationality Act and the 1962 Commonwealth Immigrants Act is frequently characterized as one in which the principle of free entry of British subjects to the United Kingdom was relinquished with great reluctance and after considerable official debate. This was not the case. On the contrary, the debate was never about principle. Labour and Conservative governments had, by 1952, instituted a number of covert, and sometimes illegal, administrative measures to discourage Black immigration (Carter, Harris, & Joshi, 1987). Additionally, throughout the 1950s the debate about immigration in Parliament and the media focused on the need to control Black immigration. In both public debate and private policy, attention was focused on the behavior of "undesirable" Black migrants, such as those involved in crime or prostitution. But the political debate throughout the 1950s was also about the desirability of letting a sizable number of West Indian or Asian migrants into Britain. The so-called race riots in Notting Hill and Nottingham in 1958 may have helped politicize this process further (Miles, 1984; Pilkington, 1988). But it is clear that, both before and after the riots, the question of control was integrated into the policy agenda.

With the growing emphasis on the control of colored immigration, the terms of ideological and policy debates about the future of Black migration turned on two themes that were to prove influential later. First, a vigorous debate took place in and out of Parliament about the possibility of revising the 1948 Nationality Act so as to limit the number of Black workers who could settle in the United Kingdom. The terms of this debate were by no means fixed by political party ideologies, and there was opposition from both Conservative and Labour politicians to the call for controls and the abandonment of the free entry principle. Second, a parallel debate developed over the problems caused by "too many colored immigrants" in relation to housing, employment, and crime. This second theme became particularly important in the years 1956 to 1958, and in the aftermath of the 1958 riots (*Hansard,* 596, 1958: Cols 1552-1597).

By linking immigration to the social aspects of the "colour problem," a theme was established that was later to prove influential in shaping both the immigration control legislation and the antidiscrimination legislation of the 1960s and 1970s. This was the argument that it was necessary to use direct state intervention to halt the "gathering momentum" of Black migration and to resolve the social problems that were perceived as linked to it.

Controls on colored immigration had been discussed as early as the late 1940s, and were seriously discussed again in 1954 and 1955. A number of arguments were used in opposition to such controls, and it was not until 1961 that a bill to control Commonwealth immigration was introduced by the government. The reasons for the reluctance to introduce controls remain to some extent a matter of speculation, although the release of government documents from early 1950s has shed some light on this non-decision-making process (Joshi & Carter, 1984; Rich, 1968, chap. 7). At least part of the reluctance to introduce controls seemed to result from a concern about whether legislation that excluded Black people could be implemented without causing embarrassment to Britain's position as head of the Commonwealth and Colonies. There were fears that such legislation would also divide public opinion, and there were doubts about the legality of controls based on color in both British and international law (Deakin, 1968; Miles & Phizacklea, 1984, chap. 2).

What is clear, however, is that the late 1940s to the late 1950s was not a period of laissez-faire in relation to Black migration. Rather, it was one of intense debate within government departments and in public circles about the effect of Black immigration on housing, the welfare state, crime, and other social problems. It is important to note that these debates were not purely about the supposed characteristics of Black migrants. They were also about the effect of Black immigration on the racial character of the British people and on the national identity. Harris (1988) makes this point clear when he argues that the debates about Black immigration during the 1950s reinforced a racialized construction of Britishness that excluded or included people on the grounds of race defined by color:

> When individuals like the Marquis of Salisbury spoke of maintaining the English way of life, they were not simply referring to economic or regional folk patterns, but explicitly to the preservation of "the racial character of the English people." We have developing here a process of subjectification grounded in a racialized construction of "British" Subject that excludes and includes people on the basis of "race"/skin colour. (p. 53)

This process was still in its early stages at this period, but it is impossible to understand the legislation passed to control Black immigration during the 1960s and 1970s without referring to the genesis and articulation of political discourse about Black immigration from 1945 to 1962.

IMMIGRATION AND RACIALIZED POLITICS

The 1958 race riots in Nottingham and Notting Hill are commonly seen as watersheds in the development of racialized politics in Britain. It is certainly true that these events helped bring to national prominence issues that had previously been discussed either locally or within government departments. The riots themselves consisted of attacks by Whites on Blacks, but this did not prevent the riots from being used as examples of the dangers of unrestricted immigration. By the 1958 riots, the mobilization of opinion in and out of Parliament in favor of controls was well advanced. The disturbances in Nottingham and Notting Hill were used by the pro-immigration controls lobby to support calls for the exclusion or even the repatriation of "undesirable immigrants." They were also used in support of the argument that Black immigration was a threat to the rule of law in the inner cities and endangered the English way of life. Lord Salisbury used the riots to justify his claim that controls should be imposed on Black immigration, and he argued that "he was extremely apprehensive of the economic and social results, for Europeans and Africans alike, that were likely to flow from an unrestricted immigration of men and women of the African race into Britain" (*The Guardian*, September 3, 1958).

Between 1958 and the introduction of the Commonwealth Immigrants Bill in 1961, a number of important debates on immigration control took place in Parliament and at party conferences (Freeman, 1979; Miles, 1984; Patterson, 1969). In Parliament, some Conservative Members of Parliament (MPs), including Cyril Osborne, organized a campaign in favor of immigration controls, though they made their case against colored migrants largely through coded language. The Labour Party, along with the Liberals, generally argued against controls, though this was by no means the case for all Labour MPs and local councilors (Layton-Henry, 1984; Reeves, 1983, chap. 7).

Outside of Parliament there was widespread coverage in both the popular and the serious newspapers of race and immigration issues. There was a flowering of popular debate about housing and social conditions in areas of Black settlement, aspects of employment and competition for jobs, and a resurgence of extreme Right groups that sought to use immigration as a basis for political mobilization. The interplay between these processes produced a wide variety of stereotypes and popular images about Black people. In September 1958, *The Times* reported that in the areas affected by the riots:

> There are three main charges of resentment against coloured inhabitants of the district. They are alleged to do no work and to collect a rich sum from the Assistance Board. They are said to find housing when White residents cannot. And they are charged with all kinds of misbehavior, especially sexual. (*The Times,* September 3, 1958)

It was precisely around such concerns that the extreme right groups focused much of their propaganda during and after the riots. There was no need in this context for such beliefs to be substantiated by evidence, but it proved equally difficult to counteract such stereotypes. This weakened attempts to resist the pressures for immigration controls.

The ambiguity in the pressure for controls became even more pronounced during the early 1960s. This was the period of the passage of the first legislative measures controlling the immigration of citizens of the United Kingdom and colonies, the 1962 Commonwealth Immigrants Act.

IMMIGRATION CONTROLS AND STATE RACISM

In the previous section, I argued that the racialization of the immigration issue during the 1950s laid the basis for the move toward the control of Black immigration, an objective that was first implemented through the 1962 Commonwealth Immigrants Act. Part of the dilemma faced by the Conservative government of the time was how to legitimize a policy that aimed to control Black immigration as a more universal measure, thereby deflecting criticism that it was essentially a racist measure. William Deedes, a Minister without Portfolio at the time, recalls that:

> the Bill's real purpose was to restrict the influx of coloured immigrants. We were reluctant to say as much openly. So the restrictions were applied to coloured and White citizens in all Commonwealth countries—though every-

body recognised that immigration from Canada, Australia and New Zealand formed no part of the problem. (Deedes, 1968, p. 10)

The racialization of the immigration issue was achieved through coded language: Commonwealth immigrants were seen as a problem, but race itself was not always mentioned as the central issue. The politicization of such terms later led to a situation where, despite the continuing scale of White immigration, popular common sense perceived all immigrants as Black, and immigration became a coded term for talking about racial questions.

Two competing explanatory models have been used to explain the move toward immigration controls. Some scholars see this shift as a response by the state to the pressure of popular opinion against Black immigration (Foot, 1965; Rose & Associates, 1969). This is also the main line of argument used by some of the chief political figures involved in the debates about control of Black migration. Others argue that the state was responding to the economic interests of the capitalist class, which required the adoption of a migrant labor system that undermined the right of Black workers to migrate and settle freely in the United Kingdom (Sivanandan, 1982, pp. 101-126).

Both explanations have been widely used in the extensive literature on the politics of immigration, but it seems inadequate to view the role of the state as purely responsive, whether to popular opinion or to economic interests. Throughout the period 1948-1962, the state was actively involved in monitoring and regulating the arrival of Black workers and helped articulate a definition of the immigration question that was suffused with racialized categories. Additionally, recent research seems to indicate that the Conservative government came close to agreeing on a policy of controls on Black immigration in 1955-1956 (Carter, Harris, & Joshi, 1987).

The demand for the control of Black immigration during the early 1950s matured from 1955 to 1962 into a concerted campaign within the cabinet, Parliament, the media, and political parties in favor of action to curb the dangers of unrestricted immigration. This in turn led to the policy debate about the formulation of legislation that could exclude Black labor from entry and settlement that led up to the introduction of the Commonwealth Immigrants Bill in 1961. This process can hardly be interpreted as a move from laissez-faire to state intervention, because the state and its institutions were already heavily involved in defining the terms of the debate about the problems caused by Black immigration.

The acceptance of the need to extend administrative controls on Black immigration into legislative action was formally announced in October 1961, when the Conservative government announced the introduction of the Commonwealth Immigrants Bill. These controls were legitimized by arguments about the need to halt Black immigration because of the limited ability of Britain to assimilate colored immigrants. Even though some MPs and commentators were reluctant to accept that the bill was simply a way of dealing with the immigration of colored workers, the Labour Party and sections of the media identified the bill as a response to racist pressures. Hugh Gaitskell, leader of the Labour Party, led a particularly strong attack on the bill in Parliament and its crude amalgamation of immigration with race (*IRR Newsletter,* May 1962; Patterson, 1969, pp. 17-20). But despite strong criticism from the Labour Party and sections of the press, the collective pressures against the entry of Black people succeeded when the Commonwealth Immigrants Act became law in 1962.

Because the act was the outcome of the sustained political campaign against Black immigration, it is not surprising that, despite claims to the contrary, its main clauses sought to control the entry of Black Commonwealth citizens into the United Kingdom. The act introduced a distinction between citizens of the United Kingdom and Colonies and citizens of independent Commonwealth countries. All holders of Commonwealth passports were subject to immigration control except those who were (a) born in the United Kingdom; (b) held UK passports issued by the UK government; or (c) included in the passport of one of the persons excluded from immigration control under (a) or (b) (Macdonald, 1983, pp. 10-12). Other Commonwealth citizens had to obtain a Ministry of Labour employment voucher to be able to enter the United Kingdom.

The creation of these different categories was legitimized as a way of controlling the number of immigrants entering the country. It was clear in both the parliamentary and the media debates about the bill that it was widely seen as a piece of legislation specifically aimed at Black migrants. In this sense, the act can be seen as the climax of the campaign for the control of Black immigration that was launched from both within and outside government during the 1950s.

Public debate about the act reflected a variety of views and was by no means all in its favor. In fact, a number of articles in the press during 1961-1962, along with sections of the Labour Party, expressed opposition to the racist thinking behind the act. Concern was also expressed about the possible consequences of the passage of the act for Britain's standing in the Black Commonwealth countries (Deakin, 1968).

THE CHANGING TERMS
OF POLITICAL DEBATE

Almost as soon as the act became law, there was a widespread political debate about its effectiveness. From 1963 to 1972, when the voucher system was abolished, there was pressure to cut back the number of vouchers allocated; this was reflected in a fall from a level of 30,130 vouchers in 1963 to 2,290 in 1972. Significantly, no controls were imposed on the entry of citizens of the Irish Republic into Britain. Nevertheless, opponents of immigration were quick to call for tighter controls; in the political climate of the mid 1960s, their voices were a major influence on the terms of political debate about race and immigration.

The opposition of the Labour Party to the 1962 act was not sustained. When Harold Wilson took office as Labour prime minister in 1964, he announced that the Commonwealth Immigrants Act would be maintained. In 1965, the government issued a White Paper on *Immigration from the Commonwealth,* which calls for controls to be maintained in an even stricter form, along with measures to promote the integration of immigrants. The White Paper represents a shift in the direction of what some have called a "Little England" policy (Rose & Associates, 1969, p. 229), and signals a convergence of the policies of the Conservative and Labour parties in favor of immigration controls.

This consensus was to be exemplified by the nature of the political debate about race and immigration from 1964 to 1970, when the Labour Party was in power. Three events represent good examples of this debate: the controversy over the electoral contest in Smethwick in 1964, the controversy over East African Asians during 1968-1969, and the political turmoil caused by Enoch Powell's intervention in this debate from 1968 onward.

The influence of events in Smethwick on the terms of national political debates about race and immigration is sometimes forgotten. It is no exaggeration to say that the political turmoil around the issue of immigration in Smethwick and the surrounding area had a deep effect on both the local and the national political scene. Popular debate and media coverage were aroused by the contest between the Labour candidate, Patrick Gordon Walker, who was widely seen as liberal on immigration, and Conservative Peter Griffiths, who fought the election largely on the basis of defending the interests of the local White majority against the influx of immigrants (Deakin, 1972; Foot, 1965). In the volatile political climate of the time, a slogan commonly heard was, "If you want a nigger for a neighbor vote Labour"; Griffiths was later to defend the use of this slogan as "a manifestation of popular feeling" about immigration in the area, and refused to condemn those who used it (*The Times,* 1968, p. 139).

The debate about the implications of Griffiths' victory carried on for some time and was influential on both the Labour Party (*The Economist,* August 7, 1965; Deakin, 1972) and the Conservative Party. Within the West Midlands region in particular, the events in Smethwick helped shift political debate and attitudes in both major parties toward a stance that emphasized their support for strict controls on Black immigration (Deakin, 1972).

During this period, the Labour government was forced on the defensive by Enoch Powell's famous "rivers of blood" speech in Birmingham in April 1968. This speech helped popularize the racial message that even tighter controls on immigration were not enough to deal with the race problem. In this speech, and in a succession of others over the next few years, Powell warned of what he saw as (a) the dangers of immigration leading to a "total transformation to which there is no parallel in a thousand years of British history," and (b) the longer-term danger of increasing racial tensions manifesting themselves in Britain on the American model. In the most infamous section of his Birmingham speech, Powell said that as he looked into the future, he felt deep foreboding about the fate of the nation if present trends continued:

> As I look ahead, I am filled with foreboding. Like the Roman, I seem to see "the River Tiber foaming with much blood." The tragic and intractable phenomenon which we watch with horror on the other side of the Atlantic, but which there is interwoven with the history and existence of the States itself, is coming upon us here by our own volition and our own neglect. (*The Observer,* April 21, 1968)

According to Powell, the long-term solution to the immigration issue went beyond the issue of immigration controls and was likely to involve the repatriation of immigrants already settled in the United Kingdom. Such a line of argument helped push political debate beyond controls as such and established repatriation as part of the political agenda. Indeed, in the same speech Powell used all his rhetorical powers to construct an image of White Britons increasingly becoming isolated and strangers in their own country:

> They found their wives unable to obtain hospital beds in childbirth, their children unable to obtain school places, their homes and neighbourhoods

changed beyond recognition, their plans and prospects for the future defeated. (*The Observer,* April 21, 1968)

Powell was able to argue that it was the failure of successive governments to act decisively to halt immigration in the 1950s that led to a
situation where more drastic measures were required to solve the problem.

The furor caused by the speech was such that Powell was forced out of
the shadow cabinet, and there was extensive media coverage of the issues
he raised throughout 1968 and 1969 and in the period leading up to the
1970 general election (*IRR Newsletter,* April/May 1968, April 1969). The
controversy acted as a focus for those calling not only for tighter controls
on Black immigration but for action to facilitate the repatriation of Black
migrants already settled.

INSTITUTIONALIZING
IMMIGRATION CONTROLS

Within the political climate created by Powell's interventions and the
ensuing political debates, the continued arrival of the dependents of
Commonwealth migrants already settled in the United Kingdom helped
keep the numbers game alive. This led to increasing calls in and out of
Parliament and the media for more action to halt immigration and to deal
with the problems that were popularly seen as associated with it. The
combined effect of those two pressures, and the use of immigration as an
electoral issue, opened up the possibility of further legislative measures.

In 1969, the Labour government introduced the Immigration Appeals
Act, which was officially based on the report of the Committee on
Immigration Appeals headed by Sir Roy Wilson (Macdonald, 1983, p. 269).
This report accepts the need for restrictions on immigration, but argues
that a system of appeal ensures that the restrictions are applied fairly.
Although this act is sometimes interpreted as a positive measure, it
institutionalized a process of deportation for those breaking conditions
attached to entry. It also legitimized restrictions on the right of entry of
those who were legally entitled to settle in the United Kingdom with the
condition that dependents seeking settlement in Britain had to be in
possession of an entry certificate. Such certificates had to be applied for
through an interview at the nearest British High Commission. Applicants
had to prove their claimed relationship to the person legally resident in

Britain; if they were unable to do so, they could be denied entry. It is under this system that many recent controversial cases have arisen.

The shift of the Labour Party toward the idea of firm immigration controls was part of a wider political process that led to the 1971 Immigration Act. During the 1970 election campaign, the Conservative Party promised there would "be no further large-scale permanent immigration." When the Immigration Bill was introduced in February 1971, it was legitimized on this basis, but as a number of speakers pointed out during the debates on the bill, it was difficult to see how it would actually reduce the number of immigrants. In essence, the 1971 act qualifies the notion of citizenship by differentiating between citizens of the United Kingdom and Colonies who are patrial and therefore have the right of abode in Britain, and nonpatrials who do not. The most important categories of patrials are (a) citizens of the United Kingdom and Colonies who have citizenship by birth, adoption, naturalization, or registration in the United Kingdom or who were born of parents, one of whom had United Kingdom citizenship by birth, or one of whose grandparents had such citizenship; and (b) citizens of the United Kingdom and Colonies who have at any time settled in the United Kingdom and who have been ordinarily resident in the United Kingdom for five years or more. Under the act, all aliens and Commonwealth citizens who are not patrials need permission to enter Britain. As before, Commonwealth citizens entering under the voucher system could settle in Britain. After the 1971 act came into force, aliens and commonwealth citizens entered on the basis of work-permits. They thus became subject to control by annual work permit, and the nonrenewal of the permit. This change of status has been defined by some scholars as a move toward the migrant worker system of other European countries. Commonwealth workers who are not patrials (and by definition almost certainly Black) were reduced to the status of short-term contract workers rather than settlers (Castles & Kosack, 1985; Sivanandan, 1982, pp. 108-112).

During the Parliamentary debates on the 1971 Immigration Act, the amalgamation of immigration with race became an issue of dispute between the Conservative and Labour parties. Although during the late 1960s the Labour Party effectively accommodated itself to a "White Britain policy," in 1971 it felt moved to question the treatment of Commonwealth immigrants along the same lines as aliens. Labour also questioned the overtly racial criteria that underlay the notion of patriality. The new act is rightly seen as racialist because it allows potentially millions of White Commonwealth citizens to enter under the patriality clause and settle in Britain, a right denied to almost all non-White Commonwealth citizens. Successive Immigration Rules issued by the Home Secretary to supplement the 1971 act have emphasized its intention to keep out Black Commonwealth citizens (Macdonald, 1983, pp. 25-30). With the exception of the Ugandan Asians who were expelled by Idi Amin in 1972, some of whom were allowed to settle in Britain during 1972-1973, this policy has been consistently pursued ever since.

The decade between 1961 and 1971 saw the introduction of three major pieces of legislation aimed at excluding Black immigrants. The 1971 act took away the right of Black Commonwealth immigrants to settle, and thus marked an important step in the institutionalization of racist immigration controls.

ANTIDISCRIMINATION POLICIES

The institutionalization of racist immigration controls represented the main strand of policy change during the 1960s and 1970s. But it was by no means the only one. During this period, three Race Relations Acts attempted to tackle aspects of racial discrimination and inequality. The 1965 and 1968 Race Relations Acts represent the beginning of this strategy, which was supported by the Labour Party. Both measures were based on the notion that the state should attempt to ban discrimination on the basis of race, color, or ethnic origin through legal sanctions, and public regulatory agencies were charged with the task of promoting greater equality of opportunity (Rose & Associates, 1969, pp. 511-530).

This dual strategy was clearly articulated in the Labour government's 1965 White Paper on *Immigration from the Commonwealth,* but it had its origins in the debates of the 1950s and the period leading up to the 1962 Commonwealth Immigrants Act. The notion that immigration was essentially an issue of race was consistent with the view (a) that the growing number of Black citizens resident in the United Kingdom was either actually or potentially the source of social problems and conflicts, and (b) that it was necessary for the state to introduce measures to promote the integration of immigrants into the wider society and its fundamental institutions.

The linking of immigration controls with integrative measures was a significant step, because it signaled a move toward the management of domestic race relations as well as legitimizing the institutionalization of controls at the point of entry. Also in 1965, the Labour government passed the first Race Relations Act, which enunciated the principle of ending discrimination against Black immigrants and their descendants on the grounds of race. Although fairly limited in its scope, the act was important in establishing the state's concern with racial discrimination and as an affirmation of the broad objective of using legislative action to achieve "good race relations" (Lester & Bindman, 1972, pp. 107-149).

Much has been written about the inherent contradictions involved in balancing racially specific controls on immigration with measures against discriminatory practices. Yet since the 1960s, the two sides of state intervention have been seen as inextricably linked. According to Roy Hattersley's famous formula, "Integration without control is impossible, but control without integration is indefensible" (*Hansard,* 721, 1965: Cols 378-385). The rationale of this argument was never articulated clearly, but it was at least partly based on the idea that the fewer immigrants (particularly Black ones), the easier it would be to integrate them into the English way of life and its sociocultural values.

The basis of these assumptions lay, as argued above, in the notion that too many Black migrants could result in racial conflict. In addition, the numbers game was tied to the idea that the cultural differences between the immigrants and the host population were a potential source of conflict. Since 1962, both the Conservative and Labour parties have accepted the need for immigration restrictions to be balanced by measures to bring about integration in the areas of housing, education, employment, and the social services.

Perhaps the high point of this strategy came during the Labour administrations of 1974 to 1979. The 1976 Race Relations Act was passed during this period, a measure that is still in force today. The most important innovations the act introduced were (a) an extension of the objectives of the law to cover not only intentional discrimination but also racial disadvantage brought about by systemic racism, and (b) the formation of the Commission for Racial Equality, a quasi-governmental agency charged with the objective of achieving greater racial equality (Lustgarten, 1980; McCrudden, 1982, pp. 336-348).

The antidiscrimination policies introduced by Labour governments during the 1960s and 1970s were and remain contradictory policies. Although they were an attempt to tackle aspects of racial discrimination, and in this sense were anti-racist, they were at the same time tied in to the immigration policies that shaped the politics of race throughout this period. There is also widespread evidence that their influence has been relatively limited in practice. But the fact that they were passed can be seen as the result of the contradictory role that the Labour Party has played in the politics of race over the past five decades.

IMMIGRATION AND RACE SINCE 1979

Since 1979, the emphasis has shifted once again. During a period when four successive Conservative administrations have been in power, political debate about race and immigration has shifted markedly to the right. In the general election of 1979, sections of the Conservative Party, including its leader Margaret Thatcher, emphasized the dangers posed to British social and cultural values by already settled Black communities. Thatcher's famous "swamping" statement in 1978 was part of a wider campaign to use race as a symbol for the neo-Conservative ideology of Thatcher's wing of the party. Even though the political language used referred to immigrants, the main reference point of this campaign was the Black communities already settled in Britain. Immigration control remained an issue of public and policy debate, particularly in relation to dependents and the marriage partners of those settled legally.

The policies pursued by the Conservative administrations since 1979 constitute a further stage in the development of immigration policy. This has involved two main policy changes. First, a number of changes to the Immigration Rules issued under the 1971 Immigration Act have been introduced, with the explicit intention of tightening controls even further. Second, the 1981 British Nationality Act was passed under the first Thatcher administration, and came into force in 1983. Debates in Parliament on both these issues give a clue to attempts by the government to circumvent further the rights of Black commonwealth citizens with a legal right to enter Britain and to construct the question of nationality along racial lines (*Hansard,* 5, 1981: Cols 765-1193; *Hansard,* 31, 1982: Cols 692-761; *Hansard,* 34, 1982: Cols 355-439; *Hansard,* 37, 1983: Cols 178-280; *Hansard* 83, 1985: Cols 893-989).

The main legislative action of the post-1979 Conservative administrations, the 1981 British Nationality Act, is a case in point. The government argued that in introducing the bill it was rationalizing existing nationality and immigration legislation to create a British citizenship that automatically gives up the right of abode in the United Kingdom. It did this by dividing the existing category of citizens of the United Kingdom and

Commonwealth into three categories: British citizens, British dependent territories citizens, and British overseas citizens. Although the government argued that the act would make immigration control less arbitrary, public and Parliamentary responses criticized the act for reinforcing racial discrimination (Layton-Henry, 1984, pp. 157-159). Indeed, the category of British overseas citizens excludes British citizens of (mostly) Asian origin from the right of abode in the United Kingdom. In this sense, the 1981 act "enshrines the existing racially discriminatory provisions of immigration law under the new clothing of British citizenship and the right of abode" (Macdonald, 1983, p. 69).

A government document prepared for the 1986 Organisation for Economic Cooperation and Development (OECD) conference on immigration policy states the broad policy objectives in traditional terms, but links them closely to other areas of concern:

> In recent decades, the basis of policy in the United Kingdom has been the need to control primary immigration—that is, new heads of households who are most likely to enter the job market. The United Kingdom is one of the most densely populated countries in Europe. In terms of housing, education, social services and, of course, jobs, the country could not support all those who would like to come here. Firm immigration control is therefore essential, in order to provide the conditions necessary for developing and maintaining good community relations. (OECD, 1986, p. 1)

In practice, therefore, the strategy pursued since 1979 has continued to legitimate the supposed link between firm controls and good community relations. The signs are that this amalgam will continue to guide the thinking of the mainstream of the Conservative Party.

At the same time, the government has steadfastly refused to strengthen the 1976 Race Relations Act or to take a more forceful stand against discrimination and racism. Even after the Scarman Report of 1981 called for a coordinated and government-led policy against racial disadvantage, a call repeated a number of times since by Lord Scarman and others, the response of the various agencies of the state has been at best limited. Rather, the government has continued to emphasize the need for tight immigration controls because "of the strain that the admission of a substantial number of immigrants can place on existing resources and services" (Leon Brittan, *Hansard,* 83, 1985: Col 893).

The logic of this approach is to displace conflicts and strains in race relations on Black communities as a whole, or specific sections of them.

This in turn has allowed the view of Blacks as an "enemy within" and a threat to social stability to take further root. The expressed rationale of the immigration laws and the race relations acts was to produce "good race relations" and integration. But by failing to depoliticize the question of Black immigration, the expressed purpose of the acts has been lost. The racialization of British politics proceeded apace during the 1970s and took on new forms in relation to specific issues or groups, for example, education, the police, young Blacks, and urban policy (CCCS Race and Politics Group, 1982; Miles & Phizacklea, 1984). The restrictions imposed by the 1971 Immigration Act and the successive Immigration Rules issued under the act have seemingly fulfilled the ostensible objective of post-1962 policies: to control primary immigration and restrict secondary immigration.

What explains this racialization of political discourses in a context of firm immigration controls? A number of issues are involved; not all of these can be analyzed in this chapter, but at least two are worth noting. First, debates about immigration and race have taken place within a broader context of social, political, and economic change that has influenced the ways in which such debates have developed. The rapid transformation of many inner-city localities over the last two decades, particularly in relation to the economic and social infrastructure, has provided a fertile ground for the racialization of issues such as employment, housing, education, and law and order (Hall, Critcher, Jefferson, Clarke, & Roberts, 1978; Phizacklea & Miles, 1980, pp. 42-68; Solomos, 1993). This racialization process has moved public and political debate beyond the question of immigration per se toward the identification and resolution of specific social problems linked to race. But the link with the immigration question is maintained at another level. It is now the size of the Black population, whether in the schools or the unemployment queue, that is identified as the source of the problem, not state racism or racial discrimination (Macdonald, 1983).

Second, the continuing racialization of British politics in the context of firm immigration controls shows how political language is often a way of emphasizing what one wants to believe and avoiding what one does not wish to face. Thus, calls for more controls on immigration are often laced with references to the number of immigrants or to the large numbers that could potentially arrive and swamp British culture. But such statements are not necessarily based on "the facts" in any recognizable sense. Rather, references to statistics and reports are often highly selective and emphasize symbolic fears. Examples of this process are the debates that occurred during the mid-1970s about the Hawley report on immigration from the Indian subcontinent (1976) and the Select Committee on Race Relations and Immigration report on immigration (1978). In both cases, the debates about these reports in Parliament, the media, and other contexts focused on the dangers of "massive" numbers of immigrants arriving and the possible social and political consequences. This debate occurred despite the fact that firm controls on immigration were implemented during the 1960s. Perhaps a more recent phenomenon is the case of the visa controls introduced in 1986. Visitors from India, Pakistan, Bangladesh, Nigeria, and Ghana are controlled as based on the number of illegal immigrants from these countries. The fact that only 222 out of 452,000 visitors from these five countries absconded as illegal immigrants in 1985 did not prevent the symbolic use of visa controls as another means of stemming the tide of immigration (*The Guardian,* September 2, 1986).

The agitation of the extreme Right-wing groups and sections of the Conservative Party in favor of stricter immigration controls and repatriation came to focus on the supposed dangers of this "alien wedge." The language used by Enoch Powell in 1968-1969 to warn of the dangers of immigration had been reworked by the late 1970s around the issue of the "enemy within." That enemy was now in many cases no longer an immigrant, but born and bred in Brixton, Handsworth, Liverpool, and other urban localities. The generation and amplification of the mugging issue in the early 1970s, confrontations between the police and young Blacks, and the identification of young Blacks as an alienated group within Black communities and British society generally helped construct a new racialized discourse about Black youth (Solomos, 1988). Increasingly, this group was identified as drifting into either criminal activities or radical political activities that brought it into direct contact, and hence conflict, with the police. In the 1950s and 1960s, the problem was focused on the need to keep Black immigrants out. Now the language of political debate seemed to shift toward the view that Black youth were a kind of social time bomb that could undermine the social fabric of the immigration and race relations amalgam and possibly society as a whole.

PROSPECTS FOR REFORM

The shift from a preoccupation with immigration and the numbers game to the question of the "enemy within" and related images of social disorder is an important development. At least in relation to the urban unrest that Britain experienced in 1981 and 1985, it highlights the complex processes through which racialized political discourses are working now. Immigration will not become less important as a political issue. Rather, the growing usage of political symbols depicting Blacks as an enemy within is inextricably linked to the history of state responses analyzed in this chapter. Indeed the post-1979 Conservative administrations have continued to mobilize the immigration question as a political symbol and to legitimate the maintenance of racially specific controls as a necessary response to fears about too much immigration.

Since 1979, however, the Labour Party and the minority parties have shown some signs of questioning this approach. The Labour Party, which introduced the 1968 Commonwealth Immigrants Act, has seemingly come round to the view that current immigration laws are racist, and it aims to introduce its own legislation when in power to ensure that controls are both nonracist and nonsexist. In a parliamentary debate on immigration in July 1985, Gerald Kaufman affirmed that the intention of a future Labour administration would be (a) to maintain firm controls on immigration, and (b) to ensure that such controls are applied equally to all immigrants regardless of race (*Hansard,* 83, 1985: Cols 909-910). He accused the Conservatives of trying to identify immigration with race, when recent history questioned this assumption:

> Viewed objectively, immigration should be neither a problem nor an issue in Britain. Substantial primary immigration ended at least a decade and a half ago, and there is no prospect of it starting again. In most years there is a net emigration from the United Kingdom. In the year [1985] only 15.5 per cent of immigrants came from the West Indies, Africa and the Indian subcontinent—the areas from which, according to the Government, there is the greatest pressure to migrate to the United Kingdom. (*Hansard,* 83, 1985: Col 910)

This approach indicates a marked shift from the actions of Labour governments during 1964-1970 and 1974-1979. But it is difficult to say what is meant by nonracist immigration controls and how a future Labour administration could break away from the logic of politics since 1962— which has been to construct Black immigration into a problem. Since the 1980s, a strong Black and anti-racist lobby has certainly emerged within the Labour Party. This lobby is pressing the party into a firm commitment to implement reforms.

In the context of the current political climate, it is hard to see how a depoliticization of questions around race and immigration can occur. Growing urban unrest and violence create a space for the Powellite imagery of a racial civil war to take root and for the real fears of the White population to be deflected on the enemy within. Promises of a break from past practice by the Labour Party must be set against the wider political background. What would be the response of Labour to a successful campaign around immigration and race by the Conservatives? The signs are not promising. Whenever the popular press accuses Labour of promising to open the floodgates to immigration from Black Commonwealth countries, as it does at election time, Labour is forced to take a strong stance against immigration. During the 1974-1979 period, the Labour government failed to take immigration out of politics; the 1979 election campaign suffered from the racialized language used by the Conservatives. Response to these pressures showed the ambiguities in Labour thinking since the mid-1960s. Whether responses in the future will be significantly different remains to be seen, but, given the entrenched nature of racist immigration controls, major structural changes are clearly required to make the promises of reform a reality.

CONCLUSION

The above discussion demonstrates that it is far too simplistic to see the British state as a reactive instrument of economic forces or popular pressures in relation to the control of immigration and the management of migrant labor. State interventions have made an independent contribution to the reproduction of the historic social relations between dominant and subordinate groups in contemporary Britain, particularly through the regulation of migrant workers and the reinforcement of racialized and ethnically based social divisions (Miles & Phizacklea, 1984). But such a generalization does not capture the complexity of the role of the state in relation to immigration and other important issues on the political agenda. Far from simply responding to pressures from the outside, the state has played a central role in defining both the form and the content of policies and wider political agendas. Indeed, the state and its agencies have become the locus of struggles over the form of the political regulation of immigration and the management of domestic race relations.

The experience of post-1945 Britain highlights the complex ways in which racism shapes social understandings of questions about race and immigration. The pressure to control and stop the arrival of Black mi-grants from the colonies and ex-colonies emphasizes the influence of racism in the making of immigration policies. At the same time, the limited influence of anti-racist initiatives highlights the problems in-volved in the development of alternative strategies for change.

In the present political climate, the question of immigration and race thus remains a live and controversial issue in British society, and may become even more so in the future. Although it is difficult to predict the specific course of political developments, it seems evident that policies about immigration are likely to remain influenced by the racialized agenda that has dominated political debate since the 1960s. At the same time, pressures for reform and stronger measures against racial discrimi-nation are likely to grow, as is evident from the new forms of political mobilization among minorities. The possibilities for any radical change of direction, however, will depend on the articulation of new political alliances and agendas that can challenge the dominant view of immigra-tion that has shaped the policies of both Conservative and Labour admini-strations during the past few decades.

What is interesting about the current situation is that a new politics of immigration has emerged in Europe as well as in other parts of the globe. As Balibar notes in relation to the situation in France and other Western European societies:

> "Immigration" has become, par excellence, the name of race, a new name, but one that is functionally equivalent to the old appellation, just as the term "immigrant" is the chief characteristic which enables individuals to be classified in a racist typology. (Balibar & Wallerstein, 1991, p. 222)

This interlinkage between the politics of immigration and race has been evident in Britain for some time. During the late 1980s and 1990s, this linkage became evident in France and Germany and a number of other European societies as well.

REFERENCES

Balibar, E., & Wallerstein, I. (1991). *Race, nation, class.* London: Verso.
Carter, B., Harris, C., & Joshi, S. (1987). *The 1951-55 Conservative government and the racialisation of Black immigration* (Policy Papers in Ethnic Relations No. 11). Coventry, UK: University of Warwick, Centre for Research in Ethnic Relations.

Castles, S., & Kosack, G. (1985). *Immigrant workers and class structure in Western Europe*. London: Oxford University Press.

CCCS Race and Politics Group. (1982). *The empire strikes back: Race and racism in 70s Britain*. London: Hutchinson.

Deakin, N. (1968). The politics of the Commonwealth Immigrants Bill. *Political Quarterly, 39*(1), 24-45.

Deakin, N. (1970). *Colour, citizenship and British society*. London: Panther.

Deakin, N. (1972). *The immigration issue in British politics*. Unpublished doctoral thesis, University of Sussex.

Dean, D. (1987). Coping with colonial immigration, the Cold War and colonial policy. *Immigrants and Minorities, 6*(3), 305-334.

Deedes, W. (1968). *Race without rancour*. London: Conservative Political Centre.

Foot, P. (1965). *Immigration and race in British politics*. Harmondsworth, UK: Penguin.

Freeman, G. (1979). *Immigrant labor and racial conflict in industrial societies*. Princeton, NJ: Princeton University Press.

Hall, S., Critcher, C., Jefferson, T., Clarke, J., & Roberts, B. (1978). *Policing the crisis: Mugging, the state, and law and order*. Basingstoke, UK: Macmillan.

Harris, C. (1988). Images of Blacks in Britain: 1930-60. In S. Allen & M. Macey (Eds.), *Race and social policy*. London: Economic and Social Research Council.

James, W., & Harris, C. (Eds.). (1993). *Inside Babylon: The Caribbean Diaspora in Britain*. London: Verso.

Joshi, S., & Carter, B. (1984). The role of Labour in the creation of a racist Britain. *Race and Class, 25*(3), 53-70.

Layton-Henry, Z. (1984). *The politics of race in contemporary Britain*. London: Allen & Unwin.

Lester, A., & Bindman, G. (1972). *Race and law*. Harmondsworth, UK: Penguin.

Lustgarten, L. (1980). *Legal control of racial discrimination*. Basingstoke, UK: Macmillan.

Macdonald, I. (1983). *Immigration law and practice in the United Kingdom*. London: Butterworths.

McCrudden, C. (1982). Institutional discrimination. *Oxford Journal of Legal Studies, 2*, 303-367.

Miles, R. (1984). The riots of 1958: Notes on the ideological construction of "race relations" as a political issue in Britain. *Immigrants and Minorities, 3*(3), 252-275.

Miles, R., & Phizacklea, A. (1984). *White man's country*. London: Pluto.

Organisation for Economic Cooperation and Development (OECD). (1986). *United Kingdom: National report for OECD conference on the future of migration*. Paris: Author.

Patterson, S. (1969). *Immigration and race relations in Britain 1960-67*. London: Oxford University Press.

Phizacklea, A., & Miles, R. (1980). *Labour and racism*. London: Routledge.

Pilkington, E. (1988). *Beyond the mother country: West Indians and the Notting Hill White riots*. London: I. B. Tauris.

Reeves, F. (1983). *British racial discourse*. Cambridge, UK: Cambridge University Press.

Rose, E. J. B., & Associates. (1969). *Colour and citizenship: A report on British race relations*. London: Oxford University Press.

Scarman, Lord. (1981). *The Brixton disorders 10-12 April 1981: Report of an inquiry by the Rt Hon. The Lord Scarman OBE*. London: Her Majesty's Stationery Office.

Select Committee on Race Relations and Immigration. (1978). *Immigration*. London: Her
  Majesty's Stationery Office.
Sivanandan, A. (1982). *A different hunger.* London: Pluto.
Solomos, J. (1988). *Black youth, racism and the state.* Cambridge, UK: Cambridge
  University Press.
Solomos, J. (1993). *Race and racism in Britain.* London: Macmillan.
The Times. (1968). *The Black man in search of power.* London: Nelson.

9

Racism and Anti-Racism
in Western Europe

Louis Kushnick

There is mounting fear for the safety and future of Europe's estimated 15 million people of Black, Third World, and peripheral country origin. This fear is based on an increasing level of racial violence and murders in Western Europe and the increasing share of votes received by far-Right political parties such as France's Front National and Germany's Republikaner Partei. Fears have also increased due to the increasingly unaccountable and undemocratic nature of decision making with regard to "racial" populations within what has been called "Fortress Europe."

Races do not exist biologically or genetically, but are defined by physical categories and from geographic locations (Gould, 1981; Stanfield, 1991; Winant & Omi, 1986). At different points in European history, groups have been defined in racial terms without having different skin color. For example, the Irish were defined as a race by the English in the 17th century during the conquest of Ireland and displacement of the Irish Catholic peasants from their land (Hechter, 1975). Although skin color has been used to determine racial hierarchy in White-settler societies, such as the

AUTHOR'S NOTE: This chapter was made possible by generous financial support from the Faculty of Arts, University of Manchester; the University of Manchester Fund for Staff Travel for Research in the Humanities and Social Sciences; and from the Small Grants Scheme in the Social Sciences of the Nuffield Foundation.

United States, Australia, and South Africa, racial dominance does not depend on different skin color. The potential for "racial" conflict exists among people with few physical distinctions, but who differ in culture, religion, and national origin.

In most European countries, a variety of identifiable groups are defined racially and treated differentially: Polish miners in France and Belgium; recently settled migrant workers from the colonial empires, such as Suranamese and Indonesians in the Netherlands; Afro-Caribbeans and Asians in Great Britain; North Africans and Africans from sub-Saharan Africa in France; and recently settled migrant workers from peripheral countries, such as Turks in Germany. Then there are settled minority populations like the Roma people in various European countries, as well as various refugees and asylum seekers (MacEwen & Prior, 1992). How these groups are defined, what subordinate roles they play in Great Britain, France, Germany, and other Western European countries, and how they are controlled come out of historic racial practices. This process, now under way in Western Europe, is the subject of this chapter.

RACE AND
THE EUROPEAN COMMUNITY

Europe, particularly the countries of the European Community (EC), has been constructing a new European identity while it has been constructing the barriers of Fortress Europe. This new identity is a racialized identity. Europe is being defined in terms of its imperialist past, with its civilizing mission in opposition to the Third World and the countries of the periphery, and in terms of Christianity in opposition to Islam. In doing so, Western Europe has excluded what has been called the EC's 13th nation, the 15 million or so descendants of other nations (Pieterse, 1991). This racist ideological construction has been paralleled by racial discrimination in terms of immigration policy, policing and criminal justice policies, education, and health and housing policies—state racism. This is a common, European racism with a common view,

which defines all Third World people as immigrants and refugees, and all immigrants and refugees as terrorists and drug-runners, [which] will not be able to tell a citizen from an immigrant or an immigrant from a refugee, let alone one black from another. They all carry their passports on their faces. (Sivanandan, 1991, p. v)

It is important to analyze the root causes of these developments and to attempt to identify their ramifications for Europe and its people. It is essential to challenge the media and politicians, who place the responsibility for the rise of racism on the victims of it—migrants, settler workers, asylum seekers, and refugees. For example, the Conservative government in Britain and most of the British media have blamed the rise of neo-Nazi violence in Germany and the rise of neo-Nazi groups in continental Europe on the invasion of bogus asylum seekers. In March 1992, Douglas Hurd, the British Foreign Secretary, linked "feeble immigration laws" with the rise of Europe's neo-Nazi Right and asserted "There is no sign that the Labour Party understands it [the tenfold increase in asylum applications in the past three years] or can be trusted to deal with it. On past form they will handle it with slogans and ambiguities" (*Daily Mail*, March 26, 1992).

The debate in Germany over racist violence has been structured by the government as a debate over Germany's constitutional obligation to receive asylum seekers. There has been an attempt to "explain" German violence as a result of the economic and social dislocations associated with reunification, particularly unemployment in the former East Germany. The newly unemployed, especially the young, facing the collapse of the old order and lacking the skills, psychological orientation, and competitive values necessary to survive in the new capitalist environment, have turned on guest workers and asylum seekers as scapegoats. It is their view that these "foreigners" are getting everything, whereas they, good Germans, are getting nothing. This explanation is not adequate and does not explain the rise of neo-Nazi violence and political activity in the former West Germany, as well as in France, which has not gone through unification. Why is the level of racist violence greater in Britain than in Germany?

ROOTS OF THE
NEW EUROPEAN RACISM

European racism was an integral part of the historical processes of nation building and economic development, which involved the conquest of large parts of the rest of the world and the construction of a world system based on slavery, plantation production, and superexploitation. Instead of being isolated in the colonies, racism and superexploitation continued after World War II as Europe sought to meet its need for cheap labor (Castles & Miller, 1993; Moch, 1992; Potts, 1990). Subsequent changes in European economies decreased the demand for labor-intensive industries. As a result, the demand for cheaper labor increased; this demand could be filled only by marginal, illegal employment in the service sector (Wallraff, 1988). Massive deindustrialization, deskilling, and underemployment of the citizen workforce reduced the demand for higher-priced domestic labor as a whole (Hollifield, 1992). As transnational corporations penetrate the Third World, they have taken European jobs with them (Gaffiken & Morrisey, 1992; Michie & Smith, 1994; Mitter, 1986; Sassen, 1988). Furthermore, social and economic dislocation in the Third World, due to European domination, has generated refugees and asylum seekers eager to enter the European mother economy.

Racial differences between the European mother country and the external colonies are now used to control and exploit the majority of the population in Western Europe (Fekete & Webber, 1994). These differences are internal. The Western European "common person" is now faced with a decline in the standard of living and more competition for fewer jobs. As in the days when Western Europe held external colonies, those responsible for exploitation are not held accountable. Instead, the crisis is due to the "racialized" immigrants, refugees, and asylum seekers.

Popular racism emerges out of and is validated by state racism. In this case, increasing class division and insecurity have led to racist stereotypes and fears. Therefore, "in our time, the seed-bed of fascism is racism" (Sivanandan, 1993, p. 69). This analysis has been supported by the findings of a number of other scholars (Dummett & Nicol, 1990; Hainsworth, 1992; MacEwen & Prior, 1992). Political and media manipulation has fostered and legitimated racialist and xenophobic ideas. The experience of those at the cutting edge, migrants and refugees, provides further validation of this crucial analysis. The Refugee Forum and Migrants Rights Action Network (1991) found that,

> it is no coincidence that countries such as Italy, which did not experience racial attacks on its North African workers, began to see vicious attacks at the time when its government began imposing immigration restrictions. Unlike wealth, racism does "trickle down" from the top, and when governments define people as unwelcome and undesirable, their populations follow. (p. 16)

This understanding is central to the development of a strategy to challenge this racism.

THE DEVELOPMENT OF
POSTWAR STATE RACISM

Working-class militancy after World War II created the political environment for welfare capitalism—the social wage—expanding the state role in providing a safety net. Working-class institutions and social democratic parties failed to build upon that militancy, and the increasing tendency of trade unionists to see themselves as an "established" middle class led to a weakening of the working class' ability to defend its gains. Imperialism and unequal international development provided populations available for recruitment to the metropolis as cheap labor. This labor was cheap not because of anything inherent, but because of the racial and national hierarchies into which it was slotted. Outsiders were brought in to do the menial work of Western society, in the hospitals, hotels, the kitchens, the foundries, on the buses, at building sites, and outside the trade unions. They arrived fully grown, fully educated, ready to work at little cost to the receiving country—thus, they represented a form of foreign aid from the periphery to the metropolis.

Immigrants work for less because the historic racist view, reinforced by political parties and trade unions, excludes rather than includes them. As in the United States, European trade unionists assumed that by keeping the "coloured" out, they were defending higher-income jobs. They were convinced that, because they were White and European, they would never have to step down to the lower-paying, dirty service jobs—the class of work beneath them. This was reflected in a variety of ways, including a refusal by the post-World War II British Labour government to confront the racist culture and take measures to incorporate Afro-Caribbeans and Asians into the polity and society. The leaders of the Labour Party acted as if the White working class was naturally racist (Carter, Harris, & Joshi, 1987; Harris, 1991; Joshi & Carter, 1984). Postwar French governments, including Socialist and Communist parties, fought brutal and fundamentally racist colonial wars in Indochina and Algeria to maintain France's position in the world and to continue to validate its civilizing mission. These wars reinforced racist assumptions and the presumed link between race and nationality. Other excolonial countries such as Belgium and the Netherlands have had similar histories and cultures, which also reinforced nationalist and racist political culture and identity.

Germany's defeat in World War II was not followed by root and branch de-Nazification—primarily because of Western Europe's preoccupation with anti-Communism. The determination to leave affairs of state in "safe" hands was accompanied by a reluctance of those safe hands to confront the ideological bases of Nazism, including its definition of what constitutes Germanness. The consequences of this failure are still playing out in Germany today. German-born children of Turkish settlers are not German citizens, yet so-called ethnic Germans from the former Soviet Union who have never lived in Germany and do not speak German are allowed entry and automatic citizenship on the basis of blood, as institutionalized in Article 116 of the German Constitution.

In the words of Oskar Lafontaine, deputy Social Democrat leader, Germany should, like France and the United States, adopt a "truly Republican understanding of nationhood," because history has shown that nationalist radicalism flourished where the "law of blood" ruled. Cornelia Schmalz-Jacobsen, the government-appointed commissioner for foreigners, has declared, "Nowhere has blood dripped so thickly into law. . . . Many of the problems we have with immigrants today would not have arisen if we had allowed people who have long formed a . . . part of our population to become Germans."

Naturalization is not granted as a rule. At the moment, only about 1,000 Turks a year manage to get through the immensely complicated process of naturalization. If automatic citizenship were granted to children of the fourth and fifth generations, 1.5 million foreigners would be living in Germany as citizens with restricted rights. Figures show that 25% of immigrants' children are under 18 years old, and that two-thirds of them were born in Germany, making up what is called "youth without a German passport" (*Guardian,* 1993).

MIGRANTS ARE AT THE LOW END OF THE TOTEM POLE

The concentration of migrants/settlers in the worst jobs with the worst working conditions at the lowest pay and status has reinforced the view that immigrants do the jobs that host country workers no longer have to do. The "native" race is raised in status—validating the race/nation hierarchy. Racial ideological stratification is thus reinforced by material stratification. Migrants lack political rights because they are not citizens, and thus their social wage is lower than the social wage of indigenous workers. They occupy the worst and most overcrowded housing, pay social security/national insurance taxes, and do not receive commensurate benefits. These workers subsidize the higher social wage of the indigenous workers. They are also more exploitable, lacking citizenship and the protection of working-class organizations. Even where migrants are skilled, or professional, a pecking order exists, with the migrant professionals occupying the lower-status sectors of the professions.

CRIMINALIZATION OF MIGRANTS

The exclusion of migrants/settlers from the political process has reinforced the processes of marginalization and criminalization of these communities by the media and the state. In Britain, Afro-Caribbeans, particularly young Afro-Caribbean males, are criminalized as muggers by the press (Hall, Crichter, Jefferson, Clarke, & Roberts, 1978; Institute of Race Relations, 1987; Smith, 1983). An important parallel to these developments can be found in the Netherlands, where in early 1993 the chief police officer in Amsterdam, Eric Nordholt, claimed on a radio program that "black youth from Surinam, the Antilles and Morocco committed 80% of street crime" and warned of Los Angeles-style riots. However, a city police spokesman admitted that the figure referred only to suspects—not those arrested and convicted—and that figures for all crimes were not available as "the police only analyzed street crime on the basis of a suspect's racial origin" (*Statewatch*, 1993, p. 3).

Similar attempts to criminalize migrants have been made by police and politicians in France, Germany, and other EC countries and have served as the basis for legitimating increasingly repressive violations of the legal rights of migrants. In 1986, the senator for internal affairs in West Berlin called refugees "drug containers" (Rathzel, 1991, p. 37). Linking migrants, refugees, and asylum seekers with drugs and crime has been central to the Rightward march of national politics and to EC-wide controls and restrictions. The TREVI group of interior ministers has as its mission the interdiction of terrorism, radicalism, extremism, violence, and immigration (hence TREVI).

Responding to the equation of migrants and criminality, Bashy Qureishy of Third World Voice in Denmark said at the Communities of Resistance Conference on November 11, 1989,

In May 1980 Mrs. Thatcher said, "I did not join Europe to have free movement of terrorists, drug traffickers, animal diseases, rabies, and illegal immigrants." I for one object to being put in the same class as a disease. At Heathrow, on my way to this conference, I was treated as a suspect by racist immigration officers. (Communities of Resistance Network, 1991, p. 11)

The combination of criminalization; bad housing; the worst jobs; high levels of unemployment; differential, racist education; and a racist criminal justice system has led to a Black male imprisonment rate in Britain twice that of White males and a Black female imprisonment rate three times that of White women. France, Germany, and other Western European countries have seen similar patterns of criminalization and stereotyping.

The channeling of young settlers into unemployment or marginal employment has become a feature of Western European life. Although the ghettos that have been created are not so racially monolithic as those in the United States, there has been a pattern of racial concentration in areas of deprivation, poor housing, and lack of amenities. This racial concentration is then turned into a blaming-the-victim syndrome, whereby the residents of these areas, who are confined to them, are blamed for their existence and identified as the outsiders who produce such alien environments.

EUROPEAN MOVE TO THE RIGHT

In France, by the early 1990s, mainstream Right-wing politicians had moved so deep into the terrain of the far-Right that Jacques Chirac, mayor of Paris and now president elect, spoke of "a family with a father, three or four wives, 20 children and 50,000 francs in welfare benefits without working." With these neighbors "and their noise and smell," French workers "would go crazy" as a result of "an overdose of immigration" (*Guardian,* June 21, 1991). In September 1991, former president Valery Giscard d'Estaing described immigration as an "invasion" and demanded the end of the automatic right of nationality by birth on French soil (*Guardian,* September 24, 1991). (This would bring France in line with Germany and Britain, which abolished that right in the Thatcher government's 1981 Nationality Act. One of the first acts of the Right-wing French government elected in 1993 was to implement d'Estaing's recommendation.) Following these comments, Jean-Marie Le Pen declared that he now considered himself to be the leader of the center.

This move to the right was in response to the extreme Right's use of racist appeals, particularly in the area of immigration control (Hainsworth,

1992). The need for the center to move to the right was articulated by Giscard ally and former Interior Minister Michel Poniatowski, who said that unless the Right allied with Le Pen, "France would become an African and socialist boulevard given over to anarchy" (*L'Humanité,* February 17, 1993; *L'Monde,* February 18, 1993). Le Pen welcomed the promise by Prime Minister Edith Cresson to fight illegal immigration with mass expulsion, including the use of charter planes—a position from which she was forced to retreat, after reviving memories of the deportation of 101 Malians on a charter plane in 1986.

EFFORTS TO FORCE MIGRANTS OUT

There was a spectacular increase in deportation orders in France under the 1989 Joxe law, which succeeded the 1986 Pasqua laws. In 1989, 9,647 people were issued deportation orders; by 1991, the figure had jumped to 32,673 and the figures for the first quarter of 1992 maintained this increase (*Le Monde,* January 14, 1993). The National Association for the Assistance of Foreigners at Frontiers (ANAFE) issued a report criticizing the conditions in which refugees and immigration prisoners are kept in detention zones. In July 1992, the French government passed the Quiles law, whereby ports and airports were authorized to set up detention zones. The judicial process for detainees and the violent methods by which people are deported was described as a "farce" (*L'Humanité,* February 17, 1993; *Le Monde,* February 18, 1993).

The construction of the migrant worker/settler as the outsider both limits migrants' rights during the period in which their labor is required and has laid the groundwork for attacks on them in this period of deindustrialization, deskilling, and resurgent mass unemployment. The European governments have tried to pressure migrants to "return" to their homelands without great success. They have even pressured migrants born in Western European countries. Attempts to buy migrants out have failed for three reasons. First, the continuing pattern of uneven economic development means that conditions for returnees in sending countries are still much worse than those in the host countries. Second, the amount of money offered was insufficient to make a fundamental change upon return to the native country. Finally, migrants have formed new social ties in their adopted countries.

All of these measures, including forced repatriation, have been insufficient to remove more than 2 million people. But state racism has been successful in labeling them as people who do not belong and reinforcing their role as lightening rods for fear and hatred, as social and economic problems have increased through no fault of the migrants'.

IDEOLOGICAL JUSTIFICATION OF REPRESSION

The ideological justifications for attempts to rid European nations of their now unwanted settlers laid the groundwork for increased racialist feeling and racist violence—racism "trickling down." As Simpson and Read (1991) conclude, there is a "momentum which seeks to describe Europe's future in terms which are increasingly white, continental and Christian. It is, in essence, the re-creation of Christendom" (p. 33). In December 1982, an editorial in the Frankfurter *Allgemeine* declared:

> the interchange between Slav, Romanic, Germanic and other Celtic peoples has become a habit. A tacit "we-feeling" has arisen in one and the same European culture. But excluded from this are the Turk-peoples, the Palestinians, North Africans and others from totally alien cultures. They, and only they, are the "foreigner problem" in the Federal Republic. (cited in Webber, 1991, p. 13)

Rathzel (1991) argues that an "unintended 'cooperation' " between Left and Right has constructed "a negative image of the migrant" (p. 38). The liberal and highly respected newspaper *Die Zeit* published an article by the general secretary of the German Red Cross, arguing that non-Central European people should be repatriated to avoid a break in German history. About the same time, the "Heidelberger Manifesto" was published. The work of a number of professors from different universities, it argues that the "mixture" of different cultures would be damaging to everybody; all people should live in their "own" place. And whereas the public version of their manifesto wrote of different cultures, the private version (leaked to the press) discussed people as biological and cybernetic systems with different traits passed on to subsequent generations through genes and tradition (see Rathzel, 1991).

On the European Community level, member states have constructed a range of institutions to control immigration refugee/asylum policies in a fashion that denies accountability to the European Parliament and facilitates the construction of Fortress Europe. Among these intergovernmental bodies are the TREVI group of ministers, the Ad Hoc Group on Immigration, and the Schengen Accord, in which participating nations set the agenda for a community-wide system of control. These structures are not subject to democratic controls or accountability by the European parliaments. Tony Bunyan, editor of *Statewatch* and keen student of policing in Europe, sees lurking behind these institutions "the beginnings of another state apparatus, made up of ad hoc and secretive bodies and separate inter-governmental arrangements, which reflects the repressive side of European political development and is largely unaccountable and undemocratic in its workings." He makes the point that,

> Crucially, [all of these intergovernment arrangements] focus on immigration in terms of a "law and order" issue and the development of international cooperation on policing. The equation of blacks with crime and drugs and terrorism, and all of that with illegal immigration, has spread across Europe so that it now forms a basis for the new European state. (Bunyan, 1991, p. 20; see also Baldwin-Edwards, 1991; Cruz, 1990; Refugee Forum and the Migrants Rights Action Network, 1991; Spencer, 1990)

Measures taken by EC countries throughout the 1980s and into the 1990s were designed to stigmatize asylum seekers as bogus and as economic rather than political refugees. The real goal is to limit the numbers who successfully gain citizenship. In fact, there is little basis in the contemporary world for a differentiation between economic and political refugees.

The Effects of Transnational Economics

A factor that blurs the apparently clear-cut differences between political and economic refugees is also a consequence of the relationship between transnational corporations (TNCs), governments, and local elites. Local elites argue that they must offer attractive conditions for transnational capital to obtain investment, especially because they are in competition with elites from other countries of the periphery for that investment. They therefore offer cheap labor and little regulation or interference with TNC activities. This ultimately places the elites in conflict with their own populations, the majority of whom pay the price of attracting and retaining the TNC investment. Governments in such circumstances have tended to become repressive to maintain order and retain power, and often create or exacerbate ethnic, tribal, or racial differences to divide and rule. People fleeing from massacres and po-groms that have been encouraged or tolerated by governments are fleeing from the consequences of economic penetration, as are unemployed migrants displaced from rural farmland. Refusal by governments to rec-ognize their involvement in the situation of migrants, refugees, and asylum seekers is purposeful and designed to limit responsibility and the rights of such people to enter their countries (Sivanandan, 1982; 1990).

Government Policies

An Amnesty International report (1991) concludes that Europe's in-creasingly restrictive approach to asylum seekers is threatening to under-mine universal standards meant to protect people who are fleeing from serious human rights violations and that, too often, would-be asylum seekers are treated as illegal immigrants. A 1992 study by the Organisa-tion for Economic Cooperation and Development (OECD) concludes that,

> The relatively high refusal rate revealed by a study of claims for asylum in several OECD countries suggests that in 1990 and 1991 claims continued to be motivated by reasons that had nothing to do with the original objectives of the asylum seeking procedure. . . . By and large, in the European OECD countries, applications are scrutinised more briefly and treated more harshly than in the past. (p. 13)

In Germany, a controversial law aimed at speeding up asylum proce-dures and allowing refugees to be housed in collection camps came into force on July 1, 1992, to deal with the estimated 400,000 asylum seekers that year. The law concentrates power over asylum seekers and deporta-tions in the central government and stipulates that applications that are "obviously unfounded" must be dealt with within six weeks, after which time unsuccessful applicants will be sent back to their homeland. The head of Germany's central office for the recognition of refugees, Norbert Von Niedig, resigned in protest of the new law. He argued that existing legislation could have dealt with the backlog of 300,000 applicants if the central government had provided funding and staff. He said the new law gave the "false impression" that all future applications would be handled in record time and would create mistaken expectations and fuel anti-foreign sentiment.

Governments have committed themselves to a regime of permanent deflation, and consequently mass unemployment. The ideological remnants of the supposed triumph of free market monetarism in countries such as Britain have added to the problem because of low inflation. These economic conditions have political consequences:

> The poor, discontented and marginalized, who are in increasing numbers paying for this, will note the apparent failure of democracy. At best they will become alienated and cynical. But more and more of them are clearly turning to authoritarian and xenophobic ideologies. (Toporowski, 1992, p. 24)

Gerald Holtham, chief economist for Lehman Brothers International, discusses in similar terms the consequences of the Thatcher-Reagan agenda, which,

> cut back access to social security and unemployment benefit, reduce[d] the latter in real terms, bust the unions, [encouraged] private state enterprises to subject their workers to "market forces," ma[d]e the workers more insecure and the labor market more competitive. That agenda, or part of it, was followed in most OECD countries. (*Independent on Sunday,* Business Section, January 10, 1993)

If immigration had not been racialized and blamed for Europe's declining standard of living, the state and private sector policies responsible for the decline would be apparent. Current levels of unemployment and job flight would not be tolerated.

TRADE UNIONS

Faced with attacks on their living standards and future opportunities, working-class Europeans have searched for support and leadership. Unfortunately, their trade unions and social democratic parties have been unable and/or unwilling to provide that leadership. A loss of militancy and awareness of interest are the outcomes of labor's participation in the welfare capitalism of the postwar period. Higher status for national labor was partly due to widespread acceptance of immigrants as non-union cheap labor. In time, European labor institutions became willing participants in their own demise. The racist compromise also led to the exclusion of the most militant and most class-conscious portions of the working class from positions of leadership within the postwar union organizations.

Migrant workers and settlers could have been valuable members of the union movement. Due to their repression and exclusion from the social benefits of compromise, they were potentially more aware of economic trends and practices that would ultimately lead to the demise of labor in Europe. Instead of being part of labor, participating in its leadership and bringing their perspective to bear, they had to fight against the racist practices of European trade unions as well as state racism.

USE OF RACE IN POLITICS

Faced with the failure of their union organizations, White European working-class people had to find explanations of and solutions to their dilemma. It is not surprising that Right-wing politicians and parties, whether within the mainstream or on the fringe of the political system, have used the race card to divert attention from the capitalist agenda (Krieger, 1986). If Blacks, Turks, Algerians, and the like are "the other," and if they (the civilized) are being swamped by alien cultures, then it is clear that the others are the cause of problems. Hordes of aliens are trying to take over their living standards and pose a threat.

The growing appeal of far-Right racist and fascist parties in Western Europe must be seen in this context. In the French regional elections of March 1992, exit polls indicated that the Front National made strong inroads into the industrial working class. The far-Right continued the pattern of winning more votes than either the Socialists or the Communists in the so-called "red belt" around Paris. The Front's 19% support among workers nationally equaled that of the Socialist Party and the conservative union. The working-class vote amounted to around 28% of the FN's total 13.9% vote, and the FN was able to gain increased support from the people in the 18-25 age range, among whom unemployment stood at 28% (*Searchlight,* May 1992, p. 18). Although the Front National did not win any seats in the 1993 National Assembly elections, and indeed lost the only seat it had held, it gained over 12% of the vote, compared to 9% in 1988, emerging as the third party in many key urban areas.

In the 1992 elections in Berlin, the fascist Republikaner Partei (REP) gained its biggest support in those working-class districts of west Berlin said to be Social Democratic Party strongholds. In elections in April 1992, 13% of the REP votes in Baden-Wurttemberg and 7.4% of the neo-Nazi Deutsche Volksunion (DVU) vote in Schleswig-Holstein were garnered in urban areas. This support was particularly heavy "among voters under 30 years of age and industrial workers in the bigger cities, where the fascists exploited resentment against foreigners with claims that 'they are taking jobs from Germans'" (*Searchlight,* May 1992, p. 15). The REP, which campaigned on law and order issues, the expulsion of "foreign criminals," and a reduction in the number of asylum seekers, increased its share of the vote in local elections in Hesse in March 1993. In Frankfurt, the REP won 10 seats on a 93-seat city council. An opinion poll carried out after these elections and published in *Der Spiegel* found support for the REP running nationwide at 6%—up from 4% before the Hesse elections—and 80% of Germans believing that it is "probable," even "certain," that the REP would gain seats in the Bundestag in the 1994 national elections (*Independent,* March 21, 1993). However, the REP vote plummeted to less than 2% (*Searchlight,* November 1994, p. 21).

The French and German political elite have pointed to these outcomes as justifications for "necessary" and "pragmatic" responses to public support for increasingly restrictive immigration controls. In May 1993, the German government, with the support of the SPD opposition, pushed through the Bundestag legislation that ended the guaranteed right of all foreigners to seek asylum. The justification, accepted by the leaders of the mainstream parties, was that the legislation was needed to preserve social peace in Germany. According to Wolfgang Schauble, parliamentary leader of Chancellor Helmut Kohl's Christian Democratic Union, "Our citizens are frightened by the unchecked refugee influx. . . . We owe them a social order that allows Germans and foreigners to live peacefully side by side" (*Guardian,* May 27, 1993).

Restrictions against racialized foreigners were seen as another crucial step toward the construction of Fortress Europe, administered by increasingly unaccountable institutions and defined by increasing control of settlers, migrants, and Blacks. The reality of the development of a common European identity—an identity based on racism—is that such measures leading to a new social order will not allow White Europeans and foreigners to live peacefully side by side. In Britain, the level of racist violence and harassment is much greater in the 1990s than it was in 1962, 1965, 1968, or 1971, when the state made attempts to enable Whites and Blacks to live peacefully side by side.

Ford (1992) estimates that there was a racial attack in Britain every 26 minutes in the early 1990s. Home Office (House of Commons, 1994) figures for England and Wales for 1992 indicate that there were nearly

9,000 reported racial attacks that year—double the number reported five years earlier (Klein, 1995). (For a general discussion of racial violence, see Brown, 1984; Commission for Racial Equality, 1987; Cooper & Qureshi, 1993; Fekete, 1988; Ginsburg, 1989; Greater London Council, 1984; Independent Committee of Inquiry, 1987; Institute of Race Relations, 1987; London Borough of Waltham Forest, 1990; Sheffield Racial Harassment Project, 1988; Tompson, 1988; Walsh, 1987.)

ANTI-RACIST STRATEGIES

Given the specific nature of contemporary European racism, it is clear that an anti-racist policy in Europe must fight for the rights of refugees and asylum seekers at the same time it is fighting for full democratic rights for settlers. Such a policy must challenge the historical definitions of "us versus them" rooted in the identities of Western Europeans. European identities are integrally connected with the history of imperialism, the slave trade, colonialism, the ideology of bringing civilization to other countries. The racist construction of European national identities has accompanied and legitimated the widening class inequalities of the capitalist nations of Western Europe. This racism has also been effective in distorting the class consciousness constructed by the European working class (Kushnick, 1981; in press).

But these racist national identities have not been internalized at all times and under all circumstances. Racism is not normal, natural, or biological. It is the product of distortion, and can be overcome by principled struggle. The very fate of Western democracy may rest on the outcome. For just as inauthentic socialist democracies in the East did not last, inauthentic capitalist democracies may fall under the weight of racism.

A principled anti-racist strategy is necessary to challenge the acceptance of the new international order at home and abroad that impoverishes people in and outside metropolitan Western Europe. The domestic policies of corporate capitalists and their political agents are racist, nationalist, and fascist. Settlers, migrants, refugees, and asylum seekers have been scapegoated by popular racism. Meanwhile, a new and more effective system of profit seeking is being put in place that is producing high unemployment and high insecurity for labor both in and outside Europe. Britain's Campaign Against Racism and Fascism (CARF) argues:

> Unity needs to be worked at. And experience shows that racism can best be challenged by working within the working class, on a long-term basis, over

issues of housing, education, employment, low pay, [and] policing football. It is around these issues that, in some areas at least, Black and White unity has become a reality. But if we are to enlarge and extend that unity, we must discard old orthodoxies and see anti-fascism not as a dogma or anti-racism as a cause, but both as being part of a creative socialist process. (*CARF,* January/February 1992, p. 4)

From a more comprehensive perspective, it is crucial to challenge the idea that racist violence can be stopped by focusing only on skinheads, neo-Nazis, and other extremists. Europe cannot rely on organizing primarily against fascists, because the popular culture of racism, deriving its sustenance and sanction from state racism, provides the seed-bed of fascism. State racism is incorporated into the German Constitution in Article 116; in the increasingly restrictive and undemocratic institutions of Fortress Europe; and in the racialized educational, health, employment, housing, and criminal justice systems of European countries. These institutions shape the lives of the settlers, migrants, and refugees in Western Europe as well as the political awareness and understanding of White working people. Thus,

the fight against fascism must begin in the fight against racism, in the community, and involve the whole community. Fighting fascism per se will not eliminate racism; but eliminating racism would cut the ground from under fascist feet. (Sivanandan, 1993, p. 69)

The new struggle must be organized from the bottom up rather than the top down. Organizations that have attempted top-down change, such as the Socialist Party in France, claim to lead the anti-racist struggle, but they have proved unable to organize and represent the settlers and migrants. Top-down organizations have proved unable or unwilling to challenge state racism. As a result, they are unable to stem the tide of popular racism and the rightward shift of European political institutions.

For example, although the FN lost its only seat in the French Parliament in the 1993 elections, the new Right-wing government of Edouard Balladur began implementing many of the FN's proposals. On his first day as prime minister, Balladur promised to crack down on "illegal immigrants" and to change the nationality law to oblige children of migrants to apply for French citizenship—long demanded by the extreme Right.

Large and well-attended protest marches may represent for many an expression of revulsion against neo-Nazi offenses, but they are reactive. The agenda has been set by the fascists, and the presence of governmental and political leaders diverts attention from the state racism that underpins popular racism. Micha Brumlik, professor of education in Frankfurt and Heidelberg, has argued that the tens of thousands of Germans who took part in the *Lichterketten,* the recent processions of candle-carrying protesters through the streets of Germany's cities,

> overlooked . . . that the heightened risk of other people being persecuted does not stem solely from torches of young arsonists, but from what took place under cold neon light—the discussions and suggestions made to change Germany's asylum laws [and] in the searchlights of the border police on the river Oder. (reprinted in the *Guardian,* February 5, 1993)

BOTTOM-UP ORGANIZING

Examples of organizing from the bottom up can be found throughout Europe. In 1991, a group of Leeds United fans decided that they could no longer allow racist and fascist recruiting activities, which had been dominant at Elland Road throughout the 1980s, to continue. They formed Leeds Fans United Against Racism and Fascism and began distributing leaflets discussing their concern about the unacceptable nature of racist behavior. They feel they have succeeded,

> where other groups like the Anti-Nazi League failed, because our campaign is based around football—for fans, by fans. . . . What we have succeeded in doing is to show ordinary fans of other clubs that racist behaviour can be successfully combated by fans themselves. (*CARF,* April/May 1991, p. 12)

In 1992, fans of St. Pauli, a German second-division club based in a multiracial area of Hamburg, organized a strong anti-racist, anti-fascist campaign against racism in German football. The symbol of the campaign has been the *St. Pauli Fans Gegen Rechts* (St. Pauli Fans Against the Right) stickers, which have appeared all over Europe. The campaign made contact with local Black communities and paraded massive anti-racist banners on match days (*CARF,* May/June 1992, p. 15).

Anti-racists have participated in campaigns against the deportation of refugees throughout Europe. In Denmark, a group of Palestinians from Lebanon sought sanctuary in a church in Copenhagen after being served with deportation orders. They were supported by a wide range of Danish people. As a result, the Danish government was forced to allow the Palestinians to stay. Others have supported campaigns initiated by settlers and migrants, such as those in Germany calling for repeal of Article 116, so that people born in Germany can become citizens and long-term residents can have access to citizenship. Gaining citizenship would enable migrants and settlers to struggle more effectively for their democratic rights and to challenge their continuing definition as outsiders. A similar campaign is being waged in Belgium. The key to the participation of anti-racists is that they are prepared to accept the leadership of settlers and migrants rather than continuing the historic pattern of Eurocentric expectations of leadership.

A number of organizations monitor and work against racism in Europe. The Early Years Trainers Anti-Racist Network, Save the Children Fund in Scotland, and the Working Group Against Racism in Children's Resources produce anti-racist resource materials. Among the other organizations that have been monitoring and organizing against both racism and fascism are the Campaign Against Racism and Fascism, with its bimonthly publication *CARF*; the Institute of Race Relations, with its European Race Audit project and journal *Race and Class*; the Runnymede Trust, with *Runnymede Bulletin*; *Statewatch,* which monitors European developments in its publication; Sage Race Relations Abstracts; Searchlight; Refugee Forum and Migrants Action Network; the Anti-Racist Initiative in Berlin; the Churches Committee for Migrants in Europe in Brussels; and the Dutch Federation of Anti-Discrimination Centres.

CONCLUSION

The economic and political crises facing Western European societies are fundamental and interconnected. The creation and maintenance of mass unemployment and the cuts in the social wage are not only producing despair and hopelessness, they are also producing conditions suitable for the spread of authoritarianism and fascism. They enable mainstream Right-wing governments to play the race card for electoral benefit and to divert systematic decisions away from the cause of social misery. The more racial stereotyping and scapegoating are used, the more historically rooted popular racism is validated.

The greater the appeal of fascists and the far-Right, the greater the danger that mainstream politicians will move farther to the right to keep up with public support. Right-wing politicians will continue to play the race card, and we may very well see the reemergence of Right-wing, fascist governments in Western Europe such as those that led up to World

War II. The other potential is the decreasing ability of the state to provide material benefits to enough sections of the White working class to buy their acquiescence and loyalty.

Increasing inequality and deskilling much of the White working class are necessary to advance transnational capitalism. Politics as usual is proving incapable of maintaining standards of living and has reduced the likelihood of transmitting high standards to the next generation. Conditions for Europe's Black and migrant/settler communities continue to worsen. The stage is set for a repeat of Europe's worst hour.

Anti-racist and anti-fascist political education and mobilization of both European Whites and people of color are desperately needed. A successful struggle depends upon its being inclusive. British miners and their families during the 1984-1985 strike learned whose interest the state serves—not theirs. A disproportionate share of the support they received came from Britain's Black communities. As a result, miners were able to see common interests with Blacks. Clearly, there is the potential for other White people to learn from these conditions and reject racism and fascism as part of the common best interest.

The choice facing the people of Western Europe is not one of White, indigenous democracies on one side and racism and authoritarianism for Blacks, migrants, and settlers on the other. An inclusive nonracist democracy must be forged that can provide a decent standard of living for all. The alternative is an authoritarian European state. Which outcome will come to pass depends on the ability of the anti-racist movements in Europe to mobilize successfully; to organize from the bottom up; to create a vision of a humane alternative; and to unify Black and White, settler, migrant, asylum seeker, and the native-born.

REFERENCES

Amnesty International. (1991). *Europe: Human rights and the need for a fair asylum policy*. Geneva.

Baldwin-Edwards, M. (1991). Immigration after 1992. *Policy and Politics, 19*(3), 199-211.

Brown, C. (1984). *Black and White Britain: The third PSI survey*. London: Heinemann.

Bunyan, T. (1991). Toward an authoritarian European state. *Race and Class, 32*(3), 19-30.

Carter, B., Harris, C., & Joshi, S. (1987). *The 1951-55 Conservative government and the racialisation of Black immigrants* (Policy Paper in Ethnic Relations, No. 11). Coventry, UK: University of Warwick, Centre for Research in Ethnic Relations.

Castles, S., & Miller, M. J. (1993). *The age of migration*. London: Macmillan.

Commission for Racial Equality. (1987). *Racial attacks—Survey of eight areas of Britain*. London: Author.

Communities of Resistance Network. (1991). *Communities of resistance, 1992; First launch report.* London: Author.

Cooper, J., & Qureshi, T. (1993). *Through patterns not our own.* London: New Ethnicities Research & Education Group.

Cruz, A. (1990). *An insight into Schengen, TREVI and other European intergovernmental bodies* (Briefing Paper No. 1, 2nd ed.). Brussels: Churches Committee for Migrants in Europe.

Dummett, A., & Nicol, A. (1990). *Subjects, citizens, aliens and others: Nationality and immigration law.* London: Weidenfeld & Nicolson.

Fekete, L. (1988). Racist violence: Meeting the new challenges. *Race and Class, 30*(2), 71-76.

Fekete, L., & Webber, F. (1994). *Inside racist Europe.* London: Institute of Race Relations.

Ford, G. (1992). *Fascist Europe: The rise of racism and xenophobia.* London: Pluto Press.

Gaffiken, F., & Morrisey, M. (1992). *The new unemployed: Joblessness and poverty in the market economy.* London: Zed Press.

Ginsburg, N. (1989). Racial harassment policy and practice: The denial of citizenship. *Critical Social Policy, 26*(26), 66-81.

Gould, S. J. (1981). *The mismeasure of man.* New York: Norton.

Greater London Council. (1984). *Racial harassment in London.* London: Commission for Racial Equality.

Hainsworth, P. (1992). Introduction: The cutting edge: The extreme right in post-war Western Europe and the USA. In P. Hainsworth (Ed.), *The extreme right in Europe and the USA.* London: Pinter.

Hall, S., Critcher, C., Jefferson, T., Clarke, J., & Roberts, B. (1978). *Policing the crisis: Mugging, the state, and law and order.* London: Macmillan.

Harris, C. (1991). Configurations of racism in the civil service. *Race and Class, 33*(1), 1-30.

Hechter, M. (1975). *Internal colonialism: The Celtic fringe in British national development, 1536-1966.* London: Routledge & Kegan Paul.

Hollifield, J. P. (1992). *Immigrants, markets and states: The political economy of postwar Europe.* Cambridge, MA: Harvard University Press.

House of Commons, Home Affairs Committee. (1994). *Third report: Racial attacks and harassment* (Vol. III). London: Author.

Independent Committee of Inquiry into Racial Harassment. (1987). *Racial harassment in Leeds, 1985-86.* Leeds, UK: Leeds Community Relations Council.

Institute of Race Relations. (1987). *Policing against Black people.* London: Author.

Joshi, S., & Carter, B. (1984). The role of labour in the creation of a racist Britain. *Race and Class, 25*(3), 53-70.

Klein, R. (1995, January 6). Where prejudice still flares into violence. *The Times Educational Supplement,* p. 9.

Krieger, J. (1986). *Reagan, Thatcher and the politics of decline.* Cambridge, UK: Polity Press.

Kushnick, L. (1981). Racism and class consciousness in modern capitalism. In B. P. Bowser & R. G. Hunt (Eds.), *Impacts of racism on White Americans* (pp. 191-216). Beverly Hills: Sage.

Kushnick, L. (in press). Political economy of White racism in the United States and Great Britain. In B. P. Bowser (Ed.), *Impacts of racism on White Americans* (2nd ed.). Thousand Oaks, CA: Sage.

London Borough of Waltham Forest. (1990). *Beneath the surface: An inquiry into racial harassment in the London borough of Waltham Forest.* London: Author.

MacEwen, M., & Prior, A. (1992). *Planning and ethnic minority settlement in Europe: The myth of thresholds of tolerance* (Research Paper No. 40). Edinburgh: Edinburgh College of Art/Heriot-Watt University School of Planning and Housing.

Michie, J., & Smith, J. G. (Eds.). (1994). *Unemployment in Europe.* London: Academic Press.

Mitter, J. (1986). *Common fate, common bond: Women in the global economy.* London: Pluto Press.

Moch, L. P. (1992). *Moving Europeans: Migration in Western Europe since 1650.* Bloomington: Indiana University Press.

Organisation for Economic Cooperation and Development. (1992). *SOPEMI: Trends in international migration.* Paris: Author.

Pieterse, J. N. (1991). Myths and realities. *Race and Class, 32*(3), 3-10.

Potts, L. (1990). *The world labour market: A history of migration.* London: Zed Books.

Rathzel, N. (1991). Germany: One race, one nation? *Race and Class, 32*(3), 31-48.

Refugee Forum and Migrant Rights Action Network. (1991). *The walls of the fortress: European agreement against immigrants, migrants and refugees.* London: Author.

Sassen, S. (1988). *The mobility of labor and capital.* Cambridge, UK: Cambridge University Press.

Sheffield Racial Harassment Project. (1988). *Because their skin is Black.* Sheffield, UK: Sheffield City Council.

Simpson, A., & Read, M. (1991). *Against a rising tide: Racism, Europe and 1992.* Nottingham, UK: Spokesman.

Sivanandan, A. (1982). *A different hunger.* London: Pluto Press.

Sivanandan, A. (1990). *Communities of resistance.* London: Verso.

Sivanandan, A. (1991). Editorial. *Race and Class, 32*(3), v-vi.

Sivanandan, A. (1993). Racism: The road from Germany. *Race and Class, 34*(3), 67-73.

Smith, D. J. (1983). *Police and people in London* (4 vols.). London: Policy Studies Institute.

Spencer, M. (1990). *1992 and all that: Civil liberties in the balance.* London: Civil Liberties Trust.

Stanfield, J. H. (1991). Racism in America and other race-centered nation-states: Synchronic considerations. *International Journal of Comparative Sociology, 32*(3-4), 243-261.

Tompson, K. (1988). *Under siege: Racism and violence in Britain today.* Harmondsworth, UK: Penguin.

Toporowski, J. (1992, September 27). Fascist spectre looms over stagnant Europe. *The Observer,* p. 24.

Wallraff, G. (1988). *The lowest of the low.* London: Methuen.

Walsh, D. (1987). *Racial harassment in Glasgow.* Glasgow: Scottish Ethnic Minorities Research Unit.

Webber, F. (1991). From ethnocentrism to Euro-racism. *Race and Class, 32*(3), 11-18.

Winant, H., & Omi, M. (1986). *Racial formation in the United States: From the 1960s to the 1980s.* London: Routledge.

10

Introduction to the Analysis
of Racism and Anti-Racism in Brazil

Rosana Heringer

Military dictatorship ended only recently in Brazil; the first civilian president was indirectly elected in 1985. Under dictatorship, it was impossible for organizations or popular movements to address racial inequalities or seek solutions actively. With civilian government and the renewal of civil liberties, popular organizations and social movements that seek to improve Brazilian society are only now beginning to emerge and become organized. Among them, different groups are dedicated to fighting racial discrimination in Brazil. These organizations, generally referred to as "the Black movement," include many different kinds of work and approaches to anti-racism. Research conducted by the Brazilian Institute of Social and Economic Analysis (IBASE) shows that in 1988, in the metropolitan region of Rio de Janeiro alone, there were 102 Black movement organizations. In all, 38 were dedicated to cultural and religious activities, whereas 34 focused primarily on researching the social and economic conditions of Black Brazilians (Heringer & Sant'Anna, 1989, p. 55).

In 1988, Brazilians "celebrated" a century since the end of slavery in their country. The commemoration was an important opportunity for Brazilian people to reflect on racism against people of African descent. The Black movement organizations had a moment to present themselves and their ideas to the nation. Their message was that, even after a century,

Table 10.1 Average Monthly Income (in Minimum Salaries)

Area	Cruzeiro
Brazil	
Whole Population	4.1*
Whites	5.3
Non-Whites (Blacks and mulattos)	2.5
Metropolitan Region of Sao Paulo	
Whole Population	7.1
Whites	8.1
Non-Whites (Blacks and mulattos)	4.2
Metropolitan Region of Salvador	
Whole Population	5.0
Whites	10.7
Non-Whites (Blacks and mulattos)	3.2

SOURCE: FIBGE. (1990). *PNAD/1987—Color da populacao* [Color of population]. Rio de Janeiro: Author.
NOTE: * 4.1 minimum salaries are equivalent to U.S. $267.

non-White people in Brazil are still victims of poor living conditions and form the majority with low incomes and poor education. Very few Afro-Brazilians are materially well-off or well-educated. In fact, the most recently available data show that 17.5% of White Brazilians do not earn more than a minimum salary (around U.S. $65), whereas this percentage among Blacks is 35% and among mulattos it is 32%. There is a similar gap in education—35% of Black people and 37% of mulattos are illiterate, whereas only 18% of Whites are illiterate (FIBGE, 1990). Average monthly salaries show the same inequality, as shown in Table 10.1.

A main strategy of the Black movement has been to denounce Brazilian racial inequalities and to point out the racial discrimination felt by non-White people in everyday, ordinary situations. These episodes of racial discrimination are often hidden and hard to identify, are never punished, and are not publicly recognized as racial prejudice. The greatest difficulty in advancing this point of view is not in whether most Brazilians acknowledge it. The main problem the Black movement has in its struggle against racism in Brazil is that many Black people do not recognize their unfavorable situation in Brazilian society as due to racial discrimination, inequality, or prejudice.

Many Blacks do not see racial discrimination because they live in a society where about 60% of the workforce, including White and non-White people, receives no more than U.S. $200 monthly salary (FIBGE, 1990, p. 14). It is difficult to notice racial discrimination amid what appears to be universal poverty. Besides, a few Black people have overcome the barriers, acquired high social status, and now appear as successful examples of equality of opportunity for all.

What is clear about the Black movement's message of racial, social, and economic inequality is that it has not created a common identity or cause among the majority of non-Whites in Brazil. But the movement is not just about redress of social inequalities. The Black movement has a second strategy of improving the status of Blacks in Brazil. It has been more successful in rescuing the positive values of Black identity. Efforts to show the positive contributions of Black people to Brazilian culture have been very well received. "Black culture" has been manifested through Afro-Brazilian religions, African history and culture, and especially Afro-Brazilian music, known as *Axe-music.*

A third strategy, adopted by Black movement organizations during the last decade, has been to use advocacy action for victims of racial discrimination. This has included denouncing injustice and giving support to victims of racial discrimination. Only a few institutions provide this service, and they are located primarily in Brazil's largest cities. This is a concrete way through which Black Brazilian victims of racial prejudice can appeal. The effectiveness of this work, however, is very much linked to the difficulties the police and the justice system in Brazil have in dealing with such cases, even when laws specifically address them.

STATE ANTI-RACISM?

The first and most important steps toward public initiatives to eliminate racism in Brazil are the enforcement of specific laws against it. According to the Brazilian Constitution, racism is a crime, punishable by imprisonment. But, as is the case with other social matters in Brazil and elsewhere, the law is not sufficient to change behaviors. People are simply not convicted for being racist in Brazil. Motta and Santos (1994) point out that the only way one could be prosecuted for racial discrimination is to declare it as a reason for mistreatment. Missing is a sense that racial discrimination in Brazil is more than the isolated actions of individuals.

In this context, Black movement organizations have recognized that their main legal defense at the time of the 1988 Constitution—the codification of racism as a crime—has not produced the positive anti-racist effects they envisioned.

A second public initiative related to the promotion of the Black population has been the creation of different consultative organizations on the local, state, and federal levels of government. The aim of these organizations is to support public policies for combating racism. Such organizations have been created during the last few years in several Brazilian states. In Rio de Janeiro, a secretary's position at the executive level of government was established, that of the Extraordinary Secretary for Defense and Promotion of the Afro-Brazilian Population (SEAFRO).

WHAT NEEDS TO BE DONE

Racism in Brazil must be given visibility. It cannot continue to be described as hidden, invisible, or disguised. Governmental and nongovernmental strategies to fight racism must take into account the necessity of making racial discrimination explicit, and showing, in each situation, how it operates and the weakness of its reasons.

The main target of this strategy would not be primarily Afro-Brazilian people, but those who mostly discriminate against them—White Brazilians. Ultimately, there must be a change in culture and ideology. Brazilians must conceive of this action in the form of specific campaigns, and use their cultural practices as well. A concrete way of changing the often negative image of Black people is their presence in advertisements and on TV shows. Not only are they in subordinate positions (maid, driver, beggar), they also have very limited roles suggesting that they cannot be more than subordinate. Blacks should be shown selling and using not just soap, but cars and computers as well. Such changes in the image of Blacks are occurring slowly. Giving visibility to racism and challenging the stereotypical images of Blacks are just two examples of the kind of action that must be put into practice to "shake up" traditional conceptions of race relations in Brazil.

In Chapter 11, Antonio Guimarães analyzes the Brazilian denial of racism that is so central to maintaining racial inequality in Brazil. What he describes is an early-20th-century racist anti-racism, where the historic realities do not fit early declarations of state racelessness that have become part of the Brazilian national character. In Chapter 12, Rosângela

Vieira takes a look at the historic Black movement. It is much more than a recently mobilized movement, as so many consider it. It comes out of the historic and contemporary reality of Afro-Brazilian community life and its consciousness of self.

REFERENCES

FIBGE. (1990). *PNAD/1987—Cor da população* [Color of population]. Rio de Janeiro: Author.

Heringer, R., & Sant'Anna, W. (1989). *Negros no Brasil: Dados da realidade* [Black people in Brazil: Statistic data]. Petropolis: Vozes/IBASE.

Motta, A., & Santos, R. (1994). *Questão racial e política: Experiências em políticas publicas* [Racial question and politics: Experiences in public policies]. Sao Paulo: CEBRAP/University of Texas at Austin/Ford Foundation.

11

Racism and Anti-Racism in Brazil: A Postmodern Perspective

Antonio Sérgio Alfredo Guimarães

Any study of racism in Brazil must begin by reflecting on the very fact that racism is a taboo subject in Brazil. Brazilians imagine themselves as inhabiting an anti-racist nation, a "racial democracy." This is one of the sources of their pride and, at the same time, conclusive proof of their status as a civilized nation.

This anti-racist claim has deep roots in both factual and literary history. Since the abolition of slavery in 1888, Brazil has not experienced legal segregation or overt racial conflicts. In literature, since the pioneering studies of Freyre in the early 1930s and Pierson in the 1940s, and as late as the 1970s, the professional research of sociologists and anthropologists has reassured both Brazilians and the rest of the world that the Brazilian pattern of race relations is relatively harmonious. In the latest edition of Cashmore's *Dictionary of Race and Ethnic Relations* (1994), the summarization of the entry on Brazil reads:

> In short, Brazil may be described as a society where class distinctions are marked and profound, where class and color overlap but do not coincide,

AUTHOR'S NOTE: This chapter benefited from a scholarship research fund granted by CAPES/Fulbright for 1993-1994, during which time I worked with the Afro-American Studies Program at Brown University. I am grateful for the comments and suggestions of Michel Agier, Benjamin Bowser, Nadya Castro, Anani Dzidzieyno, and Lucia Lippi.

where class often takes precedence over color, and where "race" is a matter of individual description and personal attractiveness rather than of group membership. (p. 9)

In this chapter, I argue that this interpretation of race and racism in Brazil is due to a certain political and social Western *problématique,* largely supplanted from the 1970s onward, but still present in Brazil. This *problématique* includes the meaning of race and racism. My main concerns are twofold: first, I argue that the language of color and class has always been used in Brazil in a racialized way. Color variations "naturalized" harsh categorical racial inequalities that could disrupt the self-image of a racial democracy. Second, I show the historical, native, and political issue of racism and anti-racism in Brazil. Although my primary sources are social scientific literary discourses, I refer to the popular, grassroots usage of these discourses as well. Before these issues are addressed, I must briefly reconstitute the idea of "race as a floating signifier" and the changing agenda of anti-racism in the West.

THE CHANGING AGENDA
OF WESTERN ANTI-RACISM

The field of scientific inquiry broadly known as "race relations" is of North American inspiration. Social scientists frequently took the U.S. pattern of race relations as a standard for comparison and contrast in their understanding of race in other societies, especially Brazil. Elevated as an archetype, the U.S. pattern molded the formation of race relations studies in Brazil. The U.S. type exhibited a segregationist, conflictive, violent pattern of relations commonly known as *Jim Crow,* which had precise rules of group affiliation based on biological reasoning that defined race. The Brazilian type, in contrast, paraded a sophisticated etiquette of distancing, sharp status, economic differentiation, egalitarian laws, and an ambiguous but very complex system of identification based mainly upon color nuances.

Why were these two systems put in sharp contrast? Why were their functional similarities unnoticed during the dominance of structural-functionalism in sociology? Three main reasons account for this dualism. First, the political agenda of anti-racism itself stressed the legal and formal status of citizenship instead of its actual organization in Brazilian society. This agenda reflected mainly the liberal interests prevailing in the

United States, South Africa, and the European colonies. In Brazil, this agenda was advanced by White, middle-class intellectuals who overlooked the popular, Black anti-racism of their time, which clashed against the barriers raised by color prejudice. By differentiating prejudice from discrimination and putting the former into the realm of individual privacy, erudite anti-racism operated, functionally, as an ideological effort to obscure real existing racism.

Second, the definition of *race* as a biological concept concealed both the actual character of color distinctions and its constructed, social, cultural dynamic in Brazilian society. If race was about concrete biological differences, so went the reasoning, then color was not a race-related notion, but a subjective and preferential notion.

Third, the search for objective realism in the social sciences that looked for definite essences and causal explanations neglected the web of slippery discursive images that concealed racism under class or status metaphors. The symmetry of the language of race and class in Brazil, although noticed, was largely misinterpreted as a proof of the insignificance of race.

The focus on formal structure and the search for objectivity were world trends. In fact, during the aftermath of World War II, anti-racism was too simple and clear-cut in its aims: to show the unscientific, mythological character of races and the barbaric, inhuman consequences of racism. Both goals operated in a field of obvious realism and vivid experience in Europe: the Holocaust and the demise of *race* as a scientific concept.

The postwar agenda of intellectual anti-racism had two obvious targets: segregation in the United States and apartheid in South Africa, the two remaining systems of formal state racism. This agenda could be measured concretely by objective change in formal social organization—the dismantling of formal legal segregation. This was a convenient logic for White Brazilians that obscured the historical assimilationist racism of Brazil.

But Anglo-American elite anti-racism was a no less active participant in the mystification and idealization of Brazil as a racial paradise. In a recent book edited by Hellwig (1992), one cannot find a single observation of racial discrimination in Brazil by African American travelers or social scientists from 1910 to 1940, and from 1940 to 1960, the registered evidence is usually explained by class reasoning.

Perceptions began to change only when civil rights laws were enacted in the United States. Only then could unequal racial opportunities be seen clearly operating and reproducing themselves through social mechanisms—schooling, unemployment, historic poverty, and urban de facto segregation. The changing perceptions of racial discrimination in the United States influenced both the Anglo-American perception of Brazil and the agenda of Western anti-racism. Thereafter, the identification of structural racial inequalities disguised in class or status terms became an important issue. Brazilian and North American racism had become much more alike.

North American Black nationalism and the feminist revolution of the 1970s shed another light on the structuring of anti-racist perceptions; the universalist and assimilationist view of postwar intellectual anti-racists was called racist because it favored the cultural annihilation of African origins and did not see the relation between cultural genocide and Black subordinate status. The women's movement stressed the way sexual differences had been historically "racialized" to naturalize and justify social and cultural hierarchies.

The historical framework of changing perceptions was completed more recently by the massive immigration of Third World people (East Indians, Caribbeans, Latin Americans, Africans, Chinese, Koreans) toward European and North American democracies. Now these immigrants are viewed as "unassimilables": colored strangers presenting sharp religious (Islam), linguistic (Arabic or Spanish speakers), or cultural (Rastafarian) threats to the native White populations. These were the ingredients for awareness of a "new racism" and a new look at race in Brazil. What is now obvious is that when it comes to race,

> culture is conceived along ethnically absolute lines, not as something intrinsically fluid, changing, unstable and dynamic, but as a fixed property of social groups rather than a relational field in which they encounter one another and live out social, historical relationships. When culture is brought in contact with race it is transformed into a pseudo-biological property of communal life. (Gilroy, 1993, p. 24)

THEORIZING RACISM

The changing anti-racist agenda reverberated in the social thinking about racism. In the 1970s, from the point of view of its structures, functions, and mechanisms, race was defined as "a group of people who in a given society are socially defined as different from other groups by virtue of certain real or putative physical differences" (Van den Berghe,

1970, p. 10). With this definition, race could no longer be distinguished from gender, ethnicity, or class.

In fact, if one examines any list of characteristics said to define and specify race, one sees that the structural and functional characteristics presented are shared by many other social hierarchies. The theorists of the 1970s, however, could not live with this ambiguity. Most of the time, even when defining race and race relations in a flexible manner, they were not conscious that their definitions encompassed other forms of hierarchy. One exception to this pattern was Van den Berghe (1970), who, reflecting on this ambiguity, wrote:

> It became increasingly clear to me over the years that the subject had no claim to a special place in a general theory of society. In other words, race and ethnic relations are not sufficiently different from other types of social relations—nor, conversely, do various types of race and ethnic relations have enough that is exclusively common—to justify special theoretical treatment. (p. 9)

In the 1980s, the tide of poststructuralism that came from France brought self-consciousness to the ambiguous definition of *race*. Deconstructionism in the social sciences favored the widespread use of *race* as a metaphor. The analysis of the discursive field of racism, both old (biological images) and new (cultural differentialism) was based on the same underlying reality disguised as different empirical phenomena.

Again, social scientists remained unable to distinguish racism from discriminations arising from other social hierarchies (gender, class, ethnicity, sexuality). To call racism any kind of discrimination based on "essentialist" or objective constructions transforms racism into a political metaphor.

Delacampagne (1990) provides a good example of this broad reconceptualization of racism and its metaphorical use:

> Racism, in the modern sense of the term, does not necessarily begin as soon as one speaks of the physiological superiority, or cultural superiority, of one race or another; it begins when one makes (alleged) cultural superiority directly and mechanically dependent on (alleged) physiological superiority, that is, when one group *derives* the cultural characteristics of a given group from its biological characteristics. Racism is the reduction of the cultural to the biological, the attempt to make the first dependent on the second. Racism exists wherever it is claimed that a given social status is explained by a given natural characteristic. (pp. 85-86)

The definition is imprecise partially because it reduces the idea of "nature" to a biological notion. But there are many ways to connect social hierarchies to biological differences. In the general sense, "natural" signifies an ahistoric or transhistoric order, devoid of related and particular interests, thus representing only one general attribute of the human species or the divinities. This presumed natural order may rest upon different bases: a theological justification (divine origin), a scientific justification (endo-determined), or a cultural justification (historical necessity).

Consequently, all social hierarchies appeal to natural order, yet they may be justified and rationalized in different ways. The economic order can be justified as a product of individual virtue (the poor are poor because they lack noble sentiments, virtues, and values); by the same token, women are said to occupy subordinate positions due to the characteristics of the female gender, and Africans or African descendants were enslaved or kept in an inferior position because their race was thought to be intellectually and morally incapable of civilization. In each case, when a natural order limits social formations, systems of rigid and inescapable hierarchies emerge. But note that in the three cases outlined, a "scientific" theory of nature (biology and genetics) was used only in the latter two cases.

This process of naturalization seems to be a necessary trait of all social hierarchies. As Guillaumin (1992) observes,

> the ideological implication of the idea of nature (and natural groups) cannot be abolished from social relations in which they occupy a central place. Ideologically hidden (since ideology lurks under "evidence"), the "natural" form, whether it is common sense or institutionalized practice, is one of the main technical means used by the dominant groups in their relations with subordinate groups. (p. 192)

Certainly, one can use racism as a metaphor for any type of naturalization resulting from systematic discriminatory practices. This, however, is a loose usage of the term, because race could be empirically absent but lending its figurative meaning to the discriminatory discourse. My presumption is that if one speaks of some discriminatory practices as sexism, class discrimination, or ethnism, that is because race is subsumed under other differences or is only a trope of irreducible differences. With this new thinking about race, the more complicated and subtle imbedding of race in class and cultural differences in Brazil comes under new attention. To use Gates' (1985) words:

Race has become a trope of ultimate, irreducible difference between cultures, linguistic groups, or adherents of specific belief systems which—more often than not—also have fundamentally opposed economic interests. Race is the ultimate trope of difference because it is so very arbitrary in its application. (p. 5)

RACE AND COLOR

In the literature relating to race relations in Brazil, as Wade (1994) points out, "the distinction between appearance and ancestry is often left unclarified and made to parallel a distinction between the insignificance and the significance of 'race' " (p. 28). In contrast to the United States, races in Brazil are not defined by the rule that there is no clear rule of biological descendance for belonging to a racial group, but rather, classifications of physical appearance and an "interplay between a variety of achieved and ascribed statuses" (Harris, 1974). This would mean that there are no racial groups in Brazil, only "groups of color" (Degler, 1991, p. 103).

Sociologists widely accepted the idea that, in Brazil and in Latin America in general, there was no racial prejudice, just "color prejudice." Azevedo (1955) writes, "Since color and somatic traits function, to a great degree, as symbols of status, resistance to inter-marriage suggests both class and race prejudice, or better, color prejudice" (p. 90). Wright (1990) is even more explicit in his discussion of Venezuela: "But Venezuelans consider only those individuals with black skin as black. Color rather than race—appearance rather than origin—play far more important roles in influencing the Venezuelans' perceptions of individuals" (p. 3).

As Fernandes (1965) points out, the idea of color prejudice is better used as a native's notion, first conceptualized by the Frente Negra Brasileira (Black Brazilian Front) in 1940. The group referred to the peculiar type of racial discrimination that oppresses Brazilian Blacks, one wherein color—viewed as a spontaneous, natural fact—and not race—viewed as an artificial, abstract, scientific concept—is decisive.

The conception of color as natural phenomenon rests on the pretense that physical appearance and phenotypical traits are neutral, objective, biological facts. But that is just the way in which in Brazil, color is a figure for race. When scholars incorporate in their discourse color as the criterion for constituting "objective" groups, they refuse to perceive Brazilian racism. Their conclusion is superficial and formalistic. Without history and clear rules of descendance, there would be no races, just spontaneous groups of color.

But there is nothing spontaneously natural about phenotypical traits or color. Gates (1985) says,

> It takes little reflection, however, to recognize that these pseudoscientific categories are themselves figures. Who has seen a black or red person, a white, yellow or brown [person]? These terms are arbitrary constructs, not reports of reality. But language is not only the medium of this often insidious tendency; it is the sign. Current language use signifies the difference between cultures and their possession of power, spelling out the distance between subordinate and superordinate, between bondsman and lord in terms of their "race." (p. 6)

This position is strengthened by the argument that nothing in skin color, hair type, width of nose, or thickness of lips is more naturally visible or discriminating than other traits, such as foot size, height, eye color, or any other physical trait. Such traits have meaning merely within a preexisting ideology (an ideology that creates the facts it organizes), and only because of this do they function as meaningful classifications or criteria.

In sum, a person can only have a color and be classified in a color group if an ideology exists in which the color of people has meaning. That is, people do not have any color except within racial ideologies, *stricto sensu*.

RACISM IN A
SOUTH AMERICAN WAY

What is the ideology that particularizes racism in Brazil? The distinctiveness of Brazilian racism, or Latin American racism in general, comes from the fact that the Brazilian nationhood was not formed, or "imagined" to use Anderson's (1992) metaphor, as a community of ethnic dissimilar individuals coming from all parts of Europe, as was the United States. Brazil is an amalgam of Creoles from different ethnic and racial backgrounds whose race and ethnicity were lost to gain Brazilian nationhood. Brazil generously offered a comfortable penumbra to hang over everyone's ancestry. Color remained the only trace of race, or better, became its coded name. Colonial racism, founded upon the idea of the ethnic purity of White settlers or conquerors, gave way after independence to the idea of mixed-blooded, mestizo nations (Skidmore, 1979; Wade,

1993; Wright, 1990), or to a *naçâo morena* in the Brazilian case, whose citizenship was granted by place of birth, not by ancestry.

Of course the United States or South Africa, for example, presents a similar place-of-birth citizenship; however, they have developed an image of themselves more as a European transplantation (the ethnic melting pot) than a multirace mixture. Their extreme sense of racial community has corresponded with nationality based upon "mixophobia"—the aversion toward racial mixture, to use Taguieff's (1987) term. To understand it further, one must comprehend how Whiteness is defined in Brazil.

The other main characteristic of race relations in Latin America is the existence of an oligarchical order in which race (color), status, and class are intimately linked. Oboler (1995) writes:

> As a result of extensive miscegenation throughout the colonies, racial classifications, social status, and honor evolved into a hierarchical arrangement that Lipschütz has called a "pigmentocracy." As Ramón Gutiérrez has described, this was a racial system whereby whiter skin was directly related to higher social status and honor whereas darker skin was associated both with "the physical labor of slaves and tributary indians" and, visually, with "the infamy of the conquered." The Spanish notion of *pureza de sangre,* or purity of blood, was thus imbedded in the New World aristocracy's understanding of the inter-related concepts of race, social status, and honor. (p. 28)

In Brazil, this system of hierarchy is layered with gradations of prestige, where social class (occupation and income), family origin, color, and formal education are buttressed by a dichotomy expressed as highborn/ rabble and elite/masses. But the hierarchy and the dichotomies are founded on the racial dichotomy of White/Black, which has sustained the slavocratic order for three centuries.

Da Costa (1988) recognizes this origin of color prejudice in Brazil when she writes about the Second Empire: "Racial prejudice served to maintain and legitimize the distance between a world of privileges and rights and one of deprivation and duties" (p. 137). The 19th-century liberal doctrine that held that the poor were poor because they were inferior found legitimacy in Brazil in the cultural destruction of Africans by European social customs and the conditions of poverty and cultural unpreparedness of free Blacks and mestiços. The servile condition of slaves, like the poverty and misery of free Blacks and mestiços, was taken as a sign of racial inferiority.

As Da Costa (1988), Fernandes (1965), and others have so well demonstrated, the entire Brazilian elite (including the Abolitionists) was prisoner to this logic, which justified social inequalities. For liberals, slavery was only an obstacle to their ideas. They did not have a critical reflection on race relations and did not care about the condition of Blacks after Abolition. The admission of universal human equality was placed on the level of theory (dogma), beyond any contact with, or commitment to, the interests of real people. As today, this theory coexisted with a great social distance and a sense of superiority in relation to Blacks, mulattos, and the general populace.

In fact, the idea of color, despite being affected by class hierarchies (thus, "money whitens," as does education), is founded upon a peculiar notion of race. This notion revolves around the dichotomy of whiteness/blackness just as in the Anglo-Saxon world. This working definition is peculiar in terms of its definition of "whiteness," that is, the rule that defines group belonging. In Brazil, Whiteness was not formed through the exclusive ethnic melting pot of European people, as in the United States (Lewis, in press; Oboler, 1995; Omi & Winant, 1986); on the contrary, "Whiteness" absorbed mixed-race, light mulattos who could exhibit the dominant symbols of Europeans: a Christian upbringing and Portuguese literacy. By extension, the rules of belonging minimized the Black pole of this dichotomy, thereby separating mestiços from Blacks. The meaning of the word *Black,* therefore, crystallized the absolutely different, the non-European. By this meaning, a real Black could not be a complete Christian (should exhibit some syncretic animist beliefs) or a cultivated man (Black women were not even considered in the identification reasoning). Therefore, in Brazil, only those with very dark skin suffer the same degree of prejudice and discrimination as Black Africans. Those with varying degrees of mestiçagem may enjoy, according to their degree of Whiteness (both chromatic and cultural, as white is a feature of Europeanness), some of the privileges reserved for Whites.

Dzidzienyo (1979) was perhaps the first to note this peculiarity of race relations in Brazil. Defining the "hallmark of the much-vaunted Brazilian 'racial democracy,' " was,

the bias that white is best and black is worst and therefore the nearer one is to white, the better. The hold which this view has on Brazilian society is all-pervasive and embraces a whole range of stereotypes, role-playing, job opportunities, life-styles, and, what is even more important, it serves as the corner- stone of the closely-observed "etiquette" of race relations in Brazil. (p. 3)

Corroborating Dzidzienyo's thesis, Cleveland Donald, Jr., a Black American journalist visiting Brazil in 1972, noted, "In fact, it does not matter that the Brazilian mulatto is not a 'Negro'; far more important is the fact that he is never White" (cited in Hellwig, 1992, p. 212).

CHANGING PATTERNS OF RACISM IN BRAZIL

Any analysis of Brazilian racism must consider at least three major historical processes: the process of nation formation; the intermingling of race in the discursive, ideological field with the other major social hierarchies of class, status, and gender; and the transformations of the socioeconomic order and its regional effects.

A discussion of nationhood is of foremost importance because in Brazil, as suggested before, the rules of nation-belonging were intended to subsume and suppress ethnic, racial, and community feelings. The Brazilian nation was first thought of as culturally uniform in terms of religion, race, ethnicity, and language. In this idea of nation, Brazilian racism could only be characterized by a fear of others, making it necessary to negate others' differences, however they may be defined (Taguieff, 1987, p. 29).

But negation of differences does not mean that universal, enlightened racism is necessarily a hidden racism, one that is ashamed to say its name. On the contrary, in the beginning of the 20th century, Brazilian fear of others was still explicit. The fundamental grounding of Brazilian racialism at this time rested upon a peculiar adaptation of scientific racism. If every racism has a particular history, whitening is what specifies Brazil's. According to Skidmore (1993), this doctrine was based,

on the assumption of white superiority—sometimes muted by leaving open the question of how "innate" inferiority might be, and using the euphemisms "more advanced" and "less advanced" races. But to this assumption were added two more. First, the black population was becoming progressively less numerous than the white for reasons which included a supposedly lower birth rate, higher incidence of disease, and social disorganization. Second, miscegenation was "naturally" producing a lighter population, in part because whiter genes were stronger and in part because people chose partners lighter than themselves. (pp. 64-65)

In summary, the particularity of Brazilian racialism resided in the importation of racist theories from Europe, excluding two important conceptions—"the innateness of racial differences and the degeneracy of mixed bloods—in order to formulate their own solution to the 'Negro problem' " (Skidmore, 1993, p. 77). White blood was thought to purify, dilute, and exterminate Black blood, thus opening the possibility for mestiços to elevate themselves to a civilized state. Whitening was the response of a wounded national pride assaulted by doubts and qualms about its industrial and economic genius. It was a way to rationalize the feelings of racial and cultural inferiority suggested by scientific racism and the geographical determinism of the 19th century.

Freyre, Pierson, and the whole project of social anthropology represented a blow against this shameless racism. Although I do not intend to discuss the academic merits or pitfalls of these works, I do examine some of their ideas in the perspective of a changing nationhood.

When Pierson (1942), Azevedo (1955), and others conducted their research, the second Brazilian-born generations of Italian, Spanish, German, and Japanese immigrants were climbing the social and economic ladder of the southern states. São Paulo would become the major industrial city in Latin America. The old stock of Brazilians, mainly from the sertão, were emigrating in large numbers to São Paulo and entering subordinate positions in the labor market. The traditionally imagined Brazilian nationality was, as a result, under profound stress. This stress came from the fact that the "new Creoles" (the native-born children of recent immigrants) did not present the same cultural uniformities as the older ones and maintained some sense of community and ethnic belonging. This novelty was far more important because these new Brazilians were situated in the consolidated, dynamic industrial and agricultural areas of southern and southeastern Brazil, toward which the cultural national axis of the country was turning—toward Rio de Janeiro, São Paulo, and Rio Grande do Sul.

The historic cultural areas of Bahia, Pernambuco, and Minas Gerais remained almost untouched in their racial composition by the new wave of immigration (Merrick & Graham, 1979; Skidmore, 1993). Freyre's work and the social anthropology of the 1940s and 1950s were done in Pernambuco and Bahia, as part of the reaction of established Brazilian-hood to the cultural challenge represented by the new economic axis of São Paulo. In this sense, racial democracy as reinterpreted by the cultural anthropology of Freyre (1938) can be said to be a founding myth of a rapidly transformed nation.

It would be an error, however, to think that the culturalist thought of the mid-20th century—after Freyre and Pierson—changed the racist assumptions of whitening. Actually, the whitening thesis was adapted to the basic tenets of social anthropology and came to signify the mobility of mestiços within the social hierarchy. On the one side, whitening was an empirical statement of fact, an upward mobility track followed by Blacks; on the other side, it presupposed a racist view of blackness to which the theory remained silent and acritical.

The Eurocentric perspective of the culturalist version of whitening can be found in Freyre (1938), Pierson (1942), Azevedo (1955), and all the most prominent and progressive Brazilian anthropologists of the 1950s:

> Through mixing and other socio-biological factors, the darker group, of black phenotype, is slowly being absorbed in the ethnic caldron; the white group is growing faster and the mestiços increase in numbers, registered in statistics as *pardos* (brown), to be ultimately submerged, through mixing, by the group predominantly of European heritage. (Azevedo, 1955, p. 51)

Whitening hereafter signified the capacity of Brazil (defined either as an extension of Europe or as a country wherein a new race was born) to absorb and integrate mestiços and Blacks. This capacity implicitly requires a willingness of people of color to repudiate their African or indigenous ancestry. Thus, whitening and racial democracy are, in fact, concepts of a new racialist discourse. The racist substance to these concepts resides in the idea, at times implicit, that there are three founding races of Brazilian nationality that have made different contributions and have qualitatively different cultural potential. The color of people, like their customs, are indexes of the positive or negative value of these races. At the core of this thought is the supposition that the mark of color is indelible not only because it signals inferior ancestry, but also because it symbolizes the presumed inferiority of this race.

It also means, implicitly, a very definitive notion of Brazilianness. Writing about the colored elites in Bahia, a city where 80% of the population has a census-declared African ancestry, Azevedo (1955) successively says:

Because of its architecture and its urban style, its antiquity, and its moderate rhythm of life, Bahia is considered today Brazil's most European city. (p. 25)

Bahia considers itself one of the most Brazilian communities in the whole country by virtue of its reduced number of foreigners and by virtue of being constituted by the original elements who settled in Brazil. (p. 38)

No other Brazilian state which has a large black population shows such a high degree of racial mixture (mestiçagem) as Bahia. This demonstrates that Bahia is probably the most important Euro-African ethnic melting pot in Brazil. (p. 48)

In these passages, the discursive slippage between Europeanness, Brazilianness, and mestiçagem clearly reveals the "European" character of this imagined nationhood, operating through the Creolization of Europeanness by the whitening of mestiçagem.

These same passages, which uncover a racialized nationhood—typical of the northeastern elites of Brazil—also unravel the strains to this nationhood brought by the European immigrant wave of 1890 to 1920, when thousands of Italians, Spaniards, Portuguese, Germans, and Japanese settlers entered the southern states in a partially official policy of whitening.

The Whiteness produced by the southern melting pot is very different from the consolidated, colonial melting pot Azevedo (1955) refers to. The main difference lies in the fact that those Whites did in truth mix in the Brazilian middle class and, to a much lesser degree, the working classes. The *paulista* (from São Paulo) working class was racially transformed through the absorption of northeastern immigrants, mainly Blacks and mestiços (Andrews, 1991). Indeed, the rapid upward mobility of European immigrants is testimony to the relative lenience of Brazilian society toward Europeans, in contrast to the subordinate assimilation of Africans.

Japanese descendants offer, in this respect, an extremely interesting case. Although placed outside the imagery of Brazilianness (they are still called *nisei*), they were not assimilated into the White-Black status gradient inherited from slavery but entered directly into the class gradient of the competitive order. As a result, they found enough leeway and arranged sufficient cultural and economic capital to make a better journey through the Brazilian society than those of African descent.

The new ethnic communities of immigrant descendants who, at first, saw and were seen by Brazilians (the traditional) as foreigners were absorbed into the Brazilian mainstream. They were also incorporated into the southern Brazilian elites and ended up redefining the racialized others, mainly working-class or underclass "traditional Brazilians," as *baianos* (Bahians) and *nordestinos* (northeasterners). Baianos and nordestinos are Black or mixed-race Brazilians from the working class; they have become the special targets of Brazil's new racism.

THEORIZING ABOUT RACISM AND ANTI-RACISM IN BRAZIL

There is something very special in this racism that comes also from the peculiar way Brazilianess is imagined. As Anderson (1992) argues, the nation in Latin America was mainly defined by "substantial landowners, allied with somewhat smaller number of merchants, and various types of professionals (lawyers, military men, local and provincial function-aires)" (p. 48). Despite the fact that all Brazilians did not gain economi-cally, the potential for conflict was averted by elite actions. This was done by incorporating mixed-race Blacks and Native Americans more "as potential recruits to mixedness" (Wade, 1993, p. 3) than as full citizens. In fact, mixed-race Blacks and Native Americans were excluded from the beginning through the very process of their emancipation, as an under-class.

Brazilian racism has a prerepublican origin. Reis (1993) shows how Africans in the mid-19th century, manumitted or not, were discriminated against in Bahia and forced back to rural areas or to Africa. Africans were the first "other," the absolute different, and when there were no Africans left but Creoles, black became a figure for Africanness.

This holds true for the upper classes and the lower classes alike. In the popular usages of Brazilianness, mainly in the soccer subculture, Creoles who do not fit the ideal mixed-race pattern of *morenidade* are called *negão* if Black or *alemão* (German) or *galego* (Galician) if White. This apparent chromatic symmetry of black and white applied by and for poor people is reversed in the chromatology of status, whereby they distinguish between a *branco fino* (those of pure European lineage) and a *branco da terra,* the mixed-Creole White (Azevedo, 1955; Pierson, 1940), thereby stressing the importance of being European.

To mark the origins of this racism, Fernandes (1965) calls it the "slave metamorphosis," to mean how black, the skin color, was used from Abolition onward as a signifier for subordinate, underclass Brazilians.

Actually, racism in Brazil has been played mainly through the contradictory game of a broadly defined citizenship, guaranteed by formal juridical rights, on the one side, but largely ignored, not enforced, and structurally limited by poverty and everyday state violence, on the other side. Racism is perpetrated through the curtailment of citizenship and the social distance created by huge economic, cultural, and social inequalities separating Blacks from Whites, poor from well-to-do, north from south.

Elites in Brazil, encompassing landowners, capitalists, intellectuals, and middle classes, represent a factual, broad compromise between wild exploitation and *bonne conscience*. On one side, elites can boast a radical, modern legislation; on the other side, it can be sure the sophisticated laws are highly inoperative. Universal franchise, for example, until recently (1988) was limited to literate people, which represented disenfranchisement for the Black illiterate mass. Still another example: Racism was first considered a misdemeanor by a Congressional Act of 1951 (Lei Afonso Arinos, no. 1390); in 1988, as a result of lobbying by the Black movement, the new democratic constitution made racism a felony. To this date, however, nobody has been sentenced on a racist charge. On the contrary, victims' attorneys opt for charges that stand a better chance for winning the case (Guimarães, 1994). This is the current Brazilian pattern of racism, which does not show its face and hides behind enlightened universalism, masking itself as anti-racism, and denying the full presence of the other, the African Brazilian or the Native Brazilian.

How does anti-racism unmask a racism that does not recognize itself as racism, that naturalizes the other through chromatic metaphors, regionalism, and class etiquette?

Marxist thought, which strongly influenced the doctrines and actions of the emerging Brazilian middle class in the 1960s, 1970s, and 1980s, did nothing to reverse this status quo. On the contrary, Marxist insistence that races are nonexistent and color is an epiphenomenon merely gave racial democracy a socialist bent. Or rather transformed it into an ideal to be achieved only through class struggle. Marxist thought adapted very well to the idea of capitalism (here a trope for Europeanness) as a civilizing force, to which the people of the entire world would naturally have to submit before reaching the socialist stage. Even when the inherent racism of these cultural theories and refined color classifications (which substitute bipolar classification) is recognized, the counterargument remains that in Brazil racism is "milder." Its mildness is suggested by the relative conformity of the Black population and the absence of legal mechanisms to thwart inequality and discrimination.

In a certain sense, the ideal of racial democracy is really a founding myth of Brazilian nationality and can only be denounced as myth, as broken promises. In fact, the studies by Andrews (1992), Castro and Guimarães (1993), Hasenbalg (1979), Lovell (1989), N. Silva (1980), P. C. Silva (1993), Telles (1992), and others unmask the mildness of Brazilian racial democracy. They show the profound inequalities that separate Blacks from other groups. They reveal a de facto job, residential, and educational segregation between White and non-White.

A critical challenge for those who struggle against racism in Brazil is to show not only inequalities, but their daily reproduction by institutions of production (public and private enterprises), institutions of public order (the police, the judicial and correctional systems), and educational and health care institutions. This is an important way through which one can hope to displace the centenarian, invisible veil that wraps the dichotomies of elite/masses and White/Black in Brazilian society.

For the African Brazilian population, those who call themselves *negros* (Blacks), anti-racism must mean first the admission of race; that is, a perception of themselves—the racialized others—as the racialized "we." It means the reconstruction of the self, drawing upon African heritage— the Afro-Brazilian culture of *candomblé, capoeira,* and *afoxés,* but also upon the cultural and political reservoir of the "Black Atlantic" legacy— the Civil Rights Movement in the United States, the Caribbean cultural renaissance, and the fight against apartheid in South Africa.

The new cultural forms of the Black movement in Latin America and Brazil (Agier, 1993; Agier & Caravalho, 1992; Wade, 1993) have stressed the process of Black reidentification in ethnic terms. It seems that only a racialized discourse can sustain a sense of pride, dignity, and self-reliance, largely destroyed by a century of invisible, universalist, enlightened racism. This ethnic resurgence is constructed upon a land to be retrieved, such as the former Maroon territories, or the transformation, largely symbolic, of poor urban areas into Black neighborhoods or new Maroons—*quilombos.* Second, there is need for the culture to redeem and repurify in contact with an imaginary Africa, the Africa brought and maintained as memory.

This concrete, popular agenda of anti-racism is still fiercely combated by Brazilian nationalists, all over the political spectrum, who believe in the official, mythological anti-racism of Brazil. They are very susceptible to what they call the reverse racism of Black organizations, or the importation of foreign categories and feelings. In truth, nothing harms the Brazilian ideal of assimilation more than the cultivation of differences. Even within the Black movement, one can hear dissident views, dissenting against a narrow definition of blackness or the essentialism involved in any ethnic formation.

Trapped at the crossroads of different types of racism, Latin American intellectuals, mainly those who view themselves through European lenses, must begin to realize that racism does not exist outside a particular history. There is no absolute, metahistorical concept of race or racism. By exploring the linkages between racism and anti-racism in the Brazilian context and situating them in the broader world system, one can hope to contribute to rescuing Brazilian race relations from its myths. That is the only way Latin American anti-racists can fight not others' but their own racism.

REFERENCES

Agier, M. (1993). *Ilê Aiyê: A invenção do mundo negro*. Unpublished manuscript.

Agier, M., & Carvalho, M. R. (1992, November 12-13). *Nation, race, culture: La trajectoire des mouvements noir et indigène dans la societé brésilienne*. Presented at the meeting "Nation, État, Ethnicité," Association des Chercheurs de Politique Africaine, Centre d'Études d'Afrique Noire, Bordeaux, France.

Anderson, B. (1992). *Imagined communities*. London: Verso.

Andrews, G. (1991). *Blacks and Whites in São Paulo, Brazil, 1899-1988*. Madison: University of Wisconsin Press.

Andrews, G. R. (1992). Desigualdade racial no Brasil e nos Estados Unidos: Uma comparção estatística. *Estudos Afro-Asiáticos, 22,* 47-84.

Azevedo, T. (1955). *As elites de cor, um estudo de ascenso social*. São Paulo: Cia Editora Nacional.

Cashmore, E. (1994). *Dictionary of race and ethnic relations* (3rd ed.). London: Routledge.

Castro, N. G., & Guimarães, J. A. (1993). Desigualdades raciais no mercado e nos locais de trabalho. *Estudos Afro-Asiáticos, 24,* 23-60.

Da Costa, E. V. (1988). *The Brazilian empire: Myths and histories*. Belmont, CA: Wadsworth.

Degler, C. N. (1991). *Neither Black nor White*. Madison: University of Wisconsin Press.

Delacampagne. (1990). Racism and the West: From praxis to logos. In D. T. Goldberg (Ed.), *Anatomy of racism* (pp. 85-86). Minneapolis: University of Minnesota Press.

Dzidzienyo, A. (1979). *The position of Blacks in Brazilian society*. London: Minority Rights Group.

Fernandes, F. (1965). *A integração do negro na sociedade de classes* (2 vols). São Paulo: Cia Editora Nacional.

Freyre, G. (1938). *Casa grande & senzala: Formação da família brasileira sob o regime da economia patriarcal.* Rio de Janeiro: Schmidt.

Gates, H. L., Jr. (1985). Editor's introduction: Writing "race" and the difference it makes. In H. L. Gates, Jr. (Ed.), *Race, writing, and difference* (pp. 1-20). Chicago: University of Chicago Press.

Gilroy, P. (1993). *Small acts: Thoughts on the politics of Black cultures.* London: Serpent's Tail.

Guillaumin, C. (1992). *"Race et nature," sexe, race et pratique du pouvoir: L'idée de nature.* Paris: Côté-Femmes Éditions.

Guimarães, J. A. (1994). *Racial conflicts in Brazilian law.* Providence, RI: Brown University, Afro-American Studies Program.

Harris, M. (1974). *Patterns of races in the Americas.* New York: Norton.

Hasenbalg, C. (1979). *Discriminação e desigualdades raciais no Brasil.* Rio de Janeiro: Gral.

Hellwig, D. J. (Ed.). (1992). *African American reflections on Brazil's racial paradise.* Philadelphia: Temple University.

Lewis, E. (in press). Race, the state and social construction: The multiple meanings of race in the twentieth century. In S. I. Kutler (Ed.), *The encyclopedia of the United States in the twentieth century.* New York: Scribner.

Lovell, P. (1989). *Income and racial inequality in Brazil.* Unpublished doctoral dissertation, University of Florida.

Merrick, T., & Graham, D. (1979). *Population and economic development in Brazil.* Baltimore: Johns Hopkins University Press.

Oboler, S. (1995). *Ethnic labels, Latino lives: Identity and the politics of re-presentation.* Minneapolis: University of Minnesota Press.

Omi, M., & Winant, H. (1986). *Racial formation in the United States, from the 1960's to the 1980's.* London: Routledge.

Pierson, D. (1942). *Negroes in Brazil: A study of race contact in Bahia.* Chicago: University of Chicago Press.

Reis, J. J. (1993). A greve negra de 1857 na Bahia. *Revista USP, 18,* 8-29.

Silva, N. (1980). O preço da cor: Diferenciais raciais na distribuição de renda no Brasil. *Pesquisa e Planejamento Econômico, 10*(1), 21-44.

Silva, P. C. (1993). *Negros à luz dos fornos: Representações do trabalho e da cor entre metalurgicos da moderna indústria baiana.* Master's thesis, Universidade Federal da Bahia, Salvador.

Skidmore, T. (1993). *White into Black.* Durham, NC: Duke University Press.

Taguieff, P. A. (1987). *La force du préjugé: Essai sur le racisme et ses doubles.* Paris: Gallimard.

Telles, E. (1992). Residential segregation by skin color in Brazil. *American Sociological Review, 57,* 186-197.

Van den Berghe, P. (1970). *Race and ethnicity.* New York: Basic Books.

Wade, P. (1993). *Blackness and race mixture: The dynamics of racial identity in Colombia.* Baltimore: Johns Hopkins University Press.

Wade, P. (1994). Race, nature and, culture. *Man (N.S.), 28,* 17-34.

Wright, W. R. (1990). *Café con leche: Race, class, and national image in Venezuela.* Austin: University of Texas Press.

12

Black Resistance in Brazil:
A Matter of Necessity

Rosângela Maria Vieira

Freedom is never voluntarily given by the oppressor; it must be demanded
by the oppressed. . . . So many of Latin America's problems have roots in
the United States that we need to form a solid, united movement, nonvio-
lently conceived and carried through, so that pressure can be brought to bear
on the capital and government power structures concerned, from both sides
of the problem at hand. (King, 1964, p. 63)

The issue of racism in Brazil is of great urgency to millions of Brazilians,
and is one of the most serious unaddressed problems in the world community. Racism is the greatest of Brazilian tragedies and speaks to the
injustices of a system that now, more than ever, impedes the progress and
social advancement of Brazil's Black majority.[1] For each generation of
African Brazilians, racism has destroyed hopes and opportunities and has
denied basic rights to Blacks. It is impossible to ignore this reality,
particularly in a country that has the second-largest Black population in
the world. Brazil is a country where Blacks live at the periphery of a
system that has rendered them invisible since colonial times.

It is important to note, however, that this subjugation has not gone
unchallenged. This chapter describes the African Brazilian challenge to
racism and surveys Black resistance in Brazil from colonial times to the
present, showing that countless African Brazilian communities have dem-

onstrated a strong sense of Black identity. This sense of personhood has led African Brazilians to struggle for survival and to reinvent themselves continuously. Black consciousness has been essential both to the African Brazilian sense of self and to the protest against injustice. The socioeconomic and political status of Blacks in contemporary Brazil is also considered so that one can see the base from which future progress can be assessed.

HISTORICAL BACKGROUND

From the 14th through the 16th centuries, Portuguese colonial rulers promoted the "suffering and humiliation of African peoples; and [were responsible] later, for the fate of Blacks in the Americas" (Rodriguez da Silva, 1987, p. 8). Dom Antâo Rodriguez was one of the first to enslave Africans. In 1444, "Rodriguez took twelve Africans from the continent as slave laborers" (Lemelle, 1992, p. 14). For the next 444 years, slavery flourished, resulting in an estimated 3,650,000 to 5,000,000 Africans being brought to Brazil. This is "a number many times greater than [the] approximately 427,000 sent to the United States" (Hellwig, 1992, p. 3).

The roots of Brazilian racism are deeply embedded in the slave-owning ideals of colonial Brazil and the need to control and exploit Africans. Racism was acquired from the Portuguese "in the same manner that Brazilians inherited their language, religion, and their habits and customs" (Silva, 1987, p. 180). Nevertheless, racism did not become rooted in Brazilian culture simply because of custom. Whether economic conditions were the cause or the effect, the racial superiority of Whites over Blacks was blessed and sanctioned by the church. Pope Nicolau V signed the Bill Romanus Pontifex on January 8, 1455, granting Portuguese navigators the rights and the power to capture Africans and hold them in perpetual servitude. The Portuguese colonizers had promised "to share half of the revenues from its colonies with the Catholic Church" (Scisinio, 1988, p. 20). In fact, profits not only motivated and justified the enslavement of Africans, it was made a Christian duty. The suffering of Africans was, in the Catholic Church's view, the price to pay for their "savagery and barbarous ways" (Rodriguez da Silva, 1987, pp. 8-11). Redemption could come only through conversion to Christianity, baptism, and resignation to a continued fate as slaves.

Africans resisted this barbarity. They struggled before, during, and after capture. While crossing the Atlantic, slaves insurrected and many committed suicide, some by "swallowing their tongues or jumping overboard" (Scisinio, 1988, pp. 60-61). According to Degler (1971) and Bastide (1978), the Black death rate and the number of suicides during colonial slavery was much greater in Brazil than in any other slave country. This fact is in direct contradiction to the notion that Brazil had "good masters" and "docile slaves," as successfully promoted in well-known writings such as Freyre's (1938) *Casa Grande e Senzala* (Masters and the Shanties) and de Holanda's *Raízes do Brasil* (Roots of Brazil). Freyre played a major role in advancing stereotypes about African Brazilians and portraying the African race as inferior and bestial.

COLONIAL TO
POST-ABOLITIONIST TIMES

As slaves, Blacks continuously organized and protested. If given the opportunity, they also worked to acquire their freedom, which was the case for Chico Rei. Chico Rei worked to free himself and his son (the only other family member to survive the Atlantic crossing). He was a tribal king, and most of his subjects had also been captured, sold to the Portuguese, and sent to the southeastern state of Minas Gerais. Through group effort and labor, Chico Rei freed his entire tribe.

Other African Brazilians resisted slavery by refusing to work efficiently during the 16-hour workdays required by their masters. Another important form of resistance was to run away and join other former slaves in the *Quilombos,* several of which became independent nations within Brazil. Quilombos were remote, self-sufficient, resistance communities founded and governed by the Black majority that fought to survive in colonial Brazil. To maintain their freedom, these communities had to be well-organized societies. Interestingly enough, the Quilombos did not exclude non-Blacks; they were examples of democratic orders and a world where "the practice of justice and the rights of participation were, in fact, accessible to all peoples, whether they were Black, Indian, or destitute and impoverished White marginalized by the colonial system" (Rodriguez da Silva, 1987, p. 21).

Eventually, all the Quilombos were wiped out by the Luso-Brazilian state. But while they existed, Quilombos distinguished themselves "for their strength in the recruitment and gathering of slaves and for maintaining their hopes to establish a free society" (Rodriguez da Silva, 1987, p. 22). Some, like Palmares, survived for almost a century. These Black nations could be found throughout Brazil, and their number is testimony to the extent and effectiveness of Black resistance in Brazil. The names of those Quilombos are unknown to most people. Each should be the topic of serious study, because we could learn a great deal about Black resistance and community in Brazil. To ignore the Brazilian Quilombos is to ignore Black resistance in Brazil.[2]

Besides the Quilombos, other Black revolts and resistance movements occurred from colonial times through the abolition of slavery. The Sastre rebellion (1798) in Bahia happened after gold was discovered following the decline of sugar production in the late 1600s. African slaves were used to extract most of the gold found in Brazil and sent to Portugal. Distressed by economic exploitation and motivated by the ideals of the French Revolution, many African Brazilians from Bahia organized to rebel against their White masters. The Sastre rebellion was,

> a democratic movement aimed at establishing a free and democratic Republican government, one accessible to all peoples. . . . [It] was discovered in its initial stages and its leaders were all [killed by hanging], and their bodies cut in pieces and disposed of like waste. (Carneiro, 1946, pp. 9-13)

The next major revolt was that of famelic slaves in Bahia (1814), which happened after Napoleon's armies began their invasion of Portugal around 1808. The Portuguese monarch, Dom João VI, fled to Rio de Janeiro, where he stayed until 1821. This was one of the worst periods for the treatment of Brazilian slaves. Starvation prevailed as never before. In desperation, slaves took to the streets to demand better treatment and freedom, only to be killed by Luso-Brazilian forces.

The period prior to and immediately after the proclamation of Brazilian independence (September 7, 1822) witnessed the Muslim Malê (1807 and 1835), the Jehad (1835), and the Black Nagos (1826-1835) revolts. These rebellions "had religious characteristics—their goal was to kill all the White masters and expel the Christian religion in the name of Alâ" (Carneiro, 1946, pp. 9-12).

The religious rebellions were followed by the Sabinada revolt (1837), in which hundreds of Black women, children, and older slaves were slaughtered by Luso-Brazilian forces with such determination and intensity that rebellion movements disappeared for some time in Bahia. Outside Bahia, the Balaio armed insurrection (1839) signaled continued resistance. The lack of long-term objectives, planning, and specific strategies allowed the revolt to be easily undermined by Brazilian forces, which, as in prior revolts, killed all the rebellion leaders. Additional revolts in the late 19th century were the Canudo and the Beata (1897), whose participants were also massacred.

Slavery ended in Brazil because it had to; African Brazilians had successfully struggled against it. In the years just before abolition, slaves were in constant rebellion. They were escaping the plantations, fleeing to the Quilombos in great numbers, and were no longer being hunted by the Brazilian army. There was also general political instability and a war with Paraguay. The entire social order was collapsing and could no longer maintain a plantation economy based on slave labor. National and international political and economic pressures also acted to abolish slavery and move toward a free society. The Brazilian state was slow to act, passing a series of self-serving laws such as the Law of the Free Womb (1871) and the Sexagenary Law (1885), which favored the interests of the White master. When freedom did come, on May 13, 1888, the victory belonged to African Brazilians, a few Abolitionists, and the international community, not to some sense of justice or benevolence from the Brazilian elites.

The years following Abolition were extremely hard for African Brazilians. Newly freed Blacks were ignored and had no opportunity to prepare for the emerging industrial economy. To survive, Blacks had to find alternatives to plantation life. Forgotten was the major role Blacks played in building the Brazilian nation and creating wealth for the elites. Instead, the 19th-century philosophical import, social Darwinism, was used to charge Blacks with natural inferiority. This alleged genetic inferiority explained Blacks' economic backwardness and supplied the justification for importing White immigrants.

At the turn of the century, the overwhelming majority of Brazilians were of African descent. The potential to become a Black nation was, even then, very clear to the White elite. The elite addressed this problem after Abolition and the declaration of the first Republic (1889) by opening the floodgates to hundreds of thousands of White European immigrants—who were given preference over Blacks in jobs, housing, and education wherever they lived, but especially in the emerging southeast. Blacks (many of whom were more skilled than the White immigrants) were pushed by European immigration into "low paying professions and unemployment" (Lopes et al., 1987, p. 23). It was also the elite's hope that White immigrants would intermarry with African Brazilians, causing Blacks to cease to exist as a race and negating the Black political potential. The powerful White minority believed the African race would disappear if enough whitening occurred. If nothing else, Blacks would be much easier to control. Through whitening, Brazil would progress into the circle of developed nations. African Brazilians were expected to vanish by neglect and design. The naiveté embedded in this goal, as well as its failure, is evident in that the African Brazilian population is estimated today at up to 75% of the total Brazilian population (Covin, 1990, p. 143). These figures are expected to continue to grow as the 21st century approaches.

RESISTANCE: EARLY 20th CENTURY TO THE PRESENT

Resistance to racism after the end of slavery was evident among Blacks by their resistance to whitening and their participation in many Black movement organizations since the early 1900s (Carneiro, 1946, pp. 9-13). Another reason for organizing and protesting was to fight against the poverty and destitution among Blacks, which have always been high. The years between World War I and the establishment of the Brazilian new state under the dictatorship of Getúlio Vargas (1930) witnessed the emergence of modern Black organizations. The expressed goals of these organizations included an improvement in living conditions and an expansion of opportunities for African Brazilians.

An extensive community-based Black press also emerged (especially in São Paulo) and played a vital role in promoting Black consciousness in the first decades of this century. The Black press was a catalyst for organizing, claiming Black rights, addressing the horrendous plight of Blacks, and fighting Brazilian racism. In the beginning, the Black press mainly promoted social events. As it became more reflective, social awareness grew, as did campaigns demanding full inclusion in Brazilian social, economic, and political life.

The record of the Black press in Brazil also leaves an important legacy of Black consciousness. These publications were mostly self-supporting and had very limited resources. Newspapers came and went with the ability of their communities to support them. The active and extensive Black press is *prima facie* evidence that African Brazilians have historic and contemporary communities, have been aware of themselves as Black people, have been conscious of their plight, and have struggled for recognition and fair opportunities in the larger Brazilian society. A people who disappeared through whitening or had no sense of themselves could not have had such an extensive and popular press.[3]

The most significant journals currently published in the United States that examine African Brazilian studies include the *Journal of Afro-Latin American Studies and Literatures,* based at Howard University and the University of New Orleans; *Journal of Black Studies*; and *Centennial Review.* Investigation of African contribution to Brazilian arts and letters is conducted through special issues of *Luso-Brazilian Review.*

Following is a list of selected Black organizations whose agendas illustrate the historical concerns for African Brazilians.

- *Centro Cívico Palmares* (Palmares Civic Center) was initially conceived in 1927 as an educational organization; it soon became a center for the fight against poverty, racial prejudice, and social inequalities.
- *Frente Negra Brasileira* (Brazilian Black Front) was founded in 1931 and became a political party in 1936, only to be outlawed by the dictator Getúlio Vargas. This group saw the need to oppose the political establishment and defend Blacks' rights to participate in all aspects of Brazilian life.
- *Teatro Experimental do Negro* (TEN) (Black Experimental Theater) was founded in 1944 by Abdias do Nascimento, one of the first and most prominent African Brazilian intellectuals to defend Black aesthetics and consciousness, and to speak out against whitening. TEN's main goals were to value and promote Black actors by using dramatic art to portray their reality and the need for social changes.
- *Primeiro Congresso do Negro Brasileiro* (First Brazilian Black Congress) was founded in 1950 to form a structured Black political constituency in Brazil.
- *Fundação da Associação Cultural do Negro* (Black Cultural Association) was founded in 1954.
- *O Movimento Black-Rio* (Black-Rio Movement).
- *Movimento Negro Unificado* (MNU) (Unified Black Movement) is one of the most important Black movements addressing issues of the African diaspora in Brazil today.
- *Fundação Palmares* (Palmares Foundation) is a statutory body of the Brazilian government founded by the Ministry of Culture on August 22, 1988.
- *Instituto de Pesquisa das Culturas Negras* (IPCN) (Institute for Research of Black Cultures).
- *Centro de Cultura e Arte Negras* (CECAN) (Center for Black Culture and Arts).

- *Grupo Palmares* (Group Palmares) proposed that Black Awareness Day be celebrated on November 20 (anniversary of Zumbi's death) rather than on May 13 (anniversary of Abolition in Brazil).

- *Federação das Entidades Afro-Brasileiras do Estado de São Paulo* (Federation of Afro-Brazilian Organizations of São Paulo) was responsible for the Black Zumbi's first community festival, still celebrated yearly in São Paulo.

- *CERCAB Nation* promotes research on racial relations in São Paulo.

- *UNegro* is a contemporary Black organization within the Brazilian Communist Party.

- *Center for the Articulation of Marginalized Peoples* (CEAP) conducts social research on issues pertaining to street children and other issues, including the forced sterilization of Black women.

- *Institute of Black Women* (GELEDÉS) is an influential organization within the Black community that examines the plight of Black women and children in Brazil.

- *OLODUM* is a group of civil rights activists that speaks out against racism and promotes the advancement of Blacks through education and organizational strength.

It is estimated that approximately 2,500 other Black organizations exist in Brazil. According to the Palmares Foundation, however, this number fluctuates between 500 and 600 active organizations at any time. They all speak against racism and promote awareness, Black consciousness, and the need to consider issues of race in the struggle to achieve social opportunities.

CURRENT STATUS
OF AFRICAN BRAZILIANS

Brazilians of African ancestry continue to live under unfavorable and oppressive circumstances. Despite being a majority of the nation's population, African Brazilians are virtually invisible in the economy and other sectors of society. Material conditions of most African Brazilians have probably deteriorated in recent years. Blacks' comparatively low social, political, and economic positions and invisibility in society cannot be explained by blaming Blacks for their plight. Many Brazilians believe that to speak of Brazilian social ills is unpatriotic. This includes speaking out against the outdated "class only" theory to explain the nature of prejudice in Brazil. In addition, many Brazilians are still firm believers in the equally discredited theory of racial harmony and democracy. African Brazilians, however, are becoming increasingly more aware that silence perpetuates their oppression and impedes the effectiveness of anti-racism campaigns. This has caused many African Brazilians to reassess their status and form united fronts against racism.

The struggle both inside and outside South Africa that has produced positive social change serves as an example to African Brazilians of what a persistent Black majority can do. But the situation in Brazil differs in many ways from that in South Africa. Racial disenfranchisement in Brazil is not enshrined in the laws or in formally acknowledged practices. This absence of widely enforceable and truly effective laws protecting Blacks from racial discrimination results in conditions reminiscent of South African apartheid—the result is probably worse in Brazil if one compares living standards.

Racism has pervaded Brazilian society for almost 500 years and is more sophisticated than racism in the United States or South Africa. In nations where racism is overtly expressed, Blacks can identify and fight their foes, but this level of openness does not exist in Brazil. In fact, the few Blacks who achieve social mobility in Brazil, primarily through sports and music, believe in the class-only character of Brazilian discrimination. Many Blacks who attain high status believe they are now equal to the descendants of their slave masters, despite all evidence to the contrary.

Whether it is acknowledged or not, the clearest evidence of racism in Brazil is in the impoverished condition of African Brazilians throughout the country. This reality suggests a direct correlation between color and poverty. Moura (1988) states that in the 1980 census, Brazilians described their racial background by 136 different racial categories. These varied from "mulatto" to a "burro when it flees." Given this reality, Moura asks:

> What is the meaning of this in a country that describes itself as a racial democracy? It means that the ideology and fundamental values of the dominant elite have been introduced, through disguised mechanisms, into many non-whites. It also means that our ethnical reality, contrary to what is said, is not equalized through miscegenation . . . on the contrary, it differentiates, and promotes hierarchies and inferiorities in such a way that non-whites attempt to create a symbolic reality where they take refuge, trying to escape from the [social, economic, and racial] inferiority conveyed through his/her color in this society. (pp. 62-63)

The vast majority of African Brazilians live in abject poverty and as a pariah class, whereas a small White minority continues to control, dominate, and grow wealthy. A few facts about living condition of Blacks in Brazil show systematic oppression.

• Data from a United Nations Report released in May 1994 show increases in poverty and the economic distance between rich and poor in the world. This report indicates that Brazil is 63rd among 163 countries in its record of human development and income distribution. This report also shows that the wealthiest 20% of Brazilians earn an income that is 32 times greater than its poorest 20%. Other research estimates that 46.94% of Blacks and 44.72% of mulattos have income at or below the current Brazilian minimum wage; the figure for Whites is 24.1% (Francisco, 1983, p. 28). This reality is made worse in a country where "69% of the population (105.3 million) does not have public sewer sanitation treatment and where 33% (52.7 million) does not have access to safe drinking water" (*O Estado de São Paulo,* 1994). This impoverished condition is aggravated further by the unsolicited appropriation of funds from the Fundo Social de Emergência (coE; Emergency Social Fund),

> by government agencies such as the Ministry of Foreign Relations, which finance some of their expenses, such as the transportation for their high ranking employees and payment of existing Brazilian debts with money that has been allotted for social programs. In the end, agencies like the coE and the Ministry of Health are left without enough funds to even purchase medicine for the poor. It is estimated that in 1995, coE's funds will total US $15.5 billion dollars. (*Folha de São Paulo,* 1994, July 10)

• Less than 2% of African Brazilians attend college and less than 1% of them graduate in a nation where the majority of the population is African Brazilian (Roland, 1988, p. 16).
• Illiteracy among Whites is at 25% (Roland, 1988, p. 16), as compared to 47.7% among Blacks and 48.05% among mulattos (Francisco, 1983, p. 28).
• Blacks are the majority of residents in the nation's *favelas*—shanty towns or modern "slave" quarters (Hering, 1994, p. 29).
• It is estimated that 78% (Oliveira, 1983, p. 24) to 88% (Hering, 1994, p. 29) of Brazilian prison inmates are of African descent. If this figure is accurate, it is the highest rate of Black incarceration in the world, far surpassing that of South Africa and the United States.

- The commercialization of African Brazilian folklore, religion, art, music, and heritage is a form of superexploitation that does not benefit African Brazilian communities. White elites also control tourism (e.g., Carnaval) and reap the profits.

- According to figures released by UNICEF, there are 50 million street children in Latin America, one-half the world's total. Of these, more than 7 million are Brazilians, the vast majority of whom are of African ancestry (CEAP—Rio de Janeiro; OAA—Organization of Africans in the Americas, Washington, D.C). These children are fair game for sexual exploitation, torture, and mutilation.

- In addition to overt violence, which results in the deaths of thousands of Afro-Brazilian street kids in the hands of off-duty police and official death squads, children in Brazil face death through malnutrition and diseases. Some 400,000 children die each year from curable illness in Brazil, and there are indications that the majority of these victims are of African ancestry. In the city of Teotônio Vilela in the state of Alagoas, the infant mortality rate is 377 for each 1,000 births (*Folha de São Paulo,* 1994, July 7). This is happening in the 11th most industrialized country in the world.

These developments are not due to coincidence or to Black inferiority or cultural differences, which are often given as explanations. It is the result of repression and a national identity that obscures reality. It is true that many *Mamelucos* (a mixture of Whites and Indians) in drought-afflicted northeastern Brazil and many blond, blue-eyed descendants of Europeans in the southeast live in wretchedly poor conditions. But these two sectors combined are much smaller than impoverished Brazilians of African ancestry regardless of their color. It is lamentable that anyone suffers poverty, but the fact that a relatively small proportion of Whites live in poverty should not diminish the gravity and awareness of the racial motivation behind the apparent correlation between color and poverty in Brazil.

CONCLUSION

The subjugation and exploitation of African Brazilians will not change unless they become agents of their own liberation with support from humanitarians, civil rights leaders, academicians, and intellectuals throughout the world, as was the case with South Africa. Brazil must awaken from its illusion of racial democracy and the class-only nature of its prejudice. Brazilian racism, which mirrors that of Latin America (or serves as its pattern), must be condemned in real terms, not just in rhetoric. African Brazilians must assert their rights and mobilize to produce broad political and economic reforms. Many African Brazilians hope that an enlightened national leadership will be supportive and take action. In the same manner, Latin America as a whole must deal with its racism and address race-driven inequality and the prejudice embedded in Latin national identities.

NOTES

1. The population of Brazil in 1993 was estimated at more than 160 million, and likely to reach 200 million within two more decades (Instituto Brasileiro de Geografia e Estatistica, 1994; *Veja,* 1994). Based on information from Black Brazilian organizations and various scholars, the estimated number of people of African ancestry in Brazil ranges from 67.8% (Oliveira, 1983) to 75% (Candido, 1983) of the total population. The Brazilian census, however, indicates that Blacks represent only 46% of the Brazilian population.

2. The Quilombos in São Paulo were Piracicaba, Itapetininga, Jundiaí, Mojiguaçu, Jabaquara, Atibaia, Santos, Campinas, Morro de Araraquara, Aldeia de Pinheiros, and Fazenda Monjolinho; in Bahia, they were Cabula, Nossa Senhora dos Mares, Cachoeira, Buraco do Tatú, Xiquexique, Andaraí, Tupim, Orobó, Campos de Cachoeira, Muritiba, Maragojipe, Jaguaribe, Jacuípe, and Urubú; in Maranhão, they were Lagoa Amarela, Turiaçu, São Benedito, and Maracassumí; in Sergipe, they were Vila Nova, Laranjeiras, Engenho Brejo, Rosário, Itaporanga, Divina Pastora, Itabarana, and Capela; in Pará, they were Arajá, Marajó, Guripi, Marajubá, Caxuí, Cametá, Alcabaça, Obidos, and Aleques; in Rio de Janeiro, the most popular Quilombo was founded by Manoel Congo and called Quilombo de Santa Catarina. The last Quilombos were founded in Amapá and were Mazagão and Oiapoque-Calçone.

3. Among many of the African Brazilian newpapers, there were *O Manelic* (1915), *A Rua* and *O Xauter* (1916), *O Alfinete* and *O Bandeirante* (1918), *A Liberdade* (1919), *A Sentinela* (1920), *O Kosmos* (1922), *O Getulino* (1923), *O Clarim d'Alvorada* (an extremely important newspaper, founded by the journalists Jayme Aguiar and José Correia Leite, one of Brazil's greatest civil rights activists). Other Black journals were *Elite* (1924), *Auriverde, O Patrocinio,* and *Progresso* (1928), *Chibata* (1932), *A Evolução* and *A Voz da Raça* (1933), *O Clarim, O Estímulo, A Raça,* and *Tribuna Negra* (1935), *A alvorada* (1936), *Senzala* (1946), *Mundo Novo* (1950), *O Novo Horizonte* (1954), *Notícias de Ébano* (1957), *O Mutirão* (1958), *Hifen* and *Niger* (1960), *Nosso Jornal* (1961), and *Correio d'Ébano* (1963; Moura, 1988, pp. 205-217). Among the journals published from the 1970s to the 1990s are *Gazeta Afro-Latina de Porto Alegre, Revista do Movimento Negro Unificado, Jornal Nagô, Jornal Nacional do MNU, Eparrei* (published by Entidade

Casa da Mulher Negra), *Jornal do Conselho da Comunidade Negra, Sinba, Jornegro, Jornal da Maioria Falante, Cecune, Jornal do Centro Ecumênico de Cultura Negra, Cadernos Negros* (published by the Group Quilombhoje, SP), *Jornal do Centro de Estudos Afro-Asiáticos,* and *Revista to Instituto das Mulheres Negras* (published by GELEDÉS).

REFERENCES

Bastide, R. (1978). *The African religions of Brazil: Toward a sociology of the interpenetration of civilizations.* Baltimore: Johns Hopkins University Press.

Bastide, R., & Fernandes, F. (1971). *Brancos e negros em São Paulo.* São Paulo: Companhia Editora Nacional.

Baptista, M. (Ed.). (1988). *Povo negro.* São Paulo: Edições Loyola.

Candido, J. (1983, Aug.-Sept.). Perfil histórico-cultural da discriminaçaõ racial e da violência urbana. *Cadernos Cândido Mendes, Estudos Afro-Asiáticos,* pp. 158-166.

Carneiro, E. (1946). *Guerra de los palmares.* Panaco, Mexico: Fondo de Cultura Económica.

Covin, D. (1990). Afrocentricity in o movimento negro unificado. *Journal of Black Studies, 21,* 126-144.

Degler, C. (1971). *Neither Black nor White.* New York: Macmillan.

Fernandes, F. (1971). *O negro no mundo dos brancos.* São Paulo: Difusaõ Européia do Livro.

Freyre, G. (1938). *Casa grande & senzala: Fomação da família brasileira sobo regime da econômica patriarcal.* Rio de Janeiro: Schmidt.

Folha de São Paulo. (1994, July 10). São Paulo: Folha de São Paulo.

Francisco, D. (1983). Comunicaçaõ. *Cadernos Cândido Mendes, Estudos Afro-Asiáticos,* pp. 26-33.

Hellwig, D. J. (Ed.). (1992). *African American reflections on Brazil's racial paradise.* Philadelphia: Temple University Press.

Hering, T. (1994). Emancipaçaõ racial no Brasil: Uma incessante continuidade histórica. *Journal of Afro-Latin American Studies and Literatures, 1,* 23-35.

King, M. L. (1964). *Why we can't wait.* New York: Penguin.

Leite, J. C., & Silva, L. (1992). *E disse o velho militante José Correia Leite.* São Paulo: Coordenadoria Especial do Negro.

Lemelle, S. (1992). *Pan-Africanism for beginners.* New York: Writers & Readers.

Lopes, H. T., et al. (1987). *Negro e cultura no Brasil.* Rio de Janeiro: Unibrade.

Moura, C. (1988). *Sociologia do negro brasileiro.* São Paulo: Atica.

O Estado de São Paulo. (1994, July 9-10). São Paulo: O Estado de São Paulo.

Oliveira, E. (1983). Manifesto à naçaõ brasileira e à comunidade negra de São Paulo. *Cadernos Cândido Mendes, Estudos Afro-Asiáticos,* p. 24.

Rodrigues da Silva, M. (1987). *O negro no Brasil.* São Paulo: Editora FTD.

Roland, E. (1988). A realidade da mulher negra. In M. Baptista (Ed.), *Povo negro* (pp. 16-29). São Paulo: Edições Loyola.

Scisinio, A. E. (1988). *Escravidaõ e à saga de Manoel Congo.* Rio de Janeiro: Achiame.

Silva, M. J. (1987). *Racismo à brasileira.* Brasilia: Thesaurus.

Veja. (1994, July 7). Rio de Janeiro: Veja.

OTHER READINGS

Macedo, S. D. (1974). *Crônica do negro no Brasil.* São Paulo: Distribuidora Record.

McAdam, D. (1982). *Political process and the development of Black insurgency, 1930-1970.* Chicago: University of Chicago Press.

McCartney, J. T. (1992). *Black power ideologies.* Philadelphia: Temple University Press.

Mintz, S. W., & Price, R. (1976). *The birth of African-American culture.* Boston: Beacon.

Mitchel, M. (1984, Summer). Cafundo: Counterpoint on a Brazilian African survival. *Centennial Review,* pp. 185-203.

Querino, M. A. (1955). *Raça africana e os seus costumes.* Salvador: Livraria Progresso Editora.

Vainfas, R. (1986). *Ideologia e escravidaõ.* Petrópolis: Vozes.

Vieira, R. M. (1994). Essays. In B. A. Tenembaum (Ed.), *Encyclopedia of Latin American history.* New York: Scribner.

Vieira, R. M. (1995). *Brave history: Black presence and power struggle in Brazil. The Afro-Latin Americans: No longer invisible.* London: Minority Rights Group.

13

Racism and Anti-Racism in the Caribbean

Ralph R. Premdas

The problem of racism and anti-racism in the Caribbean revolves around the diversity of cultures that have emerged in the region since the indigenous people were wiped out following the arrival of Columbus in 1492. At that time, the Caribbean archipelago, stretching from the Bahamas to the Guianas and encompassing thousands of islands, was already inhabited by the Arawak, Carib, and Siboney tribes, who regarded the Caribbean basin as a single integrated region. After they were subjugated, their tribes were supplanted by an assortment of colonial powers, including Spain, France, Britain, and the Netherlands. The region thus became fragmented into several European cultural spheres. The rival European powers systematically plundered the islands, mostly through one critical institution: the plantation. Key crops were cotton, tobacco, and sugar, which became preeminent.

For the land to yield bounty, abundant, reliable, and cheap labor was required; this is the variable that best explains the populating of the postindigenous Caribbean. The native people, having succumbed to the harsh regime of regimented toil, were replaced by a steady cross-oceanic caravan of indentured laborers and African slaves. Some 15 million Africans were enslaved over four centuries to work on the plantations of the Caribbean. The slaves were dehumanized as chattel. When slavery was abolished, the plantation endured, and new waves of indentured immigrants from Asia added to the proliferation of human cultures in the region. On the anvil of greed and cruelty was born the contemporary medley of peoples of the Caribbean. The imperial powers and the plantation owners reduced the imported laborers to subhuman categories in a process of racialization and racism. Eventually, when slavery was challenged and new societies of freed people were formed, this process was executed through anti-racist campaigns composed of both slaves and freed persons, Blacks and Whites alike.

This chapter examines the interplay of racist and anti-racist forces that molded the Caribbean peoples and cultures; it is divided into two parts. The first is a description of immigrants being brought to the Caribbean islands. In particular, I examine the legacy of labor recruitment, both free and indentured, to show how themes of racism and anti-racism molded the emergent social and economic character of the Caribbean states. From a historical standpoint, I then take the story from colonization through to emancipation, to self-government and independence in the 20th century. In the second part, I look at what the peoples of the Caribbean have done with their new-found liberation specifically in terms of the elimination of vestiges of racism and discrimination. Did the new political systems eradicate racism? Or were new and indirect forms of racial and ethnic differentiation invented and institutionalized so that the anti-racist struggle for equality and democracy is now caught up in an intra-Black social matrix and still needs to be won?

It is difficult to consolidate the culture and people of the Caribbean without damaging the unique experiences that constitute the fabric of the Caribbean kaleidoscope of peoples, cultures, economies, languages, music, religions, and polities. The European legacy was not simply about labor. Europeans brought different religions, values, and national styles. The immigrant labor also brought racial, linguistic, religious, and cultural differences. The new societies that emerged were not derived from the same environmental milieu from which they came. The slave experiences were not the same, and antiracist and abolitionist struggles differed from area to area.

The decolonization process also varied, and the new postindependence systems were in many respects radically different. All of this must be compressed into general patterns and trends.

THE CARIBBEAN AND COLONIALISM

The Indigenous People

When Columbus arrived uninvited in the Caribbean, he did not "discover" the indigenous people and thereby establish their existence. The Arawaks, Caribs, and Siboneys had lived in the region from time immemorial and had created viable social systems with their own religions, governments, customs, values, and economies. They did not want or seek another way of life. Upon Columbus' first encounter with the inhabitants, he immediately evaluated them in terms of servitude to fit his needs. He recorded in his journal, "They should be good servants" (Williams, 1966, p. 31). Columbus' purpose was plain. He had brought with him from Spain concepts of social organization such as the code, Las Siete Partidas, that recognized and regularized slavery. Columbus, like the early Spanish administrators, quickly stigmatized the indigenous people into preconceived subhuman categories in laying the moral basis for their servitude. He described the Caribs as cannibals and "a wild people fit for any work . . . who when they got rid of their cruel habits would be better than any other slaves" (Williams, 1966, p. 31). The noted contemporary Spanish historian, Fernando Oveido, describes them as "by nature idle and vicious, disinclined to work, cowardly, prone to evil, liars . . . sodomites, cannibals, and idolators" (Lewis, 1983, p. 47). This fiction fed into the stereotyping of the indigenous people as subhuman and deserving of enslavement and genocide.

The Spanish conquest was aimed both at the acquisition of lucre and the saving of souls. The native people were offered Christianity; on refusal, they were enslaved. They resisted the impositions of the Spaniards, but they were no match for the Spaniards' superior technology and artillery. "In despair many fled to the mountains, abandoned all cultivation and preferred to starve to death" (Williams, 1966, p. 32). Most of the indigenous people were made to pay tribute to the Spanish in gold, and were sold as property in a system of *encomiendas* and *repartmientos* (Knight, 1990; Williams, 1966). Enslavement of the native peoples met with resistance in psychological withdrawal and population decline. The native people preferred to die in dignity rather than live enslaved. The fate of the indigenous people in their dehumanization and decline was temporarily arrested by the work of Bartolemé de las Casas, a Spanish priest who officially became the protector of the Indians. He sought to demythologize the stereotype that depicted Indians as uncivilized, pointing to the fact that they possessed autonomous societies that were in many ways superior to the Spanish (see Lewis, this volume).

The saga of the genocidal decimation of the native people of the Caribbean underscores many of the salient features of the role of racism and anti-racist campaigns in the colonization and settlement of the Caribbean. Entry into the region was forced. It was met by resistance, as the conquered were systematically dehumanized by the ideologies and practices of racism. Campaigns were waged by many persons such as las Casas to save the oppressed. In the case of Indians, this did not bear much fruit, as they dwindled and practically disappeared. Today, in the insular Caribbean, residual Indian settlements exist in Dominica, Trinidad, and St. Vincent. Many places bear Indian names; they are the echoes of a civilization that once vibrantly occupied the region.

Colonization

After Columbus's arrival, Spain commanded the Caribbean without significant challenge for almost two centuries. Spanish settlements were located where there was mineral loot to be plundered, but this was in short supply in the islands. The mainland was staked out; with the discovery of large quantities of gold and silver, the Incas, Mayas, and Aztecs underwent the same dehumanization and decimation that the Caribs, Arawaks, and Ciboneys had suffered in the insular Caribbean. Spanish preoccupation with the mainland led to the Caribbean being reduced to transshipment points for cargo sent to Spain. The islands became relatively depopulated, and small-scale settlements arose mainly in Cuba, Puerto Rico, and Hispaniola. At the end of the 17th century, Dutch, French, and English intruders established rival colonies in the Caribbean.

The collapse of Spanish hegemony in the Caribbean inaugurated two dramatic changes that registered a permanent imprint on the character of the region. First, from a unified area under the Indians and then the Spanish, the Caribbean became fragmented into separate settlements controlled by various European powers. Second, the small-scale settlements were later swept away and yielded to a new mode of production—large plantations committed to the export of cotton, tobacco, and sugar. With this radical transformation came the infusion of unprecedented numbers of indentured laborers and African slaves to serve the plantations. Inherent in African slavery was racism, a degradation of humans into dehumanized chattel as a precondition to unlimited exploitation. Caribbean historian Eric Williams (1966) argues otherwise, that racist categorization came not before but after the needs of the plantation dictated the demand for servile labor.

Williams claims:

> Slavery in the Caribbean has been too narrowly identified with the Negro. A racial twist has thereby been given to what is basically an economic phenomenon. Slavery was not born of racism; rather racism was the consequence of slavery. Unfree labor in the New World was brown, black, and yellow: Catholic, Protestant and Pagan. (p. 7)

This thesis is argued on the basis that, with the introduction of large-scale plantations, White indentured laborers were initially recruited, but proved ill-adapted and expensive. Hence, Williams argues, "White servitude was the historic base upon which Negro slavery was constructed" (Williams, 1966, p. 19). Williams concludes, "Here, then is the origin of Negro slavery. The reason was economic, not racial: it had to do not with the color of the labor but the cheapness of the labor" (p. 19). Much of this argument would fly in the face of the fact that the African was portrayed in the emergent European literature of the 18th and 19th centuries as a subhuman type that provided the enslavement process with bio-social justification (Brereton, 1979, pp. 193-212).

African slavery, plantations, and sugar constituted the three pillars that engaged all aspects of emergent Caribbean society. Not all the islands came synchronistically to the experience of the plantation-slave-sugar syndrome. Although sugar was in decline in the British islands by 1834 and in the French islands by 1848, it assumed fresh life in the Spanish islands of Cuba, Puerto Rico, and the Dominican Republic. Despite variations in timing, the social system that was generated on the plantations universally was castelike, in which the slave occupied a position of humiliation that fundamentally offended the human social and spiritual form. The racist planter ideology, regardless of whether it came prior to or after enslavement, defined the role of the ruler as rooted in the best interest of the biologically inferior slave. The slave was deemed naturally inferior by God's design and was endowed with a small cranium. Slaves were considered indolent, childlike, and untrustworthy due to inherent deformity. The early Christian churches generally collaborated with the plantocracy and colonial authorities in constructing this ideology of oppression.

But the racist slave system did not go unchallenged within or outside the slave communities. From outside came intellectual disagreement and disapproval. From Europe came the agitation of the English Abolitionists and the French philosophes. The ideas of the American and French revolutions had much influence. Much of this new discourse that challenged the racist slave ideology that prevailed in Europe and the United States seeped down to the slave communities in the Caribbean. As Lewis (1983) points out, "There took place a continuous and rich intercourse of ideas between the metropolitan societies and the colonies, reaching even the slave populations, and about which the slave-owning class could do little, if anything" (p. 206). Adam Smith added artillery to the emergent antislavery dissent, pointing to the economic inefficiency of slave labor. The steady outpouring of dissonance included the works of both pamphleteers and novelists, including Montesquieu, Voltaire, Raynal, Clarkson, Diderot, Condorcet, Helvetius, and Defoe. Abolitionist struggles were also conducted within the Caribbean itself, notably in the work of Victor Schoelcher. Important fissures were opened among certain Christian clergy and missions, who would contribute to a rereading of the Bible to oppose and abolish slavery.

In due time, the Scriptures were enrolled as a main instrument in the struggle for the liberation of the slave by the slave.

From within the slave community, resistance emanated in manifold forms, ranging from overt patterns of nonviolent sabotage such as excessive deference, malingering, feigned ignorance, self-mutilation, abortion, dirt-eating, and suicide to the nurturing of a subterranean culture. The latter included reconstituted families, religious practices, economies, languages, songs, and dances fashioned from African memories. There were revolts, some brutally destroying the oppressor, which included mass escape to form autonomous Maroon villages. Slave subcultures and rebellions were prevalent throughout the Caribbean, expressed in vibrant African cults, shango, vodun, obeah, bamboo-bamboo, cambouley, and macumba. Slaves weaved alternative economic orders around small garden plots, internal marketing systems, cooperativism, and mutual aid. Secret communication networks were established; dissenting Christian churches were incorporated in the resistance. African churches became de facto secret societies. In summary, acts of resistance proliferated from the subtle to the brutal, from sycophancy to murder, in counterculture, ritual, and religion, in everything everywhere; the relentless quest for a life of freedom never ceased (Beckles, 1982; Lewis, 1983).

Abolition

Slave resistance reached its crescendo in the explosion that rocked Haiti after the French Revolution of 1789, making Haiti the first independent Black republic in the Western hemisphere (James, 1963). More than just an event particular to Haiti, it was the summit of ongoing agitation in both small and significant ways in thought and action since the first slave came to the Caribbean. The Haitian Revolution was a metaphor for salvation by aggressive self-help; Haitian independence and formal abolition of slavery followed the principle of equality embodied in the French Revolution. Early European thought against slavery was first couched in appeals to natural law, and attained practical consequence in the principles of the American and French revolutions against servitude. These principles received their finest application in Haiti, attaining reality from the efforts of the slaves who challenged the iniquitous order with unrelenting and uncompromising ardor.

In England, France, and the United States, antislavery sentiments had slowly solidified in the formation of Abolitionist societies, which lobbied for legislation that attacked the slave trade and slavery itself. The antislavery Abolition Committee headed by Wilberforce in Britain and the Société des Noirs in France offered moral and intellectual ammunition to the move for Abolition. Although Williams (1966) and others stress how reformist, ambivalent, and circumspect these efforts tended to be from the perspective of hindsight, the critical point remains that, given the tenor of the times, these initiatives were significant thrusts that accelerated the anti-racist drive toward deliverance. Facing a tidal wave of protest against the abolition of the slave trade, as well as the economic decline of the sugar industry, the plantation owners were willing to offer ameliorative transitional solutions. The threat of total loss of their slave supply led them to argue that a progressive release from bondage was in the best interest of the slaves. This rearguard action did not succeed in halting the inexorable drive for full emancipation.

In 1807, Britain abolished the slave trade; slavery itself was abolished in the British colonies in 1833. In Haiti, Napoleon Bonaparte attempted to reimpose slavery, only to invite the brutal eradication of all French planters and their families from Haitian soil. Slavery was not finally abolished in the French islands until 1848, in Puerto Rico until 1873, and in Cuba until 1886.

Although slavery was abolished in the Caribbean at different times, institutions of inequality and racial domination persisted. These emerged as the new hurdles to overcome. The anti-racist struggle now had to wrestle with an iniquitous protean monster that had become ingrained in the social structure of postemancipation Caribbean societies. A color-class system of social grading superseded the overt forms of distributing privileges, resources, and power (Braithwaite, 1953; Hoetink, 1985; Lowenthal, 1972; Smith, 1965). Things White were uniformly held superior to things Black. The social order coincided with phenotype, color, and class. Coffee-colored mulattos occupied the middle stratum of status and access to resources and privileges, underscoring the emergence of a finely tuned color continuum in the stratification system.

Continued colonial control implied racism; thus, racism embedded in the structure of Caribbean societies had to be eliminated simultaneously with the removal of colonial control. Different colonies traversed this terrain at different paces. Haiti ejected both slavery and colonial control simultaneously in a revolutionary war that culminated in victory over invading French forces in 1804. This was not the case in the remaining French, Dutch, English, and Spanish colonies. The trek to political freedom was differently paced and the modalities of struggle varied, but the trajectory toward decolonization was in one direction alone. This did not mean that anti-racist and anticolonial struggles were easy. New and ingenious forms of domination in center-periphery relationships required corresponding efforts in resistance.

In the British colonies, ex-slaves either abandoned the plantation altogether by setting up autonomous villages or rearranged their relationships as wage laborers with the plantations. A labor crisis ensued; a solution was found, not in paying better wages to the emancipated slaves or in providing better working conditions, but in recruiting indentured contract labor from Europe, India, Indonesia, and China. Again, it was discovered that European laborers were either unsuitable or too expensive in comparison with Asian and Afro-Caribbean laborers. Hence, the British inaugurated a massive transoceanic movement from India of a quarter-million East Indians from 1838 to 1917 (Samaroo, 1987). Dubbed "a new system of slavery" (Tinker, 1974), this importation of Asians, which included not only Indians but Chinese, added new cultural forms to the Caribbean (Patterson, 1977). Indian migration was significant especially in British Guiana and Trinidad. The social structure was re-created, producing culturally plural societies. The same process occurred in Suriname, when the Dutch imported large numbers of Indians and Javanese.

The drive toward independence in decolonization was radically different in the Spanish islands. The Dominican Republic attained independence in the middle of the 19th century, whereas Puerto Rico and Cuba became free from Spanish control in 1898 and fell simultaneously to American hegemony. Political change was abrupt, and, in the case of Cuba and Puerto Rico, it was accomplished through American invasion. In the British islands, political transformation was slow, involving progressive lowering of the requirements to vote, until the non-White population gained ascendancy. Even in this case, final independence was not achieved until the middle of the 20th century. The Dutch islands, apart from Suriname, remained attached to the Netherlands. The colonies of Martinique, Guadeloupe, and Dutch Guiana are still part of France. The relationships the remaining colonies maintain with their metropolitan centers are no longer coerced. The islands can choose to be independent. This is intriguing, because it breaks the old connection between colonialism and servitude. In the next section, I examine the new forms of racism and anti-racism that have emerged in the postcolonial societies of the Caribbean.

POSTCOLONIAL CARIBBEAN

The formal trappings of social differentiation and discrimination built around phenotype has been removed. But inequality and oppression still persist. Racial motifs are manifested through nuanced ways. The historical context has changed, and the victims and victimizers are differently attired. The political, social, and economic milieus have been transformed. Basic structures of struggle in the context of scarce resources and the quest for power and privileges point to a new drama in which old colonially inspired themes of distinction and discrimination are played out. The actors in the diverse Caribbean landscape are not antagonistically the same: Whites against Blacks. It is now mainly Blacks against Blacks; Blacks against browns; high browns against low browns; Africans against Indians. In most of the Caribbean, the actors are non-White.

The resources for which the new racial struggle is conducted are no longer the control of the labor of non-White persons to produce sugar, tobacco, and cotton on plantations. It is now jobs, status, and privileges in a stratified order deriving its resources from multinational corporations, multilateral aid agencies, and other international sources (Hintzen & Premdas, 1983). The tools of control are no longer slavery and indentureship, explicit laws of discrimination, residential and occupational segregation, and formal codes of deference. They are now prejudice, customs, cliqueism, clientelist networks, kin connections. This is all defended by neo-racial notions of group identity and solidarity. The overt manifestations and consequences are not always obvious. They have to be sought in the thinking, ideologies, elite structures, leadership recruitment patterns, cultural preferences, and substructural expressions of the actors. How have the new societies, having traversed the terrain to decolonization and modernity, fared with regard to the persistence of racism? How far have they proceeded in establishing societies based on merit or compassion? To answer these questions, one must examine the full kaleidoscope of cultural and political forms that have emerged in the Caribbean.

Before I discuss the cases, I must take a short detour on concepts. Racism is an ideology that seeks to justify the skewed allocation of resources in favor of a group on the basis of alleged phenotypical differences (Premdas, 1993a; Smith, 1993). What is critical about this definition is that one group deliberately discriminates against another using fictive differences. The dominant group brings into being a panoply of formal and informal practices that render other groups inferior and ineligible for equal access to the scarce resources and values of society. Discrimination may not always be based exclusively on phenotype; it is often linked to other differences such as religion, region, language, and customs. As a result, the term *ethnic* is brought into service because of its wider scope. Ethnicity refers to a collective sense of consciousness often constructed on racial, cultural, linguistic, religious, or regional claims so as to assert exclusive group identity against rival claims of other groups. Race is often a component of the phenomenon of ethnicity, but is not always present. In the Caribbean context, the racial factor is frequently present in ethnic group discrimination and differentiation.

In the Caribbean, a variety of racial and ethnic claims have emerged that carry with them the same sort of discriminatory and oppressive consequences as when master-slave racism was practiced in earlier times. To combat these practices, a different artillery of anti-racist measures has emerged. In the following sections, I shall examine the new variants and manifestations of racial and ethnic labeling and the associated countervailing actions. The first area is the culturally plural societies of Guyana, Trinidad, and Suriname. These countries contain a peculiar configuration of ethnic mixes, including Asians in significant numbers, living side by side with other groups distinguished by different institutional practices (Smith, 1965). The second area is Haiti, where a Black-mulatto struggle has superseded the old colonial Black-White structure of differentiation.

The third area is Belize, where a color-class stratification system still exists. The fourth area is the French colonies of Guadeloupe, Martinique, and French Guiana, where the policy of departmentalization has redefined the old colonial race relations. Finally, I shall look at Cuba, where a socialist regime in power for more than four decades has tried to recast intergroup relations so as to transcend the role of race.

In dealing with these specific instances of racism and anti-racism in the Caribbean, I must inevitably exclude the claims of other islands and functional groups. For instance, it could be argued that gender discrimination is a variant of racism and should be incorporated in any discourse on racial discrimination, especially in the Caribbean, where patriarchal domination is pervasive. Similarly, one could argue that certain religious groups with a racial identity, such as the Rastafarians, should be discussed. Then there are the cases of the Dutch colonies and the American Virgin Islands, as well as the Bahamas and Puerto Rico. The scope of this chapter is too constricted to accommodate all these cases. Dealing with only a select set of cases is undertaken with a view to providing a representative set of cases to gauge the diversity in which the racist-anti-racist struggle manifests itself in the contemporary Caribbean.

Guyana, Trinidad, and Suriname

Guyana, Trinidad, and Suriname constitute a unique cluster of Caribbean countries that possess multiracial populations with significant Asian components. They are unlike other parts of the Caribbean, where the norms of the colonial power were adapted into a unifying Creole culture that defined the values of the society. In Guyana, Trinidad, and Suriname, distinct and different patterns of cultural institutions have been implanted, causing national dissent, resulting in plural societies (Milne, 1982; Smith, 1965). In the colonial era, the Indo-Asian group was played against the African-descended groups; after independence was attained, the two cultural groups, suspicious of each other, competed for control of the levers of the state. In Guyana, Trinidad, and Suriname, where Indians are respectively 55%, 45%, and 33% of the population, the African mulatto groups successfully wrested control of the state and allegedly employed racist tactics to exclude Indians from equal control of the government. These were cases of non-White groups engaged in the struggle for ethnic and racial ascendancy. Guyana illustrates this well.

In Guyana, the population was bifurcated between two communities made up of African mulattos (45%) and Asian Indians (55%; Premdas,

1973). As independence approached, the leaders of the two sections constituted their own ethnically based parties and competed for the government. Forbes Burnham, who led the African mulatto-based Peoples National Congress (PNC), virtually seized power, repeatedly rigged the elections, and became abusive of the rights of his opponents, who were for the most part Indians (Premdas, 1992a). In Trinidad, where Indians and Africans were almost equal in numbers, the African-based People's National Movement, led by famed antislavery historian Eric Williams, gained control of the government and in similar fashion allocated resources discriminatorily against political adversaries, who were located for the most part in the Indian community (Premdas, 1993b). In Suriname, a military coup was led by an African-dominated army. Although Indians and Javanese constituted over half the population, they were reduced to second-class citizens. It could be argued that, in these cases, communal mobilization and ethnic discrimination were not primarily racist acts, but were intended to consolidate the gains of a middle-class elite (Hintzen & Premdas, 1983).

There were similarities in all three cases. To begin with, these societies were deeply divided along racial and institutional lines. Each racial community suspected others of harboring designs to dominate the entire society. One ethnic group grabbed power and used the apparatus of state to discriminate against the other in the distribution of jobs, contracts, privileges, and status (Premdas, 1986). Unlike the departed colonial power, the new dominant Afro-Creole group did not use open forms of discrimination such as explicit racial codes to distribute benefits. Instead, it stacked the various official statutory bodies responsible for the allocation of jobs and benefits with supporters. The effect, although originating in class interests, was the same as open racial discrimination (Premdas, 1991).

Formal equality doctrines exist in all three culturally plural societies, but informal practices by the politically dominant group make a farce of the egalitarian claims of the state. Resistance by the oppressed, which include African and Asian groups, has ranged from demonstrations, strikes, and sabotage to plots to overthrow the governments. More frequently, the oppressed vote with their feet, migrating in large numbers to other countries. The ironic aspect of these cases points to the fact that the old oppressor-oppressed categories now involve, at least on the surface, two communities that at one time were both oppressed by European power.

What makes the Guyana and Trinidad cases even more ironic is that the dominant African mulatto group legitimizes its discriminatory practices with the claim that it more resembles the norms of the departed European power in its social and cultural practices. Afro-Trinidadians were unwilling to share public resources and symbolic space with other ethnic groups, not only because they regarded these resources as scarce, but because they deemed them their legitimate right because of their earlier historic presence in the territory and the greater proximity of their culture and behaviors to the superordinate colonial culture (Ryan, 1990).

Asian Indians are regarded as "backward" and therefore deserving of being discriminated against in ways reminiscent of the manner in which European planters justified their discrimination against African slaves. The struggle of Asian Indians is similar to the resistance of the slave communities in that Indians have revitalized their Asian values in open disdain of the dominant national Creole values. The themes of the African Indian struggle are uncanny echoes of the conflict and resistance of the Europeans and Africans in the colonial period.

As difficult as it is for some to accept, the facts of political life in Guyana, Trinidad, and Suriname attest to the open communal rivalry that has deteriorated into claims and charges of ethnic oppression. It seems that the problem resides in the politics of resource allocation and fear of sectional domination. There is no reason to doubt, as has already happened with the change of government in Guyana, that Creoles would in turn charge racial discrimination under a preponderantly Indian government (Premdas, 1994).

Haiti

Haiti stands apart from the rest of the Caribbean in regard to the size of the country, its early independence, and the violent mode of its liberation. After the White population was evicted, an intense struggle ensued between Blacks and mulattos for control of the state. France occupied the western half of Hispaniola in 1660; by the end of the 18th century, Hispaniola was converted into a lucrative plantation-driven colony. Haiti had a population mix of 4,336 Whites and 2,012 African slaves in 1681. When the economy was diversified in 1789 and committed to sugar for export, Saint-Dominique had been demographically transformed into 40,000 Whites and 455,000 Blacks and mulattos (Dupuy, 1989).

The Haitian Revolution was prolonged and violent, resulting in the loss of 150,000 lives, including about 50,000 French who were sent by Napoleon to reimpose slavery. Among the distinctive features of the Haitian Revolution were the massacre in 1804 of the French remaining in the country and the declaration in the Haitian constitution that "all

Haitians would hence forth be known under the generic denomination of black" (Dupuy, 1989, p. 76). In this regard, the Haitian Revolution came to have immense symbolic significance for all Blacks in the Caribbean.

What followed after the Haitian Revolution was not an order based on equality free from racism, but one in which mulattos asserted a right to rule by virtue of their pigmentation and greater socialization in French ways. Thus, another struggle ensued between mulattos and Blacks, which became an underlying theme in the upheavals of Haitian history marked by 24 changes of government in 111 years (Dupuy, 1989). Although it could be argued that often the intrigues that led to the rise and fall of governments tended to implicate both Black and mulatto elites in the same alliance, there can be no doubt that these acts of collaboration often concealed the contest between mulattos and Blacks for political ascendancy.

Rival ideologies of color were developed: one *mulatriste* (mulatto) and the other *noiriste* (Black). Mulatristes regarded themselves as the natural heir to the French, held strong racist views against Blacks, and felt that they should rule Haiti (Dupuy, 1989). Noiristes argued that the selfishness of mulattos was the source of Haiti's difficulties (Nicholls, 1979) and therefore they should be eliminated from all positions of power. The authentic voice of the people represented by the majority Blacks should rule (Dupuy, 1989). The rival political parties that were organized to compete for power encapsulated this ethnic division, making the color issue central to Haiti's politics.

The mulatriste-noiriste antagonism has persisted into the 20th century. During the American occupations of Haiti in the early part of the century, mulattos were favored in open contempt for Blacks. During the Lescot government, sponsored by U.S. occupation forces,

> color discrimination was practiced in all aspects of social life. Color became the sole criterion of appointments to all important positions in all branches and agencies of government and the military and even in the hiring of lower level administrative and secretarial positions. Widespread exclusionary practices were followed in the social clubs of the mulatto elite and in most other secondary forms of social interaction; the color line was rigidly drawn in the choice of marriage partners from the mulatto bourgeoisie. (cited in Dupuy, 1989, p. 146)

In 1946, Dumarsais Estime became president. His victory was claimed by the noiriste forces against the mulattos. The background to this victory is important. The color question led to the founding of the Indigeniste group in the 1930s, which was linked more broadly to the international Negritude movement. Indigenist adherents depreciated European values, calling for a return to African roots in Haitian culture. Within the Indigeniste movement arose the Griots Group, which extolled the alleged peculiar personality and psychology of the African, deeming it the most appropriate for leadership in Haiti.

The Haitian case illustrates that racism does not necessarily require Blacks and Whites to be present for structures of racist discrimination to exist. In Haiti, a color-class system has evolved consisting of about 60 to 70 gradations. Color has become wedded to socioeconomic well-being, even though a large number of Blacks have ascended to middle-class status, share common economic interests with mulattos with whom they compete, and periodically collaborate to advance shared interests. Color differences serve as a surrogate for racial distinctions, on which odious discriminatory behaviors are erected.

Belize

Belize, situated on the eastern coast of Central America, belongs to the Caribbean culture sphere (Boland, 1991). Belize illustrates the effect of a major event in race and ethnic relations that has long occurred throughout the Caribbean. Belize, a former British colony, has a multiracial population of 200,000 people constituting 40% Creoles (Africans), 33% mestizos, 8% Garifunda (African Amerindian mixes), 4% Whites, 3% kekchi, and 2% East Indians. The massive movements of people out of the region is recasting the ethnic demography and upsetting ethnic political shares and relations to power. Large numbers of the Black Creole group have migrated to North America, while large numbers of native people have migrated to Belize from Guatemala, Mexico, and Nicaragua. The "balance" in favor of the Creoles has been lost, and a Latinization cultural process threatens to redefine the traditional balance of power among the ethnic groups in the country.

Young (1994) comments,

> This perceived threat to the Belizan heritage has less to do with the official allegation that the Central American refugees are responsible for an escalating crime rate and has more to do with changes in the ethnic composition of the country. With the influx of Central American refugees, the population becomes more Mestizo. (p. 116)

The contest between Creoles and mestizos is in part about ethnic shares and is apparent in the rapid increase of militant ethnic associations and revivals.

What exists in Belize is cultural pluralism with the largest indigenous Indian component in the Caribbean. Because of migration patterns, a polarized racial-cultural split has developed between Creoles and mestizos. Creoles are still the largest single ethnic cluster, but they are not a majority. They regard themselves as the group that is entitled to rule on the basis of both their numbers and their socialization in British norms. Young (1994) observes,

> Many Creoles argued . . . that Blacks are being robbed of their political power in Belize. . . . Historically, in Belize it was different, for Blacks were integrated into the political and social fabric of the country. However, a greater emphasis on the Central American heritage of the country makes many Afro-Creoles fear that they are put at a disadvantage and will lose political power in the country. (p. 117)

Martinique, Guadeloupe, and French Guiana

Since 1946, these Francophone territories have became departments of France, entitling residents to French citizenship as well as social benefits and services comparable to those available to French citizens (Hintjens, 1991). As with the Dutch islands, this status has conferred enormous economic advantages on the African and mulatto populations relative to what is available to citizens in other parts of the Caribbean. Free movement to France has resulted in the emigration of one-third of Guadeloupe, two-fifths of Martinique's, and one-fifth of French Guiana's population. In addition, large numbers of French citizens have entered these territories, upsetting the old Black-White ratios.

All of this has prompted famed Negritude advocate Aime Cesaire to accuse France of pursuing a policy of "genocide by substitution" (Hintjens, 1991). The new form of racist control has taken an odd twist, in that the Black residents are put in the difficult situation of having two choices. They can take large social welfare checks, which perpetuate their dependency on the metropolitan center on one hand, or seek dignity in outright independence on the other. But the consequence will be a dramatic drop in their standard of living.

Because of the historic imposition of French ways on the Black population, the Negritude movement in the French Caribbean sought to debunk

French culture and reorient Antilleans to their own Creole customs. Negritude constituted the ideological and programmatic mode of resistance to racism.

Despite the assimilationist pretenses of French colonial policy, a color-class system of differentiation permanently consigns Black people to a condition of inferiority (Landau, 1974). On Guadeloupe and Martinique, the *beke* planter class still dominates the economy, owning about 64% of commerce in Martinique and 25% in Guadeloupe. In reaction to French neo-colonialism by departmentalization, an independence movement has been active in Guadeloupe and has engaged in acts of violent sabotage against the government. The resistance against institutional racism and colonial control has an auspicious ancestry in the work of Victor Schoelcher, who remains, even though White, the most powerful popular symbol of the emancipation movement in the Francophone Caribbean.

The case of the French territories is structurally similar to that of the Dutch islands of Curacao, Saba, St. Eustatius, and St. Maarten, where the local population has status similar to their metropolitan counterparts, including the receipt of social welfare services and benefits. In both the French and Dutch territories, the color-class system persists, even though efforts have been undertaken to purge books, schools, and workplaces of all evidence of racial bias.

English-Speaking Caribbean and Cuba

In the remaining English-speaking Caribbean (Jamaica, Barbados, Grenada, St. Vincent, St. Lucia, the Bahamas, Dominica, Antigua, and the American and British Virgin islands), racist and anti-racist themes are quietly articulated in the color-class system of ranking (Hoetink, 1985; Lowenthal, 1972). White pigmentation is not stringently operative in conferring status and allocating benefits, as testified by the large number of Blacks who have ascended to middle-class positions. But the fact remains that the weight of color is still powerfully at play. It is not explicitly used to discriminate and exclude, but in a new order where prejudice operates indirectly, there can be little doubt that to be Whiter than Black is better for careers and life chances. A Black-mulatto bourgeoisie has acceded to power, and even though efforts have been undertaken to expurgate the obvious forms of racial discrimination, the prejudices of color inherited from the plantation period have remained deeply entrenched.

With little prompting by external manipulators, color prejudice is enacted by the children of slaves and indentured laborers. In a few cases, ethnic and race relations commissions as well as ombudsman institutions have been established to inquire into allegations of prejudice in the allocation of public employment and services. In significant ways, these English-speaking states are responding less to the residual racial prejudices in their midst and more to the problems of racism in North America. The wide diffusion of American television programs in the Caribbean, as well as the frequent ease with which Caribbean people travel to the United States, has energized anti-racist sentiments. But this anti-racist sensitivity has not addressed the internal needs of the islands, and lies more in solidarity with the problems of minorities in North America. Few Caribbean countries are as interested in racism in their own societies as they are in racial and ethnic conflict in the United States and Europe.

With regard to Cuba, reliable and systematically derived information is hard to come by. The general view is that Castro brought dramatic changes with his accession to power in January 1959 and the commitment of the Cuban Revolution to an egalitarian society. The Black population has been accorded special positions everywhere. A survey conducted among Cuban exiles from different ethnic and class backgrounds found that strong anti-racist affirmative policies have been pursued at all levels of Cuban society, enabling Black Cubans to participate fully in national life (Bernardo, 1971).

The pre-Castro Cuba was a very racist society. It fell not only under the old Spanish system of color-class biases, but under the racist practices of the United States, which occupied or dominated Cuban life for a century prior to Castro. During five centuries of settlement, a broad mulatto community constituting almost one-third of the population emerged in Cuba, with one-third Black and one-third White. There was no question that, until Castro came to power, the allocation of the powers and privileges of the society favored Whites and browns. Under Castro, special efforts have been made to parade the effects of socialism on the favorable treatment of Blacks. It is difficult to evaluate the extent to which the Cuban Revolution has eliminated the old color and race-bound prejudices of the past.

CONCLUSION

In the Caribbean, racism at the earlier stages of settlement was overt and unapologetic. Toward the end of the 20th century, as decolonization has proceeded, overt racist practices have been eliminated and indirect forms of racist and ethnic discrimination persist in subtle and ingrained ways. The diversity of people in the Caribbean is conducive to social differentiation along racial and color lines. The first people, Amerindians, were the first victims of racism. Genocide was the fate of Amerindians; only a few now exist in the insular Caribbean. Anti-racist campaigns for Indians carried out by Bartolomé de las Casas failed in the end, as Amerindians refused to live in servitude and preferred to die rather than lose their freedom and live with indignity.

Africans were next in line, as the odious slave trade witnessed the forced transfer of millions of Africans to plantations in the Caribbean. Resistance was pervasive; with the abolition of slavery, the Caribbean became the preeminent domain of majority Black settlement in the Western hemisphere.

Indentured labor added to the historic and cultural diversity, so that, along with Blacks, European Whites, Asian Indians, Chinese, and others coexist. In the modern era, with independence won and the region in the hands of the non-White population, the forms of racism and anti-racism have changed. A color-class system of differentiation pervades the Caribbean, making this area the new focus of the struggle for freedom.

REFERENCES

Beckles, H. (1982). The 200 years war: Slave resistance in the British West Indies. *Jamaican Journal of History, 13,* 1-10.

Bernardo, R. M. (1971). Moral stimulation and labor allocation in Cuba. *Studies in Comparative International Development, 6*(6).

Boland, N. (1991). Society and politics in Belize. In C. Clark (Ed.), *Society and politics in the Caribbean.* London: Macmillan.

Braithwaite, L. (1953). Stratification in Trinidad. *Social and Economic Studies, 2*(2-3), 5-177.

Brereton, B. (1979). *Race relations in colonial Trinidad, 1870-1900.* Cambridge, UK: Cambridge University Press.

Despres, L. (1967). *Cultural pluralism and nationalist politics in British Guiana.* Chicago: Rand McNally.

Dew, E. (1987). *The difficult flowering of Suriname.* The Hague: Martinus Nijhoff.

Dupuy, A. (1989). *Haiti in the world economy: Class, race, and underdevelopment since 1900.* Boulder, CO: Westview.

Grant, C. H. (1976). *The making of modern Belize.* Cambridge, UK: Cambridge University Press.

Hintjens, H. (1991). France in the Caribbean. In P. Sutton (Ed.), *Europe in the Caribbean.* London: Macmillan.

Hintzen, P., & Premdas, R. (1983). Guyana: Coercion and control in political change. *Journal of Inter-American Studies and World Affairs, 24*(3), 337-354.

Hoetink, H. (1985). Race and color in the Caribbean. In S. Mintz (Ed.), *Caribbean contours*. Baltimore: Johns Hopkins University Press.

James, C. L. R. (1963). *Black jacobins*. New York: Vintage.

Knight, F. (1990). *The Caribbean: Genesis of fragmented nationalism*. Oxford, UK: Oxford University Press.

Landau, G. (1974). Race relations in the French Caribbean. *Caribbean Issues, 1*(1), 29-48.

Lewis, G. (1983). *Main currents in Caribbean thought*. Baltimore: Johns Hopkins University Press.

Lowenthal, D. (1972). *West Indian societies*. Oxford, UK: Oxford University Press.

Milne, R. S. (1982). *Politics in ethnically bi-polar states*. Vancouver: University of British Columbia Press.

Nicholls, D. (1979). *From Dessalines to Duvalier*. Cambridge, UK: Cambridge University Press.

Patterson, O. (1977). *Ethnic chauvinism*. New York: Stein & Day.

Premdas, R. (1973). *Racial politics in Guyana*. Denver, CO: University of Denver Press.

Premdas, R. (1986). Politics of preference in the Caribbean. In N. Nevitte & P. Kennedy (Eds.), *Ethnic preference and public policy in developing states*. Boulder, CO: Lynne Rienner.

Premdas, R. (1991). The political economy of ethnic strife. *Ethnic Studies Report, 9*(2), 30-39.

Premdas, R. (1992a). *Ethnic conflict and development*. Geneva: UNRISD.

Premdas, R. (1992b). Tobago: The quest for self-determination. *Canadian Review of Studies in Nationalism, 19*, 117-127.

Premdas, R. (1993a). The anatomy of ethnic conflict. In R. Premdas (Ed.), *The enigma of ethnicity: An analysis of race in the Caribbean and the world*. Trinidad: University of the West Indies, Extra-Mural Studies.

Premdas, R. (1993b). Ethnic conflict in Trinidad. In K. Yelvington (Ed.), *Ethnicity in Trinidad*. Knoxville: University of Tennessee Press.

Premdas, R. (1994). Guyana: One year after the PNC. *Caribbean Affairs, 7*(3), 157-177.

Ryan, S. (1990). *The disillusioned electorate: The politics of succession in Trinidad and Tobago*. Trinidad: Imprint Caribbean.

Samaroo, B. (Ed.). (1987). *India in the Caribbean*. London: Hansib.

Smith, M. G. (1965). Institutional and political conditions of pluralism. In M. G. Smith & L. Kuper (Eds.), *Pluralism in Africa*. Berkeley: University of California Press.

Smith, M. G. (1993). Race and ethnicity. In R. Premdas (Ed.), *The enigma of ethnicity: An analysis of race in the Caribbean and the world*. Trinidad: University of the West Indies, Extra-Mural Studies.

Tinker, H. (1974). *A new system of slavery*. London: Oxford University Press.

Williams, E. (1966). *Capitalism and slavery*. New York: Capricorn Books.

Young, A. (1994). Belize: Challenge to democracy. In C. Edie (Ed.), *Democracy in the Caribbean*. New York: Praeger.

14

The Long Shadow
of Apartheid Ideology:
The Case of Open Schools
in South Africa

Mokubung Nkomo
Zanele Mkwanazi-Twala
Nazir Carrim

This chapter takes a new look at South African racism. The current reforms, which are purportedly designed to dismantle apartheid structures, call for an examination of the evolution of race relations and racism. There is a need to know what new configurations racism and anti-racism are likely to assume during the transition and postapartheid eras. This chapter begins with a broad historical overview, placing South Africa within the world system of racial and capitalist domination. We briefly look at the key devices of control, namely the constitution and legislation used in the implementation of apartheid ideology and the resistance campaigns to apartheid controls over the years. We demonstrate how racism has sought to adapt to new conditions. It is crucial to emphasize at the outset that, throughout the period of apartheid's construction, there was resistance of varying degrees that affected apartheid. Finally, we present, as a case study, the "open schools," to examine how recent education reforms, under the guise of safeguarding community or cultural interests, perpetuate racial and class domination.

THE EVOLUTION OF
THE APARTHEID IDEOLOGY

When the National Party came to power in 1948, determined to expunge the "liberal" and "humanitarian" attributes of British hegemony from the South African body politic, it sought to restore a socioeconomic order disrupted by British imperial rule and influence. The new order was to be "based on inherited but outmoded economic practices" (Magubane, 1979, p. 222). But this was at a time when vulgar racism in the form of Nazism had been defeated in World War II. The spirit of freedom, equality, and justice was flexing itself in the developing world, including colonial Africa, and among Blacks and other minorities in North America. The United Nations had adopted the Universal Declaration of Human Rights, which enshrined the unalienable principles of freedom, equality, and justice.

This was the world into which South Africa was thrust in 1948. The construction of apartheid ideology had to take this into account; a definitional shift was necessitated by these developments. The apartheid regime's architects moved away from ideas of "natural superiority" embedded in White supremacy ideology to emphasizing cultural differences (Magubane, 1979, p. 230). There was growing recognition of the anachronistic notion of racism as advocated and practiced in South Africa. To gain acceptance by the international community and to placate the restive Black majority, adaptations became imperative.

Difference, both socially and culturally, became the defining variable of apartheid ideology. But it is important to note that "difference" was defined and imposed by the state. To this end, the state created a mosaic of racially and ethnically defined political and geographic entities to give expression to racialism and to accommodate difference. A motley assembly of officially sanctioned linguistic constructions, such as "separate development," "cultural pluralism," "plural democracy," and "own affairs" were concocted to give credence to the new social reality created by the Afrikaner hegemony.

One should not underestimate the capacity of ideologies of domination, as with White supremacy or apartheid, to adapt and assume new forms as they confront opposition. The divide-and-rule strategy applied to the various racial and ethnic groups has also been an integral part of the adaptive character of apartheid ideology. That, in part, explains the resurgence of militant expressions of narrow nationalism and ethnic identities so evident among some of the political organizations in contemporary South Africa (Adam, 1971).

South African officials were at pains first to rid themselves of the word *apartheid* and to present their racist practices in more acceptable and palatable forms to their historical allies in the West. But, as Derrida (1986) powerfully points out, "in spite of all the verbal degenerations and lexical stratagems of the South African racists . . . whether or not the term is pronounced by South African officials, apartheid remains the effective watchword of power in South Africa. Still today" (p. 330).

The fact that South African racists manipulated language in various and degenerate ways points to one of the most central tools of racism in its attempts to persist. To create the mirage, the facade, the deception that racism no longer existed, South African racists simply spoke in a different language and called the same reality by different names. They were able to convince and delude some Whites, especially in the West, but they could not dupe Blacks in South Africa or in the Third World. This is why Third World countries consistently sought and were able to keep South Africa out of international organizations such as the Commonwealth of Nations, where South Africa was forced to withdraw its application in the face of criticism from member states in 1961; the World Health Organization, which South Africa prudently left in 1965 when the organization passed a resolution to "suspend and ultimately expel any member who is deliberately practicing a policy of racial discrimination" (Tinker, 1977); the United Nations General Assembly, which voted overwhelmingly in 1974 to reject South Africa's credentials as a member; and the United Nations Educational, Scientific, and Cultural Organization (UNESCO), which South Africa was forced to quit in 1976.

THE JURIDICAL FRAMEWORK OF APARTHEID

The Race Classification Act of 1950, also known as the Population Registration Act, gave juridical force to the belief that the people of South Africa belonged to separate racial groups. The group one was assigned to determined entitlement to correlative social benefits. Thus, apartheid not only placed Whites at the top of the body politic but also created a hierarchy of races with gradations of racism. The Boers were at the pinnacle of the social order, followed by other Whites, Indians, Coloureds, and Africans at the bottom.

It is tempting to discuss apartheid in purely racial terms. Yet, underlying these racist configurations is the economic role that each group was meant to play. The most basic laws of apartheid were essentially measures aimed at creating or securing Black labor power, on which the system of capital accumulation depends in South Africa. These laws were the racially discriminatory land laws, laws controlling the movement and settlement of Blacks, laws excluding Blacks from representative institutions of the state, and industrial relations and security control laws.

The complex ways in which racism intersected with White capitalist economic interests is made patently clear when one analyzes the Job Reservation laws. The Job Reservation Act was introduced prior to 1948 as a concession to various categories of White labor. This act, along with other customary practices in the labor market, sought to protect higher paid White wage earners from displacement by lower paid Black workers. Laws also excluded Blacks from better paid, more skilled categories of work, developing what some have called a labor aristocracy (Johnstone, 1976). The post-1948 Nationalist regime introduced two main laws in this regard: the 1951 Native Building Workers Act, section 77, and the 1956 Industrial Conciliation Act. The Native Building Workers Act imposed a statutory job color bar on the building industry, whereas the Industrial Conciliation Act provided for the establishment of an industrial tribunal with powers to make job reservation determinations in any industry or sector. Upon analysis of these laws, it is clear that they were intended to perpetuate old-fashioned racism in that they promoted White supremacy and ensured the placement of Blacks in inferior unskilled and semiskilled occupational positions. The post-1978 total strategy phase of apartheid saw a number of modifications to these laws (Davies & O'Meara, 1985), although job reservation determinations remain in force in industry and other economic sectors in South Africa.

The apartheid system cannot be perceived solely as an intentional entrenchment of racism or explained only as a system perpetuating old-fashioned racism. Nevertheless, it succeeded in doing both. These laws were so effective because they covered all aspects of South African life. Wolpe (1988), quoting Stuart Hall, argues, "race is thus . . . the modality in which class is 'lived,' the medium through which class relations are experienced, the form in which it is appropriated and 'fought through' " (p. 52).

Race occupies a specific place in South African society and cannot be seen as a mere ideological manifestation of an economic system, as class reductionist theorists are prone to argue (Rex & Mason, 1986). The "interiorization of race in class" was facilitated by the deliberate control of the movement of Blacks and the restriction of social amenities to Blacks. It is to these that we now turn our attention.

The laws controlling the movement and settlement of Blacks in White areas had as their objective the maintenance of a system of cheap Black labor through restricting the freedom of movement of Black persons so as to channel workers where employers needed cheap labor, and enforcing employment contracts by making sure that workers stayed where they were wanted (Davies, O'Meara, & Dlamini, 1984). Another objective of these laws was to keep Black people out of White areas. The most important laws in this category were the notorious pass laws.

The Reservation of Separate Amenities Act, No. 49, of 1953 provided that any person who was in charge of or had the control of any public premises or public vehicle might, whenever deemed expedient, reserve such premises or vehicle or any portion thereof for the exclusive use of persons belonging to a particular race or class. Such action could not be ruled invalid on the grounds that provision had not been made for all races, or that separate facilities provided for the various races were not substantially equal. The term "public premises" was defined to include land, the seashore, enclosure, building, structure, hall, room, office, or convenience to which the public had access, whether on the payment of an admission fee or not (Horrell, 1978). This was tied to and reinforced by the Group Areas Act.

The Group Areas Act was a cornerstone of apartheid. It ensured that people in South Africa in fact lived racially divided and separate lives. The Group Areas Act of 1950 was amended and reenacted in consolidated form in 1957. The act sought to impose control over all of South Africa with regard to interracial property transactions and interracial changes in residential occupation. The act sought, "to provide for the establishment of group areas, for the control of the acquisition of immovable property and the occupation of land and premises, and of matters incidental thereto" (cited in Carrim, 1990).

The laws controlling the movement of Blacks systematically interiorized race in class. They established the personal and interpersonal attitudes of racial difference and exclusivity based on the assumption that Blacks were inferior and thus entitled to less of society's resources and privileges. Apartheid explicitly fragmented the socioeconomic and political landscape of South Africa along racial lines. The theological and quasi-scientific justifications provided the raison d'etre for the constitutional entrenchment of racism and the proliferation of racist laws. It ideologically affected the consciousness of South Africans and cast them in racial molds. It also ensured that legally defined racial groups lived different, unequal, and separate lives. The criminal miseries it wrought on Black lives secured the economic well-being and privileges of White South Africans, Afrikaners or non-Afrikaners, in whose hands the wealth of South Africa still rests.

ANTI-RACISM STRUGGLES
IN SOUTH AFRICA

The structural functionalist account of apartheid suggests that the apartheid legislative mechanisms alone were efficient in the maintenance of White supremacy and racial capitalism, despite nuances in arguments of anticlass reductionism and the totality of racism. How did Black people, in particular, respond to such measures and what were their effects? South African history is replete with evidence of the struggles of anti-racism or resistance against apartheid.

Since the 1950s, when most apartheid laws were introduced, South Africa has witnessed the intensification of resistance to these laws. The introduction of these laws provoked the mass resistance of the Congress movement in the form of the Defiance of Unjust Laws Campaign, antiremoval marches and meetings, resistance to the Bantu Education Act of 1953, the United Front alliance, petitions and protests against women carrying passes, the adoption of the Freedom Charter on June 26, 1955, the bus boycotts, the national minimum wage campaign, the stay-at-home protests, the pass-burning campaign of the Pan-Africanist Congress, and the Poqo revolt (Lodge, 1983; Rycroft, 1987). By the mid-1960s, the government had suppressed resistance to its reactionary legislation through the police and judicial systems and by outlawing organizations such as the African National Congress and the Pan-Africanist Congress. The 1960s witnessed a decline in internal political opposition in South Africa and the establishment of a liberation movement in exile.

The 1970s saw an upsurge of different forms of anti-racist struggles. The events of June 16, 1976, and its aftermath made the talk of reform earnest and immediate. This date became internationally renowned as

Soweto Day, because it was on this day that Soweto schoolchildren took to the streets to demonstrate their opposition to the imposition of Afrikaans as a medium of instruction in their schools. They were also demonstrating against Bantu education in general. Protesting students were shot by the South African police, and 69 were killed. The massacre of children on Soweto Day surpassed that of Sharpeville in 1960, which was the turning point inaugurating the armed struggle against the racist apartheid regime.

The resistance of June 1976 occurred at the peak of the development of the Black consciousness movement in South Africa. It also coincided with the liberation of Mozambique, the rise in Black trade union activity, an increasing economic crisis, and intensification of the isolation of South Africa internationally (Molteno, 1979). There was a total rejection of old-fashioned racism, which defined Whites as inherently superior to Blacks. Blacks came to assert their identities and to promote a sense of pride in being Black.

The anti-racist struggles in South Africa suggest different conceptions of racism. The dominant position, held by the African National Congress and its allies in the Congress Movement, argues that racism is a specific phenomenon in the South African social context and is related to other forms of domination such as class and gender oppression. This position argues that both Whites and Blacks have a role to play in eradicating racist practices and highlights human identity rather than race. The Pan-Africanist Congress and the Azanian People's Organization argue for the centrality of race in their discourse. The primary form of domination for them is based on race, which in their thinking is nonreducible to other patterns of domination. Whites in this view are not seen as participants in the anti-racist struggles; Blacks must "go it alone." In addition, organizations such as the Pan-Africanist Congress emphasize the geographical location and primacy of Blacks in Africa. They hold that only people of African origin, or those who claim loyalty to Africa, are considered African. The neo-Marxists (workerists) argue that race is mainly an ideological manipulation of capitalism and economic exploitation is the essential basis for racial oppression in South Africa (Wolpe, 1975, 1988).

Developments in the 1980s further defined anti-racism in South Africa. The formation of the United Democratic Front in 1983 is the most significant development. The United Democratic Front was a broad alliance of all antiapartheid forces in South Africa. These comprised student organizations, civic groups, trade unions, women's groups, and religious and youth groups. This alliance saw racism as going far beyond legislative measures of restriction and repression, enveloping the very nature of the social fabric, individual consciousness, the quality and nature of human lives. The United Democratic Front was set up to resist the implementation of the tricameral system of parliament, where the Coloured and Indian groups were drawn into government as junior partners. The United Democratic front understood the possibility of Coloureds and Indians becoming partners in racism. It also acknowledged the possibility of Whites being opposed to racism.

This awareness had its roots in the history of antiapartheid struggles, where notable Whites were unswerving in their commitment to fighting against apartheid. In contrast, some Blacks had actively collaborated with the apartheid regime through bodies such as the Coloured Representatives Council, the South African Indian Council, and local Black Municipal authorities, and the bantustan systems. The United Democratic Front, drawing extensively on the traditions of the Congress movement in South Africa, defined anti-racist struggles in a nonracial way. The 1985 state of emergency was directed at stunting the rise of this broad antiapartheid coalition.

In contrast to the antiapartheid movement of the 1960s, the anti-racist struggles in the 1980s, including the United Democratic Front's, had a greater sense of immediacy. Achieving an end to the racist order in South Africa was seen in terms of the here and now; people wanted total change in the present, as opposed to some distant utopian future. This is significant because it also shifted anti-racist struggles away from taking protest actions to asking questions about the actual transformation of governance (Lodge & Nasson, 1991).

The conception of racism implicit in these struggles was that racism, given the complexities of apartheid machinations, was not a simple Black and White issue. Racism was seen as a set of social relations that, in complex and contradictory ways, allowed for all racial groups to develop particular racial and/or ethnic consciousness in the structural designs of White socioeconomic and political domination of a Black majority. The anti-racist struggles in and outside of South Africa were powerful weapons that forced modifications in apartheid legislation and mutations in the ideological discourse of apartheid. It was through such efforts that cracks within apartheid were made visible and the arrogance and seeming invincibility of White supremacy was irrevocably refuted. It is important to note that theories about race and race relations tend to emphasize the structural functionalist aspects of racism and tend to view the experience of racism and its persistence only from the perspective of Whites. The anti-racist struggles of South Africa demonstrate the complex ways in which both Blacks and Whites dealt with ideologies of racism and the need to persuade and win over people to an alternative, racism-free society. This process is complex, fluid, dynamic, and contradictory. The structural positions of individuals in society, or their races, do not in themselves yield answers to who, how, when, or why any individual would become a participant in an anti-racist movement. Active processes of ideological contestation (and provisions of economic incentives) are closer to yielding answers to this question. At the same time, the anti-racist struggles in South Africa point to the centrality of Black experiences in the processes of racism. The need to listen to, acknowledge, release, and legitimate Black voices is the *sine qua non* for current negotiations in South Africa.

Our discussion up to now has shown the ways in which racism in South Africa was justified theologically and pseudo-scientifically. By illustrating the ways in which the apartheid juridical processes were used to create a racially segregated society, we have shown how racial and ethnic consciousness was developed in South Africa to influence relations on personal and interpersonal levels. We have also argued that this was not a direct process. From its inception, apartheid has been actively resisted; but such resistance has not been automatic and has not come exclusively from among Blacks.

Simultaneous with the internal counter-anti-racist struggles in South Africa were equally determined worldwide and external antiapartheid movements that forced Western governments sympathetic to the South African regime to censure South Africa. These two processes contributed to the transformations of apartheid.

THE CASE OF OPEN SCHOOLS

Apartheid education laws remain intact, despite the repeal in 1990 of key apartheid legislation such as the Group Areas Act, the Population Registration Act, and the Land Act. The schools in South Africa point to the ways in which racist practices are being maintained in mutated ways. They provide a window into the ways in which racism in South Africa is being changed and the ways in which shifts to more subtle and modern forms of racism are occurring.

Apartheid Education

Apartheid education legally segregated the educational system along racial lines. There were 19 different educational departments in South Africa, including the independent states of Bophuthatswana, Transkei, and Ciskei, and the self-governing territories of KwaZulu, KwaNdebele, KaNgwane, Qwa Qwa, Venda, and Lebowa. Each department caters to its respective racial and/or ethnic group. These were established to realize the Verwoerdian maxim of separate and unequal education under apartheid (Rose & Tunmer, 1975). The Bantu Education Act was passed in 1953, which was replaced by the Education and Training Act of 1979. According to then Minister of Native Affairs H. F. Verwoerd, the guiding principles of the Bantu Education policy were that it "should have its roots entirely in the native areas and in the native environment and in the native community" (Union of South Africa Senate Debates, 1954: Cols 2593-1622).

A reality of apartheid education included gross imbalances in terms of financial allocations per racial group. At the end of 1991, every White child received $1,489 in state subsidy, whereas every African child received $566 (South African Institute, 1992). Apartheid education also meant that a White child was likely to experience schooling that was well provided for in terms of facilities such as gymnasiums, laboratories and computers, qualified teachers, and low teacher-pupil ratios.

In contrast, African schools were characterized by inadequate facilities, poor teacher qualifications, and high teacher-pupil ratios. Learning under trees, lacking textbooks, and never seeing a laboratory were commonplace African student experiences. The Coloured and Indian populations were better provided for than their African counterparts, but not to the same degree as the White population. As a result, not only was the experience of schooling under apartheid education racially segregated but it also was qualitatively different—indeed, separate and unequal. Education for Africans was deliberately inferior on the assumption that its recipients would largely remain unskilled manual laborers (Kallaway, 1986; Nkomo, 1990).

Starting in 1980, Black students throughout the country embarked on a nationwide boycott of the schools, refusing to accept apartheid education and demanding that inequities in educational provision across racial groups be rectified and that a single, nonracial, democratic educational system be established. Students linked apartheid education to apartheid capitalism, and saw themselves being trained in apartheid schools to perform low-paying jobs and remain in subordinate positions in society. This they rejected. In time, students formed alliances with trade unions, political organizations, and community-based organizations to link their struggle against apartheid education to the national liberation movement (Molteno, 1987; Wolpe et al., 1991).

The student protest reached phenomenal proportions by 1983, when the tricameral parliamentary system was being implemented and the United Democratic Front was formed. During 1984, Black education was brought to a standstill and African schools in particular were plunged into crises from which they still have not recovered. Battles with the South African army and police were the order of the day (Bundy, 1986a). Hundreds of students were detained without trial, and many left the country to join the liberation movement or armies. Many African schools were converted into "operational zones" for the army and police. It is in this context that the people's education movement was born. This movement, made up of parents, teachers, students, and community-based organizations, called for the eradication of apartheid education and the establishment of a single, nonracial, democratic education system for all South Africans, irrespective of race (Bundy, 1986a; National Education Coordinating Committee, 1990).

These anti-racist student struggles point to important shifts. What began as a specific rejection of Bantu education developed into a rejection of apartheid education in general, and then into a rejection of the apartheid capitalist system. This series of rejections led to the formulation of an alternative notion of education that went beyond the normative assumptions of apartheid education. The parents, young people, and community organizations went from seeing the need to develop a Black educational system that was qualitatively like that experienced by Whites to seeing the White educational system as inherently flawed despite its material privileges. Sisulu (1986) captures this development succinctly:

> We are not demanding the same education as whites, since that is education for domination. People's education means education at the service of the people as a whole, education that liberates, education that puts the people in command of their lives, education that prepares our people as responsible citizens of our country. (p. 110)

The opening of schools to all was partly a response to the intense struggle for a nonracial democratic education system. But many have realized that the goal of a democratic education cannot be achieved with the present system. It remains to be seen if a liberating education will be realized under a democratic government given the superficial restructuring underway.

Open Schools

Open schools in South Africa—that is, schools that have racially mixed student populations—may be traced to Catholic and other private schools in South Africa. Private schools, catering to an elite group of South Africans, have traditionally enrolled Black students. These were usually the children of African diplomats, Black South African government officials, or exceptionally wealthy Black parents. In 1976, following the Soweto student uprisings, the South African Catholic Bishops' Conference decided to defy apartheid educational legislation and to enroll Black students in Catholic schools. Initially, the bishops' defiance centered around the principle of admitting Black students into White-registered schools. Later, the Church defied the state's attempts to control the numbers of Black students admitted to Catholic schools. The state then began to impose general quotas, stipulating the admissible percentages of Black students in these schools (Christie, 1990; Cross, 1986).

Despite variations in Black enrollments in these schools, the percentage of Black students in open schools remained well below half the student population. This was partly due to government-stipulated constraints—if Black admissions exceeded 50%, the school would be forced to register with another racial group's educational department. It was also due to the admission policies of the schools themselves, which included selection tests, affiliation with particular religious denominations, and ability to pay school fees.

Fundamentally, though, both the private schools and the parochial Catholic schools were outside the mainstream educational system, to which the majority of Blacks and Whites were subjected. It was only during the de Klerk reforms of the 1990s that White state schools began enrolling Black students. The experiences of the private schools in deracializing and desegregating schooling in South Africa did encourage current attempts at opening schools.

In October 1990, the minister of White education, Piet Clase, announced the possibility that White state schools might legally enroll Black pupils. To do this, White school parent communities needed to vote on the issue, with stringent voting procedures stipulated. Schools needed to ensure that they achieved an 80% poll, out of which they needed to obtain a 72% majority. Schools were given the option to vote for one of three models; these became known as the Clase models.

Model A is the option of privatization. In this scenario, the White state school closes down as a state school and reopens as a private school. Model B is a state school option. Here the White state school remains a state school but has an "open" admissions policy. Model C is a semiprivate- semistate model. Here the state provides primarily for teachers' salaries and the rest of the school's expenses are borne by the school community. In addition, White schools could choose to remain as they are and not vote at all. In this instance they would remain all White and state aided.

Interestingly, these Clase models were recommended within the provisions of the existing apartheid constitution. As a result, all models are subject to the same conditions.

1. All White schools must maintain a 51% White majority in their population.
2. The White cultural ethos of the school should remain intact.
3. The management councils of schools have the right to determine selection criteria.
4. No school is necessarily bound to consider curriculum changes.
5. The "opening" of schools does not necessarily mean the employment of Black teachers on the staff of the schools.
6. The financing of Black pupils at open schools is the responsibility of the Black parent and pupil.

These conditions, linked to the apartheid constitution, do not enable the Clase models to challenge the foundations of apartheid education. These models do not address the Black education crisis nor do they respond to the demand for a single, nonracial, and democratic education system in South Africa (Carrim & Sayed, 1991).

At the time of their announcement, the Clase models responded to the crisis facing White education in South Africa. White education was increasingly characterized by dwindling pupil numbers, wastage of facilities, and closure of schools. Many of these developments were precipitated by demographic changes of the areas within which White schools were located. These changes were brought about by the influx of Black residents, and made possible by the scrapping of the Influx Control laws and the Group Areas Act. At the same time, many of the wealthier White families moved out of these areas. As a result, the target population of White schools was dwindling rapidly. It became economically impossible to maintain such a situation in the current recessionary climate.

At the same time as the Clase announcements in 1990, the White Nationalist government tried to appear as if it were making reforms in two ways. First, it projected itself as genuinely attempting to deracialize White schooling. This was in keeping with the main thrusts of the de Klerk reforms. Second, by allowing decisions to be made by the White school parent communities, it projected itself as being democratic, despite the fact that Black parents and pupils did not and still do not contribute to any of these decisions.

Coloured and Indian schools in South Africa began to enroll African pupils in 1985. From 1985 to 1990, such African pupil enrollments were illegal and largely depended upon the discretion of each school's principal. During the blatant repression of student activism during the 1985-1990 state of emergency, many principals were radicalized in their encounters with the police and army, who raided their schools, beat their pupils, and transformed their schools into operational zones. These experiences provided the necessary ideological and experiential bases for Indian and Coloured schools to begin enrolling African pupils in defiance of state laws. The Clase announcements signaled an official acknowledgment that African pupils were in Coloured and Indian schools and significantly boosted African enrollments at Coloured and Indian schools. This was due to the crisis in Black education generally and, specifically, to the development of the people's education movement in South Africa. The government-stipulated conditions for opening White schools are also applicable to Indian and Coloured schools, but tailored to suit their racial character. The Coloured and Indian pupils at these schools must be in the majority and the Coloured and Indian ethos of these schools should be kept intact (Carrim, 1992a).

In April 1992, the minister of White education, Piet Marais, announced that all White schools would be converted to Model C, despite the fact that 98% of those who had voted for the Clase models voted for Model B—the remaining 2% opted for Model C and none opted for Model A (Carrim, 1992; Metcalfe, 1991). (Model C is the semiprivate-semistate school.) Marais claimed that this was due to economic pressures, and if these schools were not converted to Model C, then some 11,000 White teachers would have to be retrenched. If White schools converted to Model C, only about 4,000 teachers would have to be retrenched.

The Model C conversions would dramatically increase school fees and thereby further control access to such schools. The vast majority of Black parents would be immediately excluded from Model C schools for economic rather than racial reasons. Indian and Coloured schools are currently being threatened with Model C conversions and retrenchments of teachers.

MODERN RACISM, DERACIALIZATION, AND DESEGREGATION

The way in which the government attempted to maintain apartheid in South Africa's open schools shows how it is attempting to control access of Blacks and thereby maintain White privileges. This point makes an important distinction between deracialization and desegregation. In the South African context, deracialization may be seen when both Whites and Blacks may be found in the same situation and where no discriminatory practices seem to exist. Desegregation, on the other hand, may be seen as a removal of structural mechanisms of control that prevent Blacks from enjoying the social provisions and privileges enjoyed by Whites.

The differences between deracialization and desegregation suggest other forms of racism beyond explicit forms such as apartheid. A shift from old-fashioned racism to more modern forms of racism is discernible. Modern racism, or what Hall (1981) calls "inferential racism," is evident in the open schools experience. Hall describes inferential racism as,

> those apparently naturalized representations of events and situations relating to race, whether "factual" or "fictional," which have racist premises and propositions inscribed in them as a set of unquestioned assumptions. These enable racist statements to be formulated without ever bringing into awareness the racist predicates on which the statements are grounded. (p. 28)

For South Africa, coming to terms with modern racism is both revelatory and disappointing. It is revelatory because it is the first time in South Africa's history that the struggle against racism is not simply against glaringly obvious patterns of exclusion, denial, repression, and discrimination. The struggle against racism is now also against subtle, less visible discriminatory patterns of personal and interpersonal forms of racism. It is precisely because of this realization that the new "freedoms" are disappointing. After decades of struggle against racism, South Africans are again called upon to continue struggling against racism. A slightly different struggle, but a continuing struggle nonetheless.

The "opening" of schools in South Africa attempted to desegregate schools but not to deracialize them. This is evident in three ways: on the macrostructural level; through admission policies and levels; and by how these problems have been conceptualized

Macrostructural Level

Two important mechanisms of control simultaneously reinforce each other. First is a shift from racial criteria for admissions to a social class emphasis. The private and Catholic schools provided education for a clientele that could afford to pay the school fees. It was for this reason, more than any other, that these schools were outside mainstream educational provisions. The conversion of White state schools to Model C schools, patently controlling access to such schools on an economic basis, shifts emphasis away from race criteria to considerations of being able to afford tuition.

Secondly, these reforms maintain the particular religious and cultural ethos of the school. Each school can now argue that it is for Catholic, Jewish, or Muslim children, or Portuguese, Greek, or Indian children. Black pupils who can afford to attend are forced to become part of schools whose ethos is not about or for them. This assimilationist approach has the effect of legitimating the White, Coloured, and Indian cultural and normative frameworks historically constituted by apartheid. It also continues to secure White, and to a lesser extent Coloured and Indian, interests and privileges. South Africans desegregate in ways that render schools elitist and exclusionary; but by being cast in assimilationist molds, they do not deracialize the ethos or Eurocentric normative frameworks and assumptions of the schools. The obverse of this is equally significant. Black South African worldviews and experiences are made illegitimate and, at best, are stereotyped.

The normative assumptions that inform legitimate knowledge in the schools are defined by the cultural, religious, and social class ethos of the schools. Black experiences and histories do not influence such systems of knowledge, and structurally nothing in the way the school is designed will necessitate such considerations. Black knowledge constructions remain marginalized (Carrim, 1992b; Metcalfe, 1991). If such schools see themselves as accountable only to White, Indian, or Coloured communities, then they have no need to be accountable to Black communities and interests. The school may very well be desegregated, in that Blacks are not segregated in exclusionary ways, but the school remains racialized.

Here lies the complexity of modern racism in South Africa. On the one hand, people of different races tend to be of different cultural backgrounds. In this regard, the struggle against racism in South Africa has consistently maintained the right of individuals to free cultural expression in a democracy. The only provision has been that such cultural expression should not foster racism. On the other hand, cultural expressions are likely to be camouflage for racism. The open schools experience suggests this. Cultural exclusivity in South Africa has the inevitable effect of being racially exclusive. The Model C conversions structurally enable communities in which a particular racial group predominates to establish schools within a particular cultural framework. A school that has been historically Indian, for example, can justify its Indian-only character as a voluntary choice of the school community to maintain, foster, and promote an Indian cultural identity through the school. The result: The school remains Indian only. Racism or cultural democracy? Whatever the answer may be, the unavoidable implication is that the apartheid structure, which was explicitly racist, remains unchanged.

These experiences also point to the need to enlarge the understanding of racism. Racism is not simply a White versus Black issue. There are variations in experiences of prejudice within the Black community and gradations of prejudice among them. The tendency to homogenize all Black people into the category of "Black" obfuscates the racial or ethnic dynamics within the Black population itself. It is only through a complex conception of racism that one can see how Indian and Coloured schools perpetuate racism and segregation.

At the macrostructural level, the school is desegregated, albeit in limited ways, but it is not deracialized. In the South African context, desegregation has a very specific meaning. Establishing a unitary, nonracial, and democratic education system for all South Africans is the aim of desegregation. This is the opposite of the segregationist educational goals of apartheid. The educational reforms to date do not address the cultural complexities of South Africa or the cultural exclusion of Africans. A multicultural approach to knowledge is needed that includes an anti-racist dimension to redress the legacy of apartheid and cultivate citizenship in a nonracial South Africa (National Education Policy Investigation, 1992).

Admission Policies and Levels

All White state schools, 77% of Indian schools, and 39% of Coloured schools use selection tests for Black applicants. These include tests in proficiency in English and mathematics, standardized intelligence quotient tests, and tests in particular subjects, such as physical science. No White, Indian, or Coloured pupil is subjected to such tests, but gains automatic entrance into such schools. In general, African pupils at White, Coloured, and Indian schools do not exceed 10% of the total pupil population (Carrim, 1992a; Metcalfe, 1991).

The assumptions inherent in the admission tests themselves are loaded with racist implications. Is the intelligence of Africans being tested for diagnoses of educational strengths and weaknesses or to determine admission? The former may be educationally defensible, but the latter infringes on a child's right to be educated. How different are such tests from the obviously racist tests used historically by colonialists? What signals of racial difference are conveyed to Black and White children who witness some of their peers being tested and some not? Will these "open schools" justify the use of admission tests as a means to uphold educational standards? The calculated consequence of such practices is to maintain discriminatory practices that place Africans in subordinate positions without using the word apartheid. The admission tests are a striking example of the ways in which racist discourses consistently belie their outcomes. The tests are seemingly ways to include Blacks in desegregated schools. Yet they are used to exclude Blacks. Those that do get in are a minority, easily assimilable, whereas the majority remain outside, a distant "other."

Conceptions of Problems

Apartheid education has seriously affected the educational performances of all students in particular and all Black students in general. In concrete terms, this has been reflected in the high failure and dropout rates of African students, the poor levels of educational performance by Black students, the low rates of admission of Black students into postsecondary institutions, and the emergence of academic support programs (ASPs) at all levels of education. Teachers in open schools are confronted by the ill-equipped and disadvantaged educational backgrounds of the few Black students who enroll. How do they respond to these problems?

The primary purpose of ASPs has been to provide the necessary support for Black students to cope with and succeed at the educational tasks with which they are confronted. As a result, ASPs have been institutional responses to the diversity of educational levels and backgrounds. The initiative to establish ASPs has primarily been at White English-language universities. ASPs are found in primary and secondary schools; tertiary institutions, including Black universities and colleges; and nongovernmental establishments. The recent opening of White, Coloured, and Indian schools to people of all races has given an additional impetus to the establishment of ASPs at schools (National Education Policy Investigation, 1992).

The curriculum taught in open schools is not inclusive or multicultural. These schools are not only Eurocentric, but biased in favor of Afrikaner nationalism and White supremacy as well. Teachers are recruited from the same cultural population and designated race as their students and have no reason to question their curriculum with regard to sensitivity to other groups (Jansen, 1991; Nkomo, 1990). The way in which the curriculum is conceptualized has affected the way in which ASPs are defined. Eurocentric content is at the core of the curriculum; ASPs are social constructs reinforcing apartheid values. Thus, this education is against the worldview, cultures, and morals of Black students and their communities (National Education Policy Investigation, 1992).

Furthermore, ASPs tend to view the student as the problem. This entails viewing the student as having a deficit, simultaneously implying that existing curricula, teaching methods, and learning demands are not problematic. The Black student is seen as being inherently unable, deficient, and inferior. This obviously reinforces racist assumptions about Blacks (National Education Policy Investigation, 1992).

It is useful here to point out other ways in which ASPs have been practiced in South Africa, because it offers an example of how such racist assumptions about the nature of the pedagogical problems being experienced may be contested and changed. In some instances, conceptions of the ASPs have undergone refinement and the general understanding of ASP issues have become socially and politically influenced. The student is not so much seen as a problem with a deficit, but the problem is understood to be caused by the unequal and racist nature of the apartheid educational system. This understanding has led to some curricular innovation and change, a reexamination of admissions and evaluation criteria, and a consideration of the quality and nature of teaching itself (National Education Policy Investigation, 1992).

Yet open schools still operate within a deficit understanding of the nature of the educational problems Black students experience. If the school and its staff view the problems in these ways, then Black students are labeled "deficient," treated as deficient, and made to believe that they are the problem and that the problem is individualized. As research on labeling processes indicates, mechanisms that so assess students not only divide the schoolrooms but also have the capacity of being self-fulfilling prophecies (Giddens, 1989; Meighan, 1986). Thus, although White teachers are now teaching Black students in previously White schools in South Africa, racism is still prevalent in South African education in ways that insinuate that Blacks are unable, unsuitable, deficient, inferior, ill-equipped, or simply incompetent. Schools are desegregated but they are not deracialized.

CONCLUSION

In pointing out the distinction between desegregation and deracialization in the open schools experiences in South Africa, we are able to show that racism in South Africa continues to operate in education. The continued racialization of schools occurs through the use of mechanisms such as exclusionary admission policies, single racial and cultural ethos schools, and schools that view Black students as academically and individually deficient. The apartheid ideology and legacy continues to cast its long shadow in mutated and subtle ways. Desegregation erodes visible, explicit forms of old-fashion racism, but deracialization becomes the fulcrum around which struggles continue.

It is important to point out that, to the degree that apartheid ideology is socially constructed, it is equally deconstructible. South Africa offers new opportunities for social reconstruction informed by a genuine democratic ethos. Each emergent mutant form of racism, although more sophisticated, is weaker than its predecessor and can be further weakened in the thick of determined contestation. Global and local efforts to eliminate racism are mutually reinforcing. Ultimately, the solution lies in the transformation of power relations of the sort that is genuinely democratic, not only in the education field, but in other commanding spheres of the political economy.

POSTSCRIPT

When we first wrote this chapter, the first nonracial and democratic election in South Africa had not yet occurred. On April 26-28, 1994, Black South Africans for the first time voted the government of their choice into power. Equally important, Whites voted with Blacks in the same election on a common voters' roll. This is a milestone in South African history.

Nelson Mandela became the first Black president in South African history. His party, the African National Congress (ANC), won convincingly by 62% nationally. The ANC was followed by F. W. de Klerk's National Party, with 22% of the electorate; Buthelezi's Inkatha Freedom Party, with 10%; and the Democratic Party, with 1% (Cohen, 1994). A government of national unity, working under an interim constitution, was put into power through these elections. But even with an interim government, the ANC-led government is now able to put into place the necessary legislation to facilitate the reconstruction and development of South African society. This has not yet happened, but such legislation is likely in the near future.

The educational situation in South Africa is still very much the way it has always been, although the constitution calls for a unitary, nonracial, and democratic education system. No legislation has been enacted yet to effect this constitutional provision. As a result, all the racially defined education departments described in this chapter still exist. It is becoming increasingly apparent that most educational matters are being decided on the provincial level, rather than by the central government.

The interim constitution allows individual provinces to decide upon the nature and content of their educational systems. Section 32 guarantees that,

> Every person shall have the right (a) to basic education and equal access to educational institutions; (b) to instruction in the language of his or her choice where this is reasonably practicable; and (c) to establish, where practicable, educational institutions based on a common culture, language or religion, provided that there shall be no discrimination on the grounds of race. (Greenstein, 1994; Interim Constitution, 1994)

Communities could legitimately argue for using their schools to protect their class, culture, and ethnic interests, provided that the Bill of Rights and other constitutional clauses are not infringed upon. These particularistic and parochial tendencies have not changed for most schools, although the scenario at Model C schools has changed. The number of Black students at these open schools has increased. In many Model C schools, Black students now represent nearly 50% of the student body. Some schools have Black majorities, pointing to two important changes (Stewart, 1994).

First, more critical and sophisticated approaches are being tried with regard to admissions criteria and selection tests, suggesting greater fairness in racial and educational terms. Second, because Blacks are a majority in some schools, social relations among students and between students and teachers have changed.

Although many of these schools are still operating from the assimilationist model, some are moving rapidly toward a more integrated approach with a multicultural framework. These schools are no longer individualizing problems with Black students and thereby marginalizing them. Blacks are being provided for within mainstream education programs. This integration of academic support into the mainstream also means that these schools' curricula, teaching methods, and assessment are also being reviewed. These changes are most welcome.

The changes in the schools are important ones, but they need to be treated with caution. They are the exception rather than the rule, and do not point to a national trend toward deracializing education in South Africa. In this chapter, we argue that there is a distinction between desegregation and deracialization. The changes in the schools are desegregation, but they are not deracialization. Further research needs to be conducted to ascertain the degree to which they are deracialized as well.

The educational experiences of the majority of Black South Africans remain essentially unaltered. Many continue to attend inferior and segregated schools. Until provincial educational ministries are vested with power through the federal legislature, very little can change. Only then can the challenges of reconstructing society at large, and the education system in particular, be attempted with greater purpose and success. Until then, the continued subordination of Blacks will persist.

REFERENCES

Adam, H. (1971). *Modernizing racial domination: The dynamics of South African politics.* Berkeley: University of California Press.

Bundy, C. (1986a, January 10). Schools and revolution. *New Society, 75,* 52-55.

Bundy, C. (1986b, January 3). South Africa on the switchback. *New Society, 75,* 7-11.

Carrim, N. (1990). *Fietas: A social history of Pageview: 1948-88.* Johannesburg: Save Pageview Association.

Carrim, N. (1992a). *Desegregation in Indian and Coloured schooling* (Education Policy Unit Report). Johannesburg: University of Witwatersrand.

Carrim, N. (1992b). Open schools: Problems and possibilities. *Democracy in Action, Institute for a Democratic Alternative for South Africa, 6*(2), 18-19.

Carrim, N., & Sayed, Y. (1991, May). Open schools: Reform or transformation? *Work in Progress.*

Christie, P. (1990). *Open schools: Racially mixed Catholic schools in South Africa, 1976-1986.* Johannesburg: Ravan.

Cohen, T. (1994, February 9). South Africa is no basket case, Manuel tells G-7. *Business Day.*

Cross, M. (1987). The road to non-racial education in South Africa: The case of the Catholic "open" schools in the Transvaal, 1976-1986. In *Criticique-Vision-Strategy: Proceedings of the Kenton-at-Helderfontein Conference.* Johannesburg: University of Wiwatersrand.

Davies, R., & O'Meara, D. (1985). Total strategy in South Africa: An analysis of South African regional policy. *Journal of South African Studies, 11*(2), 183-211.

Davies, R., O'Meara, D., & Dlamini, S. (1984). *The struggle for South Africa.* London: Zed Books.

Derrida, J. (1986). Racism's last word. In H. L. Gates (Ed.), *Difference* (p. 300). Chicago: University of Chicago Press.

Giddens, A. (1989). *Sociology.* Cambridge, UK: Polity.

Greenstein, R. (1994). *Evaluation of the status of the state and state-aided school models* (Education Policy Unit Research Paper). Johannesburg: University of Witwatersrand.

Hall, S. (1981). The Whites of their eyes: Racists' ideologies and the media. In G. Bridges & R. Brunt (Eds.), *Silver linings: Some strategies for the eighties* (pp. 28-52). London: Lawrence & Wishart.

Horrell, M. (1978). *Laws affecting race relations in South Africa.* Johannesburg: South African Institute of Race Relations.

Jansen, J. (Ed.). (1991). *Knowledge and power in the world system: The South African case.* Johannesburg: Skotaville.

Johnstone, F. (1976). *Race, class, and gold.* London: Routledge & Kegan Paul.

Kallaway, P. (Ed.). (1986). *Apartheid and education.* Johannesburg: Ravan.

Lodge, T. (1983). *Black politics in South Africa since 1945.* Johannesburg: Ravan.

Lodge, T., & Nasson, B. (1991). *All, here, and now: Black politics in South Africa in the 1980s.* New York: Ford Foundation.

Magubane, B. (1979). *The political economy of race and class in South Africa.* New York: Monthly Review Press.

Meighan, R. (1986). *A sociology of education.* London: Cassell.

Metcalfe, M. (1991). *Desegregating education in South Africa: White school enrollment in Johannesburg, 1985-91: Update and policy analysis* (Educational Policy Unit Report 2). Johannesburg: University of Witwatersrand.

Molteno, F. (1979). The up-risings of 16th June: A review of the literature on events in South Africa 1976. *Social Dynamics, 5*(1), 51-89.

Molteno, F. (1987). Students take control: The 1980 boycott of Coloured education in the Cape Peninsula. *British Journal of Sociology of Education, 8*(1), 51-89.

National Education Coordinating Committee. (1990, March 29-30). *National conference report and programme.* Durham: University of Durham-Westville.

National Education Policy Investigation. (1992). *Academic support and the curriculum* (NEPI Working Paper). Oxford: Oxford University Press.

Nkomo, M. (Ed.). (1990). *Pedagogy of domination.* Trenton, NJ: Africa World Press.

Rex, J., & Mason, D. (1986). *Theories for race and ethnic relations.* Cambridge, UK: Cambridge University Press.

Rose, B., & Tunmer, R. (1975). *Documents in South African education.* Johannesburg: Donker.

Rycroft, A. J. (1987). *Race and law in South Africa.* Kenwyn: Juta & Company.

Sisulu, Z. (1986). People's education for people's power. *Transformation, 1,* 96-117.

South African Institute of Race Relations. (1992). *Annual survey 1991-1992.* Johannesburg: Author.

Stewart, G. (1994). *A future education strategy and the role of state-aided schools.* Unpublished paper submitted to the PWV Provincial Education Ministry, South Africa.

Tinker, H. (1977). *Race, conflict, and the international order: From empire to United Nations.* New York: St. Martin's.

Wolpe, H. (1975). The theory of internal colonialism: The South African case. In I. Oxaal et al. (Eds.), *Beyond the sociology of development* (pp. 229-252). London: Routledge & Kegan Paul.

Wolpe, H. (1986). Class concepts, class struggle and racism. In J. Rex & D. Mason (Eds.), *Theories of race and ethnic relations* (pp. 110-130). Cambridge, UK: Cambridge University Press.

Wolpe, H. (1988). *Race, class and the apartheid state.* Paris: UNESCO Press.

Wolpe, H., Unterhalter, E., Botha, T., Badat, S., Dlamini, T., & Khotseng, B. (Eds.). (1991). *Apartheid education and popular struggles.* Johannesburg: Ravan.

15

Racism in the Modern World Community

Benjamin P. Bowser

In the 14 prior chapters, racism and anti-racism were reviewed in history and in the present in six different world communities. A casual reader might conclude that if racism is so extensive, it must be an innate human characteristic that has always existed, despite Snowden's (this volume) argument to the contrary. A casual reader might also conclude that racism will be with us for a very long time. Indeed, the scope of racism as a world phenomenon may seem overwhelming and suggests that the casual reader may be right. But another conclusion is more consistent with the views presented in this book: Racism is a historic and cultural belief (in one race's inferiority and in another's superiority) that has been used by national elites to maintain social stratification in their favor (see, in this volume, Solomos, Kushnick, Vieira, and Premdas). Racism has been very useful in obscuring economic class interests by keeping opposing racial identities more important than class differences. To maintain the opposing racial identities that becloud important class differences, it is necessary to have institutional practices that produce and justify unequal and differential racial outcomes.

Through racialized social identities, individual expressions of racism are learned, justified, and reinforced by cultural and institutional practices. In fact, the trilevel organization of racism suggests that individual racism commonly acted out in one generation could not pass on to subsequent generations or find expression in another nation without reinforcement by cultural and institutional practices. Those who see racism as having only physical and inherited origins ignore its cultural and institutional characteristics. As Wood (this volume) and Lewis (this volume) illustrate, modern racism is part of the Western European legacy of African and Indian slavery and world colonization. Finally, the over-looked occurrences of White anti-racism are additional evidence that racism is not innate (Aptheker, 1992). That some more privileged people of European descent were not racist and even opposed it strikes at the core of the claim that Europeans or any other group are innately racist.

Instead, racism is a historically defined dynamic interrelation between culture, institutions, and individual behaviors. Racism is a context and explanation for why race under specific conditions and circumstances triggers the human capacity to hate, fear other people, and treat them with disdain. A fundamental lesson from a century of social and behavioral scientific theory (Zeitlin, 1994) and research (Robboy & Clark, 1983) is that groups of individuals who come together as part of a collective identity act not simply as individuals but as historic and social beings. There is nothing innate or inevitable about acting out racial hatred or solidarity with others. What makes behavior human is that it is socially derived (Mills, 1961).

Each author in Part III who provides a description of racism and anti-racism also provides a unique history. In this sense, each case seems exceptional. Yet each case has two things in common. First, in all cases the central motive for maintaining the race myth is the same: to use government and the economy to maintain and justify social stratification where racial identity has a history of being used to confer advantage and disadvantage. Second, national elites define and redefine institutions to maintain their advantage and show no reluctance to use the race myth to maintain their privileged status and to avoid attracting attention and challenge to themselves. In the United States, Brazil, and South Africa, the powerful minorities continued use of race has been essential to obscure their separate class interests and dominant role by creating competition and conflict between racial and ethnic groups (see Guimarães, this volume; Nkomo, Twala, & Carrim, this volume). The majority of people of European descent in each nation have had a minimal capacity or circumstance to plan, define, manage, and redefine government and business practices that have perpetuated and redefined racism over the past century. The role of the majority of Europeans has been largely and consistently reactive, as was the case of common non-slave-holding Whites in colonial North Carolina (Cecil-Fronsman, 1992). These conclusions may not be apparent because the evidence is multinational and cuts across two centuries of history and social change. Further explanation is needed.

PATERNALISTIC RACISM AND ANTI-RACISM

Major changes in social organization have led to major changes in relations between races. Changes in race relations judged as landmark improvements were desegregation, antidiscrimination laws in the United States, and the enfranchisement of a Black majority electorate in South Africa. But these reforms have as much to do with changes in social organization as they do with successful anti-racist movements. Van den Berghe (1969) refers to the midcentury changes in race relations world-wide as reactions to the transition of world communities from paternalistic to competitive societies. There is mounting historical and contemporary evidence from modern world systems and global economics that such a transition has occurred. But this transition in the social order and in race relations has not eliminated racism, nor are the creation, management, and re-creation of institutional practices across history that result in changes in race relations due to the equivalent of a natural law or process such as a race relations cycle (Thompson, 1968). Changing race relations and the continuity in racism across multiple times and places are outgrowths of human decisions among those with the influence and power to maintain social systems where inequality is an essential built-in feature.

The period of paternalistic racism ran from slavery and direct colonialism through the end of World War II and the 1950s. Especially important were the years between the end of slavery and the emergence of Third World national states. In Part III, Vieira (this volume) points out that slavery ended in Brazil with the Portuguese colonial planter class still in possession of the land and capital and dominating the national government. What does a minority do that has been in control for centuries, has no intentions of surrendering its power and privilege, no longer owns the labor and bodies of the majority (Covin, 1990; Skidmore, 1974), and professes to have a liberal democratic government? Do nothing, and the former slaves would demand and agitate for market-value wages for their labor, as they did. They would also eventually dominate the government and erode, if not end, exclusive elite class privileges. From 1888 through the mid-20th century, the descendants of the planter class invested in industrialization; purposefully located the main site of the new economy in the south, farthest away from the major African Brazilian population centers; and aggressively recruited European immigrants as industrial labor. European immigrants were not needed because of a labor shortage; there was sufficient labor among impoverished African Brazilians. The new Europeans were needed to negate the large numbers and the political potential of African Brazilians and the possibility that they could gain strategic prominence in the new economy as labor rather than as outcasts.

A similar social transformation took place in the United States after the Civil War. The major difference is that the Southern planter class was defeated in war and initially lost both land and capital. Its major task was to gain back the land, get control again of former slaves' labor, and solidify its power by dominating state governments. The nightriders and Ku Klux Klan who killed opposing Blacks and anti-racist Whites alike did just that (Bloom, 1987, chap. 1). They took back the land and then hired displaced Blacks and poor Whites as sharecroppers—excellent case studies have been made on the Mississippi Delta (Brandfon, 1967; Cobb, 1992). The nightriders and oppressive race codes did not arise out of some wellspring of racial hatred among common Southern Whites. Prior to and during the Jim Crow codes, there were too many cases of Whites and Blacks working together to improve their wages and living in community (Bruce, 1959; Debs, 1923; Foner, 1955; Harris, 1982). It took people with know-how and deeply opposing interests to promote widespread reigns of terror and at the same time persuade the federal government to abandon the former slaves and the post-Civil War reconstruction of the South. The new laws subordinating Blacks, disenfranchising them from participation in government, restricting their land ownership, and regulating their everyday interactions with Whites originated with the defeated class of Southern planters, not the larger number of poor White farmers (Bloom, 1987, chap. 1). Jim Crow paternalism remained until the mid-20th-century challenge posed by the Civil Rights Movement.

Similarly, the end of slavery in the Caribbean posed a challenge to erstwhile colonialists. Former slaves set up autonomous villages and demanded to be fairly compensated for their labor (Tinker, 1974). The response of former slave masters, now plantation employers, was to import East Indian and Chinese laborers to compete with Black labor. As in Brazil, there was no shortage of Afro-Caribbean laborers, only an unwillingness to allow them to monopolize labor and thereby gain control over living wages. The second tactic to maintain planters' control was to recruit Blacks away from the Caribbean to the colonial mother countries as entry-level labor. Potential discontent and frustrated ambitions could be displaced to White majority countries (Levine, 1987). Experiments with local control and supervision of labor and property after emancipation created a local Afro-Caribbean managerial elite that would eventually govern the Caribbean nations as part of a larger worldwide neo-colonial system in the second half of this century (Ambursley & Cohen, 1983).

The turn of the century found a very different situation in South Africa. The Zulu threat to Dutch expansion of settlements in the interior had finally been suppressed, but now the struggle as to who would define and control South Africa was between English and Dutch colonialists. The Boer Wars temporarily settled the outcome. The English colonial agenda would nominally prevail until the end of World War II. By this time, Black South Africans were the base of the South African industrial and agricultural workforce. Racial discrimination existed, as did racial segregation, but it was not so pervasive as it was in the American South after 1880. Racial restrictions were driven more by rural and Boer cultural racism, characteristic of European settler societies. It was not until the end of World War II that something decisive had to be done to negate the Black population majority with its aspirations for democratic rights as the nation's majority. It was at this point that Dutch Boer South Africans researched Jim Crow in the American South and used it to create apartheid to negate both the Black majority's potential to control government and its threat to White privilege (Cell, 1982; Fredrickson, 1981).

Race was not a major historic issue in the heartland of Great Britain and Western Europe. The presence of Africans and other Third World peoples was minimal. But wherever they were concentrated, as in Liverpool and Marseilles, there were periods of racial tensions over job competition and relations with European women (Fall, 1986; Scobie, 1972). Clearly, the colonial presumption of European racial supremacy was not uncommon among the European rank and file and put an additional edge on interethnic conflict and competition. Race relations in Great Britain and Europe prior to the rise of Nazi Germany are of particular importance because they show how Europeans responded to people of color primarily based on cultural racism without institutional reinforcement. There was no elite manipulation of colonial beliefs or adjustment of social institutions to produce racially distinct and unequal outcomes.

Paternalistic racism was not due only to elite manipulation. The elites could not have been so successful in Brazil, the United States, the Caribbean, and eventually South Africa if there was not another important factor. The survival of the colonies and their slave-based economies required the social construction of "White people" out of the nonelite and poor Europeans from many different and historically conflicting cultures and nationalities (Allen, 1994). It also required a complementary social construction of "Black," "Indian," and generalized "others" from the national and cultural differences among Africans and native people. The redefining of vast differences into purposefully opposing collective identities was essential to controlling slaves, Indians, and freed slaves and to gaining the allegiance of nonelite European colonialists from many nations and cultures (Bennett, 1965; Cecil-Fronsman, 1992; D'Emilio & Freedman, 1988; Sobel, 1987). Immigrant Europeans redefined with a fictional superior identity could then be used to defend elite "Whiteness" and oppose the aspirations of Indians and Africans whose claim to citizenship and participation in the national life preceded that of European immigrants.

Three hundred years of institutional practice based on the fiction of distinct races and racial superiority and inferiority has now encoded European racism (the presumption of White superiority and non-White inferiority) in Western cultural beliefs. This belief system has been used very effectively to reconstruct racism from period to period to prevent popular challenges to those who make long-term economic decisions, control state policies, and consistently benefit across time. The creation of conflicting races and their separation have been essential to elite control. Slave and Indian revolts were dangerous enough, but far more frightening was the potential power of slaves, Indian, and poor Europeans together in rebellions. These majority rebellions in the United States and Brazil had the potential to overthrow the colonial system and the elite privileges that colonial slavery was based on (Aptheker, 1983; Price, 1979). Likewise, coalitions between Black and White labor in the American South after the Civil War posed the greatest threat to elite efforts to reclaim control of the Southern economy and state governments (Debs, 1923; Foner, 1955; Harris, 1982).

FROM PATERNALISTIC
TO COMPETITIVE RACISM

An agricultural economy requires a large number of workers spread over vast rural tracts of land. In contrast, the initial industrial economy required large numbers concentrated in cities. It was well-known in Europe that "cities make men free" (Vance, 1977). Urban freedom was also evident in the difficulty masters had controlling slaves in cities (Wade, 1964). Indeed, the most dangerous and dramatic slave rebellions originated in U.S. and Brazilian cities and towns (Aptheker, 1983; Price, 1979). How could an elite minority maintain control over thousands of industrial workers in rapidly expanding cities? It would be impossible to control directly the day-to-day actions and behaviors of workers outside plants or to determine what they read or heard.

A second critical problem with the transition to an industrial economy was whether or not to use the already available, English-speaking, and often skilled Black labor force in the United States, Brazil, and the Caribbean. This would have done three things. First, it would have lifted Blacks out of poverty, increasing their already large population and encouraging their survival and the threat they posed to elite control and privilege. Second, Blacks would be able to participate fully as citizens in the nation's political life. Finally, it would have put Blacks in a position to monopolize industrial labor and demand higher wages. These developments would have been disastrous for elite control and for profits. It was therefore necessary to create a new social order and new race relations to take advantage of industrialization as an engine to maintain elite control.

The new social order could be created in the following way. Import from many countries large numbers of poor Europeans and East Indians displaced by mechanization, commercial farming, and poverty. In the Caribbean, East Indian immigrants were brought in to compete with the large numbers of Blacks already there for plantation jobs, and in the United States and Brazil, European immigrants were used to defuse the Black industrial labor and political potential. Immigrants did not come because native Whites wanted them, nor did immigrants simply invite themselves. Native White opposition to immigration clearly shows that the average White American or Brazilian did not organize, want, encourage, or pay for the immigration of thousands of Europeans to the United States and Brazil. Competition with hundreds of thousands of new Europeans was not in their best interest. Not only were Blacks displaced from the initial industrial workforce, many native poor Whites were as well.

System maintenance in the urban competitive world appeared to be based on the following principle: The more immigrants there were and the greater their variety of national origins, the more the ethnic competition and the less likely a fully class-conscious integrated labor force would emerge. Ethnic competition would keep wages low, because every new ethnic group would be a reserve labor force prepared to work for less than those already in the workforce ahead of them. Using European ethnic groups as the industrial workforce produced a historic irony. Instead of European immigrants being used to threaten an already established Black citizen and industrial labor force, the opposite happened. Already available Blacks were used in the United States and Brazil as a reserve labor force to threaten immigrant European industrial workers. Not only was the Black political and labor threat defused, the potential immigrant threat to organize more effectively and demand higher wages was too. Controlling business interests (elites) could count on Blacks and recent European immigrants to fight against one another and not against them.

With such a self-regulating system, it was not necessary to control everyday behaviors. Everyone could enjoy personal freedoms in their own ethnic and class neighborhoods. Blacks could be used to keep White labor in check, and European immigrants who now had "White" status conferred on them and the better jobs would keep Blacks in check. Anger, hostility, riots, and hatred would be directed across race and ethnic lines, not at the controlling class. Class differences would be secondary, and the minority in control to whom profits flowed would be virtually ignored. This new system did not require directly controlling every aspect of subordinates' lives, nor did it require subordinates knowing who was in control and acknowledging that fact. In fact, immigrants and Blacks could even vote, because who was in office and who elected them was less important than what resources these officials had access to and whose interests and agendas they served.

Ethnic competition succeeded in the United States and was used to undercut the application of liberal ideals of individual rights, freedoms, and potentials. By 1890, the Black proportion of the U.S. population had dropped dramatically because of the large volume of European immigration (U.S. Bureau of the Census, 1979). Brazil succeeded in industrializing its south, but did not completely offset the Black majority with immigrants. Instead of racializing all social identities, as in the United States, the Brazilian power elite did the opposite. It deracialized social identities by acknowledging and encouraging interracial mixing between poor immigrant Whites and Blacks. The goal was to "whiten" the Black population (Guimarães, this volume; Vieira, this volume). A large mulatto middle identity would buffer minority White elites from the majority Black threat (Covin, 1990). Mulattos served the same role in Brazil as European immigrants did in the United States. The British importation of East Indians into the Caribbean between 1838 and 1917 created ethnic rivalry and competition that benefited colonial interests (Patterson, 1977; Tinker, 1974). In South Africa, the Boers opposed the English strategy of bringing East Indians and other Europeans in as industrial workers to offset the Black majority (Cell, 1982). The Boers feared that their prominence would be diminished by adding large numbers of other nationalities to the English-Boer competition to dominate the nation. With the exception of South Africa, the results were the same in each nation—greater personal freedom for exslaves, political enfranchisement with limited effect, continued elite control, and profits unimagined in the paternalistic world of plantations, slavery, or sharecropping.

Finally, it must be understood that the transition from paternalistic to competitive societies did not occur uniformly. Sao Paulo and Chicago were ahead of Salvador and Birmingham in transforming from paternalistic to competitive racism. Uneven transition had everything to do with the timing and the success of the Civil Rights Movement in the American South, the absence of a similar movement in Brazil, and the successful movements for national independence in the European colonial world after World War II. For example, most of the United States after the war was well along in its transition to a national economy. The South was the exception. The Southern Civil Rights Movement enjoyed relative success after World War II because the Jim Crow South was already an anachronism by 1950. Agriculture was being mechanized, rural population was dispersing into cities, and cash crops were declining as a share of the total Southern economy (Bloom, 1987, chap. 1). Investments in the South and new enterprise were coming increasingly from the North and Midwest, and were concentrating in Southern cities where Blacks were important consumers. When Blacks challenged Jim Crow racial segregation, they faced a considerably weakened Southern agrarian controlling class and were able to leverage support from other powerful national interests. Urban businesses, national chain stores and employers, and finally the federal government were willing to sacrifice de facto segregation in the face of national protests televised worldwide. Urban business interests relied on Blacks as consumers throughout the United States, and the federal government was concerned about the international image of the United States due to cold war competition with the Soviet Union.

By 1950, it was clear in the U.S. South that formal racial segregation was no longer necessary to maintain elite control or to continue a way of life that could be so visibly and easily challenged. In contrast, civil rights challenges in the decades prior to the emergence of the new national and industrial social order were soundly resisted and did not generate the support of powerful outside interests (Branch, 1988, chap. 1). In Brazil, the uneven development between the paternal north and the competitive industrial south never became a target for massive Black discontent. A rigid distinction between Black and White did not exist, and there was no formal and rigid system of racial separation. The Black population was trapped in poverty, treated with benign neglect, and deracialized, and social mobility was based not on merit but on patronage (da Costa, 1990).

At the same time that segregation became an anachronism in the United States and Brazil, an important innovation in colonialism occurred. With the economies of Third World countries set up to produce resources and provide cheap labor for their motherlands, it was not necessary to control national governments (Amin, 1973; Ghosh, 1985). Postwar nationalist sentiment could be accommodated by granting former colonies political independence. But just as the urban laborer enjoyed the new-found freedom of the city, the newly independent colonies were still economically dependent on their former colonial masters. By midcentury, a new social system had been put in place to accommodate popular aspirations for freedom as well as the colonial elite's need to maintain control and assure continued privilege.

ANTI-RACISM IN THE PATERNALISTIC AND COMPETITIVE WORLDS

Aptheker (1992) has shown that not only did anti-racism exist in the United States through 1900, but that opposition to racism by Whites was not uncommon or unknown. Some Indians, Blacks, and Whites opposed individual acts of racism, opposed institutional practices that perpetuated racism, and rejected the cultural belief of racial superiority and inferiority. Similar historical research needs to be done in Brazil, the Caribbean, and South Africa. In the paternalistic world, opposition to racism was clear because racism was visibly and formally institutionalized. John Brown led an armed rebellion against the institution of slavery; thousands of Whites in the United States voted against their states becoming slave states during the 1840s because they opposed racism and slavery; the Quilombos of Brazil were anti-racist Black communities that did not exclude anti-racist Whites. Anti-racist Blacks and Whites took action against the institution of Jim Crow segregation, where all aspects of Southern life were rigidly segregated by race. Anti-racism in South Africa was in opposition to the institutional practices of apartheid. In all the paternalistic societies, planters, governors, and other leading personali-

ties who represented and symbolized maintenance of a formally structured and racialized way of life became targets of effective anti-racist
actions.

In the new urban, industrial, and competitive world, there are no formal
institutions whose purpose is to maintain the subordinate status of "inferior" groups. State governors, industrialists, and other important public
figures do not directly stand for or represent the superiority of one or the
other race. Anyone can vote and hold public office. There are laws against
racial discrimination and efforts to hire members of historically underrepresented groups. Unlike the prior social systems, where everything was
racialized, nothing is racialized in the competitive one except social and
economic outcomes. Yet, racial inequalities, exploitation, and victimiza-
tion—outcomes of institutionalized slavery and colonialism—have some-
how continued in the new social order.

How do anti-racists attack a racism of consequences? When Martin
Luther King, Jr., went to Chicago to protest and organize action against
racialized economic inequalities, civil authorities did not oppose the
protest, as they had done in the paternalistic South. Chicago accommodated it. Economic inequality as an outcome is not a formal institution set
up to perpetuate racial segregation. King's efforts went nowhere because
there were no institutional targets. Instead, protesters were confronted with
the most violent collective opposition they had experienced to date—
Northern White ethnics, the sons and daughters of European immigrants.

We live in this new competitive social order and, with the exception of
South Africa, no anti-racism movement in any of the nations studied has
effectively challenged modern racism. Anti-racists in the United States
are faced with the same puzzle as anti-racists in Brazil—racism in consequence but not by formal institution. The collapse of Jim Crow in the
American South eliminated the last formal institutional target of racism
in the United States, just as the collapse of apartheid in South Africa
brings in a new social order without formal racial institutions. Nkomo,
Twala, and Carrim (this volume) provide initial evidence that the new
South Africa continues to perpetuate racism in consequence.

Virtually all of the anti-racist efforts over the past three decades in the
United States have been framed by the past. To understand and respond to
racism in the present, one must take a new look and new actions. To view
and respond to the present social order as if it were the old is inadequate.

The pervasive presumption of European superiority (cultural racism)
and racialized social identities have continued from the colonial past into

the present. What is different is the way in which people of color, in particular people of African descent, are marginalized in the workforce and viewed and treated as a reserve workforce. These are essential factors that must be examined very carefully in a comprehensive, specific, and sensitive analysis of the present social order to understand how racism in consequence is produced and what can be done about it.

Virtually all of the present analyses of racial inequality are victim centered, and fundamentally misunderstand racism as a dynamic phenomenon (see Bowser, this volume). Neither anti-racist Blacks or Whites alone have the full perspective, insight, experience, or resources to make such an assessment and take effective action. This is why discussion of how we might break down the categorical barriers to transracial anti-racist coalitions that Blauner and Dugger explore in this book are so important. Broad-based coalitions of anti-racists and antipatriarchists are needed not only to take action but to build a consensus on the nature of the problems as well as where and how actions can be taken. This is precisely what has been missing in the United States since the 1960s civil rights efforts in the South.

POSTMODERN AND GLOBAL RACISM

Although there has not been an adequate anti-racist response to the specific character of racism in contemporary competitive societies, there is evidence that a third social transformation is underway. The first cue of major change came in the early 1970s, when it became clear that business and jobs were fleeing U.S. cities (Goldsmith & Blakely, 1992). This development was known as "job and White flight." Supposedly because of the concentration of Blacks in large U.S. cities, the desegregation of housing and schools, and the Black economic riots of the 1960s, many businesses and White residents moved out of U.S. cities. This trend was explained by race—the menacing Black presence. Jobs were supposedly being moved to rapidly expanding White suburbs as well.

The fact is that businesses, jobs, and Whites were leaving U.S. cities in the 1950s well before the racialization of U.S. cities and riots (Kasarda, 1976). A primary reason for Black riots was the lack of employment in a rapidly declining industrial base (Kerner, 1968). It also turns out that not all of the displaced jobs were moved to the suburbs. In the 1990s, it became clear that U.S. industrial and manufacturing jobs are being moved overseas to other countries (Bocage, 1980; Magaziner & Patinkin, 1989). This is not a development that happened overnight. It required corporate board decisions at least a decade in advance and acquiescence from the federal government. While the American public was led to believe that jobs were fleeing urban Blacks for the suburbs, an unspecified proportion of these jobs were fleeing the nation. Long-term investment and labor policies in the United States were abandoning White Americans as well as Blacks.

Although the White middle and working classes thought the major social geography was race, the class basis of their relative affluence and privilege was being undercut—enterprise within U.S. national boundaries. This has happened because European Americans have uncritically aligned their interests based on common race (being White) with those who make decisions and have decided to transform U.S. business interests into a world economy that does not include or necessarily benefit the average White American. The timing and manner in which the U.S. economy is internationalizing are subjects of debate and analysis (Bosworth, 1993). Regardless of whether the trend is just starting or far along, the economic basis of the U.S. White middle and working classes is in decline. Not only is the long-term fate of African Americans dependent on transracial coalitions as Blauner (this volume) suggests, the long-term fate of European Americans is also dependent upon transcending the race myth.

The movement of capital and jobs from Great Britain and Western Europe into the global economy has been facilitated by using racism in the same way it has been used in the United States—to obscure class interests (Solomos, this volume; Kushnick, this volume). The difference is that, in Europe, the racial scapegoats were imported. Afro-Caribbeans and East Indians in Great Britain and Turks and North Africans in France and Germany were used to perform service jobs in Europe after the war—just as Mexican immigrants have been used to do agricultural work in the United States. Immigrants of color are also a reserve labor force that can be used to undercut British and Western European domestic labor, to help forge a false racial unity by invoking European racial supremacy, and to be blamed for the declining European standard of living and job losses. Again, White unity obscures conflicting class interests that would be much more obvious without racial scapegoats. As in the United States, this is not a cosmic social dynamic. This use of race is the consequence of decisions made by small groups of investors and managers with the power and influence to create enterprise and to have the state and media support their decisions.

The recent dismantling of apartheid is not due to White South African altruism or to mounting anti-racist opposition. It is a strategic move acknowledging that sufficient economic barriers are already in place to keep Black South Africans subordinate and to maintain general White privilege. The effectiveness of economic barriers as a way to maintain racial-class barriers has already been demonstrated in the United States, Great Britain, Brazil, and Western Europe. Dismantling apartheid acknowledges that the economy and the media are the primary institutions that define and control society, not the state. Without apartheid, South African business elites can now freely plan and execute the integration of the resource-rich South African economy into the global economy and leave the waning power of the state to the Black and colored majority. This is a bold move that may have a future application in Brazil if African Brazilians become a political force in their own right.

The Caribbean is also part of the transition from colonial to industrial to global social systems. Political independence has given rise to a Afro-Caribbean broker class (Gomes, 1980; Greene, 1993; Smith, 1984) that does not have the power or the resources to plan and execute long-term economic development. Its role is to facilitate external investments and interests. Caribbean regional economic development is totally dependent upon North American, British, Western European, and Japanese investments (McDonald, 1973). By limiting the major investor countries' investments to tourism, many in the Caribbean population have had no way to support themselves in the rural areas. Poverty and lack of opportunities have forced many to emigrate to Caribbean cities, the United States, and Great Britain for service jobs and as a reserve labor force (Levine, 1987). Thus, the Caribbean has served as a source of cheap labor for the industrial world. It is likely that when depopulation has gone far enough, selected islands will be developed for affluent White resettlement. Communications technologies now make it possible for global executives and their families to enjoy the tropics while directing, creating, and managing from afar. The Caribbean broker class that controls the governments stands to benefit when this redevelopment begins.

Western capital and jobs are now mobile. Lower-end manufacturing and assembly jobs and facilities can be moved any place in the world (Bosworth, 1993)—wherever there is political stability and cheap labor costs. If a government demands unacceptable tax levels or labor demands higher wages, facilities and jobs can be moved to another country (Bocage, 1980; Ghosh, 1985). Instead of one race or ethnic group in one nation serving as a reserve labor pool to discipline the demands of another, the entire world is in reserve. If the corporation is large enough, taxes, high wage demands, dependence on labor, and government interference are things of the past. This is why stock markets can continue to show steady growth while tax bases in the Western world erode, more and more workers are underemployed and unemployed, and more and more people are homeless. The United States, Great Britain, and Western Europe are decreasing their reliance on national states or domestic labor and decreasing their benefits to specific governments or classes of White workers. These developments have major societal consequences and could not happen without racism as a distraction and source of a continued false identity.

Postmodern Racism:
A Convergence of Experiences?

Given the variations in how racism has been used in Brazil, the United States, the Caribbean, South Africa, Great Britain, and Western Europe, there is little reason to think that common connections between how racism is expressed exist. Each national expression of racism would have to be addressed locally and with individually designed strategies, as has been the case in the past. But the assumption that national racism is independent of others runs contrary to the merging of economic and social orders. Furthermore, racism is not a static unchanging phenomenon, nor is it unaffected by changes in larger social systems. The national racial expressions described in this book are slowly and subtly converging because the underlying economic and social organizations that racism supports are also converging.

The United States, the Caribbean, Brazil, Great Britain, Western Europe, and South Africa are all part of an emerging postmodern world economic system. Although each nation and region has a long history of trade and exchange with one another, past contacts have been based on exchange between nationally bound economies and governments. To a large extent, national boundaries replicated cultural ones. The trend toward a global economy suggests that national economic boundaries are being superseded by groups of nations in interconnected and interdependent regional economies. What goes on economically in China or Brazil also affects daily life in the United States or Italy.

A first consequence of this world economic trend is the decline in the centrality of national states. The absolute authority and centrality of federal states are reduced when the major sources of jobs, income, tax revenue, and general prosperity are no longer bound by historic customs, nativist sentiments, national laws, and political boundaries. The larger and more international corporations become, the less dependent they are on any national states or workforces. The more independent corporations are of national boundaries, the greater their ability to extract concessions from state and national governments as well as from labor. The most rapid economic growth in the world community today is through the internationalization of businesses led by North American and Western European industries (Beeman & Frank, 1988).

A second consequence of the modern world economy is what Kushnick describes (this volume). The movement of plants, points of assembly, and manufacturing from the United States, Western Europe, and now Japan into the Third World is further dislocating domestic and regional economies that have already been shattered by historic colonial dependencies. People who are dislocated from African, Asian, and Latin American rural communities are forced into Third World cities and into the North American, British, and Western European immigrant labor forces. The depopulation of the Caribbean is just one example. The emerging modern world economic system is corporate colonialism without the historic leadership or necessity of the state or church. The new role of the state is to service the international business sector rather than national populations. One of the most important state services now is to maintain political stability and social control to encourage investment from the international business community.

THE ROLE OF COMMUNICATIONS

During slavery, order was maintained by force of arms, as Vieira (this volume) describes in early Brazil. Slavery in North America was reinforced by social identities that ignored diversity among Europeans, assigned Whites superior status, and set Whites against Blacks (Allen, 1994; Bennett, 1965). By the turn of this century, control of European colonies was maintained by pitting rival nations and religions against one another and the creation of dependent Western native elites. During this century, the necessity of racial dominance was transformed into national security during the cold war, where political subversion was added to the list of system maintenance strategies in the Third World (Morris, 1967; Radosh, 1969). Now the use of Western force of arms is out of the question except against the smallest island nations or the most disorganized countries—Grenada, Haiti, or Somalia. How is control maintained in the emerging postmodern global world and what implications do the new controls have for maintaining or challenging racism?

The postmodern global world is dependent upon electronic communications that make international coordination and agreements easy to enter into and execute. It is no longer necessary to be in the same city or the same country or even to speak the same language to manage, make decisions, and communicate with others in one's own or other corporations or governments. A business can be run, instructions can be given, orders can be filled, opinions can be rendered, and decisions can be made any place on earth for activities any place else on earth. Corporation management can be in New York State, research and development in California and Europe, and production in Mexico, Hong Kong, or Singapore. North American auto manufacturers can have parts made in Korea, Japan, and Spain; steel produced in Brazil; and cars assembled in Mexico and Canada and then shipped to the United States. Business and government elites in one nation can selectively, instantaneously, and continuously coordinate their investment and disinvestment policies with other elites in other nations. Entire industries, economies, and governments can work together invisibly to shape material and perceptual realities for the larger public.

When communications and cooperation are central, invisible, and selective, it is insufficient to have human and material resources produce a product, bring it to market, and then make, hold, and invest the profits. A nation must have much more than natural and human resources to develop economically. Success is based upon becoming part of larger, often invisible, communications networks that make essential connections between potential partners. Investors need to be connected to product developers, manufacturers, retailers, and government supporters. Communications control knowledge and access that in turn control what one can or cannot do.

Despite increasing competition from Pacific Rim nations, the United States and Western Europe dominate and largely control communications in the modern world system. They control both the technology and its application. This means that North American and Western European elites define the dialogue as to how the world system is set up and works. This is largely because of the hold that North Americans and Western Europeans have over computers, air travel, telephone, television, movies, radio, print news, and popular entertainment.

Racism in Communications

If communications is at the heart of the emerging world system and is essential to it, then the most powerful and continued uses of racism can be expected to come out of communications. McLean (this volume) describes how the movie and television industries in the United States have perpetuated racist images at home and abroad. The significance of this point cannot be overemphasized; communications technologies are on the threshold of quantum leaps in the ability to absorb attention and define consciousness. Communications have heavily influenced social awareness. In the next century, they may very well define it. We can anticipate the obsolescence of single-dimension media (voice and/or vision) and the emergence of interactive multimedia (multidimensional voice and vision).

Virtual reality technologies have the potential to blur the boundaries between imagination and reality. The use of crude racial imagery is already apparent in the prototypes of advanced game and computer systems. Social habits that took two centuries to produce can be reinforced or challenged in one very successful, widely spread virtual reality system. If racism is part of the culture from which these communications systems are created, it is naive to think that racism and all other "isms" will not be perpetuated through the new technologies. Racial messages will be far more effectively conveyed as North Americans' and Western Europeans' images of themselves dominate the rest of the world. McLuhan's statement, "the medium is the message," is more prophetic than anyone imagined.

That *The Birth of a Nation* was a sell-out favorite in Russia and Sambo dolls were the rage in Japan is evidence of North American racist socialization through exported media. People who have no modern contact, history, or experience with people of African or North American Indian descent learn—and have no immediate reason to question—the "Black" and "Indian" physical and/or cultural inferiority in relation to "Whites." Africans and African Americans can now be called "nigger" any place on earth. Whatever has been done to change race relations in the United States in the past three decades cannot compare to the unseen racial damage from North American dominance of world movie and television entertainment. That racism finds expression in the Western world is bad enough, but the worldwide assumption of White dominance over people of color is far more disastrous.

EFFECTIVE ANTI-RACISM IN THE POSTMODERN WORLD

Colonial wars of liberation and public defiance of formal racial segregation helped end the direct subjugation of people of color in the United States, the Caribbean, and South Africa. To gain political control of governments that participate in a world economy defined and controlled by elites that use racism to maintain control does not have nearly the same promise it did in the 1950s. In the same way, picketing, sit-downs, and public protests do not change societies where governments can pass as many laws as they like, but ultimately do not control the central institutions in citizens' lives—the economy and the media. The most effective struggle against racism in the next century will have to center on who controls local and global economies (Brecher, Childs, & Cutler, 1993). A parallel and equally important struggle must be waged over the images conveyed by communications media both at home and abroad. If modern racism is perpetuated through mass media and multimedia, it must be combated in the same way. McLean (this volume) describes a time when movies were used against racism in the United States. Modern media have the potential to show the world what racism is and to isolate and wipe out its acceptance. Modern media have the potential to unseat racism and the other "isms" within Western national cultures.

In addition to focusing on central economic control and the use of the media to combat racism, a number of other related measures are suggested by the authors in this book.

1. Bowser and Kushnick speak of the need to challenge and reconstruct national identities in the United States and Western Europe that have created artificial and inaccurate polar national identities—Black versus White, citizen versus noncitizen. Vieira writes of a similar need in Brazil. But the Brazilian racial identity is purposefully diffused from polarities to obscure the large African presence in Brazil.

2. Dugger suggests that the categorical view of race and gender as distinct sources of historic exploitation pits the racial and women's struggle against each other, when in fact progress cannot be made on one

front without progress on the other. The very way in which race and gender are conceptualized defeats a common struggle for human liberation. There is a need to recognize differences in views and experiences and engage in a common discourse where each struggle can be personally embraced regardless of race and gender. Through discourse, men can learn about women's experience; women can see what men know and fear; people of color can come to see Whites as people; people of European descent can come to know what it is like to be Black, Indian, or Asian; and people of color can understand each other. Dugger's description of postmodern feminism is close to classic European liberalism, but without the problematic emphasis on individualism.

3. There is a need for bottom-to-top organization, where specific social issues are addressed by anti-racists (Brecher, Childs, & Cutler, 1993; Kushnick, this volume). Working-class Europeans and European Americans are contributing to their own decline by focusing discontent on other races and foreigners. Direct, long-term, and local work within the working class is required to get it to see that their false social identity as "Whites" obscures their real interests. The working class needs to focus attention on the economic decision-making and investment policies that force people from Third World nations to immigrate to the United States and Western Europe and to deport living-wage domestic jobs overseas. Organizing from the bottom is the only way to reach and influence this crucial sector.

4. Once colonial and fictional identities are questioned, multicultural coalitions are possible. Politically effective and international coalitions with the interest and motivation to organize and challenge the real government (international corporations) are not possible as long as participants continue to be racially identified. Multicultural working coalitions are vital to negate and address the institutional strategy of pitting one racial, ethnic, or cultural group against the other.

5. Domestic anti-racist social movements in one country must be allied and work with anti-racist movements in other countries. Distance, language barriers, and national boundaries that limit nonelites are being used to advance inequalities around the world. If these barriers are also eliminated for anti-racists, there would be no place for racist institutional interests or international economic exploitation to hide. Furthermore, anti-racists from around the world could draw upon each others' information, skills, tactics, talents, resources, and experiences.

6. Effective anti-racism requires long, careful, and critical examination of lost opportunities, groups, and interests that should be allied but

are not, and what can be done to bring and keep together coalitions that can make a difference. This will require as much reflection and listening as action and hard work.

7. The free rein of international corporations to exploit poverty and inequality anywhere on earth must be addressed. World labor laws and enforcement will reduce labor exploitation and the concentration of extraordinary wealth in the hands of a few at the expense of large numbers of people. This will require the expansion of United Nations and World Court type of roles.

8. There is a need for authentic dialogue where people of historically conflicting identities may speak their minds and have their experiences and perspectives listened to and understood. This will require being more precise and careful in how generalized labels are used.

9. Not only does dominant group racism have to be addressed, subordinate group racism does too. One racism cannot exist without the other. To challenge one effectively requires challenging the other.

10. As Blauner (this volume) asserts, effective anti-racism requires working with the positive potential of nonelite Europeans to be anti-racist for reasons of basic self-interest. The maintenance of racial supremacy comes with a heavy price in loss of community, personal and economic insecurity, moral compromise, hatred, and being hated. Most Whites have not and will not benefit from race interests where their role is to defend the privilege of elites who exploit them as well. Whites will see the absurdity of their position and defense if they are convinced of their social class vulnerability and if given the opportunity to understand how they are exploited as well. They can become allies in a mutually beneficial anti-racist struggle.

CONCLUSION:
A NEW RESEARCH AGENDA

A very different research agenda is called for. The social order will change and racism will be re-created as an outcome of the struggle of elites to maintain control and opposition to that control. A number of research topics are suggested.

1. What are the specific institutional practices that produce racism in Brazil, the United States, the Caribbean, Great Britain, Western Europe, and South Africa? One practice is hiring people of color last and using

their lesser seniority as a basis to fire them when downsizing is called for—ignoring the initial discrimination that put people of color at the end of the job queue. Tracking in schools and unequal-per-student expenditures in education produce generational inequality. If educational outcomes are racially unequal, then inequality can be "legitimately" carried over to produce long-term racial inequality in employment. Research into such practices has been ongoing in the United States and Great Britain, but what are the parallel practices in other racialized social orders? How do they compare? What are effective anti-racist solutions?

2. To what extent have living-wage jobs in specific industries in the United States, Great Britain, and Western Europe been moved overseas, and what have these jobs been replaced with? What has been the consequence of these specific jobs moving overseas for both the communities that lost them and the communities that gained them? Globalization of jobs may not be as advanced or have had as negative an effect as suggested by Bowser (this volume), Solomos (this volume), and Kushnick (this volume).

3. Can major changes in the economy be traced to purposeful (elite) planning and decision making in business, which are supported in turn by related elites in government? Are the social and racial consequences of these plans and decisions known in advance? If the elite hypothesis is correct, then who are the decision makers, and when, where, and how did they act to produce current outcomes? Alternatively, changes in the social order and race relations may indeed be outcomes of impersonal social and historic dynamics.

4. Does identification as White in contra-distinction with Black, Asian, Indian, or others obscure economic class differences and interests among European ethnic groups in the United States, Brazil, South Africa, Great Britain, and Western Europe? Does identification as Black in contra-distinction with White obscure economic class differences and interests? These questions address the broader issue of whether or not specific social identity contributes to maintaining a racialized social order.

5. Are there experiments or experiences in how one might effectively deracialize and degender subordinate and dominant group social identities? If so, what are the personal and institutional consequences of deracialized and de-genderized social identities?

6. Are there any historic or contemporary cases where progress has been made against racism without related progress in challenging patriarchy, or successfully challenging patriarchy without also challenging racism?

7. What is the nature, extent, and dynamic of subordinate group racism in the United States, the Caribbean, Brazil, South Africa, Great Britain, and Western Europe?

8. Does dominant and subordinate group racism interact to perpetuate cultural and institutional racism? If so, how has it done so in different nations and at different times?

9. As Blauner (this volume) suggests in the United States, do large potential anti-racist coalitions exist in Brazil, South Africa, Great Britain, and Western Europe? If so, what will it take to mobilize these potential coalitions?

10. For existing anti-racist coalitions in all of the national areas looked at in this book, what are their strategies, membership composition, successes, and failures? Are there any lessons to be learned within and across global areas?

11. How do Western racial stereotypes and imagery affect overseas viewers? Do they pick up the dominant-subordinate messages? To what extent are these messages internalized and who identifies with them?

If liberalism is essential to and a necessary factor of a successful anti-racist coalition, a new liberalism must be defined that can effectively deal with the collective ways in which people are oppressed and the collective realities of historic identities and behaviors. The West's secular religion will become an effective blueprint in creating an anti-racist future where individual and group rights and freedoms can be balanced and maintained through a global and truly well-informed democratic process. Postmodern feminism may very well lead the way for such a reformulation of classical liberalism.

REFERENCES

Allen, T. (1994). *The invention of the White race.* London: Verso.

Ambursley, F., & Cohen, R. (1983). Crisis in the Caribbean: Internal transformations and external constraints. In F. Ambursley & R. Cohen (Eds.), *Crisis in the Caribbean.* New York: Monthly Review Press.

Amin, S. (1973). *Neo-colonialism in West Africa.* New York: Monthly Review Press.

Aptheker, H. (1983). *American Negro slave revolts.* New York: International Publishers.

Aptheker, H. (1992). *Anti-racism in U.S. history: The first two hundred years.* Westport, CT: Praeger.

Beeman, W., & Frank, I. (1988). *New dynamics in the global economy.* New York: Committee for Economic Development.

Bennett, L. (1965). Miscegenation in America. In C. M. Larson (Ed.), *Marriage across the color line.* Chicago: Johnson Publications.

Bloom, J. (1987). *Class, race, and the civil rights movement.* Bloomington: Indiana University Press.

Bocage, D. (1980). American-Caribbean economic interdependence. In V. R. McDonald (Ed.), *The Caribbean issues of emergence: Socio-economic and political perspectives.* Washington, DC: University Press of America.

Bosworth, B. (1993). *Savings and investment in a global economy.* Washington, DC: Brookings Institution.

Branch, T. (1988). *Parting the waters: America in the King years, 1954-63.* New York: Simon & Schuster.

Brandfon, R. (1967). *Cotton king of the new South: A history of the Yazoo Mississippi Delta from reconstruction to the twentieth century.* Cambridge, MA: Harvard University Press.

Brecher, J., Childs, J. B., & Cutler, J. (Eds.). (1993). *Global visions beyond the new world order.* Boston: South End.

Bruce, R. V. (1959). *1877: Year of violence.* New York: Bobbs-Merrill.

Cecil-Fronsman, B. (1992). *Common Whites: Class and culture in antebellum North Carolina.* Lexington: University Press of Kentucky.

Cell, J. W. (1982). *The highest stage of White supremacy: The origins of segregation in South Africa and the American south.* New York: Oxford University Press.

Cobb, J. (1992). *The most southern place on earth: The Mississippi Delta and the roots of regional identity.* New York: Oxford University Press.

Covin, D. (1990). Afrocentricity in *o movimento Negro unificado. Journal of Black Studies, 21,* 126-144.

da Costa, E. V. (1990). *The Brazilian empire: Myths and histories.* Belmont, CA: Wadsworth.

Debs, E. (1923). *The Negro worker.* New York: Emancipation Publications.

D'Emilio, J., & Freedman, E. (1988). *Intimate matters: A history of sexuality in America.* New York: Harper & Row.

Fall, M. (1986). *Les Africains noirs en France.* Paris: L'Harmattan.

Foner, P. (1955). *History of the labor movement in the U.S.* (Vol. 2). New York: International Publishers.

Fredrickson, G. (1981). *White supremacy: A comparative study in American and South African history.* New York: Oxford University Press.

Ghosh, B. (1985). *Political economy of neo-colonialism in Third World countries.* New Delphi: Sterling.

Goldsmith, W., & Blakely, E. (1992). *Separate societies: Poverty and inequality in U.S. cities.* Philadelphia: Temple University Press.

Gomes, R. C. (1980). Class, status, and privilege: The objective interest of the new elite in Guyana. In V. R. McDonald (Ed.), *The Caribbean issues of emergence: Socioeconomic and political perspectives.* Washington, DC: University Press of America.

Greene, E. (Ed.). (1993). *Race, class, and gender in the future of the Caribbean.* Kingston, Jamaica: University of the West Indies, Institute of Social and Economic Research.

Harris, W. (1982). *The harder we run: Black workers since the Civil War.* New York: Oxford University Press.

Kasarda, J. (1976). The changing occupational structure of the American metropolis: Apropos the urban problem. In B. Schwartz (Ed.), *The changing face of the suburbs.* Chicago: University of Chicago Press.

Kerner, O. (1968). *Report of the National Advisory Commission on Civil Disorders.* New York: Bantam Books.

Levine, B. B. (Ed.). (1987). *The Caribbean exodus.* New York: Praeger.

Magaziner, I., & Patinkin, M. (1989). *The silent war: Inside the global business battles shaping America's future.* New York: Random House.

McDonald, V. R. (Ed.). (1973). *The Caribbean economies: Perspectives on social, political, and economic conditions.* New York: MSS Information Corp.

Mills, C. W. (1961). *The sociological imagination.* New York: Grove.

Morris, G. (1967). *CIA and American labor.* New York: International Publishers.

Patterson, O. (1977). *Ethnic chauvinism.* New York: Stein & Day.

Price, R. (1979). *Maroon societies: Rebel slave communities in the Americas.* Baltimore: Johns Hopkins University Press.

Radosh, R. (1969). *American labor and U.S. foreign policy.* New York: Random House.

Robboy, H., & Clark, C. (Eds.). (1983). *Social interaction: Readings in sociology.* New York: St. Martin's.

Scobie, E. (1972). *Black Britannia: A history of Blacks in Britain.* Chicago: Johnson Publishing.

Skidmore, T. (1974). *Black into White: Race and nationality in Brazilian thought.* New York: New York: Cambridge University Press.

Smith, M. G. (1984). *Culture, race, and class in the Commonwealth Caribbean.* Mona, Jamaica: University of the West Indies, Department of Extra-Mural Studies.

Sobel, M. (1987). *The world they made together: Black and White values in eighteenth century Virginia.* Princeton, NJ: Princeton University Press.

Thompson, E. (1968). *Race relations and the race problem: A definition and analysis.* New York: Greenwood.

Tinker, H. (1974). *A new system of slavery.* London: Oxford University Press.

U.S. Bureau of the Census. (1979). *Current population reports: The social and economic status of the Black population in the U.S.: An historical view, 1790-1978* (Special Studies Series P-23, No. 80). Washington, DC: Government Printing Office.

Van den Berghe, P. (1969). *Race and racism: A comparative perspective.* New York: John Wiley.

Vance, J. (1977). *This scene of man: The role and structure of the city in the geography of Western civilization.* New York: Harper.

Wade, R. (1964). *Slavery in the cities.* New York: Oxford University Press.

Zeitlin, I. (1994). *Ideology and the development of sociological theory.* Englewood Cliffs, NJ: Prentice Hall.

Name Index

Subject Index

About the Authors

Herbert Aptheker has participated in anti-racism and anti-war struggles for more than six decades. He received a Ph.D. in history from Columbia University, and is the author or editor of 80 books, including *American Negro Slave Revolts* (1943), *To Be Free* (1991), and *Anti-Racism in U.S. History* (1992). He is the editor of the complete correspondence and writings of W. E. B. Du Bois.

Bob Blauner is Emeritus Professor of Sociology at the University of California at Berkeley and author of the best-selling *Black Lives, White Lives: Three Decades of Race Relations* (1989).

Benjamin P. Bowser is Professor of Sociology and Social Services at California State University at Hayward and Associate Editor of *Sage Race Relations Abstracts* (London). He is co-editor of *Impacts of Racism on White Americans* (1981), *Black Male Adolescents: Parenting and Education in Community Context* (1991), and *Toward the Multicultural University* (1995).

Nazir Carrim is Lecturer in the Education Department at the University of Witwatersrand in Johannesburg, South Africa.

Karen Dugger is Associate Professor of Sociology and Department Chair at Bucknell University. She is also Director of Bucknell's Race and Gender Resource Center, and has published work on the intersection of race and gender.

Antonio Sérgio Alfredo Guimarães is Adjunct Professor of Sociology at the Universidade Federal da Bahia in Salvador, Brazil. He has been a research fellow at the CNPq (Brazilian Research Foundation), is one of two editors of *Revista Apro-Asia*. He holds a Ph.D in sociology from the University of Wisconsin. He is also the author of numerous studies on industrial labor in Brazil.

Rosana Heringer is Assistant Professor of Sociology at the Universidade Federal de Vicosa, Minas Gerais, Brazil. She has been for ten years a sociologist affiliated with the Brazilian Institute of Social and Economic Analyses (IBASE) in Rio de Janeiro. Her work focuses on urban violence and human rights issues.

Louis Kushnick is Senior Lecturer in American Studies at the University of Manchester and has been editor of *Sage Race Relations Abstracts* (London) since 1980. He is Vice-Chair of the Institute of Race Relations in London. He has published extensively in journals on race and class in the United States and Great Britain and has been a visiting scholar at a number of universities in the United States.

Laura A. Lewis recently received a Ph.D. in anthropology from the University of Chicago, and currently teaches at the University of Rochester. She is author of *Race, Witchcraft, and Power in Colonial Mexico* (forthcoming) and articles on race and gender in 16th- and 17th-century Mexico. She has also done field work among Afro-Mexicans on Mexico's southern Pacific coast.

Polly E. McLean is Associate Professor in the School of Journalism and Mass Communication at the University of Colorado, Boulder. She teaches and publishes in the areas of media, popular culture, and international communications. She has a Ph.D. from the University of Texas.

Mokubung Nkomo is on the faculty of New School for Social Research and directs the South Africa Partnership Program. He is editor of *The Pedagogy of Domination* (1990) and author of *Student Culture and Activism in Black South African Universities* (1984).

Ralph R. Premdas is Professor of Political Science at the University of the West Indies, St. Augustine, Trinidad, and Tobago. He holds

Ph.D.s in political science and religion. His most recent works include *The Enigma of Ethnicity in the Caribbean* (1993), *Ethnicity and Development* (1991), and *Arthur Lewis: His Economic and Political Thought* (1990). He has published widely on ethnic conflict in the Caribbean.

Frank M. Snowden, Jr. is Emeritus Professor of Classics at Howard University. He has been a Fellow of the Woodrow Wilson International Center for Scholars, cultural attaché for the American Embassy in Rome, Italy and since retiring from Howard University, at one time a visiting professor at Georgetown University and Vassar College. His books include *Blacks in Antiquity* (1970), *Before Color Prejudice: The Ancient View of Blacks* (1983), and *The Image of the Black in Western Art I* (1976) (as co-author).

John Solomos is Professor of Sociology and Social Policy at the University of Southampton. He has published widely on aspects of race and racism in Britain and Europe. His most recent books are *Race and Racism in Britain* (1993) and *Racism and Migration in Western Europe* (1993).

Zanele Mkwanazi-Twala is a researcher at the Educational Policy Unit of the University of Witwatersrand in Johannesburg, South Africa.

Rosângela Maria Vieira is Professor in Modern Language and Literature at Howard University. She is a founding editor of *The Journal of Afro-Latin American Studies and Literatures,* and has written on Afro-Latin writers and cultural identity.

Peter H. Wood is Professor of History at Duke University, where he specializes in early American and Native American history. His first book, *Black Majority: Negroes in Colonial South Carolina From 1670 Through the Stono Rebellion* (1974), was nominated for the National Book Award. His most recent book is *Strange New Land: African Americans 1617-1776.*